The Comparative Politics of Immigration

Many governments face similar pressures surrounding the hotly debated topic of immigration. Yet, the disparate ways in which policy makers respond is striking. *The Comparative Politics of Immigration* explains why democratic governments adopt the immigration policies they do. Through an in-depth study of immigration politics in Germany, Canada, Switzerland, and the United States, Antje Ellermann examines the development of immigration policy from the postwar era to the present. The book presents a new theory of immigration policy making grounded in the political insulation of policy makers. Three types of insulation shape the translation of immigration preference into policy: popular insulation from the demands of the unorganized public, interest group insulation from the claims of organized lobbies, and diplomatic insulation from the lobbying of immigrant-sending states. Addressing the nuances in immigration reforms, Ellermann analyzes both institutional factors and policy actors' strategic decisions to account for cross-national and temporal variation.

Antje Ellermann is Associate Professor of Political Science, Founding Director of the Centre for Migration Studies, and Director of the Institute for European Studies at the University of British Columbia. Her award-winning research focuses on the politics of migration and citizenship in liberal democracies. She is the author of *States against Migrants: Deportation in Germany and the United States* (2009).

Cambridge Studies in Comparative Politics

General Editors
Kathleen Thelen *Massachusetts Institute of Technology*

Associate Editors
Catherine Boone *London School of Economics*
Thad Dunning *University of California, Berkeley*
Anna Grzymala-Busse *Stanford University*
Torben Iversen *Harvard University*
Stathis Kalyvas *Yale University*
Margaret Levi *Stanford University*
Melanie Manion *Duke University*
Helen Milner *Princeton University*
Frances Rosenbluth *Yale University*
Susan Stokes *Yale University*
Tariq Thachil *Vanderbilt University*
Erik Wibbels *Duke University*

Series Founder
Peter Lange *Duke University*

Other Books in the Series

Christopher Adolph *Bankers, Bureaucrats, and Central Bank Politics: The Myth of Neutrality*

Michael Albertus *Autocracy and Redistribution: The Politics of Land Reform*

Michael Albertus *Property Without Rights: Origins and Consequences of the Property Rights Gap*

Santiago Anria, *When Movements Become Parties: The Bolivian MAS in Comparative Perspective*

Ben W. Ansell *From the Ballot to the Blackboard: The Redistributive Political Economy of Education*

Ben W. Ansell and Johannes Lindvall, *Inward Conquest: The Political Origins of Modern Public Services*

Ben W. Ansell and David J. Samuels, *Inequality and Democratization: An Elite-Competition Approach*

Adam Michael Auerbach *Demanding Development: The Politics of Public Goods Provision in India's Urban Slums*

Ana Arjona *Rebelocracy: Social Order in the Colombian Civil War*

Leonardo R. Arriola *Multi-Ethnic Coalitions in Africa: Business Financing of Opposition Election Campaigns*

David Austen-Smith, Jeffry A. Frieden, Miriam A. Golden, Karl Ove Moene, and Adam Przeworski, eds., *Selected Works of Michael Wallerstein: The Political Economy of Inequality, Unions, and Social Democracy*

Continued after the index

The Comparative Politics of Immigration

Policy Choices in Germany, Canada, Switzerland, and the United States

ANTJE ELLERMANN

The University of British Columbia

CAMBRIDGE
UNIVERSITY PRESS

CAMBRIDGE
UNIVERSITY PRESS

University Printing House, Cambridge CB2 8BS, United Kingdom

One Liberty Plaza, 20th Floor, New York, NY 10006, USA

477 Williamstown Road, Port Melbourne, VIC 3207, Australia

314–321, 3rd Floor, Plot 3, Splendor Forum, Jasola District Centre, New Delhi – 110025, India

79 Anson Road, #06–04/06, Singapore 079906

Cambridge University Press is part of the University of Cambridge.

It furthers the University's mission by disseminating knowledge in the pursuit of education, learning, and research at the highest international levels of excellence.

www.cambridge.org
Information on this title: www.cambridge.org/9781107146648
DOI: 10.1017/9781316551103

First published 2021

A catalogue record for this publication is available from the British Library.

Library of Congress Cataloging-in-Publication Data
NAMES: Ellermann, Antje, 1971– author.
TITLE: The comparative politics of immigration : policy choices in Germany, Canada, Switzerland, and the United States / Antje Ellermann.
DESCRIPTION: Cambridge ; New York, NY : Cambridge University Press, 2021. | Series: Cambridge studies in comparative politics | Includes bibliographical references and index.
IDENTIFIERS: LCCN 2020039502 (print) | LCCN 2020039503 (ebook) | ISBN 9781107146648 (hardback) | ISBN 9781316601617 (paperback) | ISBN 9781316551103 (epub)
SUBJECTS: LCSH: Emigration and immigration–Government policy–Case studies. | Comparative government.
CLASSIFICATION: LCC JV6271 .E55 2021 (print) | LCC JV6271 (ebook) | DDC 325/.1–dc23
LC record available at https://lccn.loc.gov/2020039502
LC ebook record available at https://lccn.loc.gov/2020039503

ISBN 978-1-107-14664-8 Hardback
ISBN 978-1-316-60161-7 Paperback

In memory of my grandparents, Johanna and Martin Gruhler,
whose roots ran deep

Contents

Figures

Tables

Acknowledgments

While writing this book was largely a solitary process, it could not have happened without the many conversations I have had with colleagues and friends over the past ten years. It was a question asked by political science colleagues at the University of British Columbia ("What immigration text would you assign to comparative public policy students?") that first planted the idea for this book in my mind. At the project's early stages, discussions with Ellen Immergut during a sabbatical stay at Humboldt University in Berlin convinced me to adopt an arenas model of policy making. Not long after, Roger Waldinger and Hiroshi Motomura at the University of California, Los Angeles (UCLA) persuaded me to integrate the role of foreign governments into my analytical framework. Without these conversations, this book would have looked much different. I also owe a debt of gratitude to both Phil Triadafilopoulos at the University of Toronto and Alan Jacobs at the University of British Columbia whose many comments on the manuscript uncovered analytical blind spots and improved its empirical rigor. Thanks also to Daniel Tichenor and Etienne Piguet for fact-checking the US and Swiss chapters, respectively; any remaining mistakes are my own, of course. Earlier drafts greatly benefited from presentation and discussion with colleagues at the Berlin Social Science Center; Humboldt University of Berlin; Johns Hopkins University; Lund University; University of British Columbia; University of California, Los Angeles; University of Michigan; University of Sussex; and University of Toronto. At Johns Hopkins University, a special thank you to Steven Teles and Erin Chung, and also to Yunchen Tian for fantastic discussant comments. I am also grateful for all the feedback received on earlier drafts at annual meetings of the American Political

Science Association, the Canadian Political Science Association, and the International Studies Association.

This research could not have happened without the financial and logistical support of many organizations. I gratefully acknowledge generous funding from the Social Sciences and Humanities Research Council of Canada (Standard Research Grant #410-2008-00210). Thank you to Ellen Immergut at Humboldt University of Berlin and to Ruud Koopmans and Marc Helbling at the Berlin Social Science Center for generous institutional support during two Berlin sabbaticals. Reference staff members at numerous institutions have freely shared their time and knowledge with me. This included staff at the Political Archive of the Federal Foreign Office (*Politisches Archiv des Auswärtigen Amtes*) in Berlin, the Swiss Federal Archives (*Schweizerisches Bundesarchiv*) in Bern, the Swiss Social Archives (*Schweizerisches Sozialarchiv*) in Zurich, and the Documentation Center at the Swiss Forum for Migration and Population Studies in Neuchatel. Back at the University of British Columbia, the award of a Hornby Island Residency made possible the first of a series of writing retreats that were so critical for completing this project.

I was lucky to work with an amazing team of graduate and undergraduate research assistants who have supported this project over the years by conducting literature reviews, collecting data, and copyediting: Alberto Alcaraz, Graeme Bant, Camille Desmarès, Valerie Freeland, Matthew Gravelle, Sandra Schinnerl, and Aim Sinpeng. Two anonymous reviewers provided many constructive suggestions that made for a much stronger book. At Cambridge University Press, Sara Doskow masterfully steered the project from manuscript to print. A big thank you to Kathleen Thelen for her encouragement and support of this project. Dania Sheldon created the index at a time when COVID-19 was turning our lives upside down.

Parts of Chapters 3 and 4 originally appeared in *World Politics* 65(3) (2013): 491–538 and the *Journal of Ethnic and Migration Studies* 41(8) (2015) 1235–53, and some tables of Chapter 5 originally appeared in *International Migration* (2019) (https://doi.org/10.1111/imig.12645). I thank the editors for their permission to reuse these materials.

My deepest gratitude goes to Alan and Ruby. Thank you for putting up with my physical absences during writing retreats, and with some of the mental absences in between. Having you in my life means the world to me. My grandparents, Johanna Gruhler (1920–2018) and Martin

Gruhler (1908–2014), passed on while I was working on this book. While I never managed to persuade either of them that academic writing was real work, this book reflects the lessons of resilience and grit that they imparted to me throughout their lives. It is to their memory that I dedicate this book.

Introduction

Immigration is one of the most politically charged policy issues of our day. As the uncertain prospects of immigration reform in many democracies illustrate, makers of immigration policy often find themselves between a rock and a hard place. On the one hand, immigrant recruitment presents policy makers with possible solutions to domestic labor shortages and the fiscal pressures of aging populations. Opening up channels for family migration and refugee resettlement allows policy makers to answer the humanitarian imperatives created by economic migration and forced displacement. On the other hand, public apprehension about the cultural integration of diverse migrant populations and popular concern about the risk of adverse labor market and welfare state impacts often render immigrant admissions a politically risky undertaking. Strikingly, while governments across the liberal democratic world operate under a comparable set of pressures, their policy responses have diverged widely. Whereas some states have sharply tightened immigration rules, others have chosen to open their borders to select groups of immigrants. While some countries have decided to admit permanent residents, others have opted for temporary labor recruitment. And where some states have prioritized family-based immigration, others have favored economic entrants. What can account for this variety of policy choices? And why do countries experience radical changes in immigration policy at certain points in time while showing striking resilience at others?

This book seeks to account for the variety of immigration policies adopted by democratic governments. Through the comparative study of Switzerland, Germany, Canada, and the United States, the book examines and explains the evolution of immigration policy in these democracies over the past six decades. By comparing policy choices across countries and over time, this book pursues two principal objectives. Its primary purpose is the development of a theoretical framework for the comparative study of the politics of immigration policy making in liberal democracies. The second objective is to provide a nuanced understanding of the political dynamics that have shaped policy development in these four countries which, in 2017, collectively were home to 27 percent of the world's 258 million international migrants.[1]

In focusing its lens on the variety of policy choices adopted by democratic governments, this book departs from existing scholarship in political science and sociology, which tends to examine immigration policy through the lens of the "control gap" (Hollifield et al. 2014). This debate grapples with two distinct gaps: the gap between restrictionist public opinion and liberal immigration policy, and the divergence between immigration policy and its actual outcomes. Rather than engaging with this debate and examining immigration policy as a puzzle of policy liberalism or as a case study of limited state capacity, this book examines the making of immigration policy *as an area of interest in its own right.* Understanding the policy dynamics of immigration policy is not only of theoretical but also of empirical value. Immigration policy affects immigration flows (Helbling and Leblang 2019) and simultaneously is shaped by and shapes political contestation. Policies of immigrant selection mold societies by favoring certain newcomers over others and by creating differential conditions of welcome and inclusion. Thus, while all the countries examined in this book over the past decades have become transformed into multiethnic immigration societies, the experience and impact of mass immigration has varied across national contexts.

As a study of immigration policy making, this book examines the policy dynamics that account for the *diversity of policy choices* adopted by democratic governments. Studying immigration reform over the *longue durée* and across national contexts, this book demonstrates significant oscillation between liberalizing and restrictionist policy impulses, rather than a consistent pattern of policy expansionism. Conceptually speaking, this study represents a move away from treating immigration policy as a unitary and coherent whole, in favor of an understanding of immigration policy as a "visa mix" (Boucher and Gest 2017) of discrete

---

[1] Based on data from the Migration Policy Institute's Migration Data Hub, www .migrationpolicy.org/programs/migration-data-hub.

admission policies, each premised on a distinct logic and able to move in separate directions. Hence, the book's paired comparison of Swiss and German immigration policy is based on the differentiation between temporary ("guest worker") and permanent economic immigration, while the Canadian and US cases focus on the mix between family and economic visas. This disaggregation allows for a systematic tracing of equivalent policies over extended periods of time and across comparable national contexts. Finally, this study of "policy choices" is premised on a broad understanding of immigration policy. In addition to legislative statutes, which are most commonly associated with immigration policy, this study also accounts for the making of bilateral treaties and executive regulations. Moreover, the book's analysis of policy choices extends to both successful and unsuccessful cases of immigration reform. In other words, when reform initiatives fail, policy "choices" maintain the policy status quo.

Of course, these substantive choices come at some cost. Most obviously, the book's theoretical scope is limited to the Global North. Because it is premised on institutional characteristics common to advanced democracies, its framework will not carry over to illiberal or nondemocratic regimes, at least not without major revisions. Likewise, focusing on some subsets of policy comes at the cost of excluding others. While the study encompasses family immigration, temporary foreign worker recruitment, and permanent economic immigration, other policies – pertaining to asylum and refugee admissions, migration control, and immigrant integration and citizenship – are beyond the book's empirical scope (though, as we will see in Chapter 7, not beyond its explanatory scope). In a similar vein, the book is limited to the study of policy making at the national level. Given the selection of cases, supranational (European Union) policy making is of little consequence to the developments examined here; similarly, with the partial exception of Canada, subnational governments play little role when it comes to deciding on family and economic immigrant admissions. Chapter 7 will address the question of how to adapt the study's theoretical framework to the study of supranational and subnational policy making. This introductory chapter will now proceed by situating the study in the broader literature, and providing an overview of its argument. We then move on to a discussion of case selection, including a detailed description of the institutional features of the four country cases that provide the building blocks for the empirical chapters. The chapter then concludes with a methodological section and an overview of the book's remaining six chapters.

THE CASE FOR A COMPARATIVE THEORY
OF IMMIGRATION POLICY

In a mid-2000s survey of the state of immigration research in political science, one of the field's leading scholars concluded the following: "We have a long way to go before we have in hand well-developed and widely tested theories that purport to explain and predict the role of state regulation of migration [and] the dynamics of the politics of immigration" (Freeman 2005, 111). Despite the proliferation of migration scholarship since, we have yet to develop a comprehensive and comparative theory of immigration politics that would allow us to understand the diversity of policy choices adopted by governments across the Global North. This persistent gap in migration scholarship is not the result of a lack of scholarship on the dynamics of immigration politics. However, the vast majority of works in political science and political sociology that have grappled with immigration policy and its impacts have focused on a single or small set of explanatory variables, rather than examining how the constitutive parts of a political system interact to produce immigration policies. Accordingly, scholars have identified variables that can be usefully grouped under the rubrics of interests, institutions, and ideas. This brief literature review will identify the most prominent factors that have been argued to drive immigration politics – either by shaping policy outputs (immigration policies) or policy outcomes (immigration flows). While these largely single-factor analyses do not amount to an overarching framework, they nevertheless provide important building blocks for the development of a theory of immigration policy making. The discussion will conclude by examining the few notable scholarly works that have followed a more comprehensive approach to the study of immigration politics.

Interests

Gary Freeman, one of the pioneers of interest-based approaches to the study of immigration politics, placed the role of pro-immigration interest groups at the very center of immigration policy making. It is because of the political influence of pro-immigration lobbies, he argues, that immigration politics is defined by an "expansionary gap" between expansionist (liberalizing) immigration policy, on the one hand, and restrictionist public opinion, on the other (Freeman 1994, 1995).

Institutions

Political institutions simultaneously empower and constrain policy makers as they seek to realize their preferences on immigration. Thus, in systems with judicial review, courts have been argued to provide a counterweight to the populist pressures bearing on elected representatives, thereby constraining policy restrictionism. Students of political behavior, on the other hand, have focused their arguments on the role of partisanship in accounting for legislators' policy choices on immigration. Lastly, the study of bureaucracies has shifted the focus of analysis from the judicial and legislative arenas to the bureaucracy and have argued that, under certain conditions, policy making is best understood as a result of bureaucratic activism.

Courts

Cornelius et al. (1994) coined the puzzle of the "control gap paradox" to draw attention to the gap between the goals of immigration policy, on the one hand, and its actual results, on the other. Where interest group approaches emphasized the power of business in generating this "expansionary drift," institutionalist scholars have pointed to the role of liberal institutions in generating this gap. Thus, scholars have identified the role of the courts in protecting the rights of noncitizens, thereby compromising the state's ability to control immigration (Joppke 1998b, 1999, Guiraudon and Lahav 2000, Guiraudon 2000a). Christian Joppke's seminal work on "why liberal states accept unwanted immigration" (1998b) firmly established the courts at the center of the liberal state's "self-limited sovereignty," which takes its clearest expression in the state's inability to fully close its borders to immigration. Unlike elected officials who are "chronically vulnerable to populist anti-immigrant sentiments," judges are "shielded from such pressures, as they are only obliged to the abstract commands of statutory and constitutional law" (1998b, 271). Contrasting the institution of judicial review in Germany with its absence in Britain, Joppke examines a number of pivotal court rulings by the German Constitutional Court to account for the inability of Germany's policy makers to prevent the settlement of guest workers and their families. Thus, by virtue of their extensive powers of judicial review, German courts were able to force the hand of recalcitrant policy makers to establish residence rights and ease access to family unification.

Recently, however, a number of historically and contextually embedded studies have challenged the common association of judicial review with a categorical immigration expansionism (Ellermann 2013, Bonjour 2016, Johannesson 2018). Saskia Bonjour's nuanced analysis of family immigration policy making in Germany between 1975 and 1990 paints a far less sanguine pattern of judicial activism than that offered by Joppke. By studying the entirety of immigration-related court rulings during this pivotal period, her analysis shows that courts sometimes sided with, but more often against, immigrant advocates. Bonjour's finding of a "general scarcity, variability, and multi-interpretability of jurisprudence" (2016, 345) challenges prevalent conceptions of judges as reliable converters of liberal principles into legal policy-making constraints. "The impact of the judiciary on immigration policies," she concludes, "has been simultaneously overestimated and underestimated" (Bonjour 2016, 328). While courts were often unwilling to encroach upon democratic sovereignty, Bonjour finds that the courts' most significant impact has instead been indirect: courts matter to the extent that their rulings provide immigrant advocates with discursive weapons. Thus, whether in government, parliament, or civil society, immigration liberals have strategically engaged in a highly selective interpretation of court rulings and utilized the legitimacy attached to the language of rights to pursue their claims in the political arenas. Studying judicial decision-making in the context of asylum adjudication in Sweden, Johannesson (2018) similarly defies the expectation of a consistent liberal judicial activism. Rather than adopting the role as "guardians of human rights," she finds that judges instead rely on norms of impartiality. This results in a skeptical approach to asylum adjudication that rejects what judges view as widespread and emotionally tinged expressions of solidarity with asylum seekers.

Political Parties

With the rising political salience of immigration over the past three decades, immigration and integration issues have become subject to party competition. Where parties adopt distinct positions on immigration, we would expect the making of immigration policy to be shaped by the partisan composition of policy-making institutions. Yet, while there is broad scholarly agreement about the electoral significance of immigration (Kriesi et al. 2008, Bornschier 2010), there is no consensus on whether the relationship between parties' left–right positioning and their position on immigration follows reliable and cross-nationally generalizable patterns. In particular, the widespread tendency in the literature to aggregate distinct areas of immigration and integration policy has likely obscured variation in partisan positioning across issue areas, making it more difficult to theorize the impact of partisanship on immigration policy making.

In two large cross-national analyses (fifteen and twenty-two countries, respectively), van der Brug and van Spanje (2009) and Cochrane (2011) find that parties' left–right positioning largely corresponds to their positioning on immigration, with parties to the left holding more favorable views about immigrants than parties to the right. Lahav's (2004) and Hix and Noury's (2007) work on party positioning on immigration and integration in the European Parliament confirms this pattern, with parties to the left being more supportive of liberal immigration and integration policies. This being said, Cochrane's analysis (2011) shows a considerable degree of cross-national variation among center-right parties, a finding confirmed by Kriesi et al.'s (2008) and Bornschier's (2010) analyses of party positioning on immigration and integration in France, Germany, Switzerland, the Netherlands, and Britain, with center-right liberal parties exhibiting the greatest degree of variation. This finding is echoed in Carvalho and Ruedin's (2019) study of seven Western European countries, which finds a strong left–right cleavage for parties' immigration and integration positioning, and confirms greater polarization on integration issues among centrist and right-wing as compared to mainstream left parties (though this finding only holds for five out of seven countries).

In contrast, Givens and Luedtke's (2005) analysis of French, German, and British parties finds no significant differences in parties' positions on immigration while confirming a partisan divide on questions of integration. Similarly, Duncan and van Hecke (2008) find that left–right partisan differences only hold for parties' positions on integration and not for immigration control. For the latter, the (restrictionist) position of Social Democrats is indistinguishable from those taken by Conservatives and Christian Democrats, whereas Liberal and Green parties adopt a less restrictionist position. A number of single-case analyses lend further support to the argument that positions on immigration (as distinct from integration) cross left–right ideological lines. Black and Hicks (2008) find that Canadian parties across the political spectrum are supportive of immigration, with partisan differences only emerging at a highly disaggregated level. Thus, the center-right Conservatives are more supportive of investor class immigration whereas the center-left New Democrats distinguish themselves by their strong support for family reunification and refugee admissions. Looking at Norway, Gudbrandsen (2010) finds that parties across the political spectrum support increases in immigration, in particular in refugee admissions.

Single-party studies further complicate our understanding of parties' positioning on immigration because both center-right and center-left parties are exposed to cross-cutting pressures. Whereas left-of-center parties struggle to retain the support of working-class voters while holding on to socially liberal values, right-of-center parties face cross-cutting pressures from social conservatives and economic liberals. Thus, Hinnfors et al. (2012) find that the Swedish Social Democrats support restrictive economic immigration policies in order to accommodate organized labor, and Bucken-Knapp (2009) argues that center-right parties push for policy liberalization in response to business pressure. Bale and Partos (2014) show a similar pattern for the British Labour Party. Analyses of center-right parties in Britain and Germany (Boswell and Hough 2008, Bale 2013, Bale and Partos 2014) show that these parties seek to win working-class votes from center-left parties by embracing anti-immigration positions. Van Kersbergen and Krouwel (2008) find that Dutch center-right parties have adopted restrictionist immigration and integration positions, especially when faced with electoral competition from the far-right.

In sum, while we would expect partisan positioning on immigration to influence the direction of immigration policy, conflicting findings within the literature suggest that we should exercise caution when theorizing about the impact of partisanship on immigration policy, especially when moving from the aggregate to the country level. Intersecting with the cross-cutting pressures faced by centrist and mainstream right parties is the issue of electoral competition – a challenge that varies across countries, in part due to differing electoral rules and party systems. There is much evidence to suggest that the rise of far-right parties has forced mainstream parties to the left and the right to harden their stance toward immigration and immigrants (Bale 2003, van Kersbergen and Krouwel 2008, van Spanje 2010). Scholars generally agree that center-right parties respond to electoral competition from the far-right by co-opting the latter's anti-immigrant positions (Marthaler 2008, Green-Pedersen and Krogstrup 2008). Findings on the impact of far-right parties on the left are less consistent. Whereas some argue that far-right contagion affects center-left parties in the same way – though to a lesser degree – than center-right parties (van Kersbergen and Krouwel 2008, Bale et al. 2010, van Spanje 2010), other studies find no discernible impact (Coffé 2008, Meguid 2008, Bornschier 2010, de Lange et al. 2014, Ackermann and Freitag 2015, Carvalho and Ruedin 2019).

Bureaucracies

Studies of immigration bureaucrats – while still relatively rare in the migration literature – have revealed an oftentimes important, and virtually always distinct, role played by government bureaucrats in the politics of immigration (Calavita 1992, Magaña 2003, Ellermann 2009, Eule 2014, Boucher 2016, Paquet 2016). Immigration bureaucrats have been found to distinguish themselves from other policy makers by their specialized knowledge of this complex policy area (Boucher 2016), their capacity for policy learning (Ellermann 2015), and the relatively depoliticized nature of decision-making in bureaucratic institutions (Guiraudon 2000b, Bulmer 2011). Moreover, in an important contribution, recent work by Mireille Paquet (2015) and Anna Boucher (2013) clearly shows that the role of bureaucratic actors is not limited to implementing immigration policies, but also extends to initiating and shaping the making of immigration policy itself.

In her study of venue shopping and the making of high-skilled immigration policy in Australia and Canada, Boucher defines bureaucratic control as a function of "the extent to which the bureaucracy is protected from political challenge from outside interests that may seek to elevate conflict to more open political venues in order to realize their political goals" (2013, 349). Boucher finds significant cross-national variation in the ability of bureaucrats to maintain bureaucratic control in the 1990s and 2000s, with important implications for policy adoption. Whereas immigration bureaucrats in Australia successfully contained policy making within the bureaucracy by relying on regulations and limiting opportunities for legal review, their Canadian counterparts failed to stop immigration activists and lawyers from moving points system regulations into the legislative venue by demanding that these regulations be subject to legislative review. As a result, Australia adopted a more selective points system than Canada, with stricter language and educational requirements and a higher point threshold.

Paquet's study of bureaucratic policy entrepreneurship, which refers to the "autonomous actions of bureaucrats that [bring] about policy change" (2015, 1815), examines the role of Canadian immigration bureaucrats working at the provincial (subnational) level in developing subnational immigration and integration policies. She shows that the unprecedented institutionalization of pro-immigrant policy agendas at the provincial level in the 1990s occurred in the absence of interest group lobbying or changes in public mobilization. In fact, the political dynamics that resulted in the development of new and quantitatively significant economic immigration pathways by the provinces followed "a model of client politics, without clients" (2015, 1831). In other words, provincial policy development took place in the safety of bureaucratic institutions and was driven by bureaucratic activism, rather than by interest group lobbying. In sum, arguments about the role of bureaucratic actors in the politics of immigration policy offer alternative explanations to accounts that highlight the role of interest groups and political parties in the making of immigration policy.

Ideas

Political action is driven not only by interests but also by the ideational commitments and values that actors bring to bear on the political process, as ideational structures, values, and beliefs shape both individual and collective identities. Thus, scholars of political development have argued that the ideational legacies left behind by pivotal historical events can continue to shape immigration politics well into the future. Whereas these accounts emphasize cross-national divergence in immigration and citizenship policies, students of global norms have examined ideational processes of convergence. Whether focused on universal human rights norms, the securitization of migration, or the paradigm of human capital, these scholars emphasize the power of global norms in shaping policy making across national contexts, ranging from shared understandings of the moral obligations of liberal states to conceptions of desirable and undesirable immigrants.

National Identity

Historically embedded accounts of immigration politics have long posited that as expressions of national identity, immigration and citizenship policies are shaped by the legacies of the past. The causal significance attributed to historical legacies is reflected in the emphasis that typologies of immigration politics have placed on the timing and the nature of a country's first experience with large-scale migration (Freeman 1995, Joppke 1998a). These legacies, it is argued, continue to shape contemporary policy making because they mold fundamental attitudes and institutions. Accordingly, ideational legacies are understood as "patterns of political and social thought that shape thinking on questions of migration" (Koven and Götzke 2010, 178) and delineate the range of legitimate and viable policy responses in a given national context. Historically grounded legitimation approaches to migration speak of "ideologies of immigration" (Boswell 2003), "philosophies of integration" (Favell 1998), or traditions of "citizenship and nationhood" (Brubaker 1992) that set the parameters within which immigration continues to be debated and policy made.

As one of the most prominent examples of historically grounded ideational approaches, Rogers Brubaker's *Citizenship in France and Germany* (1992) contends that differences in the sequencing of nation building and state building in the two countries gave rise to distinct understandings of national identity: whereas the French created a nation within an already strong state, Germany existed as an ideal of cultural connectedness long before any large state embodied that ideal. By the early twentieth century, then, each country had in place distinct citizenship laws that reflected these differing paths of political development. Whereas French citizenship was based on a civic understanding of nationhood and allowed for the acquisition of citizenship by territorial birth, German citizenship was based exclusively on the principle of descent, reflecting an ethnocultural conception of national identity. Brubaker shows how the basic logic underlying these early citizenship acts remained fundamentally unchanged until the early 1990s.

While few would contest the claim that national immigration ideologies constrain policy making, historically embedded immigration narratives fare better at explaining policy stasis than change. Thus, while Brubaker provides a compelling explanation for the absence of policy change for close to a hundred years, his argument cannot adequately account for the passage of citizenship reforms after the early 1990s, which marked important departures from previous policy and moved citizenship policies toward cross-national convergence, rather than divergence. Thus, ideational arguments that focus on the path-dependent properties of historical legacies reach their limits when confronted with either nonincremental policy change or cross-national policy convergence.

Global Norms

Whereas arguments about the role of nation-building legacies speak of the power of ideas in driving cross-national *divergence* in immigration policy, global norms approaches describe ideational processes that push toward policy *convergence*. The dominant account within this literature examines the power of *liberal norms*, specifically the postwar emergence of norms of universal personhood and human rights that were propelled by the horrors of the Holocaust and the wave of decolonization that spread across the Global South in the 1960s and 1970s. Given their deterritorialized logic, the emergence and institutionalization of universal human rights provides a critical check on national sovereignty. Some accounts of normative liberal constraint locate the source of this normative power in the international arena (Jacobson 1996, Sassen 1998). For instance, Yasemin Soysal's work on post-national membership (1994) posits that the authority of nation-states over citizenship policy has been curtailed by universalistic conceptions of individual rights and their legitimation through international conventions.

While few dispute the emergence of human rights norms, skeptics have questioned the impact of these global norms on the making of immigration policy at the national level. Instead, these scholars argue that liberal norms are grounded in domestic, rather than international, institutions and discourses (Joppke 2001, Triadafilopoulos and Schönwälder 2006, Bonjour 2016). Thus, Bonjour's analysis of family unification policies in Germany (discussed above) identifies the "language of rights" as an influential discursive weapon wielded by immigrant advocates within state institutions and civil society (2016). In a similar vein, Bonjour's study of Dutch family immigration policies (2011) over the latter half of the twentieth century shows that pivotal pro-immigrant actors within parliament and the Ministry of Social Affairs were motivated by individual ethical considerations. Of course, global and domestic approaches to the study of norms are not necessarily mutually exclusive. Triadafilos Triadafilopoulos's (2012) comparative study of the liberalization of immigration reform in Germany and Canada develops a "variation within convergence" argument that brings together global and domestic accounts of normative constraint. While the emergence of a new global human rights culture exerted equivalent liberalizing pressure on policy makers in both countries, he argues, the pace of reform differed cross-nationally because it was mediated by domestic traditions of nationhood and political institutions.

While attention to the power of liberal norms in driving policy liberalization has been integral to the North American immigration literature from its inception (see Hollifield 1992), European scholars have tended to emphasize the power of discursive processes of *securitization* in accounting for policy restrictionism. In stark contrast to the liberalizing power of universal human rights norms, then, the "securitization" of migration has been used as an ideational construct and discursive process that pushes toward closure, rather than openness (Waever et al. 1993, Huysmans 2006). As migrants are constructed as potential threats to identity, economic, or environmental security, the defense of state sovereignty is seen to take precedence over adherence to human rights norms. Jef Huysmans, for instance, shows how the abolition of internal border controls within the European Union went hand in hand with the institutional integration of migration policy into the EU's internal security framework. Thus, what started out as the "socio-economic project of the internal market" soon morphed into "an internal security project" (Huysmans 2000, 760). In a similar vein, Phillipe Bourbeau's (2011) analysis of discursive securitization in Canada and France examines the role of elected politicians and the media in institutionally integrating migration into policing and defense frameworks.

Whereas liberal norms arguments posit convergence toward liberalization while securitization arguments identify convergence toward closure, recent work has relied on ideational arguments to explain convergence toward *selective* liberalization. Selective liberalization describes the simultaneous pursuit of high-skilled and deterrence of low-skilled – that is, family and humanitarian – immigration. While these accounts of "selecting by merit" (Shachar 2016) complement existing political economy accounts that emphasize the structural demand for high-skilled labor in global knowledge economies (see above), in linking the pursuit of "the best and the brightest" with the simultaneous warding off of low-skilled immigrants, ideational arguments fill an analytic void left by labor market accounts that cannot explain the undesirability of low-skilled immigrants in the face of continued structural demand for unskilled labor. Elsewhere I have used the concept of *human capital citizenship* (Ellermann 2019) to argue that as states' imagination of their citizens has shifted from that of bearers of rights to bearers of human capital, economic attributes such as education, skill, and self-sufficiency have become imbued with cultural significance. Thus, as states have constructed what Elrick and Winter have termed a "middle-class national identity" (2018), the high-skill bias of economic immigrant selection has spilled over into noneconomic immigration streams and resulted in increasingly selective policies of family admissions.

Existing Frameworks of Immigration Politics

While the works discussed above examine a limited subset of variables, over the past decade a small body of immigration scholarship that seeks to offer more comprehensive explanatory frameworks for the study of

immigration policy choices has emerged.[2] Christina Boswell's article
"Theorizing Migration Policy: Is There a Third Way?" (2007) rests on
the premise that immigration policy making is fundamentally driven by
the functional imperatives of the state. Rejecting political economy and
institutionalist approaches that crowd out any space for agency, she
instead proposes a "third way" that considers societal interests and
institutions as constraints that are mediated by the state's need to
maintain legitimacy. As a "function of the compatibility of political
actions and practices with the expectations and values of a particular
public" (Boswell 2007, 88), state legitimacy rests on the ability of state
actors to perform four basic functions: maintaining the state's territorial
integrity and the physical security of its citizens (security), safeguarding
economic growth (accumulation of wealth), protecting the rights and
socioeconomic well-being of its citizens (fairness), and preserving its
democratic and liberal institutions (institutional legitimacy). Given these
wide-ranging functional imperatives, how do states deal with the risk of
losing legitimacy because they are unable to fulfill all four imperatives
simultaneously? In particular, Boswell identifies a deep-seated tension
between the imperatives of economic accumulation and institutional
legitimacy, which favor liberalized immigrant admissions, and imperatives of security and fairness, which favor closure and protectionist
policies. She argues that state actors can reconcile these competing
imperatives either by means of intentional policy incoherence, which
allows competing groups to claim policy credit, or by pursuing the more
politically contentious route of elevating one function over others.
Boswell does not specify the conditions under which state actors will
decide on a given strategy, or how they will decide on which function
will trump others. While these kinds of elaborations are likely outside

---

[2] There are several additional notable texts that pursue different goals from this analysis.
Most prominently, Hollifield et al.'s *Controlling Immigration* (2014) offers a comparative
analysis of trends in immigration policy and its enforcement across the Global North.
Rather than accounting for specific policy choices, the volume examines two hypotheses:
first, that of cross-national convergence in the policies and instruments of immigration
control, and second, an increase in the gap between policy output, on the one hand, and
policy implementation, on the other. Castles et al.'s *The Age of Migration* (2014). examines migration movements and their effects on sending and receiving countries, while only
briefly touching on the politics of immigration policy making. Similarly, Messina's *The
Logic and Politics of Post-WWII Migration to Europe* (2007) does not seek to offer a
policy framework but instead explores the impact of immigration on European societies
and politics through the lens of state sovereignty. Like Castles et al., Messina has little to
say about the role of institutions in shaping immigration politics

the scope of a single article, Boswell's insights into the motivations of state action provide an important building block on which to build a more differentiated theory of immigration policy making.

Similarly, James Hampshire's *The Politics of Immigration* (2013) offers a sweeping theoretical framework of the politics of immigration and immigrant integration in liberal democracies spanning national, regional, and international levels of policy making. The basic logic of his analysis mirrors Boswell's in being grounded in four fundamental, partially contradictory, "facets" of liberal statehood that give rise to a "liberal paradox" suspended in the tension between closure and openness. Thus, whereas public opinion (representative democracy) and national identity (nationhood) generate pressures for closure and exclusion, constitutionality and liberal norms (constitutionalism) as well as economic imperatives (capitalism) push for openness and inclusion. It is because of these intrinsic contradictions of liberal statehood that we can understand "the intractable nature of immigration policy [as] not a failure of governance, but rather a reflection of contradictory imperatives of the state" (Hampshire 2013, 2).

Hampshire chooses not to focus on a particular country, or even region, but instead posits a basic logic of immigration politics shared across liberal democracies. As a result of this "panoramic" perspective, *The Politics of Immigration* "cannot do justice to the complexities of individual countries" (Hampshire 2013, 2). While Hampshire concedes that individual countries will somewhat vary in their positioning on the openness–closedness spectrum, his framework does not theorize drivers of this variation, whether cross-nationally or over time. In other words, while there is much value in a perspective that transcends country-level politics and distills complex phenomena into a few key claims – claims that will need to be taken seriously by any theorist of immigration politics – the liberal paradox framework does not allow us to study variation in immigration politics. Moreover, the framework is designed to explain patterns of immigration politics, rather than – as is the purpose of this study – to account for policy choices. To do that, we would also need to theorize the mechanisms that mediate the basic imperatives of liberal statehood and the policy process. While filling this gap is clearly beyond the scope of Hampshire's study, a final point of omission points to a curious oversight in an otherwise global and state-centric framework: the role of foreign governments in shaping immigration politics. Even though Hampshire's analysis excels in combining multiple levels of analysis, his examination of international actors is limited to international organizations, ignoring the possibility that the actions of foreign states may amplify or subdue particular features of liberal statehood.

By contrast to Hampshire's global approach, Martin Schain's book *The Politics of Immigration* (2008) is based on in-depth case studies of the development of immigration policy in France, Britain, and the United States. Placing the framing of immigration by party elites at the center of his analysis, Schain argues that political parties frame the issues of immigration as the result of "electoral considerations." Accordingly, party leaders make strategic decisions about whether or not to politicize immigration as a threat to national identity, depending on whether they seek to mobilize anti-immigrant voters or appeal to immigrant constituencies. While Schain also considers the role of institutions and interest groups, these variables mostly feature in the empirical chapters, whereas in the theoretical chapter they are integrated into the literature review rather than serving as the building blocks of theory.

A final, important contribution to a comprehensive theorization of the politics of immigration policy is Tariq Abou-Chadi's article "The Political and Institutional Determinants of Immigration Policies" (2016). Unlike the previous works mentioned, which theorized broad patterns of immigration politics, Abou-Chadi's quantitative analysis focuses on the making of immigration policy and, more precisely, the likelihood of policy liberalization. Combining a veto point argument with a number of political and electoral variables, he finds that the passage of liberalizing immigration reform hinges on a left-of-center government ruling in the absence of executive and legislative veto points. Moreover, the likelihood of liberalizing immigration reform is significantly reduced when a far-right party is represented in the legislature, when electoral competitiveness is high, and when the issue of immigration is politically salient.

Abou-Chadi's analysis points to populist mobilization as a key obstacle to liberalizing immigration reform and makes a compelling case for the adoption of a veto point framework in accounting for variation in reform success. At the same time, given the variable constraints inherent in quantitative analysis, the framework is by necessity reductionist, attributing all liberalizing reform impulses to one source: left-of-center party ideology. This assumption not only misses the importance of societal and economic interests as sources of reform impetus, but its usefulness depends on the study of recent cross-national aggregates. In other words, looking at the ideological commitments of left-of-center governments will be of little help when studying policy reform in time periods before parties adopted distinct positions on immigration (the postwar period), when studying specific areas of immigration policy where the left cannot be assumed to be more liberal (temporary foreign worker recruitment), or when studying policy making in party systems where parties are internally divided on immigration (United States) or where there is a cross-party consensus on the desirability of immigration (Canada). To understand policy developments in these contexts, a more fine-grained analysis is necessary.

PREVIEW OF THE ARGUMENT

The institutional framework developed in Chapter 2 seeks to account for two distinct aspects of immigration reform. First, using a theory of political insulation the framework seeks to account for the *direction* of policy change. In other words, it seeks to answer the question: under what conditions will policy reform move toward greater openness as opposed to tighter closure? Second, the framework builds on veto point arguments in order to theorize the *magnitude* of policy change. It asks: under what conditions will immigration reform take the form of a radical (or paradigmatic), rather than incremental, departure from the policy status quo? This section will provide an overview of these arguments.

Theorizing the Direction of Policy Change: The Importance of Insulation

The book's theoretical framework builds on Ellen Immergut's work on institutions, arenas, and veto points, which conceives of political systems as "sets of interconnected arenas" (1990, 396) marked by distinctive rules of representation. In Immergut's framework, the policy process is likened to a path that winds through the arenas. While largely determined by constitutional rules, its course is also shaped by political strategy. Because each arena has a distinct political logic, the course of a given policy path matters greatly for policy reform. Looking at the making of immigration policy, I argue that the most salient question concerning the logic of policy arenas is the extent to which they provide policy makers with three distinct types of political insulation: *popular insulation* from the demands of the unorganized public, *interest group insulation* from the claims of organized lobbies, and *diplomatic* insulation from the lobbying of foreign states. Premised on this insulation logic, variation in policy paths will engender variation in the direction of policy reform. Whereas some paths will lead to policy liberalization, others will end in immigration restrictionism.

Three Types of Insulation

What distinguishes immigration policy from many other policy fields is the cross-cutting nature of the pressures bearing on policy making. Policy makers regularly find themselves between a rock and a hard place as the demands of the organized and unorganized publics push in opposing directions. The unorganized (general) public typically favors a restrictive stance on questions of admission and stay. Recent research on what drives public attitudes on immigration suggests that cultural factors are a primary determinant of public opinion. Public opposition to immigration is strongly driven by concerns about the protection of the national culture and thus fuels emotionally charged and essentially protectionist immigration debates. It follows that policy makers who pursue proposals that seek to liberalize immigration policy will most likely succeed under conditions of *popular insulation*. A second way in which societal influence bears on policy makers is through the lobbying efforts of organized interests. Because the benefits of immigration are concentrated and its costs diffuse (Freeman 1995), organization is strongest among pro-immigration groups, in particular among business associations. In contrast to restrictionist public opinion, then, organized interests typically demand a liberalization of immigration policy. Policy choices that emerge from contexts of low *interest group insulation* will point in the direction of policy liberalization.

Finally, because immigration policy sits at the intersection of domestic politics and international relations, policy makers will often find themselves confronted with the demands of *immigrant-sending* states with a stake in the immigration policies enacted by receiving states. For countries that struggle with economic stagnation and slack labor markets, emigration serves as a vital safety valve to relieve employment pressures at home and to provide much-needed foreign currency through migrant remittances. Given the social, economic, and monetary benefits of emigration – and the tendency to discount its long-term societal costs – we can assume that sending states will strongly favor policies that facilitate the emigration of their nationals while opposing policies that would result in their return. It follows that policy makers who seeks to restrict immigration will be most likely to succeed under conditions of *diplomatic insulation*, with one exception. In situations where unregulated migration threatens to destabilize immigrant-receiving regions, policy makers are likely to find themselves confronted with lobbying from fellow *immigrant-receiving* states to tighten migration controls. In this instance, policy restrictionism will be facilitated by the absence of diplomatic insulation.

Insulation in the Policy Arenas

Policy arenas differ in their degree of popular, interest group, and diplomatic insulation, both in relation to each other and in cross-national comparison (for a discussion of the latter, see the "Case Selection and Description" section later in this chapter). The *executive arena* provides the highest degree of popular and interest group insulation. Not only are deliberations in cabinet meetings effectively shielded from public view, but few organized societal interests – with the exception of business – are sufficiently powerful to have access to the highest level of the executive. At the same time, diplomatic insulation is weakest among executive officials as they bear primary responsibility for foreign affairs and the conduct of diplomatic relations. Unlike legislators, executive actors can ill afford to ignore the diplomatic repercussions of immigration reform.

In the *legislative arena*, policy making takes place in a context of intermediate popular and interest group insulation. A larger array of interest groups can exert influence on individual decision makers because the threshold for access is lower than in the executive arena. To the extent that legislators are elected on the basis of candidate-focused, rather than party-focused, campaigns, they will be vulnerable to popular pressure throughout their tenure, especially in contexts with short legislative terms. While the legislative arena is marked by greater diplomatic insulation than the executive arena, sending-state officials may nevertheless succeed in exerting some influence by lobbying individual representatives, particularly in candidate-focused legislatures.

The *electoral arena* distinguishes itself by the virtual absence of popular insulation. Given that public opinion on immigration typically favors restriction, popular mobilization at the polls or during referendum campaigns will increase pressure on policy makers to restrict immigration. Interest group insulation, by contrast, is greatest in the electoral arena because popular influence overrides expansionist interest group demands. This is not to say that electoral campaigns do not provide interest groups with a window of opportunity for influencing policy. But as long as policy passes through the electoral arena, officials will seek to distance themselves from the demands of organized lobbies. Finally, diplomatic pressure is unlikely to gain traction in the electoral arena, where campaign agendas and promises will focus on the national interest, rather than the challenges confronting foreign states.

The significance of the *judicial arena* in the politics of immigration policy making varies depending on the constitutional provisions for judicial review. In systems with *concrete* judicial review – where judges adjudicate cases brought by claimants adversely affected by the implementation of a statute – interest groups can play a role not only in setting the court's agenda, but also in influencing the substance of its rulings. Given our earlier arguments about the nature of interest group mobilization, we would expect litigation and the filing of amicus curiae briefs[3] to be dominated by pro-immigration groups. Judges in countries with institutions of *abstract* judicial review, by contrast, will enjoy weaker popular insulation. Abstract review is initiated by politicians who refer legislation directly to the court. It thus provides the parliamentary opposition, or in some cases subnational governments, with a veto point. To the extent that opposition parties file for abstract review in order to instrumentalize immigration policy for partisan purposes, constitutional review lessens the popular insulation of governing majorities. Finally, because immigration law falls under domestic law, judges deliberate in contexts of strong diplomatic insulation.

Theorizing the Magnitude of Policy Change: The Importance of Veto Points

More often than not, policy reform is incremental in nature: it results in minor policy adjustments or the adoption of new policy instruments without, however, altering the overarching goals of policy. Yet from time to time, radical – paradigmatic – policy change does occur. On those rare occasions, when the ideational foundations of the policy status quo have crumbled, policy makers succeed in adopting policy reforms that reflect a new immigration paradigm. Under what conditions is paradigmatic immigration reform possible?

Paradigmatic reform constitutes a profound disruption of the policy status quo. As a first and necessary condition, paradigmatic policy change is preceded by the loss of congruence between an existing paradigm and its environment. Lessening congruence initially can be of little consequence, given the path-dependent logic of institutionally embedded

---

[3] Amicus curiae briefs are submitted to the court by a third party who offers its expertise or insight on a given issue.

paradigms. With the passage of time, however, the gap between a paradigm and its environment will continue to widen, resulting in what Triadafilopoulos (2010) calls policy "stretching," followed by policy failure. At this point, the normative consensus regarding the desirability of a paradigm's continued reproduction will fall apart and open the door to new understandings of immigration policy. Once a paradigm is discredited, policy makers will turn to alternative paradigms in order to legitimate the pursuit of nonincremental policy reform. Unlike incremental change, paradigmatic change is more "sociological" and "political" in nature (Pierson 1993, 614). Because embracing a new paradigm involves rethinking basic aspects of policy, the consideration of alternative paradigms will usually take place in the context of broad-based debate. In other words, a new paradigm needs to resonate with a broad range of actors in order to be accepted as legitimate.

While there often is a broad consensus that an old paradigm has outlived its purpose, the adoption of a new paradigm is usually a far more contentious process. Once a paradigm has lost its legitimacy, alternative paradigms will emerge and compete for recognition. Importantly, because of its need for legitimation, a new immigration paradigm cannot be institutionalized solely within the executive arena but ultimately will need to also be affirmed through legislative debate. As a result, paradigmatic reform depends upon the absence of veto points. This is especially critical where paradigmatic change promises to liberalize immigration, as its opponents will seek to appeal to popular restrictionism and exploit veto points for partisan gains. As a result, where the proponents of opposing paradigms have access to veto points, a paradigm shift cannot be completed. Conversely, it is only in the absence of veto points – when reformers are firmly in control of the policy making process – that paradigmatic immigration reform is possible.

CASE SELECTION AND DESCRIPTION

The book's four empirical chapters examine the politics of immigration policy making from the immediate postwar era to the present in four major countries of immigration: Switzerland, Germany, Canada, and the United States. This selection of cases is based on two sets of considerations. First, these countries constitute paired cases that represent distinct regimes in the migration literature: guest worker and settler colonial regimes. Typologies of immigration regimes have long emphasized the role played by a country's first experience with mass immigration in shaping the ideational and political contours of present-day immigration politics. Instead of treating historical accounts at face value, however, I argue that they are best understood as narratives that exert their ideational influence through a highly selective reading of national history. Selecting paired cases with similar immigration narratives – Switzerland and Germany, Canada and the United States – allows us to compare policy making in contexts with comparable orientations toward immigration and, as a result, similar policy challenges. While this first criterion ensures the selection of comparable cases, a second criterion allows us to test the theory of political insulation developed in Chapter 2: variation in political institutions. Thus, on most indicators the four countries selected for this study represent the full range of institutional variation observable across advanced democracies: Canada's Westminster parliamentary system, Germany's coalition government parliamentary system, the US presidential system, and the Swiss semi-presidential system of direct democracy.

Historical Legacies

In its most basic form, the distinction between setter colonial and guest worker states posits that historical legacies matter. Immigration policy is not made on a tabula rasa but is shaped by the ideational and political legacies of the past. Yet, as Christophe Bertossi reminds us, the taxonomies that give expression to historical legacies are not factual accounts of the past but rather "represent a performative cognitive construction of social reality" (2011, 1574). Too often, taxonomies of immigration mistake the construction of historical narratives for history itself. For instance, in one of the most influential formulations, immigration in settler colonial states is argued to be "integral to their founding and development as nations. They are prototypical countries of immigration, and they stand alone today in encouraging mass immigration for permanent settlement" (Freeman 1995, 887). By contrast, in guest worker states, "mass immigration occurred when they were already fully developed national states" (Freeman 1995, 890). These narratives at best represent a highly selective reading of the past, and at worst a misinterpretation of immigration history. Likewise, self-referential terms such as "country of immigration" (settler colonial states) and "non-immigration country" (guest worker states) do not necessarily tell us anything about actual immigration flows. As Figure 1.1 shows, at no point in time does the relative size of the foreign-born population adhere to the analytical

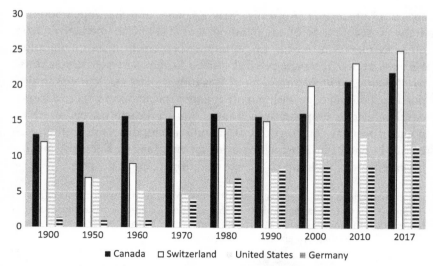

FIGURE 1.1 Foreign-born as percentage of population, 1900–2017.

distinction between settler colonial (Canada and the United States) and guest worker (Switzerland and Germany) states. While in 1900 Switzerland, Canada, and the United States had comparable foreign-born percentages, five decades later Switzerland and the United States clustered, whereas from 1970 onward a pattern of two analytically cross-cutting pairs emerge: Germany and the United States on the one hand, and Switzerland and Canada on the other.

This is not to argue that immigration narratives do not matter – on the contrary. The power of immigration narratives is discursive in nature, as they are "used, imagined, negotiated, affirmed, contested, and challenged by different types of people" (Bertossi 2011, 1572). In other words, immigration narratives shape the politics of immigration through their power of framing national identity and its relationship to immigration.

The Settler Colonial States: Canada and the United States
Canada and the United States share a common mythology of being nations of immigrants. In both countries, the nation-of-immigrants narrative constructs immigration as the norm, rather than an aberration, and references the contributions made by past waves of immigrants to justify present-day immigration. In one of the earliest immigration regime taxonomies, Freeman thus describes the "English-speaking settler

societies" of Canada, Australia, New Zealand, and the United States as archetypal countries of immigration that distinguish themselves from other immigration regimes by promoting permanent mass immigration. He attributes a "receptive cultural context for further waves of migrants" to a "politics of immigration [that] was forged years ago and was institutionalized during eras when population movements were vital to national development or even survival" (1995, 887). Freeman's account echoes popular postwar constructions of national identity in these "settler societies." In one of its most telling articulations, John F. Kennedy, making his case for the abolition of the national origins quotas, wrote:

[E]very American who ever lived, with the exception of one group, was either an immigrant himself or a descendant of immigrants. ... And some anthropologists believe that the Indians themselves were immigrants from another continent who displaced the original Americans – the aborigines.

(Kennedy 1964, 2)

Challenging those who mistake this immigration folklore for a historically grounded identity, historian Donna Gabaccia (2010) has shown that the celebratory conception of an ethnically inclusive American identity only emerged during the Cold War era. During the early colonial period, English-speaking settlers in Canada and the United States used the term "emigrant" to refer to and celebrate European colonizers, and it was only in the late ninteenth century that newcomers, who by now increasingly came from regions outside of Northern and Western Europe, were commonly referred to as "immigrants." Contrary to what the immigration folklore would expect us to believe, however, for many decades this term carried negative connotations and was the preferred terminology of restrictionists, who used it when advocating for Chinese exclusion and the restriction of Southern and Eastern European immigration. In other words, "the term 'immigrant' initially built a poor foundation on which to begin to create a celebratory portrait of the United States as a 'nation of immigrants'" (Gabaccia 2010, 17). It was only with the beginning of the Cold War that inclusive narratives of settler colonial states as "nations of immigrants" won out and, by the 1960s, came to be successfully employed by immigration progressives (such as John F. Kennedy) to demand the abolition of the old ethnoracial order.

Like all narratives of nationhood, the invention of settler states as inclusive countries of immigration requires acts of willful forgetting. As settlers became transformed into immigrants and the settler nation became reinvented as a nation of immigrants, Indigenous dispossession and displacement were written out of the national narrative. Legal scholar Leti Volpp has described the invention of the nation of immigrants as "the settler's alibi." Accordingly, "[i]mmigration is responsible for indigenous dispossession. But it also provides the alibi. Thus, immigration functions as both the reason for – and basis of – denial. The settler state is naturalized as the nation of immigrants" (Volpp 2015, 325). The country-of-immigration narrative thus fulfills two critical and interconnected functions: it subsumes settler colonial identity at the same time as it erases Indigenous nationhood by constructing Indigenous populations as immigrants themselves (Byrd 2011). Just as John F. Kennedy made reference to Indigenous peoples as "immigrants from another continent," Canadianization campaigns during the Cold War constructed Indigenous peoples as "immigrants, too" and subjected them to assimilation campaigns modeled after those directed at immigrants (Bohaker and Iacovetta 2009). Thus, at the same time as the nation-of-immigrants narrative transforms settlers into immigrants, it constructs the "Indigenous as alien" (Volpp 2015).

The historical narrative of Canada and the United States as "countries of immigration" not only erases their foundational constitution as settler colonial states, but also obscures the profound impact ideologies of racial and cultural superiority have had on each country's immigration politics and policy. With the development of federal immigration policy in the latter half of the nineteenth century, immigration policy came to be explicitly premised on racial and ethnic selection, engendering prohibitions on black as well as Asian, in particular Chinese and Japanese, immigration, literacy tests designed to discourage Southern and Eastern European immigration, and government refusals to admit Jewish refugees. The power of racist ideology was so pervasive that it even trumped economic considerations. Even though Canada faced perpetual problems in attracting and retaining sufficient numbers of immigrants – offering a much less attractive climate than its competitors, the United States and Australia – it pursued a highly ethnically selective admissions policy (Fitzgerald and Cook-Martín 2014, 141).

The recognition that the legacy of settler colonialism constitutes an integral part of American and Canadian political development offers an important corrective to their sunnier narratives of countries of immigration. Immigration was not only the engine of territorial and economic domination, but also enabled ethnically selective nation building. Alongside the erasure of Indigenous presence and the exclusion of non-white immigrants, the settler imperative rested on the promotion of

European immigration. Thus, by contrast to Europe's guest worker states, by the end of World War II the desirability of European immigration was firmly institutionalized through policies of family unification and economic recruitment policies. As a result, the most pressing question facing policy makers in the postwar era and into the twenty-first century was not the principle of immigrant settlement, but rather the *composition* of immigrants. Should immigrant selection continue to privilege European countries of origin? And what should be the balance between family and economic admissions? The empirical analysis of immigration policy making in the two settler colonial states in Chapters 5 and 6 will thus focus on these policies of permanent immigrant admissions.

The Guest Worker States: Switzerland and Germany

The politics of immigration in Switzerland and Germany are commonly said to be defined by the experience of unintended and large-scale guest worker settlement in the postwar era. As Freeman argues,

[t]he distinctive feature that sets Great Britain, France, Germany, Belgium, the Netherlands, Sweden, and Switzerland apart from the settler societies is that their modern experience of mass immigration occurred when they were already fully developed national states. They enter the current period chiefly conditioned by their experiences of migration during the years after World War II, a migration that was narrowly economic and, for certain states, a largely unintended after-effect of colonialism.

(1995, 889)

While Freeman is correct in identifying the experience of unintended immigrant settlement in the decades following World War II as a critical influence on the subsequent politics of immigration, his narrative ignores the fact that guest worker immigration was not by any means the first experience of large-scale immigration. While both countries had closed their borders to immigrants for the three decades prior to the beginning of guest worker recruitment – reflecting the security imperatives of two world wars and the economic turmoil of the Great Depression – prior to World War I both countries experienced large-scale immigration under radically different policy regimes.

In the last decades of the nineteenth century, rapid economic development and demographic change in Switzerland and the German Empire led to the large-scale recruitment of workers from neighboring countries. By 1910, the number of foreign nationals exceeded half a million in Switzerland (Vuilleumier 1992, 42) and 1.2 million in the German Empire (Herbert 2001, 23). Because of Switzerland's small population base, of course, immigrants accounted for a much larger population share: 14.7 percent in 1910, compared to 1.9 percent in the German Empire. This inflow of foreign workers was governed by strikingly different policy regimes. The Swiss government entered into numerous bilateral agreements with its neighboring countries that provided for freedom of movement and settlement. With the exception of political rights, foreign nationals were placed on an equal footing with citizens and were encouraged to naturalize after just two years of residence (D'Amato 2001). In the German Empire, by contrast, protectionism prevailed over liberalism, and migration policy was dominated by Chancellor Bismarck's concern with the "Polonization" of Eastern Prussia. After some early recruitment efforts, Bismarck closed the eastern border and ordered the expulsion of 40,000 Polish workers, a third of whom were Jewish. Yet agricultural labor shortages quickly worsened, and Bismarck instituted a seasonal agricultural worker policy for Eastern Prussia that was based on strictly enforced worker rotation. Thus, when the outbreak of World War I shut down immigrant recruitment across Europe, both countries had already experienced large-scale economic immigration and, in the case of Switzerland, large-scale immigrant settlement. As we see in Chapters 3 and 4, these earlier migration experiences shaped the ways in which guest worker recruitment was regulated in the two countries.

Whereas the "country of non-immigration" narrative interprets the postwar recruitment of guest workers in Switzerland and Germany as a novel and historically unprecedented defining moment, the historical record allows for an alternative narrative that posits foreign worker recruitment as the norm, rather than the exception. In other words, it is the halting of (voluntary[4]) migrant labor flows between 1914 and the end of World War II that is the exception, not the resumption of recruitment in the postwar era. Moreover, the striking liberalization of Swiss pre-World War I immigration policy challenges the argument that, historically speaking, state-sponsored encouragement of immigrant settlement is limited to contexts where nation building is not yet complete and requires immigrants to shore up the population. Just as the characterization of settler colonial states as "countries of immigration" is best understood as an ideational construct, so is the portrayal of Western European guest worker states as newcomers to the experience of immigration. As a political narrative, the importance of remaining a "country of non-

---

[4] Both world wars marked the shift from voluntary to forced labor recruitment.

immigration" defined the contours of immigration politics for many years. This narrative distanced guest worker statehood from "classic countries of immigration" and ensured that rather than debates over the composition of immigrants, the most pressing political question was whether or not to allow immigrant settlement. Hence, Chapters 3 and 4 examine the politics of immigration policy making in the two guest worker states through the lens of temporary versus permanent immigrant admissions.

Political Institutions

The theory of political insulation developed in this book posits a logic of policy making that is fundamentally shaped by competing popular, interest group, and diplomatic pressures bearing on the making of immigration policy. Thus, the policy choices arising from this process will vary depending on whether or not policy makers are insulated from the three types of pressure. Political insulation from these pressures, in turn, is shaped by the institutional configurations within which policy makers operate. Not only can the institutional loci of policy making vary over the course of the policy process and between policy reform episodes, but institutional conditions of policy making also vary cross-nationally. Hence, the degree and type of insulation is contingent on a proposal's path through the policy arenas, on the one hand, and the constitutional context within which it is set, on the other. Otherwise identically situated policy makers will seek to pursue their policy preferences under greatly varying conditions of political insulation. Of the three types of insulation theorized here, only popular and interest group insulation are expected to vary across constitutional contexts. Any cross-national variation in diplomatic insulation, by contrast, will be the result of *noninstitutional* factors (such as geopolitical positioning) and hence will not factor into case selection.

Popular Insulation and Electoral Institutions
While popular insulation is weakest in electoral arenas everywhere, it is weaker in some countries than in others. Switzerland, unique among the four cases in having both cantonal and federal institutions of direct democracy, represents the bottom end of popular insulation. Popular pressure is regularly mobilized through referendum campaigns and popular initiatives.[5] The meteoric rise of the populist far-right Swiss People's

---

[5] Popular initiatives are referendums launched as a result of public petitions.

Party (SVP) since the early 1990s has no doubt been aided by institutions of direct democracy. The launching of popular initiatives has allowed the party to promote their anti-immigrant agenda, including the successful initiatives "For the Expulsion of Criminal Foreigners" (2010), "Against Mass Immigration" (2014), and, most prominently, "Against the Construction of Minarets" (2009). In 2003, the SVP won a historic victory in forcing the first ever reshuffle of the "magic formula," which since 1959 has divided the seven executive seats of the Federal Council between the four ruling parties. Having won 27 percent of the popular vote, the SVP was assigned a second seat at the expense of the center-right Christian Democrats. Today, the SVP is not only the most successful populist far-right party in Europe but the electorally most successful party in Swiss politics since the introduction of proportional representation in 1919. In the 2015 election it won a record of 29 percent of the votes and one-third of the seats in the lower house of parliament.

The presence of far-right parties in a party system is a major reason for cross-national variation in popular insulation. Of the four cases examined here, Switzerland lies at one extreme and Canada at the other, with Germany and the United States in between. Canada, which is widely considered an "exceptional" case (Bloemraad 2012), distinguishes itself by the absence of anti-immigration party platforms at the federal level,[6] with the notable exception of increasing asylum restrictionism, especially within the Conservative Party. Canadian party politics is characterized by a well-entrenched cross-party consensus that favors high levels of immigration and multicultural immigrant integration. In part, this consensus reflects the comparatively strong electoral clout of immigrant and ethnic minorities as a result of high levels of immigration, exceptionally high naturalization rates, and the advantages enjoyed by geographically concentrated voting blocs in a single-member plurality electoral system (Westlake 2018). This is especially the case for the center-right

---

[6] With the exception of the populist Reform Party (dissolved in 2000), which in its early years ran on an anti-multiculturalism agenda and later on merged with the center-right Progressive Conservatives to form the Conservative Party of Canada. At the provincial level, Quebec stands out due to its traditionally more assimilationist orientation. In 2018 the Coalition Avenir Québec (CAQ), established in 2011 and running on an immigration restriction and anti-Islam platform, won a decisive electoral victory that propelled it from third place to majority government. While the CAQ demands cuts in immigration, it nonetheless supports relatively high immigration levels. So far these differences between Quebec and Anglophone Canada have had no discernable impact on federal debates over immigration.

Conservative Party, which has held immigration restrictionism in check for strategic, rather than ideological, considerations. Even though the party's traditional base holds restrictionist views, the need to capture seats in a demographically rapidly diversifying electorate mandates that the party also appeal to immigrant voters. To illustrate, in 2006 foreign-born residents in the provinces of Ontario and British Columbia, which together account for 48 percent of all federal seats, constituted over 20 percent of the population in over half of all districts and over 40 percent of the population in over a quarter of districts (Marwah et al. 2013, 98). As a result, and in telling contrast to the restrictionist Reform Party of the 1990s (see note 6), since the 2000s the Conservative Party has aggressively courted immigrant and ethnic minority voters.

By contrast to Switzerland, the constitution of the Federal Republic of Germany restricts the use of plebiscites in order to prevent the recurrence of the political extremism that led to the demise of democracy during the Weimar Republic. Immigration only started to enter the electoral arena after it became subject to partisan contestation in the 1980s, with the center-right Christian Social Union (CSU) in particular adopting highly restrictionist positions on immigration. In a second contrast to Switzerland, despite electoral rules of proportional representation far-right parties have until recently been absent from German federal politics, as the 5 percent electoral hurdle – designed to counteract the openness of proportional representation to radical parties – succeeded in preventing the entry of anti-immigrant parties into parliament. The election of 2017 marked the first time in the Federal Republic's history that a far-right party entered the Bundestag, with the populist Alternative for Germany (*Alternative für Deutschland*) winning close to 13 percent of the popular vote. While this latest development is too recent to factor into the case studies of this book, we would expect that for as long as there is a sizable parliamentary far-right faction in the Bundestag, popular insulation in Germany's electoral arena will be at a postwar low.

In the United States there is no constitutional provision for referendums at the federal level. The US two-party system is based on majoritarian electoral rules that have precluded the rise of a far-right third party. The positioning of Democrats and Republicans on major issues of immigration, however, has changed considerably over time. During the postwar era, positioning on immigration followed regional, rather than partisan, lines. Whereas Democratic and Republican representatives of urban, immigrant-heavy constituencies in the North sought to abolish race-based immigrant admissions, Southern Democrats opposed immigration reform. It was only in the 1980s, after Southern Democrats were replaced by Republicans, that immigration became a partisan issue, albeit one that was marked by changing and oftentimes cross-cutting coalitions. Thus, immigration reform would often be driven by "strange bedfellow" coalitions that cut across partisan lines, reflecting alliances between business and ethnic interests, in addition to a new regional division between interior and border states (Gimpel and Edwards 1999). The formation of cross-cutting immigration coalitions in the US system is institutionally facilitated by the relatively weak party cohesion and partisan discipline that is characteristic of separation-of-powers systems. To the extent that immigration produces cross-cutting coalitions, popular insulation in the electoral arena remains relatively high as neither party stands to gain from politicization of the issue. With the growing influence of the Tea Party movement within the Republican Party since 2009, however, immigration has become progressively polarized. The immigration agenda of Tea Party Republicans bears a strong resemblance to those of populist far-right parties in Europe. With the election of Donald Trump as president of the United States, the balance of power between Tea Party and moderate Republicans has shifted decisively toward the former, drastically widening the partisan gap and ensuring a virtually constant politicization of immigration. Thus, whereas popular insulation in the electoral arena was relatively high until the 1980s, followed by an intermediate – though highly variable – period from the 1980s to the 2010s, it has reached a historic low in the Trump era.

Popular Insulation and Legislative Institutions

Institution-driven variation in popular insulation in the legislative arena is largely a function of the length of electoral cycles and the strength of the personal vote. The shorter the legislative term, the greater the need for legislators to consider their constituents' views when casting their vote on a given issue. In a similar vein, the stronger the "personal vote" or, put differently, the weaker party discipline is, the greater the accountability of elected representatives to their constituents. In contexts of strong party discipline, by contrast, legislators have little choice but to vote the party line and thus cannot be expected to be held individually accountable to their constituents. On both counts, then, the US House of Representatives stands out as providing much less popular insulation than the Canadian House of Commons or the German Bundestag. Members of the House of Representatives not only operate in a context of weak party discipline, but their two-year terms are only half as long as those of Canadian and

German legislators. As far as the US Senate is concerned, we would expect senators to enjoy greater political insulation than members of the House solely by virtue of their six-year terms, though this advantage may be offset by the larger visibility of their office and greater competitiveness of Senate elections (Jacobson 2012). The comparatively weak popular insulation of US legislators is all the more significant because of congressional dominance in the making of immigration policy, which contrasts with the executive–legislative balance of policy making in parliamentary regimes, which tilts toward the executive.

Compared to US legislators, members of the German Bundesrat enjoy a great measure of popular insulation because they are delegates of the *Länder* governments (usually cabinet members) rather than being directly elected. In Canada, senators are appointed by the governor general on the advice of the prime minister and hold their seats until age 75, which renders them exceptionally insulated – though this insulation is not particularly politically consequential, as the Senate of Canada is a far weaker institution than the American, German, and Swiss upper houses. While it holds the power to veto bills, it has not used this power since 1939, instead limiting itself to making minor amendments to proposed legislation.

In Switzerland, members of both houses of the Federal Assembly are directly elected: members of the National Assembly (the lower house) through rules of proportional representation, legislators of the Council of States (the upper house) by majoritarian vote. Even compared to US representatives, and despite serving four-year terms and enjoying greater party discipline (though less than Canadian and German legislators), Swiss parliamentarians operate in a context of exceptionally weak popular insulation. Given the Federal Assembly's "militia" tradition, its members lack the time, information, and professional competence typically associated with professional legislators (Kriesi 2001). Most importantly, the direct democratic opportunities to contest legislation mean that policy making always takes place under the threat of referendum, even when a referendum or popular initiative has not (yet) been called. In other words, "the menace of the referendum introduces an atmosphere of doubt into parliament and fundamentally limits its freedom of action. As a result, the Federal Assembly has traditionally been unenterprising and rather timid" (Kriesi 2001, 61).

Popular Insulation and Executive Institutions

Across countries, executive arenas are marked by greater popular insulation than legislative and electoral ones. Whereas much of legislative deliberation and the voting record of individual legislators is part of the public record, executive policy making takes place behind closed doors and is shielded from the eyes of even attentive publics. There is minor variation in popular insulation between presidential, including the Swiss semi-presidential, and parliamentary systems, based on governments' security of tenure. While the US president and the Swiss Federal Council cannot be dismissed by the legislature, and thus enjoy safety of tenure until the next election, the Canadian prime minister and German chancellor rely on the confidence of their parliaments. At the same time, dismissal by parliament is the fate of exceedingly few governments, and it is unclear to what extent, if at all, this constitutes a genuine vulnerability. The single exception to a pattern of strong executive insulation is the Swiss Federal Council, for the same reason that makes the Federal Assembly so vulnerable to popular pressure: the threat of popular referendum. In fact, making the unique structure of the Swiss government work has been linked to the ever present referendum threat. In the absence of this threat, it is argued, this arrangement would run the risk of instability, as instead of dividing power between a prime minister and a cabinet, the Federal Council is a non-hierarchical body of seven councilors elected by parliament according to the "magic formula," who rotate the position of federal president on a yearly basis. This structure of power sharing "is intended to produce solutions acceptable to a sufficiently large majority in parliament as well as by popular votes for the risk of the optional referendum to be reduced" (Linder 2009, 573).

Popular Insulation and Judicial Institutions

Judges who review the constitutionality of immigration policy typically deliberate under conditions of high popular insulation. As political appointees who oftentimes enjoy lifetime tenure, they may take into account – but certainly are not meaningfully constrained by – public opinion. The only institutional context where popular insulation can be indirectly compromised is where constitutions provide for the exercise of abstract review, the constitutional review of legislation in the absence of a concrete legal case. For the four cases, the only country with the provision of abstract review is Germany. The United States and Canada only recognize concrete (case-driven) review, whereas the primacy of popular sovereignty in Switzerland precludes the possibility of judicial review altogether. In Germany, abstract review is typically initiated by members of the parliamentary opposition (or else by members of a *Land* government) who refer an immigration statute to the court in order to exploit immigration policy for partisan reasons. Where a liberalizing law is under review, abstract review in effect provides a means through which the parliamentary opposition may mobilize popular fears, thereby indirectly lowering the popular insulation of the judicial arena. Courts with the power of abstract review have thus been referred to as "the extended arm of the opposition" (Stüwe 2001). While the use of abstract review is rare, it features prominently in one of the case studies examined in Chapter 4.

Interest Group Insulation and Electoral Institutions

While electoral institutions are designed as conduits of popular pressure, the financial demands inherent in electoral campaigns also provide openings for interest group influence (Witko 2011, Kalla and Broockman 2016, Powell and Grimmer 2016). The strength of interest group insulation depends on candidates' dependence on financial donations. Where electoral campaigns are candidate focused rather than party focused, candidates are heavily reliant on donations and, by extension, vulnerable to interest group influence. By contrast, where candidates can rely on strong, publicly funded parties, interest group insulation is stronger. Thus, the interest group insulation of electoral institutions will be strongest in Canada and Germany and weakest in the United States and Switzerland. Germany was a pioneer in the public funding of political parties, driven by the need to strengthen democratic institutions after the end of the Third Reich. In Canada, campaign finance reform in 2004 significantly increased interest group insulation by banning corporate and trade union contributions to political parties and candidates. By the late 2000s, Canada's four major parties received between 55 and 70 percent of their income from public funds (IDEA 2014, 271), compared to about one-third of income of German parties (IDEA 2014, 224).[7]

By comparison, American and Swiss electoral campaigns take place under starkly different conditions. Public party funding in Switzerland is nonexistent and, in the United States, negligible (covering about 0.6 percent of campaign expenses in 2012) (IDEA 2014, 272). US campaigns stand out by the enormous costs associated with candidate-centered campaigns. Unlike Germany and Canada, the United States does not offer free or subsidized airtime to parties or candidates,[8] nor are there any limits on campaign spending. Switzerland, in turn, distinguishes itself by

---

[7] Germany's "matching funds" rule stipulates that public subsidies cannot exceed the amount of private money raised by the party (IDEA 2014, 224).

[8] Switzerland does not allow electoral advertising on television.

the absence of campaign finance legislation, including the requirement for parties to disclose their campaign funding. The longstanding financial and organizational weakness of Swiss parties goes hand in hand with greater reliance on interest groups for campaign funding. Parties are further weakened by direct democratic institutions: in referendum campaigns, the resources of interest groups and social movements by far exceed those of political parties. Moreover, the importance of referendums in the electoral arena has given rise to institutionalized pre-parliamentary processes of stakeholder consultation, which provide organized interests with additional policy influence (Linder 2010, Papadopoulos 2013). In sum, while all four countries share the weak popular insulation so characteristic of electoral arenas, only Swiss and American electoral institutions operate in a context of weakened interest group insulation.

Interest Group Insulation and Legislative Institutions

Patterns of interest group insulation in the legislative arena closely map to those observed in the electoral arena. The differential representational logics of weak versus strong parties and candidate-centered versus party-centered campaigning shape the relationships between individual legislators and interest lobbies, creating significant vulnerabilities to interest group influence in contexts of weak parties and candidate-centered campaigning. Because interest groups have the institutional resources to track the voting records of individual legislators, they can threaten to withhold their financial support for future campaigns should legislators vote against their interests. Moreover, strong bicameralism – as is the case for the United States, Switzerland, and Germany – further decreases interest group insulation because of its institutional access points for lobbyists (Baumgartner and Jones 1993). While German and Canadian parliamentarians are not immune to interest group pressures – Germany in particular has been singled out for its weak lobbying regulations (Transparency International 2015) – the combination of strong parties and concentration of political power in the executive, which is typical of parliamentary systems, means that lobbyists will usually target the executive arena. However, in presidential systems, such as the United States, interests will target both arenas simultaneously. As a result, German and Canadian parliamentarians enjoy greater interest group insulation than their American and Swiss counterparts.

To argue that Swiss legislators are only weakly insulated against interest group pressure fails to capture the prevalence of "double loyalties" (Linder 2005, 217) among members of the Federal Assembly, which renders the very notion of interest group insulation meaningless. Swiss parliamentarians represent not only their party, but also specific interest associations, corporations, and nongovernmental associations. Because of the Federal Assembly's historical origins as a militia government, even today most legislators fulfill their office on a part-time basis and supplement their meager parliamentary income through more lucrative professional positions, including prominent positions in interest associations (even in peak-level employer association) and on corporate boards. In the 2010s, the average parliamentarian self-declared membership in eight (in the lower house) and ten (upper house) interest groups – memberships that oftentimes closely corresponded to a representative's parliamentary committee membership (Transparency International Schweiz 2019, 20). As a result, "[t]he parliamentarians' loyalty in nominal votes with regard to the interest associations they represent in parliament is virtually as high as it is with regard to their parties" (Kriesi 2001, 68). Swiss councilors themselves have described their position as a "merger of parliamentarian and lobbyist" (Transparency International Schweiz 2019, 20).

Interest Group Insulation and Executive Institutions

Lobbying within the executive arenas of the four countries is structurally shaped by two contrasting structures of interest representation: neocorporatism in Switzerland and Germany, and interest group pluralism in Canada and the United States. Neocorporatism describes the formalized and routine representation of business and labor peak associations on ministerial advisory boards and other executive institutions. In contrast, under interest group pluralism the state plays a less interventionist role in regulating interest group access, which results in lobbies competing for access to the policy-making process. Given the "privileged" position of business (Lindblom 1977), which arises not only from its superior resources but also from the dependence of elected officials on favorable economic development, business will always have the upper hand among interests in pluralist systems. In neocorporatist systems, however, the pre-eminence of business is tempered by the insider status of organized labor.

While both Swiss and German executive actors operate in contexts where government and economic interests are tightly integrated, and decision-making is premised on a process of consultation and consensus building, union strength varies between the countries. In Germany's system of social neocorporatism, unions are centralized and hold a relatively strong status. In Switzerland's liberal neocorporatist system (Katzenstein 1987a), by contrast, a weak state and feeble central institutions have prevented the institutionalization of strong, centralized trade unions. Instead, Swiss business holds a decisive organizational advantage over labor, even though both social partners formally participate in the pre-parliamentary decision-making process (*Vernehmlassung*) (Schmitter Heisler 2000) and are routinely consulted throughout the policy process. Given the "capitalist bias" of the Swiss system – the director of the Swiss employer association *Economiesuisse* (formerly *Vorort*) has been described as the eighth federal councilor (Eichenberger and Mach 2011, 63) – meaningful influence by organized labor is typically limited to social, rather than economic, issues (Kriesi 1982).

How, then, does the strength of interest group insulation compare across the executive arenas of the four countries? The answer depends on which interests seek representation. As far as business is concerned, insulation will clearly be weakest in Switzerland. The routine and formalized consultation with business under German neocorporatism ensures that its influence is significant and steady, whereas in the pluralist systems of Canada and the United States business influence will be significant though somewhat haphazard. Organized labor, by contrast, is in by far the strongest position in Germany, though the much weaker Swiss unions are at least guaranteed a seat at the bargaining table – unlike their Canadian and American counterparts. Finally, the influence of noneconomic interests will vary depending on their resources and insider contacts in the US and Canada, while having less access in Germany and Switzerland, where the inclusion of social partners comes at the cost of excluding other interests.

Interest Group Insulation in the Judicial Arena

In constitutional contexts of judicial review, organized interests can either bring litigation on behalf of a claimant adversely affected by a legal statute or they can intervene as a third party by filing an amicus curiae brief. The filing of amicus briefs is often likened to lobbying, as it provides organized interests with the opportunity to signal their preferences and share their expertise and information pertinent to a case with judges (Collins 2007). While research on the influence of amicus briefs across national contexts is virtually nonexistent – the vast majority of studies focus on the US Supreme Court – there is reason to believe that to the extent that amicus curiae briefs influence judicial decision-making, their

TABLE I.I *Institution-driven insulation in cross-national comparison*

Popular insulation			
Arenas	Switzerland	Germany	Canada	United States
Electoral	Low	Intermediate	High	Intermediate (variable)
Legislative	Low	High	High	Low
Executive	Intermediate	High	High	High
Judicial	N/A	Intermediate (rare)	High	High
Interest group insulation			
Arenas	Switzerland	Germany	Canada	United States
Electoral	Low	High	High	Intermediate
Legislative	Low	High	High	Intermediate
Executive	Low (business) Intermediate (others)	Low (social partners) High (others)	Intermediate	Intermediate
Judicial	N/A	High	High	Intermediate

impact will most likely be felt in the United States, given its litigation-prone adversarial legal culture and strong civil society.

To sum up, Table 1.1 provides an overview of the impact of institutions in shaping the strength of policy makers' popular and interest group insulation in the four countries. Note that the insulation scores in each cell are based on a cross-national, rather than cross-arena (see Chapter 2), comparison. Put differently, the scores express cross-national variation in the strength of insulation for a given policy arena. Thus, Swiss institutions stand out for the lack of insulation they offer to policy makers, whereas the opposite is the case for Canada, where policy makers operate in an institutional environment conducive to both popular and interest group insulation. Germany and the United States are both in-between cases. The next section elaborates on the book's methodology, after which the chapter concludes with a brief outline of the subsequent chapters.

METHOD OF INQUIRY

Given the complexities and contingencies that so often bedevil attempts at theorizing policy reform, studying immigration reform over the *longue durée* allows us to see the kinds of policy patterns that crystallize only with the passage of time. Echoing Howlett and Cashore's assessment that "any analysis of policy development must be historical in nature and cover periods of years or even decades or more" (2009, 35), this study examines the development of immigration policy from the immediate postwar period to the 2010s. There is no question that the end of World War II marked a historical turning point in the politics of immigration across the Global North as it ushered in a much-altered global environment – economically, politically, and ideologically. While this watershed was most dramatic for Germany, it also fundamentally altered the immigration regimes of Switzerland, Canada, and the United States. In Canada and the United States, the horrors of the Holocaust resolutely discredited the biological racism that had been so influential in shaping immigration policy since its inception across settler colonial states. Meanwhile, in Europe the need to rebuild a continent devastated by war set the scene for the large-scale foreign labor recruitment that even today lives on in the term guest worker (*Gastarbeiter*). While no break with the past can ever be absolute, and certain continuities always remain, the dynamics that migration scholars associate with "the politics of immigration" by and large have their origins in the postwar era. It is in this sense, then, that the book provides the longest possible historical coverage of the politics of immigration policy making.

The study of the *longue durée* in four countries was only possible owing to the empirically rich (English-, German-, and French-language) immigration literature. Much of the data that this book's empirical chapters draw on are borrowed from existing scholarship. Whenever necessary, these data were supplemented with original archival data (most importantly for the Swiss case), a close reading of legislative transcripts and government reports, news articles, and other nonscholarly publications. Gathering these qualitative data allowed for the telling of a causal story of immigration reform by means of process tracing, a tool widely used for qualitative within-case analysis (Bennett and Checkel 2014). Process tracing allows for the identification of causal mechanisms that link proposed explanatory variables to a given outcome of interest. While each case study examined in this book digs deep into the historical record, focusing on three causal mechanisms – popular, interest group, and diplomatic insulation – allows the analysis to proceed in a relatively parsimonious manner. Each case study looks for observable implications of the three proposed mechanisms, while also considering alternative explanations for policy choices. This allows for the evaluation of the goodness of fit between the theoretically generated expectations, on the one hand, and the case-by-case observations, on the other. The paired nature of the chapters also adds a cross-national comparison to this task and provides us with additional leverage. While ideally the case studies should be read in pairs – Switzerland and Germany as one pair, Canada and the United States as the other – the chapters can also stand alone for those interested in a particular case.

Finally, in the interest of parsimony, this study's theoretical framework does not seek to predict the preferences and, by extension, the substance of initial reform proposals. These are inductively determined by means of case-by-case analysis. The framework's theoretical scope starts at the point of a policy proposal and identifies the direction (liberalization or restriction) and scope (incremental or paradigmatic) of the proposed reforms. It then identifies the conditions – both institutional and strategic – that will determine whether or not (or to what extent) a proposal is expected to succeed. In other words, this book's framework allows us to account for the distance – or lack thereof – between a reform proposal, on the one hand, and the final policy choice, on the other.

BOOK OVERVIEW

Chapter 2 presents the book's policy arenas framework, which seeks to account for the direction and magnitude of immigration reform. After introducing the different institutional arenas through which immigration policy can travel, the chapter begins by theorizing the direction of policy change. Whether policy reform will liberalize or restrict immigration will depend, I argue, on policy makers' insulation from four sets of actors with distinct sets of preferences: domestically, the general public and interest groups; internationally, immigrant-sending states and immigrant-receiving states. Whereas insulation from popular pressure and from diplomatic pressure by receiving states will allow for policy liberalization, insulation from interest groups and sending states will move policy in the direction of immigration restriction. Importantly, which of these pressures policy makers are exposed to will vary across policy arenas because each policy arena has a distinct combination of popular, interest group, and diplomatic insulation. As policy paths can vary across episodes of immigration reform, different policy paths will produce variation in policy choice. The chapter then turns its attention to the policy path itself, distinguishing between constitutional rules and political strategy. Constitutional rules, which define the arenas through which a policy proposal must minimally pass, vary both across countries and across types of policy. Beyond constitutional rules, the policy path is shaped by political strategy, as policy makers and external actors alike face incentives to alter or contain a policy's path. Oftentimes informed by policy learning, political strategy can account for variation in policy paths over time in a given constitutional context.

The chapter then moves on to theorize the magnitude of policy change by distinguishing between incremental and paradigmatic immigration reform. Policy arenas matter not only because of their distinct insulation logics, but also because they constitute veto points for opponents of reform. The theory posits that because incremental reform does not seek to alter fundamental assumptions of policy it can oftentimes be enacted in a single arena. By contrast, because of its greater magnitude, paradigmatic reform will have to pass through a greater number of policy arenas, each of which can serve as a potential veto point to policy reform. The success of paradigmatic immigration reform therefore will depend upon a highly restrictive set of conditions, most importantly the absence of reform opponents with veto power.

Chapter 3 lays out the making of Swiss economic immigration policy from the late 1940s to the mid-2010s. It begins with the establishment of Switzerland's guest worker regime with the signing of the Swiss-Italian recruitment treaty in 1948. Premised on the principle of worker rotation, recruitment policy reflected a process of policy learning from the late nineteenth century, when unregulated labor migration had resulted in large-scale immigrant settlement and triggered violent popular backlash. By choosing rotation, policy makers thus sought to balance the disparate goals of economic expansion, on the one hand, and the prevention of immigrant settlement, on the other. Throughout the 1940s and 1950s, the need to prevent "overforeignization" – a term that describes the association of immigrant settlement with sociocultural threat – served as an important check on guest worker recruitment.

The second case study traces a series of regulatory reforms over the course of the 1960s, culminating in the creation of the global ceiling system in 1970. Whereas in the early recruitment period only the stay, but not the overall number of workers, was subject to state control, by the early 1960s guest workers started to qualify for residence permits. This incipient settlement process triggered sustained popular mobilization against "overforeignization." Caught between popular pressure for closure and interest group pressure for openness, the government passed a series of incremental reforms that capped guest worker recruitment at the firm level. With the success of the populist Schwarzenbach Initiative in forcing a referendum on immigration, however, pressures for closure gained the upper hand, and policy makers decided to override the preferences of business and impose a "global ceiling" that capped the overall number of guest workers. In doing so, policy makers were able to avert defeat at the referendum, as voters rejected the initiative.

The chapter's third case study is set during a period marked by historic changes in Switzerland's international environment. With the construction of the European Union's single market, in the early 1990s, Switzerland had to decide whether or not to join a new European Economic Area (EEA) that would allow for the free movement of goods, persons, capital, and services. While EEA membership would provide Switzerland's export-oriented industries with open market access, it was incompatible with the annual quotas imposed under the global ceiling system. Anti-immigration groups quickly mobilized against EEA membership, arguing that it would lead to higher levels of immigration and a loss of sovereignty. After a long search for new policy models, the government enacted the Three Circles Policy, which sought to reconcile the diplomatic imperative of free movement of European workers with the populist calls for closure. While an inner circle of EU and European Free Trade Area (EFTA) immigrants would enjoy freedom of movement, recruitment beyond this circle would be limited to citizens of "culturally similar" (i.e., Western) countries. Unlike in 1970, however, these concessions failed to placate populist groups, in particular the far-right SVP, and, in a mandatory referendum, voters rejected Switzerland's EEA membership.

The chapter's final case study examines policy making in the 2000s, as Switzerland continues to grapple with the tension between the economic imperative of market integration and populist calls for immigration control. Committed to securing access to the European market, the Swiss government opted for a treaty-based approach to market integration, which, at the European Union's insistence, included a Free Movement Agreement. In order to neutralize the referendum threat, policy makers appealed to the SVP, whose economic wing supported market integration, with the argument that bilateral treaties do not infringe on Swiss sovereignty in the way that regional membership would have done. At the same time, the government courted trade unions, promising significant labor market protections in exchange for union support of the treaty package. The government's strategy paid off when, at a referendum organized by anti-immigration groups in 2000, a majority of voters endorsed the treaties. Eight years later, the Swiss parliament passed a new immigration act that codified the policy changes enacted through bilateral treaties or executive directives over the previous years. Questions about the direction of Swiss immigration policy seemed to be settled until, in 2014, a new anti-immigration initiative was put to the people. Adopted by a majority of voters, the Mass Immigration Initiative presented policy makers with the impossible choice between legislating the people's will or maintaining its bilateral treaties with the European Union. Policy makers decided in favor of the latter, leaving Switzerland's immigration policy acutely vulnerable to future popular challenge.

Chapter 4 examines Germany's politics of economic immigration policy making over the course of five decades. The first case study examines the establishment of Germany's guest worker system through a series of bilateral treaties in the 1950s and 1960s, followed by the 1973 recruitment stop. Intent on rebuilding its severed diplomatic and economic relations after World War II, Germany initially entered into recruitment treaties because of diplomatic pressure from Mediterranean sending states. Not long into recruitment, growing domestic labor shortages provided the impetus for expanding guest worker employment. For most of the recruitment period, policy makers assumed that guest worker recruitment would be reversible and failed to put into place policy safeguards to prevent immigrant settlement. When the government shut down recruitment in response to mounting social and political tensions in the early 1970s, policy makers were able to seize the oil crisis as a window of opportunity to shut down recruitment, against the expressed preferences of sending states. After the recruitment stop, political elites used the experience of unintended and large-scale immigrant settlement to construct a national narrative of Germany as a "country of non-immigration," allowing for the maintenance of the recruitment stop even after the oil crisis.

The second case study examines the reopening of guest worker recruitment channels – this time with Central and Eastern European sending states – in the 1990s. Once again, diplomatic considerations provided an important impetus for recruitment, as the German government was concerned to facilitate economic and political regional stabilization after the end of the Cold War. By contrast to the postwar era, this time recruitment was firmly premised on worker rotation to ensure the reversibility of recruitment. Thus, policy makers engaged in policy learning to allow for the reopening of temporary foreign worker recruitment without, however, challenging the paradigm of non-immigration.

It was only in the new millennium that the non-immigration paradigm came under sustained attack. The chapter's third case study examines the

Green Card program of 2000, which marked Germany's first foray into high-skilled immigration and, despite its limited recruitment success, marked the beginning of a debate that sought to reframe (high-skilled) immigration as being in Germany's national interest. Calls for Comprehensive Immigration Reform which would necessitate a paradigm shift from non-immigration to country of immigration, mounted. Our final case study examines the passage of the 2004 Immigration Act by Germany's first Social Democratic-Green government. The Act signifies the failure of paradigmatic reform: rather than being a historic milestone, it left in place the recruitment stop and provided for the admission of high-skilled immigrants only on the basis of regulatory exemptions. While paradigmatic reform easily passed the lower house, *Land*-level elections turned the upper house into a veto point for social conservatives who objected to the new immigration paradigm. Constant electioneering turned modest disagreements into a partisan gulf, producing a legislative stalemate in the upper house that prompted the bill's referral to the Constitutional Court, who ruled in the opposition's favor. As a result, rather than ushering in a new immigration paradigm, the Immigration Act of 2004 affirmed the decades-old recruitment stop and held on to the view of immigration as the exception rather than the rule. Subsequent legislative reforms have continued along the path of nonparadigmatic policy reform by incrementally liberalizing the admission of high-skilled and, since 2019, skilled, foreign workers.

Chapter 5 studies the development of Canadian family and economic immigration policy from the late 1950s to the mid-2010s. The first case study examines the end of the White Canada policy in favor of an immigration policy that selected on the basis of skills and family ties rather than national origin. This far-reaching change was first passed in two rounds of regulatory change in 1962 and 1967, before being legitim-ated in the legislative arena with the passage of the 1976 Immigration Act. It was driven by diplomatic pressure and made possible by a high degree of popular insulation. The 1976 Act followed in the wake of a period of consultation and consensus building among societal and political elites, opening up the policy process to interest group influence for the sake of public legitimation. In doing so, policy makers were forced to make important concessions to immigrant constituencies on the question of family immigration.

In a second case study, the chapter examines a series of reforms passed between the mid-1980s and early 2000s that transformed the size and composition of Canadian immigrant admissions. In a first change, this period marked the transition from an economic admissions policy aimed at filling short-term labor market shortages to one designed to ensure Canada's competitiveness in a global knowledge economy. As economic admissions became uncoupled from the state of the economy, immigration levels were set and maintained at historic highs. The raising of overall immigration levels laid the groundwork for a second policy shift that tilted the balance of immigrant admissions from family to economic immigration, creating a policy regime that is – and remains – defined by economic immigration. In a dynamic similar to that leading up to the 1976 Act, these paradigmatic reforms were first passed in the form of regulation, before becoming institutionalized with the Immigration and Refugee Protection Act of 2001. In contrast to the 1976 Act, however, increasing immigration levels allowed policy makers to frame the reforms as pro-immigration, shielding reformers from interest group pressure to reverse plans for cutting family immigration.

The chapter's third case study examines a succession of reforms enacted under a conservative government between 2006 and 2015. Whereas previous reform efforts had been marked by a lack of partisanship, the newly constituted Conservative Party espoused a distinct policy agenda of market liberalism. Determined to fully exploit the executive's policy-making autonomy, the government shifted the logic of economic admissions from human capital to employer demand, sidelined the centrality of permanent immigration in favor of temporary foreign worker recruitment, and curtailed the sponsorship of extended family members. Even when policy moved into the legislative arena, the government shunned the consensus-oriented policy-making style that had characterized previous rounds of immigration reform. While the absence of legislative veto points allowed the government to enact its policy agenda without making major concessions to societal interests, it did so at the cost of policy legitimacy, thereby rendering immigration reform vulnerable to future reversal.

Chapter 6 investigates the politics of US immigration reform from the early 1950s until the mid-2010s. The passage of the 1965 Immigration and Nationality Act marks the beginning of a policy regime anchored in family ties and occupational skills. As the United States came to embrace its position as a Cold War superpower, the White House's diplomatic insulation weakened, and diplomatic pressure to end national origins-based admissions mounted. Yet unlike the Canadian cabinet, the White House could not repeal the national origins quotas by means of regulatory change but instead had to rely on congressional cooperation to pass legislative change. With restrictionist Southern Democrats in control of key congressional committees, however, reform was blocked throughout the 1950s and into the 1960s. It was only after the restrictionist coalition was weakened by generational turnover that immigration reform got under way, albeit with major concessions made to congressional restrictionists. As a result, while the 1965 Act abolished the quotas, it fell short of the original vision of the executive–congressional reform coalition. Most significantly, it imposed a ceiling on western hemisphere immigration and created an immigration system dominated by family reunification, rather than employment-based admissions.

The second case study examines the political process leading up to the 1990 Immigration Act, which enacted historically unprecedented levels of admissions. Originally intended to tilt the balance of admissions from family toward high-skilled immigration – including a firm cap on overall numbers – the 1990 Act instead liberalized economic admissions through an increase in overall visas, rather than by, as had been intended, a reduction in family-based visas. The 1990 reform clearly illustrates the lack of interest group insulation of members of Congress. Because legislators were not sufficiently insulated to impose costs on organized interests – in particular ethnic lobbies – the policy solution was an overall increase, rather than a redistribution of, visas. This case study thus stands in notable contrast to the ability of Canadian policy makers to create a human capital-based immigration policy.

The chapter's third case study analyzes three failed attempts to pass Comprehensive Immigration Reform – which encompasses economic admissions, family admissions, temporary foreign worker recruitment, border enforcement, and, most controversially, the legalization of undocumented immigrants – under the Bush and Obama presidencies. While some reform attempts were more successful than others, reflecting variation in interest group support, in the end all three attempts failed because of the growing influence of immigration restrictionists within the Republican Party. Tea Party Republicans made sure that Republican legislators would come to see any step toward immigration liberalization as a potential electoral liability. Under both the Bush and Obama presidencies, the legalization of undocumented immigrants in particular became the third rail of immigration reform. Impossible to exclude from the reform agenda because of the size of the undocumented population, legalization became the focus of Republican obstructionism. Even though the growing electoral strength of Latino voters provided an important impetus for reform, in the end legislators' lack of insulation from popular restrictionism came to determine the outcome of reform.

Chapter 7 sums up the book's key theoretical claims and empirical findings before exploring the extension of its argument beyond the cases examined in the empirical chapters. The chapter first applies the argument to additional migration-related policy areas, including asylum, refugee resettlement, migration control, immigrant integration, and citizenship policy. It then ventures beyond the national level of policy making by using the insulation framework to shed light on the logic of immigration policy making in the European Union, followed by subnational policy making. The chapter concludes with an appraisal of the future politics of immigration policy.

Theorizing Immigration Policy

Veto Points and the Insulation Logics of Policy Arenas

This chapter presents a theoretical framework for the comparative study of the politics of immigration policy. It provides us with the analytical tools to engage in two distinct types of comparison: comparison of policy choices across countries and over time. Both types of comparison are necessary if we are to develop a well-grounded understanding of the dynamics driving the making of immigration policy. Studying policy making in cross-national perspective enables us to confront the puzzle of why liberal democracies that share broadly similar migration challenges oftentimes adopt remarkably different policy solutions. At the most basic level, countries vary in their orientation toward the desirability of immigration. Whereas some states actively embrace immigration by recruiting permanent residents from abroad, others welcome foreign nationals on a strictly temporary basis only, while yet others seek to keep out as many migrants as possible. In addition to maintaining distinct orientations toward immigration, states also direct openness and closure toward different immigrant groups. Of those policy regimes that broadly embrace immigration, some direct their openness toward economic migrants while others prioritize family-based immigration instead. The comparative study of policy making thus allows us to identify and explain variation in policy choice across liberal democracies. A cross-national comparison also deepens our understanding of immigration politics in individual countries, as it allows us to distinguish between policy dynamics that are generalizable and those that are sui generis.

Just as cross-national comparison illuminates the determinants of policy choice, so does the study of policy making over time. Adopting an intertemporal perspective allows us to account for both policy *stasis* and policy *change*. Thus, by studying the politics of immigration policy over time we can identify the mechanisms of policy reproduction that yield striking policy stability over long time periods. By adopting a long time horizon, we can understand the ways in which present policy choices are conditioned by those of the past. At the same time, intertemporal analysis allows us to identify not only the conditions under which policy changes, but also the magnitude of policy change. While most of the time policy reform makes only modest changes to the status quo, under rare conditions paradigmatic policy change ushers in a novel appraisal of immigration (Hall 1993). Studying policy choice over time thus allows us to identify the outer bounds of imaginable policy reform, and to gauge the significance of a given case of policy reform. Building on arguments in historical institutionalism, this chapter's policy arenas framework allows us to understand both the *magnitude* and substantive *direction* of immigration policy reform.

AN ARENAS FRAMEWORK OF IMMIGRATION POLICY MAKING

Historical institutionalist scholars have long recognized the substantive and strategic impact of institutions on public policy (Immergut 1990, Steinmo et al. 1992, Hall and Taylor 1996, Scharpf 2000). The institutions from within which policy makers operate represent distinct substantive mandates that shape how actors conceive of a given policy issue, decide among competing policy goals and trade-offs, and define the range of appropriate actions. Institutions both shape actors' substantive preferences and equip them with strategic knowledge for how best to pursue their preferences. Simultaneously empowering and constraining, institutional rules delineate the range of constitutionally and politically viable action and allow actors to anticipate the actions that competing actors are likely to pursue. If actors are able to navigate their institutional environment successfully, then their preferences will be reflected in enacted policy.

Before we examine the role political institutions have in the shaping of immigration policy more closely, we will establish the basic imperatives – or interests – that underpin state action in liberal states. While the policy arenas framework is premised on the institutional disaggregation of the state, we nevertheless need to recognize that even though their salience may vary between institutional locations, certain imperatives are collectively shared by policy makers *across* institutional contexts. These imperatives endow policy makers with distinct preferences and mark them as subjective actors in their own right, rather than as neutral arbiters among competing societal interests. Even where the preferences of policy makers happen to coincide with those of societal actors, state actors' preferences cannot be reduced to those of societal groups.

I follow Christina Boswell in arguing that the making of immigration policy intersects with several core functions of the state that are at the heart of its "quest for legitimacy" (Boswell 2007, 88). First, one of the state's most basic imperatives is the provision of security for its citizens. With the securitization of migration (Bigo 2002, Huysmans 1998), immigration control has become part of this core function, to the extent that the state's capacity for immigration control is now a critical test case for its legitimation as security provider. Second, and again following Boswell, the pursuit of economic growth – the "accumulation of wealth" (2007, 89) – constitutes another core function of the state. In market economies, this entails the creation of business-friendly environments including, where necessary, the recruitment of foreign workers to meet labor shortages. As a third imperative, and here I depart from Boswell,[1] the liberal democratic state derives legitimacy from representing the popular will. Because of the state's representational function, its officials seek to make policy in ways that will gain and maintain the public's confidence. Hence, the state's representational mandate will make policy makers particularly cautious about pursuing immigration policies that are visibly at odds with public attitudes. Finally, the legitimacy of liberal states is contingent on their normative integrity.[2] Therefore, any treatment of non-nationals that fundamentally violates the liberal principles on which the state's domestic order and its foreign relations are built presents a threat to its moral legitimacy.

The interests and preferences of policy makers do not only follow functional imperatives. Executive and legislative state actors both carry into office partisan affiliations and ideological orientations. Without denying the influence of partisan ideology, however, this analysis treats partisanship as exogenous to its theoretical framework. Returning to our earlier discussion of political parties' positioning on immigration (see Chapter 1, "Political Parties"), one of the conclusions that emerges from

---

[1] I exclude Boswell's third state function – the fair distribution of rights – because it pertains to integration, not immigration, policy.

[2] Boswell's fourth state function is that of institutional legitimacy, which closely corresponds to my use of normative integrity. Unlike Boswell, however, who exclusively focuses on the domestic sphere, I conceive of the legitimation challenge of normative integrity as spanning both the domestic and the international spheres.

this literature is that while immigration positioning maps onto a left–right spectrum divide *in the aggregate* (with the left being more supportive of immigration), this pattern often falls apart once we scale down, either by examining subsets of immigration policy or by investigating specific countries. Not surprisingly, then, the policy challenges examined in this book do not consistently map onto a left–right divide: while center-left parties are more likely to take a restrictionist stance on temporary foreign worker recruitment, center-right parties are more likely to favor restricting family-based immigration.

Most importantly, at least two of the four countries examined in this book defy partisan expectations. Whereas Canada is an outlier because of its cross-party pro-immigration consensus, Switzerland stands out by the unique partisan stability induced by its "magic formula" (see Chapter 1, "Popular Insulation and Electoral Institutions"), which locks in the partisan composition of governments. In other words, in neither country does partisanship serve as a reliable predictor of the direction of proposed immigration reform. On a final note, partisanship quickly loses its explanatory power once we examine more historically distant episodes of immigration reform. Distinct partisan positioning on immigration only emerged with the politicization of immigration, which is a relatively recent phenomenon. For these reasons, this chapter will not theorize the partisan preferences of policy makers. While the partisan affiliations of policy makers matter, we cannot predict their impact across all country cases and subfields of immigration policies. Instead, we treat partisanship as exogenous to this theoretical framework and instead examine its impact inductively in the book's empirical chapters. We now move beyond the substantive preferences of policy makers to theorize the institutionally embedded dynamics of immigration policy making.

The policy arenas framework developed in this chapter builds on veto point arguments in the historical institutionalist literature.[3] First

---

[3] This framework builds on veto point arguments within historical institutionalism, rather than on veto player theory as developed within rational choice institutionalism (Tsebelis 2002). Despite significant overlap between the two approaches, the highly formalized and deductive nature of veto player theory is ill-suited for an empirically grounded comparative policy analysis. In a first limitation, veto player theory focuses largely on incumbent partisan veto players and ignores the role of interest groups and societal groups, which are central to both Immergut's and this analysis. Second, whereas the inductive nature of veto point arguments allows for the identification of policy content, veto player theory is silent on both the location of the policy status quo and the direction of policy change because of the difficulty of determining these a priori (for a more detailed comparison of the two approaches, see Jochem 2003).

developed by Ellen Immergut (1990, 1992), this approach conceives of political systems as sets of institutional arenas, or "institutional sites for policy making" (Timmermans 2001), through which policy travels. The policy process thus resembles a path that winds through certain arenas while circumventing others. The path of a given policy, then, is of critical importance for the outcome of immigration reform for two distinct reasons. First, arenas are potential veto points – that is, they constitute "points of strategic uncertainty where decisions may be overturned" (Immergut 1992, 27). It follows that with each additional arena a policy travels through, the risk of reform failure increases. Second, arenas matter because they embody distinct political logics. Policy arenas, I argue, play a critical role in shaping the *direction* of immigration policy because they present policy makers with distinct types of *political insulation*. For the makers of immigration policy, political insulation is a much-cherished good, as they operate in often highly politicized environments marked by the competing demands of the public, interest groups, and foreign states. I argue that the direction of policy change is fundamentally shaped by four types of political insulation. Whereas domestically, *popular insulation* will shield policy makers from public pressure for policy restrictionism, *interest group insulation* is necessary if policy makers are to enjoy a reprieve from demands for policy liberalization. At the international level, *diplomatic insulation* from immigrant-*receiving* states will provide a buffer from restrictionist demands, whereas *diplomatic insulation* from immigrant-*sending* states will deflect pressure for policy liberalization.

Because arenas differ in the types of insulation they provide, policy choices will vary not only across countries but, in contexts where political actors can manipulate the institutional locus of policy making, also over time. The institutional context in which immigration policy making is set encompasses four policy arenas: the executive arena, the legislative arena, the electoral arena, and the judicial arena. First, the executive arena consists of the national government and the upper echelons of the executive bureaucracy. Second, the legislative arena comprises one or two legislative chambers. Third, the electoral arena is defined by electoral campaigns and, in some constitutional contexts, popular referendums and initiatives. Lastly, the judicial arena, which is significant only in systems with judicial review, comprises constitutional courts that have the power to strike down policy. We begin our discussion of the policy arenas framework by theorizing the role of political insulation in the making of immigration policy.

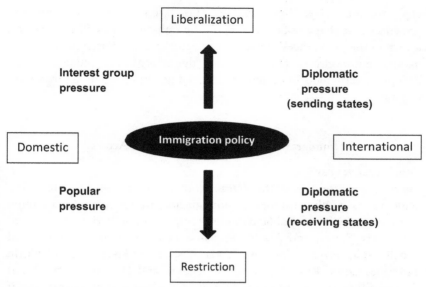

FIGURE 2.1 Immigration preferences of external actors.

THEORIZING THE DIRECTION OF POLICY CHANGE: THE INSULATION LOGIC OF POLICY ARENAS

In the realm of immigration, a policy arena's most critical attribute is the degree to which it provides policy makers with political insulation. Put differently, policy arenas gain significance as they provide openings for non-policy makers – whether domestic societal actors or foreign states – to influence policy decisions. When it comes to the making of immigration policy, the pressures confronting policy makers are fundamentally cross-cutting in nature. Whereas the general public and other receiving states push for national closure, organized interests and sending states will lobby for the liberalization of immigration (Figure 2.1). We therefore need to distinguish between four types of political insulation: *popular insulation*, which shields policy makers from the demands of the general public; *interest group insulation*, which provides reprieve from the lobbying efforts of organized interests; *diplomatic insulation* (from *sending states*), which buffers policy makers from the demands of immigrant-sending states; and *diplomatic insulation* (from *receiving states*), which wards off political pressure from fellow immigrant-receiving states. Before we can examine the conditions under which policy makers will enjoy the four types of political insulation, we first need to identify the pressures that shape policy making in their absence. Specifically, we will ascertain the preferences of each set of actors who threaten the decision-making autonomy of policy makers: the unorganized public, interest groups, governments of sending states, and governments of fellow receiving states.

Immigration Preferences of External Actors

Public Preferences

There is a consensus in the literature that across immigrant-receiving democracies, public attitudes on immigration are restrictionist, meaning that a majority of the public commonly supports a lowering of immigration levels (Simon and Alexander 1993, Esses et al. 1998, Simon and Lynch 1999, Fetzer 2000, Lahav 2004, Kessler and Freeman 2005, Citrin and Sides 2008, Rustenbach 2010, Segovia and Defever 2010). What drives this pervasive public restrictionism? Under what conditions, if any, will its strength vary? Does it reflect a categorical opposition to immigration, or does the public differentiate between different forms of immigration? In other words, are there any conditions under which the public might support the liberalization of immigration policy?

Public opinion scholars have identified two contextual[4] factors that impact the strength of public opposition to immigration. First, the state of the economy affects the intensity of public restrictionism. In times of economic downturn, the public is more likely to express hostility toward immigration than during times of growth – a finding that, significantly, holds across countries (Palmer 1996, Citrin et al. 1997, Lee and Ottati 2002, Wilkes et al. 2008, Meuleman et al. 2009, Aksoy 2012). Second, the public makes distinctions among immigrant groups based on socio-economic characteristics, assessing immigration based on its perceived economic impact (Hainmueller and Hopkins 2014). In particular, the public consistently prefers high-skilled over low-skilled immigration (Hainmueller and Hiscox 2010, O'Connell 2011, Hainmueller and Hopkins 2012).

---

[4] We will focus on contextual rather than individual-level factors. Individual-level variables that have been shown to impact attitudes toward immigration – most importantly educational attainment – do not help us to predict when hostility toward immigrants will increase, and what kind of immigrants are more likely to be the targets of hostility.

While economic factors clearly play a role in shaping public opinion on immigration, there is compelling evidence to suggest that cultural fears are a prominent driver of anti-immigration attitudes. Recent research suggests that cultural fears are better predictors of attitudes toward immigration than is the state of the economy (Sniderman et al. 2004, McLaren and Johnson 2007, Hainmueller and Hiscox 2010, Ford 2011, Hainmueller and Hangartner 2013, Hainmueller and Hopkins 2014). Card et al. find that compositional concerns about immigration's impact on a country's cultural and social life are two to five times more important than concerns about immigration's economic impact on wages and taxes (2012). One important limitation to our understanding of cultural drivers of immigration attitudes – and in particular of the role played by ethno-cultural group characteristics – is the problem of social desirability bias in survey research. Thus, Iyengar et al. (2013) find no evidence that ethno-racial attributes shape attitudes toward individual immigrants. In a similar vein, Harell et al. (2012) find that Canadians and Americans differentiate between immigrants on the basis of skill level but not based on skin tone, though Americans (but not Canadians) differentiate on the basis of immigrants' regional origin. These sanguine findings about the lack of significance of ethnocultural attributes are, however, challenged by behavioral studies. Most prominently, Hainmueller and Hangartner's (2013) natural experiment involving Swiss voting behavior finds that naturalization referendums are strongly driven by taste-based ethnic discrimination, with applicants' country of origin serving as the strongest predictor of naturalization decisions. Hainmueller and Hangartner's finding that the preferences revealed at the polls greatly differ from those expressed in survey responses suggest that survey research grossly underestimates the role of ethnocultural attributes in shaping immigration attitudes.

At the same time, Harell et al.'s (2012) finding that Americans but not Canadians differentiate on the basis of region of origin points to potential cross-national variation in immigration attitudes. There is some evidence that public restrictionism is weaker in Canada than in Europe and the United States (Simon and Lynch 1999, Hiebert 2006, Adams 2007, Citrin et al. 2012). Explanations for Canadians' seemingly more open attitudes toward immigration have generally focused on the country's more economically selective (high-skilled) immigration policy, its geographic distance from immigrant-sending regions, its comparatively proactive integration and multiculturalism policies, and the relatively strong electoral clout of its ethnic and immigrant minorities (Kymlicka 2003,

Bloemraad 2006, Harell 2009, Marwah et al. 2013). Theorizing the immigration preferences of the public certainly requires us to consider the possibility that, under certain conditions, ethnic minority electoral strength can provide a counterweight to the majority's immigration restrictionism. As Westlake (2018) argues, ethnic minority electoral strength – operationalized as a function of the size of the foreign-born population and the ease of access to naturalization – can matter in countries where electoral rules reward geographically concentrated voting blocs (i.e., in single-member district systems). Of the countries examined in this book, Canada stands out by its relatively high ethnic minority electoral strength.[5] Thus, Westlake finds a relationship between Canada's ethnic minority electoral strength and its strong multiculturalism policies. At the same time, we would expect the impact of ethnic minority electoral strength to vary across policy areas, mattering most for multiculturalism and integration policies and least for temporary foreign worker recruitment. Thus, while the Canadian case does not warrant a categorical departure from the assumption of popular restrictionism (Rheault 2013), it does prompt us to consider the possibility of cross-national variation in the strength of anti-immigration attitudes. In particular, culturally driven arguments against immigration may be less effective in mobilizing the public in some countries than in others. Despite this caveat, given that public attitudes consistently favor the restriction of immigration over its expansion, we can posit that whenever public opinion is mobilized, it will exert pressure in favor of policy restrictionism and against policy liberalization.

Interest Group Preferences

A second way in which societal influence can bear on immigration policy is through the lobbying efforts of organized interests. Gary Freeman (1995) has argued that, because the benefits of immigration are concentrated and its costs diffuse, organization and mobilization is strongest among pro-immigration groups, in particular by employers who stand to gain from the increased supply of labor. Interest group pressure therefore is liberalizing in nature: it will point in the direction of opening up immigration to select groups of immigrants. For instance, we would expect corporate lobbying to correspond positively to the admission of temporary foreign workers (Rheault 2013). While Freeman's argument

---

[5] It is highest in Australia, followed by Canada and New Zealand (see Westlake 2018, 426).

works well for the settler colonial states in which it was developed, it requires some revision to be applicable to nonsettler countries. Most fundamentally, Freeman's argument is premised on a pluralist system of interest representation – shared by all settler colonial states – where interest groups rely on self-organization to compete against each other for access to the policy-making process. In these contexts, business with its "privileged position" (Lindblom 1977) and superior financial and organizational resources is by far the most powerful interest group.

However, looking at the kind of neocorporatist systems of interest representation that are prevalent across much of Europe, Freeman's assumptions do not fully hold. In neocorporatist systems the state supports certain interests – principally labor and business – in solving the collective action problem of mobilization. The state not only assists these groups in establishing structures of interest representation but also guarantees them a seat at the bargaining table. In doing so, it strengthens the relative position of labor and lowers the hurdle to mobilization in cases where the costs of immigration may be diffuse. As a result, when it comes to influencing policy labor is more likely to serve as a counterweight to the interests of business, and we would expect pressures for policy liberalization to be more restrained in neocorporatist countries than in pluralist systems of interest representation.

Sending-State Preferences

Immigration is a quintessentially intermestic[6] policy field. Sitting at the intersection of domestic politics and international relations, immigration policy made in one country often has far-reaching social and economic implications for others. Far from indifferent to the policy choices of receiving states, sending governments face strong incentives to influence immigration policy making, thereby turning immigration from a domestic policy issue into one of international relations. While we know far less about the preferences of immigrant-sending states than those of immigrant-receiving countries (Rosenblum 2004), there is no question that sending states have a clear stake in what kind of immigration policies are enacted by receiving states. For countries that struggle with economic stagnation and slack labor markets, emigration serves as a vital safety valve to relieve employment pressures at home. Even more critically, emigration is a source of much-needed foreign currency, and migrant

---

[6] Following Manning (1977) I use the term to describe a process in which domestic policy making is either influenced by or has an impact at the international level.

remittances constitute the second largest capital flow to the developing
world after foreign direct investment (World Bank 2014). While emigration also imposes long-term costs in the form of brain drain and
depopulation, sending states are likely to discount them in favor of the
more fungible and immediate economic benefits of international migration (Rosenblum 2004).

Given the social, economic, and monetary benefits of emigration, we
can assume that sending states will strongly favor policies that facilitate
the emigration of their nationals while opposing policies that would result
in their return (Ellermann 2008). We can further expect sending states to
contest policies that discriminate against or infringe on the rights of their
nationals. As Fitzgerald and Cook-Martín have argued in the context of
racially selective immigration policy in the Americas, "the nation- state ...
is based on the principle that the state represents a particular people.
Governments of countries of origin do not complain about discrimination
so much because they care about the welfare of particular migrants,
but because they have a desire to avoid international shame" (2014,
28). In sum, we can assume that countries of emigration will favor the
enactment of liberalizing and nondiscriminatory immigration policies in
receiving countries.

Receiving-State Preferences

While diplomatic pressure most often emanates from immigrant-sending
states, under certain conditions immigrant-receiving states will follow suit
and seek to influence policy in other receiving states in the region. Unlike
sending states, however, pressure from receiving states will point in the
direction of policy restrictionism rather than liberalization. Essentially,
immigrant-receiving states will place restrictionist demands on other
receiving states if they consider their security interests to be compromised
by the latter's actions (or inaction). This is most often the case where
border control is compromised after a sudden influx of asylum seekers or
other irregular migrants. As state sovereignty is premised on effective
border control, uncontrolled immigration poses a serious political liability
for any democratic government. Uncontrolled immigration puts into
question the efficacy of the policy status quo, thereby threatening not
only to undermine its legitimacy but also to trigger popular backlash.
Where compromised border control can be attributed to the actions of
other receiving states – such as ineffective border controls that facilitate
the transit movement of refugees into other neighboring states – policy
makers will demand that receiving states restore effective control of their

borders. Diplomatic insulation from receiving states thus matters most in the politics of border control and asylum policy. While this framework theorizes both sending- and receiving-state diplomatic pressure, receiving-state pressure does not feature in the book's empirical chapters. Because the case studies focus exclusively on economic immigration and family immigration, diplomatic pressure emanates only from sending, not from fellow receiving, states. We will now take a closer look at how popular and interest group pressure, as well as sending-state and receiving-state pressure, operate in the four policy arenas.

Popular Insulation in the Policy Arenas

By definition, popular insulation is weakest in the *electoral arena*, where mobilization threatens to impose high political costs on policy makers. Popular pressure is generated as the public is mobilized in anticipation of a referendum or popular initiative, or in the lead-up to an election. Note that the mere anticipation of political costs can suffice for the electoral arena to constitute a viable veto point. In other words, a referendum may not have to be called for popular influence to exert its power. As Aubert has argued with reference to Switzerland, "[t]he most successful referendums are those which do not take place. The circles which might have fought the law do not do so because it contains what they want. ... [P]arliament does not make laws in a sovereign way but always under the threat of a referendum" (Aubert 1978, 48–9). Where immigration becomes politicized in the lead-up to an election, a party's refusal to support popular demands for restrictionism can easily threaten its electoral success. This is the case where mainstream parties compete with far-right parties for votes. Typically, mainstream parties will seek to avoid the politicization of immigration unless they pursue policies that are unlikely to trigger pervasive immigration restrictionism, such as high-skilled worker recruitment or the legalization of the children of undocumented immigrants. Where their agenda control is threatened by far-right populist parties, or by regional or internal party factions, however, mainstream parties will likely feel the need to exploit the issue (Perlmutter 1996). In other words, mainstream political parties will co-opt restrictionist policy agendas if not doing so poses a credible threat to their electoral success.

The salience of the electoral arena – and the associated degree of popular insulation – is, first and foremost, a function of political institutions and, as a result, will vary cross-nationally (for a detailed cross-national institutional comparison of the book's four country cases, see

Chapter 1). Where policy makers operate in institutional contexts of direct democracy, policy will regularly move beyond the executive and legislative arenas into the electoral arena. As a result, policy making in systems of direct democracy is marked by the virtual absence of popular insulation. That is, policy makers have to navigate a political environment where popular pressure for immigration restrictionism is ubiquitous. Shifting our focus from referendums and initiatives to elections, we would expect popular insulation to be weakest in jurisdictions with short and fixed electoral cycles (Scharpf 2000). Where electoral cycles are short, legislators are perpetually on the campaign trail, forced to pander to public opinion. Where electoral cycles are fixed, governments cannot create buffers from unfavorable public opinion by controlling the timing of elections. Finally, as argued above, immigration policy is far more likely to become politicized during election season in the presence of far-right parties, or where mainstream parties are marked by internal or regional factions. Whatever the case may be, public mobilization generally spells bad news for policy makers intent on liberalizing the policy status quo.

Contrary to the electoral arena, the *executive arena* is marked by a high degree of popular insulation. While it could be countered that in this age of the "permanent campaign" (Blumenthal 1982) no elected official is ever truly insulated from popular pressure, the fact that governments represent national constituencies means that executives need to balance populist pressures against other imperatives, such as the nation's broader economic, security, and diplomatic interests (Rosenblum 2004). Given the pervasiveness of policy linkages between immigration and these other areas of public policy, the pursuit of an unabashedly populist agenda of immigration restrictionism would constitute an enormous liability for executive policy makers. The political insulation of executives will be most compromised in cases where governments pursue policies that are at odds with their partisan ideological commitments and, hence, party platforms. At the same time, executives are closely attuned to their political environment and will seek to anticipate any political fallout of potentially unpopular policies. To do so, they have at their disposal various tools of damage control that serve to protect their popular insulation. Perhaps most importantly, executive policy making takes place behind closed doors, and, as a result, even attentive publics are usually kept in the dark about what transpires in cabinet and intraministerial meetings. Executives will further seek to control the timing of going public with any potentially unpopular policies. In a similar vein, where constitutionally empowered to do so, chief executives will seek to prevent the politicization of immigration in the popular arena by manipulating the timing of elections.

Policy makers in the *legislative arena*, by contrast, operate in contexts of weaker popular insulation. It is weakest in presidential systems with majoritarian electoral rules where individual legislators are elected through the personal vote and answer to their constituents, rather than to their party's leadership. Where legislators operating in these contexts also face the challenge of short legislative terms with their associated "permanent campaign[s]" (Blumenthal 1982), popular insulation will be decidedly weak. By contrast, legislators in parliamentary systems who are elected under rules of party-list proportional representation will enjoy much greater popular insulation than their congressional counterparts. This occurs because in parliamentary systems, legislators' political fortunes are closely tied to those of their party. In other words, they are accountable first to their party leadership and only secondarily to their constituents. It follows that while popular insulation is weaker in the legislative arena vis-à-vis the executive arena, it is also highly variable across constitutional contexts.

The judicial arena constitutes a policy arena only in countries where judges are empowered to review the constitutionality of federal policy. In these contexts constitutional judges operate under conditions of high popular insulation. As political appointees with oftentimes life tenure, judges are not beholden to public opinion. Their popular insulation can be indirectly compromised in the rare – but potentially significant – instances where judges engage in abstract review. Abstract review, which is common across European legal systems but does not exist in the United States, involves the constitutional review of legislation in the absence of a concrete legal case. It is initiated by politicians who refer legislation directly to the court. Courts cannot reject a case, and governments cannot prevent the courts from reviewing their legislation (Stone 1990). Even though abstract review rarely occurs, it can have far-reaching policy consequences as it provides the parliamentary opposition or, in some cases, members of subnational governments, with a veto point. It is thus viewed as the true final stage of the legislative process.

Not surprisingly, then, constitutional courts that exercise abstract ex post review have been referred to as "negative legislators" (Kelsen 1928), "third legislative chambers" (Stone 1990), "the extended arm of the opposition," and "veto players" (Stüwe 2001). Constitutional review lessens the popular insulation of governing majorities, to the extent that opposition parties file for abstract review in order to exploit immigration policy for partisan purposes. Where reform proposals seek to liberalize immigration, the prospect of constitutional reform provides a conduit for the mobilization of popular fears by the opposition, even in cases where the government holds a solid parliamentary majority. Naturally, just as in the case with popular referendums, the possibility of abstract review with its threat of future censure can also have a strong indirect influence on policy making. Constitutional review creates incentives for parliamentary majorities to concede to certain demands of the opposition in order to avoid constitutional censure and its associated political costs (Stone 1990). We now turn to interest groups as the main domestic counterweight to popular demands for immigration restrictionism. Just as policy makers' popular insulation varies across the policy arenas, so does their interest group insulation.

Interest Group Insulation in the Policy Arenas

Under what conditions will interest groups shape the making of immigration policy? Which interests will be most likely to pressure policy makers? I start from the premise that among the profusion of interests, business will have the upper hand. More than any other group, business brings to the table critical information, expertise, and financial resources (Austen-Smith and Wright 1994). Business represents and exerts control over important constituencies and can offer – or withhold – its cooperation in the implementation of policy. Because its goals and resources dovetail with policy makers' preferences and needs (Bouwen 2004, Eising 2007), business occupies a privileged position (Lindblom 1977) that confers disproportionate access to policy makers. Notwithstanding its privileged position, however, the political influence of business can be tempered – though not fully offset – by strong unions. Labor will enjoy greater institutionalized policy-making access in neocorporatist systems of interest representation than in pluralist, noncorporatist, states. Yet even in neocorporatist regimes, the influence of unions will be limited, given business' position as the quintessential insider group with comparatively open access to policy makers (Binderkrantz et al. 2015). We now take a closer look at the interest group insulation of policy makers across the four policy arenas, starting with the executive and legislative arenas.

Broadly speaking, the *executive arena* is marked by a much higher degree of interest group insulation than the *legislative arena*. The executive arena boasts fewer points of access for interest groups for the simple reason that there are fewer cabinet members (and only one head of government) than there are legislators. In the words of a Washington, DC insider, "there are 535 opportunities in Congress and only one in the White House. Where would you put your effort?" (cited in Light 1999, 94). There is no question that the demands on the time and attention of a small group of cabinet members are much greater than those experienced by legislators. Moreover, individual legislators, especially in systems with weak parties, face stronger incentives to respond to interest group demands because they depend on their support for public endorsement and campaign funding. Furthermore, while cabinet and ministerial deliberations are typically shrouded in secrecy, legislative transcripts and roll call votes are public information and commonly dissected by interest groups, thereby further weakening legislators' interest group insulation.

Beyond these differences, the legislative arena is also marked by a larger number of institutional access points. The highly differentiated institutions of Parliament and Congress – most importantly their committees and subcommittees – provide many more access points than the more centralized institutions of government. The number of institutional access points is further increased in bicameral legislatures. If a chamber holds veto power over legislation, then lobbyists may succeed in one chamber after having failed in the other.

A further source of cross-arena variation in interest group insulation lies in their differing representational logics. Executives represent the general interest, whereas legislators represent geographic constituencies. Given their national mandate, executives are significantly constrained when it comes to catering to "special" interests, although in neocorporatist systems the institutionalized triad of state, business, and labor gives legitimacy to the demands of the social partners. Yet, to a much greater degree than legislators, executives have to justify their decisions with reference to the general interest, and decisions are more likely to take into account a broad range of interests. As a result, executives tend to play a more dominant role in their relationship with interest representatives than members of the legislature. Unlike Congress and the courts, for instance, White House lobbying often operates from the inside-out. That is, it is initiated by the president and his staff, rather than by lobbyists (Holyoke 2004). As a result, "[o]rganized interests, especially those that possess real clout, do not control the amount, direction or tempo of contact with the White House" (Burdett 2009, 405).

Moving beyond the executive and legislative arenas, interest group insulation is greatest in the *electoral arena* where popular influence –

the main counterweight to liberalizing interest group demands – rules supreme, as politicians seek to cater to public opinion to win votes. This is not to say that electoral campaigns do not provide interest groups with a window of opportunity for influencing policy. Given politicians' dependence on financial campaign contributions, this is most certainly the case. But for as long as policy passes through the electoral arena, officials will seek to distance themselves from the demands of organized lobbies. As a result, we should expect any concessions made to business during campaign season to be enacted with a significant time lag. That is, we should expect immigration reform to follow the electoral cycle. Policy makers will be most likely to pursue liberalizing immigration reforms after, and never in the lead-up to, elections. Conversely, policy makers will be most likely to pursue restrictionist immigration policies in the lead-up to elections.

In political systems with institutions of direct democracy, referendums and popular initiatives[7] provide additional channels of societal influence. This is particularly pronounced in contexts where these institutions can be activated from below (as is the case with popular initiatives), and therefore cannot be fully controlled by policy makers. I argue that in a manner analogous to elections, interest group insulation will be greatest in the lead-up to referendums and initiatives, as the latter typically give voice to populist demands for immigration restrictionism that conflict with the liberalizing preferences of interest groups. This is the case even though the referendum threat in Switzerland, as the direct democracy par excellence, has given rise to institutionalized pre-parliamentary processes of stakeholder consultation[8] which provide organized interests with an important avenue of policy influence (Linder 2010, Papadopoulos 2013). Similarly, popular initiatives, which are typically organized by outsider interests, can trigger a process of (ex post, rather than ex ante) negotiation and provide interests with policy influence, even if the initiative is eventually withdrawn. Yet, when it comes to issues of immigration it is far from obvious that these institutional mechanisms serve to weaken interest group insulation. Because the referendum threat effectively provides the public with a legislative veto, the restrictionist demands of the public will trump the liberalizing influence of organized lobbies. In the

---

[7] Referendums seek to overturn existing laws, while initiatives put forward new proposals.
[8] The *Vernehmlassungsverfahren* is a process whereby subnational governments and major societal groups are invited to comment on the first draft of a bill.

electoral arena, interest group insulation will only be compromised where interest group preferences align with, and thereby amplify, popular demands for restrictionism. This is most likely to be the case where populist campaigns are not articulated in xenophobic terms and trade unions can represent the restrictionist interests of their members without incurring the risk of being associated with xenophobia. Trade unions will be most likely to lend their support to campaigns that only *indirectly* impinge on immigration policy – such as labor market policy or questions of European integration – and therefore are less likely to be tainted by xenophobia. Setting aside this possibility, however, we can posit that in systems with institutions of direct democracy, referendums and initiatives will significantly weaken popular insulation without activating counter-vailing interest group pressures.

Turning to interest group insulation in the *judicial arena*, immigration policy can travel not only along the path of abstract review, as discussed above, but also along the path of concrete review, where judges rule on cases brought by claimants adversely affected by the implementation of a legal statute. In cases of concrete review, societal influence typically is exercised by organized interests. Interest groups either decide to bring litigation – thereby moving policy into the judicial arena – or else file amicus curiae briefs, which offer expert opinion on the broader policy implications of a legal decision. The role played by amicus briefs for justices is comparable to that played by lobbyists for legislators: they provide legal and substantive information and signal the preferences of other actors (Collins 2007). The filing of amicus briefs not only increases the likelihood that a court will grant review (Caldeira and Wright 1988), but in cases where a court decides to rule it can even exert influence on the ruling's ideological direction (Collins 2007). Where concrete review is exercised, then, interest groups play an important role not only in setting the court's agenda, but also in influencing its substantive ruling. Given that individual cases are most likely to be brought by claimants who consider their rights to have been infringed upon, we would expect rulings that depart from the legal status quo to move policy in the direction of liberalizing, rather than restricting, immigration. The same expectation holds once we consider our earlier arguments about the nature of interest group mobilization, which predict that litigation and amicus filings will be dominated by pro-immigrant groups. We will now turn our attention to the international arena and examine the extent to which foreign governments are able to influence policy making in the four policy arenas.

Diplomatic Insulation in the Policy Arenas

Under what conditions should we expect the interests of foreign states to have an impact on immigration policy making in receiving states? In other words, what determines the degree of diplomatic insulation enjoyed by policy makers in receiving states? At its most basic level, diplomatic insulation is a function of the degree of interdependence between states. Interdependence, of course, can take many forms. Sending states have leverage over immigration policy making in receiving states if the latter have strategic security interests in the sending region or rely on market access for their exports. Similarly, where immigrant-receiving states face severe sectoral labor shortages, sending states will have bargaining power to influence admissions conditions for their nationals. It follows that the more receiving states depend on the cooperation of sending states, the weaker their diplomatic insulation. Turning to the relationship between immigrant-receiving states, rather than being the exception, interdependence constitutes the rule. Given the depth of economic and political integration, both regionally and globally, among advanced democracies, the condition of interdependence is virtually always met. It follows that where fellow receiving states decide to exert diplomatic pressure and make immigration policy the object of bilateral bargaining, they will likely do so in a context of low diplomatic insulation.

In addition to bilateral dependence, diplomatic insulation can be weakened by the imposition of reputational costs. As "dramaturgical acts" designed "to build a country's international brand" (Fitzgerald and Cook-Martín 2014, 21), migration policies oftentimes are highly symbolic in nature. As a result, immigrant-sending governments in particular can impose what Greenhill (2011) has termed "hypocrisy costs" on receiving states whose policies are incongruent with the image they seek to project. The extent to which the imposition of hypocrisy costs presents a threat to the diplomatic insulation of policy makers depends not only on how far a given policy strays from a state's projected image, but also on a country's international standing. Here, liberal states with a strong international standing are better placed to absorb hypocrisy costs than peripheral democracies or liberal democracies that seek to improve their international standing.

A third challenge to diplomatic insulation stems from externalities associated with policy developments in other immigrant-receiving countries that change the environment within which a state's immigration policy functions. If, for instance, neighboring recruiting states liberalize their admission of skilled foreign workers, the state's policy status quo may no longer be effective in attracting sufficient skilled labor. Conversely, a tightening of immigration controls in the region will inadvertently create pressures for other states to follow suit in order to ward off unwanted immigration. In other words, confronted with external shifts in migration flows, immigrant-receiving states will often have little choice but to adjust their policies to align with those of other states, a process that Fitzgerald and Cook-Martín have termed "strategic adjustment" (2014, 26). In many ways, the need for strategic adjustment presents the greatest threat to diplomatic insulation because it presents policy makers with a fait accompli.

In what ways, then, does diplomatic insulation vary across the four policy arenas? There is no question that diplomatic insulation, whether from the demands of sending or receiving states, is weakest in the *executive arena*, where officials bear the primary responsibility for foreign affairs and the conduct of diplomatic relations. It is executives who are charged with negotiating and setting the terms for bilateral agreements, including labor recruitment treaties, and it is diplomatic officials who have to grapple with the complexity of policy interdependencies in bilateral negotiations. Likewise, the representational logic of the executive branch pushes cabinets to "think in grander terms about social problems and the national interest" (Moe and Wilson 1994, 11). Thus, executives face much stronger incentives than legislators to weigh up how policy choices in one area, such as immigration, will impact other aspects of foreign relations, such as international trade. The need to consider the bigger picture will also make executives more likely to recognize the need for strategic adjustment in the light of policy developments abroad. Finally, given the moral authority and high visibility associated with the office of the chief executive, presidents and prime ministers will bear the brunt of reputational costs incurred in the process of immigration policy making, both domestically and abroad.

Whereas executive officials operate in contexts of low diplomatic insulation, we would expect diplomatic insulation in the *legislative arena* to be greater, albeit with some cross-national variation. Both sending-state and receiving-state officials may seek to influence policy by lobbying individual legislators; they may even adopt "cross-level" lobbying strategies (Knopf 1993) by mobilizing transnational advocacy groups. By conceiving foreign officials as lobbyists, we would expect the diplomatic insulation of legislators to approximate their interest group insulation. Accordingly, legislators in parliamentary systems will enjoy high diplomatic insulation, while members of Congress will operate in institutional contexts of intermediate diplomatic insulation. In the *electoral arena*, diplomatic insulation is dependably high. Because immigration policy strikes at the heart of national sovereignty, the public is unlikely to modify their preferences in the light of the interests of foreign governments. On the contrary, where policy change is perceived to be driven by diplomatic pressure, it is likely to be met by public hostility. Finally, the *judicial arena* is equally marked by high diplomatic insulation. Judges who are charged with reviewing the constitutionality of domestic laws have little reason to consider the ways in which they may impinge on the interests of foreign states.

Table 2.1 sums up the relative strengths[9] of popular, interest group, and diplomatic insulation across the four policy arenas and their likely impact on the direction of policy development. Accordingly, in the *executive arena* external pressure is most likely to move policy toward liberalization, given the combination of low (diplomatic) and intermediate (interest group) insulation from pressures for liberalization, and high (popular) insulation from restrictionist demands. The one scenario where we would expect a shift toward policy restrictionism is where diplomatic pressure is exercised by receiving, rather than by sending, states, although any such move may be moderated through liberalizing interest group pressure. Turning to the *legislative arena*, societal pressure will likely produce variable policy impacts. Given that popular and interest group pressure are usually cross-cutting in nature, we would expect the emergence of policy compromises – cases of selective liberalization or restriction – that include both liberalizing and restrictionist provisions. In the *electoral arena*, by contrast, pressure by external actors will firmly move policy toward restrictionism, given the relative absence of popular insulation paired with strong insulation from liberalization pressures. Finally, turning to the *judicial arena*, we need to distinguish between the institutions of concrete and abstract review. Where judges exercise their powers of concrete review, policy will likely move toward liberalization, given that review is initiated by aggrieved individuals who see their rights violated by the state. In political systems with the institution of abstract

---

[9] Note that the strength of insulation is measured in relation to other arenas in the same political system. This does not preclude the possibility that, in a given arena, insulation may vary over time, either as a result of strategic action or through changes in its political environment. Likewise, there is significant cross-national variation in arena insulation (see Chapter 1). Cross-national and intertemporal variation in insulation will be examined in the empirical chapters.

TABLE 2.1 *Strength of political insulation in the policy arenas*

	Popular insulation	Interest group insulation	Diplomatic insulation	Policy direction
Executive arena	High	Intermediate	Low (sending)	Liberalization
			Low (receiving)	Restriction
Legislative arena	Intermediate	Low	Intermediate to high	Variable (Selective liberalization, selective restriction)
Electoral arena	Low	High	High	Restriction
Judicial arena				
Concrete review	High	Intermediate	High	Liberalization
Abstract review	Intermediate	High	High	Restriction

review, by contrast, legal review of immigration policy is typically used as a political weapon of the parliamentary opposition in ways that pander to public opinion. As a result, we would expect the exercise of abstract review to move policy toward restriction, and not liberalization.

Policy arenas, I have argued, are critical to our understanding of immigration policy making because they reflect distinct logics of political insulation. Because they vary in the degree to which they shield policy makers from the competing pressures of the public, interest groups, and foreign states, different policy arenas will shift policy in distinct directions. In other words, different policy paths through the arenas will produce different policy choices. What, then, determines the path that a given reform proposal will take? I argue that the nature of the policy path is determined by two sets of factors: constitutional rules and political strategy. The following section will begin to theorize the policy path by examining the role of constitutional rules.

THEORIZING THE POLICY PATH

The Role of Constitutional Rules

The institutional context of immigration policy making is made up of four policy arenas: the executive arena, the legislative arena, the electoral arena, and the judicial arena. While a policy's path is not necessarily constitutionally predetermined, constitutional rules nevertheless define the arenas through which a given policy must *minimally* pass. These rules not only vary across national contexts but also depend upon the specific form that policy reform takes, whether it is passed as regulation, legislation, or in the form of international treaties. This section describes the four policy arenas and sketches the constitutionally mandated path of each type of policy through the arenas.

Executive Arena
As the most frequently traversed policy arena, the executive arena encompasses both the national government and the upper echelons of the executive bureaucracy. Because immigration can serve a broad range of policy goals, policy making oftentimes involves a number of ministries: in addition to immigration bureaucrats, immigration policy is also made by labor market, trade, and diplomatic officials. The executive arena distinguishes itself among other arenas in that all policy has to pass through it. Where policy takes the form of regulation, constitutional rules only

require passage through the executive arena. Where policy is pursued as legislative reform, it has to pass through both the executive and the legislative arenas. The constitutionally mandated policy path of bilateral treaties, by contrast, varies depending on the nature of the treaty. Whereas in some cases treaties are required only to pass through the executive arena, in others they have to navigate the legislative arena as well. Where policy making is required to pass through both arenas, the executive plays a dual role as agenda setter and veto point. Governments can set the policy agenda either through their right of legislative initiative, as is common in parliamentary systems, or by finding legislative backers for their proposals, as is more often the case in presidential systems. In presidential systems the executive's veto power takes the form of the presidential veto of congressional bills. In parliamentary systems, in the rare case that party discipline fails to assure the government of parliamentary support for its proposals, prime ministers can seek to force their policy agenda by moving a vote of confidence.

Legislative Arena

The legislative arena comprises one or two legislative chambers. The legislative arena constitutes a veto point in cases where legislators can overturn an executive decision (Immergut 1990). The risk of legislative veto thus varies significantly across countries and over time. In presidential systems, where Congress and the president have separate electoral mandates and party discipline is weak, the legislative arena constitutes a veto point any time that policy requires congressional approval. The threat of legislative veto is particularly acute during times of divided government. In parliamentary systems, by contrast, the legislative arena oftentimes does not constitute a viable veto point. Because executive and legislative arenas share the same electoral mandate and are controlled by the same party in contexts marked by strong party discipline, the threat of legislative veto is typically small (Scharpf 2000). However, in countries with strong bicameralism the veto threat is high when the second legislative chamber is controlled by a different partisan majority from the executive (Krehbiel 1996). In a similar vein, the legislative arena constitutes a veto point where executives head minority governments and therefore cannot rely on the support of a parliamentary majority.

Electoral Arena

Constitutional rules rarely require a policy proposal to travel through the electoral arena. The electoral arena comprises a constitutional veto point only in contexts of direct democracy where institutions allow for the popular ratification of policies, or offer the possibility of popular agenda-setting by means of initiative. In systems where all legislation is subject to popular referenda, the electoral arena constitutes a formidable constitutional veto point. In these contexts, the electoral arena not only presents a reactive veto point, but voters can also engage in proactive agenda-setting by means of popular initiative. Popular initiatives effectively place voters in the position of policy maker because, if passed, they require parliament to pass corresponding legislation.

Judicial Arena

The judicial arena is the least traveled arena. Whereas policy is made in the executive and legislative arenas, it is in the judicial arena that, occasionally, it is unmade. In political systems with the institution of constitutional review, policy may, but need not, travel through the judicial arena as judges are empowered to strike down policy provisions or, less commonly, entire legislative statutes. In contexts of abstract review, elected officials can refer a statute to the courts before its enforcement, even in the absence of a concrete judicial case. As a result, in these contexts the parliamentary opposition can exploit the judicial arena as a veto point.

Having outlined the ways in which constitutional rules determine the minimum number of policy arenas through which a proposal must travel, we now turn to the role of political strategy as a policy path's determinant. While constitutional rules can account for cross-national variation in policy paths, political strategy allows us to account for variation in policy paths not only across countries, but also over time. In contrast to constitutional rules, which lay out a predictable policy path, political strategy introduces uncertainty into the policy process because, if successful, it produces policy spillover into arenas that are not constitutionally prescribed.

The Role of Political Strategy

Given the arenas' insulation logics, political actors have a great stake in the path that a proposal takes. In Immergut's words, "the ability to force a decision from one arena to another may significantly alter the policy deliberations and their outcome" (1990, 398). Because some policy paths are more conducive to policy liberalization while others favor immigration restriction, policy makers and external actors alike will seek to alter or contain a policy's path. Where actors pursue their immigration preferences by strategically manipulating the policy path, they can be said to engage in arena (or venue) shopping. The term venue shopping, developed by Baumgartner and Jones (1993) and later applied to asylum politics by Guiraudon (2000b), describes policy makers' decision to circumvent political obstacles in one institution by moving policy into a venue that will be more amenable to their preferences. While venue-shopping arguments typically describe the movement of policy out of hostile into friendly environments, I argue that venue shopping can also take the form of strategic containment. That is, it can describe efforts to *prevent* the movement of policy out of friendly arenas. We will now examine the arena-shopping strategies pursued by the range of actors in the politics of immigration policy, beginning with the makers of policy.

Executives as Policy Makers

In the politics of immigration policy making, executives play a critical role as initiators of policy reform. Where a policy proposal originates in the executive arena, executives will seek to contain its path by preventing, if constitutionally possible, what I refer to as *policy spillover* – policy movement into other arenas. Executives will seek to prevent policy spillover into the legislative (and, potentially, electoral) arena by pursuing reform in the form of regulation rather than legislation. Given the strategic advantages of the executive arena, especially its protection from public scrutiny and the absence of institutionalized opposition, policy output (such as regulations) that does not require legislative approval has a much greater likelihood of surviving intact than policies that take the form of legislation.

As a second containment strategy, executive policy makers can employ policy learning to maximize their room for maneuver within the confines of incremental policy reform. As we will discuss below, incremental policy reform (in contrast to paradigmatic reform) alters immigration policy in ways that do not alter its fundamental assumptions. Because of its relatively modest scope, incremental reform can – depending on the behavior of opposition actors – be passed without legislative approval. Thus, executives seeking to prevent policy spillover will shy away from paradigmatic reform and instead find ways of maximizing room for maneuver within existing policy parameters. Policy learning is one such tool that provides policy makers with greater maneuverability within the paradigmatic status quo. Among the range of policy makers, executives are best placed to reflect on and learn from past experience. As Heclo (1974) has shown, "puzzling" and policy learning is most likely to emerge from technocratic contexts, where decision-making has a strong evidence-based logic and, because it takes place behind closed doors, is relatively unconstrained by politicization. As "meaningful reactions to previous policies" (Skocpol and Weir 1985, 119), policy learning is typically failure-induced – it emerges after a process of reflection on policy failure in the past. Past policy failure matters because it sensitizes policy makers to the possibility of future failure, thus serving, in the words of Peter May (1992), as a "trigger" for rethinking policy design. Policy learning thus provides executive actors with the opportunity of developing new policy tools that can bring about policy change without necessarily requiring the policy path to lead through the legislative arena.

A third way in which executive actors can prevent policy spillover is by manipulating the timing of immigration reform. Given the volatility of the electoral arena, executive actors will be particularly concerned with preventing spillover into the electoral arena. The risks of spillover are most pronounced in the case of liberalizing immigration reform, where the prevention of politicization is most critical. As a result, unless a policy initiative is designed to assuage popular concerns about immigration, executive policy makers will seek to pursue immigration reform only after, and not in the lead-up to, elections.

Opposition Legislators as Policy Makers

Among the universe of policy makers, opposition legislators are most critical in mobilizing opposition to the policy initiatives originating from the executive arena. The arena-shopping strategies of opposition legislators will be diametrically opposed to those of executive actors. Where executives pursue policy containment within the executive arena, opposition legislators will pursue policy spillover into the legislative, electoral, and judicial arenas. For instance, opposition legislators may seek to move policy from the executive to the legislative arena by demanding that policy take the form of statutory instead of regulatory change. If opposition legislators can make a persuasive case that the changes pursued in the form of regulatory reform are too far reaching to be passed without legislative input, then they may even mobilize support from governing party legislators who will be sensitive to concerns of legislative sidelining.

One of the most common strategies of policy spillover adopted by opposition legislators is the politicization of immigration in the electoral arena. Because so much of the success of executive-driven reform hinges on policy containment, opposition legislators stand to gain from politicizing immigration in the lead-up to an election or a referendum. Politicization can take many forms, ranging from legislative debate and public discussion to incorporating immigration policy into campaign platforms. If successful, policy spillover into the electoral arena will, to use Schattschneider's famous words, "socialize conflict" (1975) and broaden its scope, thereby potentially empowering policy losers.

A third, though rare, strategy of arena shopping is to move policy into the judicial arena. This is possible in systems of abstract constitutional review, where legislators are empowered to refer legislation to the courts before its enactment. Only opposition legislators have the incentives to avail themselves of this power, however, and the courts engaging in abstract review effectively serve as "the extended arm of the opposition" (Stüwe 2001). Because opposition legislators typically file for abstract review in order to exploit policy reform for partisan purposes, abstract review can considerably undermine the popular insulation of executives even where courts end up deciding in the government's favor. We now shift our focus to the arena-shopping strategies of external actors.

Pro-immigration Lobbies as External Actors

The arena-shopping strategies of pro-immigration lobbies, most prominently organized business, are partially aligned with those of executive policy makers. Like government executives, pro-immigration interests will seek to prevent the politicization of immigration by preventing policy spillover into the electoral arena. Unlike executives, however, pro-immigration lobbies will favor policy spillover into the legislative arena whenever they cannot gain access to government officials or where the latter are insufficiently responsive to their concerns. Given its many institutional access points, lobbyists are likely to fare better in the legislative arena. Where the policy path leads through both arenas, interest groups will strategically lobby both executive and legislative policy makers. Regardless of which arena they target, however, pro-immigration interests will prefer to wield their influence behind closed doors, reflecting the logic of client politics (Wilson 1980, Freeman 1995), in order to avoid public exposure and the associated risk of politicization. It is only when interest groups are unsuccessful in politically insulated areas and when their demands lend themselves to a humanitarian framing that they may seek to politicize a given issue in order to raise consciousness and bring about ideologically based solidarity.

Anti-immigration Entrepreneurs as External Actors

As the engine of popular pressure, anti-immigration entrepreneurs seek to solve the collective action problem of mobilizing the unorganized public. They seek to give voice to the public's immigration restrictionism by directing the policy path into the legislative and, most importantly, electoral arena. Like policy entrepreneurs more generally (Wilson 1980), anti-immigration entrepreneurs will do whatever is in their power to politicize policy reform and impose costs on policy makers for disregarding public opinion. They will take on the role of lobbyist in the legislative arena, where they will closely track and publicize legislators' positioning on immigration. Moreover, anti-immigration entrepreneurs will mobilize their supporters to communicate their immigration preferences to elected representatives.

The most formidable tool at the disposal of anti-immigration entrepreneurs, however, is the pursuit of policy spillover into the electoral arena. Policy entrepreneurs will seek to move immigration to the center of public debate, forcing political parties to position themselves on matters of immigration during campaign season and forcing popular referendums or initiatives where constitutionally possible. Among the policy venues, it is the electoral arena that is most favored by anti-immigration entrepreneurs. Once policy has moved into the electoral arena, any efforts by policy makers to reassert control over its path and move immigration reform out of the electoral arena are unlikely to succeed.

Foreign States

In important ways, the strategic behavior of foreign governments mirrors that of domestic interest groups: they will favor policy containment to maximize their leverage as lobbyists in the executive and legislative arenas. To a much greater extent than domestic lobbies, however, foreign diplomats will favor the executive arena as a site of policy making. Not only is foreign policy largely made in the executive arena, but diplomatic institutions also provide well-entrenched access points to executive officials. Like domestic interest groups, foreign diplomats will refrain from pursuing their policy preferences in the electoral arena. This will even be the case where diplomatic pressure originates from receiving, rather than sending, countries, and is therefore restrictionist in nature. Even though receiving states will share with the public a preference for immigration restrictionism, engagement in the electoral arena would likely provoke popular backlash against what would be perceived as illegitimate meddling with domestic affairs.

The policy arenas framework developed in this chapter has theorized the direction of policy change as a function of an arena's popular, interest group, and diplomatic insulation. In turn, we have argued, the policy path through the arenas is shaped by constitutional rules, on the one hand, and the strategies of policy makers and external actors, on the other. In the final section, the chapter examines the magnitude of policy change. We ask: under what conditions will policy makers be able to enact policy change that fundamentally transforms the policy status quo?

THEORIZING THE MAGNITUDE OF POLICY CHANGE: POLICY ARENAS AS VETO POINTS

The basic parameters of immigration policy display remarkable resilience over time. When policy change occurs, most of the time it takes the form of incremental change, which leaves the overarching goals of policy intact. Yet occasionally, fundamental policy change does happen, and immigration policy departs from the trajectory it has been traveling along. Before we theorize the conditions under which this kind of paradigmatic policy change is possible, we more closely investigate the logic of ideational path dependence that makes paradigmatic reform so challenging.

The Path-Dependent Logic of Immigration Paradigms

As the ideational legacies of a country's immigration history, immigration paradigms convey a particular understanding of the relationship between immigration, national identity, and the national interest. Like paradigms more generally, they constitute

> frameworks of ideas and standards that specif[y] not only the goals of policy and the kind of instruments that can be used to attain them, but also the very nature of the problems that they are meant to be addressing ... [A] framework is embedded in the very terminology through which policy makers communicate about their work, and it is influential precisely because so much of it is taken for granted and unamenable to scrutiny as a whole.
>
> (Hall 1993, 279)

Immigration paradigms can contain both descriptive elements – such as causal claims about the consequences of immigration – and prescriptive assertions about what policy should be like. Immigration paradigms thus set the parameters within which immigration continues to be debated and policy made. While competing paradigms will coexist in a given place and time, typically one paradigm will be hegemonic in setting the terms of political debate.

As ideational structures, immigration paradigms perform both cognitive and political functions. As cognitive mechanisms, ideas provide policy makers with mental models that direct attention to certain lines of reasoning and away from others (Jacobs 2009). This process of selection and simplification is particularly important in situations marked by informational and causal complexity. Once adopted, a mental model will be cognitively self-reinforcing, as policy makers will weigh most heavily information and arguments that confirm their model while disregarding disconfirmatory experiences (Jacobs 2009).

In addition to providing elites with cognitive mechanisms for navigating complexity, paradigms also perform a political function by legitimating – or delegitimating – policy choice. Given the publicly contested nature of immigration politics, policy models that fit within the dominant paradigm will have a far greater likelihood of adoption than proposals that violate a paradigm's basic assumptions. Because the adoption of a paradigm, to quote Thomas Kuhn, "end[s] the constant reiteration of fundamentals" (Kuhn 1970, 18), it engenders an ideational path dependence by providing actors with the broad parameters within which policy is considered and within which it is deemed appropriate and legitimate. Each policy choice made within these parameters will fuel support for its reproduction (Mahony 2000). Over time, then, increasing legitimation processes feed into a positive feedback cycle, and past judgments about a policy's appropriateness become the basis on which future decisions about appropriateness are made. While there is clearly scope for policy maneuvering within the bounds of a paradigm, radical policy reform is contingent on a shift in paradigms.

Veto Points and Paradigmatic Policy Change

Given the path-dependent logic of paradigms, what are the conditions under which paradigmatic change can emerge? Immigration reform that profoundly disrupts the policy status quo is contingent on a set of highly restrictive conditions. As a first condition, the hegemonic power of a paradigm can only be disrupted once it comes to be widely regarded as incompatible with its environment. Here it is important to recognize that external challenges need not be targeted at an immigration paradigm per se but may also be directed at intersecting paradigms with spillover effects on immigration policy, such as labor market paradigms. Regardless of which paradigm is under threat, the process of environmental change typically follows an incremental logic, though on rare occasions it can take the form of an exogenous shock that suddenly and profoundly alters a policy's environment. Where environments shift incrementally, changes accumulate over time. While the confirmatory bias of policy makers' mental maps will initially prevent the recognition of an emerging gap between a paradigm's fundamental assumptions, on the one hand, and realities on the ground, on the other, over time this gap will widen until it is sufficiently large to overrule the cognitive bias of policy makers. In Triadafilos Triadafilopoulos' words, exogenous change will lead to, first, policy "stretching," followed by policy "unraveling" (2012). While paradigmatic change can often be slow and incremental, where environmental change takes the form of an exogenous punctuation, paradigms can become delegitimized in a relatively short period of time (Howlett and Cashore 2009). Regardless of the tempo of environmental change, once fissures in the congruence between a paradigm and its environment have become sufficiently large, the normative consensus regarding the desirability of a paradigm's continued reproduction will fall apart and open the door to new understandings of the role of immigration policy.

As a second condition for paradigmatic change, paradigm shifts – the move from one paradigm to another – typically emerge after a process of broad-based debate. In contrast to incremental change, which often occurs in technocratic and depoliticized contexts, paradigmatic change is more "sociological" and "political" in nature (Pierson 1993, 614). For a new paradigm to be institutionalized, not only does it have to assure policy makers that it will serve as a catalyst for the development of effective policy, but its normative ideals have to signal to both elites and the public that they are congruent with the basic values of the polity (Schmidt 2008). Because debate on the continued viability of a given paradigm involves the rethinking of fundamental aspects of policy, it will emerge in the context of widespread *societal* debate and involve a range of state and civil society actors. Because, ultimately, paradigmatic change cannot remain hidden, the adoption of new policy goals in the absence of societal debate constitutes a colossal political liability, especially where the adoption of a new paradigm has liberalizing implications and runs counter to popular restrictionism. The institutionalization of paradigmatic change thus needs to resonate with, and engage, significant segments of society, albeit with one caveat. Initially the pursuit of a new paradigm may take place in the context of popular insulation. Executive policy makers might seek to enact paradigmatic changes in the form of regulation rather than legislation, either strategically as a trial balloon to gauge its resonance with elites more broadly, or naïvely in the hope that it will escape public scrutiny. Given its enormous implications, however, paradigmatic reform cannot remain hidden beyond the short term and will require much broader political support, and thus spillover into other arenas, for its institutionalization.

Finally, and building on the previous point, paradigmatic policy change is unlikely to become institutionalized in the presence of institutional veto points. Even where paradigm failure has become a generally accepted fact, there is unlikely to exist a broad consensus on what paradigm to adopt in its stead. Once an old paradigm begins to weaken, alternative paradigms that in the past held little legitimacy begin to occupy the space vacated by the retreating paradigm. However, if a new paradigm spearheaded by policy reformers is politically contested, then its institutionalization will be contingent on the absence of veto points. In Hall's words, "[t]he movement from one paradigm to another will ultimately entail a set of judgments that is more political in tone, and the outcome will depend, not only on the arguments of competing factions, but on their positional advantages within a broader institutional framework, on the ancillary resources they can command in the relevant conflicts, and on exogenous factors affecting the power of one set of actors to impose its paradigm over others" (Hall 1993, 280).

Politicization is a particular threat to paradigmatic change if the newly emerging paradigm promises to open up immigration. In this case, partisan veto players face strong incentives to mobilize against reform and capitalize on public opposition to immigration. As a result, if the proponents of competing paradigms have access to veto points the paradigm shift will remain incomplete. Conversely, if supporters of a new paradigm can secure control over legislative policy making and move to institutionalize the new paradigm in the form of legislation – or, alternatively, where elite consensus is institutionalized, such as under the Swiss concordance system – then paradigmatic policy change is possible.

On a final note, in the presence of these three conditions – the loss of congruence between a paradigm and its environment, the presence of broad-based debate, and the absence of institutional veto points – paradigmatic change is often facilitated by a shift in power in the form of government turnover. Power shifts serve as mechanisms for ideational change because members of the opposition are more likely to offer unorthodox perspectives and push for radical reform. Moreover, in comparison with incumbent governments, opposition members face weaker credibility problems when departing from a previously entrenched paradigm.

The policy arenas framework developed in this chapter allows for the comparative study of immigration policy making across space and time. In order to capture meaningful cross-national and intertemporal variation in policy, we have distinguished between the *direction* of policy change (liberalization versus restriction) and its *magnitude* (incremental versus paradigmatic). We have argued that the direction of policy change is first and foremost a function of the degree to which policy makers enjoy insulation from four sets of actors: domestically, from the general public and from interest groups; internationally, from sending and receiving states. Insulation from popular pressure and diplomatic pressure by receiving states will allow for the pursuit of policy liberalization, while insulation from interest groups and sending states will facilitate immigration restrictionism. Because each policy arena has a distinct combination of popular, interest group, and diplomatic insulation, different policy paths will produce different policy choices. Differences in policy paths, in turn, originate from differences in constitutional rules and the arena-shopping strategies of political actors.

Policy arenas matter not only because they reflect distinct insulation logics, but also because they constitute veto points for the blockage of reform. While incremental policy change can sometimes be enacted in a single arena, the policy path of paradigmatic reform will lead through at least two arenas. The greater the number of arenas, however, the greater the number of veto points, and the lower the likelihood of policy change. It follows that paradigmatic reform will only take place under highly restrictive conditions, at moments when the stars align, so to speak, and reform opponents lack veto power. We now move on to the empirical chapters and apply this framework to a variety of liberal democracies (including both settler colonial and guest worker countries) and time periods, ranging from the postwar era to the present. If the policy arenas framework is to allow for the broad theorizing of the politics of immigration policy it will need to account for cases of policy stability and change across these diverse institutional, ideational, and historical contexts.

3

The Making of Swiss Immigration Policy

Explaining Permanent and Temporary Economic Admissions

This chapter examines four episodes of Swiss economic immigration policy making from the 1940s to the 2010s. Our analysis begins with the conclusion of the 1948 Swiss-Italian recruitment treaty, which set the terms of admission for the first two decades of Swiss guest worker recruitment. Reflecting a process of policy learning from Switzerland's past failure to prevent the settlement of foreign workers, Swiss recruitment policy was based on the principle of rotation. Past policy failure provided postwar policy makers not only with lessons for policy design but also with the determination to prevent settlement. Thus, the experience of unintended and large-scale immigrant settlement in the late nineteenth century gave rise to the "overforeignization" paradigm that, since the early twentieth century, has provided a critical impetus for immigration control.

The chapter's second case study extends from the early 1960s to 1970, a period in which the rotation system came under intense stress because of the cross-cutting pressures engendered by the drastic decline in policy makers' diplomatic and popular insulation. Buoyed by Europe-wide competition for Italian labor and a booming domestic economy, the Italian government demanded liberalized terms of recruitment for its nationals. At the same time, Swiss anti-immigrant groups organized a series of "overforeignization initiatives" that threatened to halt recruitment. The Federal Council navigated these pressures by liberalizing the residence and family unification rights of Italian workers while simultaneously restricting the number of new recruits.

Our third case study, the Three Circles Policy of 1991, once again underscores the significance of the lack of diplomatic and popular insulation for the making of Swiss immigration policy. Driven by pressures of

84

"strategic adjustment" to a rapidly integrating European market, the Three Circles Policy offered free movement to European workers at the same time as it closed the door to nationals of "culturally distant" countries. Yet this policy compromise failed to placate the Swiss public, and the Federal Council soon found itself under reform pressure once again.

The chapter's fourth case study examines the adoption of the Two Circles Policy and the ratification of the Agreement on the Free Movement of Persons with the European Union, both of which were written into law with the passage of Switzerland's 2008 Immigration Act. With this latest legislation, the Federal Council institutionalized the free movement of European labor while at the same time overriding the interests of labor-intensive business by limiting the immigration of third-country nationals to highly skilled workers and their families. Despite these legislative successes, the Federal Council in 2014 was once again confronted with its lack of popular insulation after a majority of voters supported the Swiss People's Party's (SVP) Initiative against Mass Immigration. Caught between the diplomatic imperative of upholding its bilateral legal commitments, on the one hand, and the public's vote for immigration cuts, on the other, policy makers decided to implement the referendum in a way that accommodated its diplomatic constraints, leaving the policy vulnerable to continued popular challenge.

THE POSTWAR GUEST WORKER ROTATION SYSTEM (1948–1961)

When, after World War II, Swiss policy makers pondered the possibility of recruiting workers from abroad, they were fully aware that if left unchecked recruitment would carry the risk of permanent immigrant settlement. Less than forty years earlier, under a paradigm of economic liberalism, loosely regulated labor migration had led the country's foreign population share to double from 8 to 16 percent. This experience of unintended immigrant settlement left behind a deep-seated and pervasive sense that large-scale immigration presented a threat to Swiss identity. There was a consensus that to be politically feasible, future foreign worker recruitment would have to be strictly regulated by the state to ensure that the economic benefits of labor recruitment would not be diminished by the social and cultural costs of settlement.

Prewar Legacies: Switzerland's Open Borders Policy (1862–1914)

In 1862, and in marked contrast to Prussia (see Chapter 4), Switzerland instituted an open borders policy. This policy liberalization was in keeping with a European era of free movement that began around 1860 and lasted until the outbreak of World War I. The (re)institution of visa- and passport-free travel across most of the continent corresponded to a broader paradigm of economic liberalism that marked the second half of the nineteenth century, one which had become feasible after the political upheavals of the revolutions of 1848 had subsided (Lucassen 2001). By 1914, Switzerland had entered into bilateral treaties with twenty-one countries and established a reciprocal regime of free movement and settlement for migrant workers and their families (Niederberger 1982).

By the turn of the century, however, rapid immigration had come to trigger xenophobic responses, most famously the 1896 Zürich pogrom against Italian migrants, who were feared as economic competitors and potential strike breakers. Even more pronounced than economic fears was the notion that foreigners posed a threat to social cohesion and national identity. Around the same time as the Zürich pogrom, a new word, which would later become the foundation of the country's postwar immigration paradigm, entered the Swiss political vocabulary: "overforeignization"[1] (*Überfremdung*) (Niederberger 1982). Initially, since it was the country's largest immigrant group, the term was only applied to the German community. Given its economic successes, political elites feared that popular admiration for an immigrant group with monarchical ties would dilute the *Schweizer Eigenart* ("Swiss unique characteristics" or "Swissness") and weaken native democratic norms. Before long, however, the term came to be used much more widely to express fears that high levels of immigration would weaken Swiss culture and national identity.

Despite increasing popular opposition to its open borders policy, the Swiss government undertook no attempts to regulate the entry or settlement of foreign workers until the external shock of World War I marked the end of the age of free mobility across Europe. For one, the federal government's constitutional powers were notoriously weak in the decades following Swiss Confederation in 1848. At least as important, however, was the fact that the Federal Council was severely constrained by its lack of diplomatic insulation. Because of the size of the Swiss diaspora – more than 300,000 Swiss citizens had settled abroad, and Swiss emigration

---

[1] This chapter conceives of "overforeignization" as a discursive construction rather than as a matter of fact. For stylistic reasons, however, for the remainder of the chapter the term will be used without quotes.

continued well into the twentieth century – the government had little choice but to reciprocate liberal immigration and settlement provisions and extend the rights afforded to the Swiss émigrés to foreign nationals living in Switzerland. By 1914, the country's first experiment with large-scale labor migration had opened the doors to the arrival and settlement of close to half a million of migrants, 16 percent of the country's population (Vuilleumier 1992).

World War I constituted an ideological and policy watershed for Europe's migration regime. It marked the end of the age of free mobility, as strict travel controls were imposed across the continent. In Switzerland, controls on the movement and settlement of foreign nationals – initially intended as temporary – remained in place after the war, and the economic troubles that marked the interwar period further pre-empted the resumption of labor recruitment. As a result, the combined effect of war mobilization, strict settlement controls, and high unemployment resulted in a steady decline of the foreign population. By 1941, its share (5.3 percent) had returned to pre-1880 levels.

Policy Learning in the Executive Arena: The Rotation System of the Late 1940s and 1950s

In 1945, with much of Europe's economy in a shambles, Swiss administrative officials braced themselves for high levels of unemployment. By early fall, however, employer associations started to warn of worsening labor shortages in several industries (Schweizerischer Metall- und Uhrenarbeiterverband June 6, 1946). In October, after the Department of Economic Affairs recommended the recruitment of temporary migrant workers, the Federal Council authorized employers to recruit foreign workers (Cerutti 2005). While the government's recruitment preference was for French, Austrian, and German workers, these states had lost too many men during the war to allow for state-sanctioned emigration. As a result, the Federal Council approached Italy and, after close to three years of informal recruitment, in 1948 the Swiss-Italian recruitment agreement was signed. While the political process leading up to the conclusion of the 1948 treaty was marked by a broad consensus between Swiss political elites and employer associations, labor unions – the potential cost bearers of increased labor supply – feared that recruitment would exert downward pressure on native wage and work conditions (Cerutti 2005, Niederberger 1982). These concerns were assuaged by the Federal Council's guarantee of equal work and pay conditions for Swiss and foreign workers, which allowed union representatives to go along with the decision to recruit foreign labor.

When the agreement was signed, the new recruitment system stood in stark contrast to Switzerland's pre-World War I policy of free movement and settlement. Founded on the principles of reversible migration, numerical control, and prevention of settlement, migrant workers were only issued with temporary work permits. In the case of seasonal workers – who accounted for roughly half of all admissions until the early 1960s – permits were valid for a maximum of nine months, with administrative practice oftentimes more restrictive.[2] Seasonal workers could neither bring in their families nor adjust to non-seasonal status. Non-seasonal permits,[3] by contrast, were issued for a year at a time and were renewable (Piguet 2006a). Annual permit holders, however, were only eligible to apply for permanent residence after ten years of uninterrupted stay. Family unification was possible after three years of residence, but applications generally were handled restrictively (*Neue Zürcher Zeitung* November 21, 1960, Boscardin 1962).

This radical departure from past recruitment policy, I argue, was motivated by a process of reflection on the pre-World War I legacy of immigrant settlement – a process that ultimately facilitated paradigmatic change. As early as the turn of the century, political elites had begun to conceive of large-scale immigrant settlement as a threat to Swiss identity. It was during this period that the term overforeignization was born, denoting "the influence and alien ideas of unassimilated or insufficiently assimilated members of foreign cultures ... that are sufficiently strong to displace the essential and foundational ideas of one's native culture, so that the native population can no longer live according to its own, autonomous, traditions" (Bundesamt für Industrie, Gewerbe und Arbeit 1964, 136, my translation).

By the end of World War I, overforeignization had come to be perceived as not only a cultural threat, but also a political one. The following excerpt from the 1964 report of the government-appointed Expert Commission for the Study of the Problem of Foreign Labor is worth citing at length because it speaks to the lasting power of the association of

---

[2] For instance, in 1950 cantons were instructed to issue permits for three months, after which, depending on economic conditions, they could be revoked without warning (see Eidgenössische Fremdenpolizei December 28, 1950). However, until the early 1970s, when the introduction of the Swiss Register for Foreigners allowed for the centralization of enforcement data, there was significant local-level variation in administrative practices.

[3] *Bewilligung B, Jahresaufenthalter.*

overforeignization and national security well into the postwar period. Detailing the policy lessons learned from the previous open borders policy, the report stated that:

the dangerous consequences of "spiritual overforeignization" (*geistige Überfremdung*)[4] were clearly observable before World War I. We didn't recognize this danger at the time, because we succumbed to the illusion that politics and culture could be separated, that we could remain Germans, French, and Italians in a cultural sense, and still remain Swiss. We doubted and even denied the existence of a sense of "Swissness" (*Schweizer Eigenart*). [... As a result, during World War I] the majority of German Swiss supported Germany, while the majority of French Swiss supported the Entente.

(Bundesamt für Industrie, Gewerbe und Arbeit 1964, 133, my translation)

Thus, by the time Switzerland embarked on its postwar recruitment program, the overforeignization paradigm – which associated immigration with settlement and settlement with threat – was well entrenched in Swiss political discourse and shared by a diverse set of actors. As a result, when the issue of foreign worker recruitment resurfaced in the mid-1940s, it was immediately viewed through the lens of overforeignization. While it appears that policy makers did not (yet) attempt to define a numerical threshold of overforeignization, there was a consensus about "a causal link between the number of foreigners, and the threat to Swiss identity" (Mahnig and Wimmer 2003, 141). In 1948, the year in which the Swiss-Italian agreement was signed, the Federal Council credited the strict immigration controls of the interwar period with "having averted the previous alarmingly high threat of overforeignization" and cautioned that "we need to continue to be vigilant, especially today, where Switzerland once again is immensely attractive to foreigners" (Buomberger 2004, 34, my translation). Similarly, despite relatively small numbers in the early recruitment period, trade unions warned that "our country is threatened with overforeignization" (Schweizerischer Metall- und Uhrenarbeiterverband 1955, 7, my translation) and recommended a long list of "protective measures against overforeignization" (Schweizerischer Metall- und Uhrenarbeiterverband 1955, 8–9, my translation). Even employer associations, the unequivocal beneficiaries of recruitment, considered it necessary to pay lip service to the threat of overforeignization

---

[4] This term has no English equivalent and is closest in meaning to "the spirit of a person." It conjures up an image of foreigners as seeking to infiltrate the minds of the Swiss in order to destroy Swiss values (Riaño and Wastl-Walter 2006).

and warned of the limits of the "assimilation capacity" of the Swiss people (Buomberger 2004, 35).

Not only were the goals of the postwar guest worker system circumscribed by the overforeignization paradigm, but its policy instruments also reflected the lessons from the past. In an instance of failure-induced policy learning, elites had clearly come to associate loosely regulated economic migration with immigrant settlement. Because the very idea of uncontrolled immigration was inimical to the consensus that overforeignization had to be prevented at all costs (*Neue Zürcher Zeitung* November 13, 1946, Cerutti 2005, Schweizerische Arbeitgeber-Zeitung June 20, 1947), it was imperative that recruitment not result in settlement. In the words of the Federal Council, first in 1924 but reiterated since, "we do not object to the immigration of foreign nationals, provided they do not settle in Switzerland" (Eidgenössischer Bundesrat, March 26, 1924, 517, cited in Mahnig and Piguet 2004, 68, my translation). These imperatives, then, gave rise to a recruitment policy that was firmly premised on the rotation principle. Accordingly, BIGA (*Bundesamt für Industrie, Gewerbe und Arbeit*) – Switzerland's labor market agency – considered the adoption of policy measures to prevent long-term residence and family unification as indispensable to the prevention of overforeignization (Bundesamt für Industrie, Gewerbe und Arbeit March 31, 1953, my translation).

Looking at the conditions under which the Swiss guest worker system was established, we find that they closely correspond to those identified as conducive to policy learning (Heclo 1974). Policy making took place in the executive arena, where the Federal Council and labor market technocrats negotiated policy details with the social partners while bypassing the legislative arena, where little attention was paid to the matter. The shared preferences of the Federal Council and the employer associations for temporary foreign worker recruitment emerged in a relatively conflict-free and politically insulated context of decision-making, a process supported by the fact that the unions, after securing wage guarantees, were not sufficiently opposed to recruitment to pursue its broader politicization. These factors, combined with the memory of past policy failure and the hegemony of the overforeignization paradigm, allow for a notable degree of elite constraint even in the absence of popular pressure for recruitment controls. Thus, by choosing rotation as the basic principle of recruitment policy, policy makers sought to balance the disparate goals of economic expansion, on the one hand, and the prevention of overforeignization, on the other.

Remarkably, throughout the drastic expansion of the migrant worker population in the 1950s, the rotation system remained firmly in place. The Federal Council continued to balance the goal of economic expansion against concerns about overforeignization, arguing that a market-driven admission policy could only extend "up to the limit demanded by the avoidance of *Überfremdung*" (Geschäftsberichts des Bundesrates 1958, 42, cited in Niederberger 1982, 42, my translation). Throughout the economic boom of the mid-1950s, BIGA gave instructions to the cantonal authorities to issue seasonal, rather than annual, work permits whenever possible and to handle requests for family unification restrictively (Bundesamt für Industrie, Gewerbe und Arbeit March 31, 1953). Administrative practice was often considerably more restrictive than official regulations. In the early 1950s, for instance, a number of cantons only allowed family unification after ten (rather than the official three) years of residence (Eidgenössisches Justiz- und Polizeidepartement December 12, 1956).

As a result, throughout the 1940s and 1950s Switzerland's rotation policy was largely successful in preventing settlement. Despite the high costs of rotation incurred by many employers, annual labor turnover in some firms remained as high as 40 percent (Buomberger 2004, 18). Similarly, as late as 1959 – more than a decade into recruitment – the vast majority of even non-seasonal migrant workers continued to leave the country after two to three years, with only a quarter of all foreigners having resided in the country for more than three years (Buomberger 2004, Schweizerischer Metall- und Uhrenarbeiterverband 1962).

THE ROTATION SYSTEM UNDER STRESS: RECRUITMENT CAPS, TREATY REVISION, AND THE GLOBAL CEILING SYSTEM

Starting in the early 1960s, the rotation system came under mounting threat. Swiss employers were becoming increasingly hostile to fielding the costs of constant worker turnover at a time of sustained economic growth. Meanwhile the Federal Council was cognizant that, with demand for foreign labor unabated since the early 1950s, the first guest workers started to qualify for permanent residence, thereby raising the specter of immigrant settlement. At the same time as the Federal Council came under pressure at home, it confronted mounting international competition for foreign labor from its European neighbors, which significantly compromised its diplomatic insulation. The Italian government was quick to recognize its bargaining advantage and demanded the renegotiation of the terms of its 1948 recruitment agreement with Switzerland. Seeking to secure a continued flow of foreign labor while limiting settlement, the Federal Council agreed to liberalize the residence and family unification rights of Italian workers at the same time as it embarked on a trial-and-error process of imposing numerical ceilings on guest worker recruitment.

Declining Rotation and the Imposition of Recruitment Caps

With the economic boom showing no sign of abating, by the early 1960s employers tried to avoid the efficiency losses of rotation by retaining non-seasonal workers. In a similar vein, cantons that heavily depended on recruitment sought to defy BIGA's instructions to issue seasonal rather than annual permits. As a result, despite the high hurdle of the ten-year residence requirement, some guest workers started to qualify for permanent residency. While the numbers were small – in 1960 permanent permits were issued to 1,000–1,500 foreign workers (*Neue Zürcher Zeitung* November 21, 1960) – the very fact of settlement defied the rotation principle. Thus, even though the relative size of the Swiss seasonal worker population continued to be significant, by the early 1960s they no longer accounted for over half, but just under a third of foreign workers (Bundesamt für Industrie, Gewerbe und Arbeit 1964, March 31, 1953). These developments had important political ramifications. With the beginning of settlement, it became progressively difficult to justify high levels of immigration to an increasingly xenophobic public (Piguet 2006a).

Aware of this predicament, in 1962 the Federal Council appealed to employers to voluntarily restrict the number of employees. After no cooperation was forthcoming, the government instituted a cap (*Plafonierungsmassnahme*) on the employment of foreign workers. Largely drawn up by BIGA, the ceiling measure stipulated that the number of workers employed in a given firm in 1962 was not to be exceeded by the hiring of foreign workers (Cerutti 2005). Despite the cap, however, new arrivals increased by 4.5 percent the following year (Mahnig and Piguet 2004, 127). The main culprit for the continued increase in numbers was the employer associations, which had successfully lobbied the Federal Council to exempt the agricultural and hospitality sectors from the cap. Moreover, at the cantonal level many employers were able to negotiate additional firm-level exemptions (Mahnig and Piguet 2004). While the Federal Council continued to fine-tune its control measures, the government-appointed Expert Commission for the Study of the Problem of Foreign Labor issued its report, *The Problem of Foreign Workers*, which received widespread attention. Arguing that Switzerland was in "acute danger of overforeignization" (Bundesamt für Industrie, Gewerbe und Arbeit 1964, 137, my translation) and faced an excess of "foreign penetration," its authors commended a reduction in guest worker recruitment. In contending that a "satisfactory" level of economic growth could be achieved with a workforce of 500,000 non-seasonal guest workers by 1970, political elites for the first time had sought to quantify a desirable immigration target (Cerutti 2005, 103).

What is remarkable about the Federal Council's attempts to reign in recruitment in the early 1960s is the fact that it occurred at a time of unparalleled economic growth and labor demand. No other European guest worker country – including Germany – sought to implement recruitment checks before the economic slowdown of the 1970s. While there was also some concern about economic overheating, the Swiss ceiling measures of the early 1960s are best understood as motivated by the recognition of gradual guest worker settlement and the associated fears of overforeignization. While policy making was still confined to the executive arena, popular fears of overforeignization were on the rise. The salience of these fears is evident in an analysis of Swiss media coverage in the mid-1960s: the two dominant discourses of guest worker recruitment were "economic necessity of guest worker recruitment" and "overforeignization" (Niehr 2004, 243). Of particular interest is the degree to which the notion of overforeignization had become ideologically naturalized: of all articles employing this discourse, over 44 percent did so in a neutral, factual manner (Niehr 2004, 243).

Weakening Diplomatic Insulation and the Renegotiation of the Swiss-Italian Agreement

Curtailing recruitment during a time of continued employer demand for foreign workers was not the only challenge facing policy makers, however. Ironically, at the same time as the Federal Council sought to slow down recruitment, guest worker supply started to dry up. Not only had other European countries – most importantly Germany – entered into recruitment agreements with Italy, but with the signing of the 1957 Treaty of Rome free mobility and the harmonization of social insurance schemes was starting to become a reality for members of the European Economic Community. Consequently, Switzerland lost in attractiveness as a destination for migrant workers and faced pressures for strategic adjustment

(Fitzgerald and Cook-Martín 2014) of its recruitment policies. Aware of Switzerland's predicament, the Italian government demanded a renegotiation of the 1948 agreement, including a lowering of the waiting period for family unification from three years to one, and for permanent residence from ten years to five. After three years of protracted diplomatic conflict, in 1964 the two countries reached agreement on two critical amendments. First, the waiting time for family unification for workers with non-seasonal permits was to be lowered from three years to eighteen months. Second, seasonal workers who had worked in Switzerland for five successive seasons were now entitled to apply for yearly permits (Piguet 2006b).

From the Federal Council's perspective, these concessions – which, after all, reflected a compromise between the two governments – were necessary to keep recruitment channels open (Cerutti 2005). Yet the government realized that the agreement's revision threatened to dilute the fundamental principle of rotation and would not be met with popular approval at home. The liberalization of the family unification clause in particular constituted a political liability, given the widely recognized relationship between family unification and settlement. In order to deflect potential conflict, the Federal Council decided to move the provision into an annex to the agreement, thereby exempting it from parliamentary approval (Cerutti 2005). The agreement was slated to come into effect in November 1964, before ratification by parliament. Little did the government realize that the time of executive-centered decision-making was about to come to an end.

The Rise of Populist Politics and the Global Ceiling System of 1970

When the Federal Council made the revised Swiss-Italian agreement public and submitted it to the legislature all hell broke loose. For the first time in the postwar era, immigration became the subject of sustained public debate, with a newly founded Zürich-based anti-immigrant group, the Swiss Popular Movement against Overforeignization (*Schweizerische Volksbewegung gegen die Überfremdung*), fanning the embers of xenophobia. Opponents of the revised agreement portrayed the Federal Council as a puppet of the Italian government and argued that the new agreement would lead to unacceptable levels of overforeignization (Cerutti 2005).

Arguing that ratification would carry the risk of popular initiative, the National Council – Switzerland's directly elected lower house, who to this point had shown little interest in the issue of guest worker recruitment – refused to vote on the matter until the government had satisfactorily addressed its concerns. Desperate to secure the National Council's support, the Federal Council promised further recruitment reductions and decreed stricter entry controls at the border.[5] The strategy paid off and, in March 1964, the National Council ratified the agreement (Cerutti 2005). Having averted the threat of legislative veto, the government followed up on its promise to further restrict immigration. The "double ceiling" system (*doppelte Plafonierung*) of 1965 not only limited the overall number of foreign employees in a given firm but also required a 5 percent reduction in a firm's permanent foreign workforce. The measure reflected BIGA's assessment that overforeignization would be most effectively tackled by a reduction of non-seasonal workers in particular.[6] In contrast to previous cap measures, the double ceiling succeeded in reducing the number of arrivals by 40,000 (Cerutti 2005, 128).

Yet despite these administrative successes, the ratified Swiss-Italian agreement continued to serve as a lightning rod for anti-immigrant voices. Just over a year after its ratification, the first overforeignization initiative (*Überfremdungsinitiative*) was submitted by the Democratic Party of the canton of Zürich, a small and nationalist party which had gathered 60,000 signatures. The initiative demanded that the total number of foreign nationals be reduced to 10 percent of the country's resident population at a time when 15 percent of Switzerland's resident population was foreign (Mahnig and Piguet 2004). The Federal Council expressed agreement with the basic concerns of the action committee – the threat of the overforeignization of Swiss society – but rejected the initiative's demands as economically irresponsible. The government appealed to the public to reject the initiative and pledged to find new ways of curbing immigration.

Thus, even though it was faced with mounting opposition from employers who protested the double ceiling system, under the threat of popular initiative the Federal Council decreed an additional 5 percent reduction in economic admissions in 1966. Now that the government enjoyed neither interest group nor popular insulation, its response to cross-cutting societal demands was to impose increasingly restrictive numerical controls, without, however, dismantling the system. After this

---

[5] Foreign nationals arriving at the border from now on would be required to be in possession of a work permit prior to entry.

[6] In addition, sectoral cap exemptions were reduced.

fourth order, employer associations, supported by some cantonal governments, aggressively lobbied the government for a break from recruitment
reductions and argued that the government's control measures were
inflicting serious economic harm. The Federal Council, supported by the
unions, nevertheless decided to push ahead with a fifth order that stipulated an additional 2 percent reduction. Employers – in particular in
cantons with expanding, labor-intensive economies – became increasingly
restive. Yet the government, still under the threat of popular initiative,
vowed to plow ahead and announced further reductions: 3 percent by late
1968, followed by a further 2 percent by the end of 1969. After this last
announcement, the Democratic Party decided to retract the initiative.

While the initiative's withdrawal marked an important victory for the
Federal Council, it did not allow for a permanent retreat into the relative
safety of the executive arena. By late 1968, the number of migrants with
non-seasonal and permanent permits had increased by 4.8 percent,
thereby pushing the foreign population share over the previous historical
peak of 16 percent (Mahnig and Piguet 2004). Several months later, a
second initiative against overforeignization seized upon this increase and
gathered 70,000 signatures. Organized by the National Action against the
Overforeignization of Nation and Home (*Nationale Aktion gegen die
Überfremdung von Volk und Heimat*), and named after its instigator,
national councilor James Schwarzenbach, the initiative's demands were
even more far-reaching than those of its predecessor. Not only was the
proportion of foreign nationals to be capped at 10 percent in any canton
other than Geneva, but family unification was to be severely curtailed.
The Federal Council – supported by both houses of parliament and the
social partners – rejected the initiative, maintaining that its demands
would not only cause significant economic harm but would also violate
Switzerland's bilateral agreements and contravene the European
Convention on Human Rights.

Three months before the critical vote, the Federal Council decreed a
global ceiling on immigration (*Gesamtplafonierung*). The global ceiling,
which unlike previous caps was not limited to the firm level, was to be
based on an annual contingent for new recruits that would be calculated
against the expected number of migrant departures (Piguet 2006b).
Cantons and employer associations strongly objected to the measure,
while trade unions were in support. The government decided to implement the cap over the opposition of employers and cantons and, presenting the global ceiling as the magic bullet to curb immigration, promised
the public to keep the system in place even after the popular vote.

The vote of June 7, 1970 is considered one of the most significant in postwar Swiss history. Not only were the government's stakes exceedingly high – spanning both economic concerns and matters of high politics in the international arena – but with a turnout of 74 percent, public mobilization reached a record high. In the words of BIGA director Grübel:

> It was a historic vote. Newspapers called it "a shot across the bows," "a unique declaration of no-confidence," "a fateful turnaround"! What remains beyond doubt is that for decades no electoral campaign has been fought with a comparable degree of tenacity and passion. ... The public attended countless political events in unprecedented numbers. The presence of the mass media even exceeded that observable during major sports events.
>
> (Mahnig and Piguet 2004, 78–9, my translation)

To the government's great relief, its gamble had paid off. The initiative was rejected by 54 percent of voters and twenty out of twenty-seven cantons.[7]

The global ceiling system of 1970 marked the end of two decades of market-driven labor recruitment. As the major losers, employers and those cantons heavily dependent on foreign labor were hardest hit by the new policy regime. By contrast, unions and the public, who had long been supportive of capping immigration, emerged as the winners. Ironically perhaps, so did the Federal Council. Even though the Schwarzenbach Initiative put the government in a politically precarious position, it also provided the Federal Council with the necessary leverage to overrule the employer associations as the most powerful interest group player in Switzerland's liberal corporatist system. The global ceiling can be seen as the final conclusion of a succession of capping measures pursued by governments since the early 1960s. The option of a global ceiling had been debated within BIGA as early as 1965 but, given the strength of employer opposition, was discarded as politically infeasible. Thus, had the country not experienced the radical public backlash of the late 1960s it is doubtful that the Federal Council would have taken on employers and cantons over the institution of a global cap. In the words of BIGA director Grübel, "[w]e had to utilize the increasing political pressure that emanated from public opinion to overcome the resistance of industry" (cited in Niederberger 1982, 88, my translation).

To what extent did the new system succeed in reigning in immigration? The measure was clearly successful in regulating the number of seasonal

---

[7] Passage would have required a double majority.

and annual permits. Whereas in 1970, 70,000 annual permits were issued, this number dropped to 50,000 in each of the three following years – well before the oil crisis put an end to unbridled labor demand. It follows that under the global ceiling system, the Federal Council was well positioned to control the number of workers subject to permit renewal. When the oil crisis hit, the number of seasonal and annual workers fell precipitously as authorities stopped issuing and renewing permits. In fact, by 1975, for the first time since the early 1950s, we observe a decrease in the size of Switzerland's foreign population (see Figure 4.1).

Most importantly, the institution of the global ceiling system marked the end of a decade of highly charged immigration politics dominated by the popular arena. When, in 1972, a third overforeignization initiative was introduced, the public firmly rejected it, giving credence to the government's argument that the global ceiling system's policy of "stabilization" was the only economically and politically viable way forward. The initiative's popular rejection led to a weakening of xenophobic circles, a success that can be attributed to the Federal Council's quota policy (Mahnig and Piguet 2004). For the better part of the next two decades the new policy was successful in mollifying fears of popular overforeignization while ensuring a steady supply of foreign labor. Like the recruitment policies of the immediate postwar era, the global ceiling system remained premised on the idea of rotation – a feature that German policy makers had come to term "the Swiss model" (Straubhaar 1989, 30) – even if its ability to prevent settlement was becoming increasingly constrained. While the global ceiling was well suited to regulating the number of new workers, it was unable to slow the pace of settlement. In fact, the foreign-born population continued to grow from 17 percent of Switzerland's resident population in 1970 to 18.4 percent only three years later. This increase reflects the influence of factors well beyond the global cap's regulatory scope, most importantly the amended 1964 Swiss-Italian recruitment agreement, which, reflecting Switzerland's weakened diplomatic insulation in a Europe-wide competition for migrant labor, entitled seasonal workers to apply for annual permits, thereby accelerating the pace of family unification.

POLICY EXPERIMENTATION IN THE 1990S:
THE THREE CIRCLES POLICY

In the latter half of the 1980s, historic changes in Switzerland's international environment, driven by the rapid pace of European economic integration, increasingly called the global ceiling system's viability into question. Whereas in the 1970s and 1980s little attention was paid to questions of labor migration, as immigration politics was dominated by a highly charged asylum debate, questions of labor migration were now once again at the forefront of political debate. The 1990s came to be marked by a sustained search for new policy models, which was driven by the need for strategic adjustment to the European Union's single market and took the form of a process of trial-and-error experimentation with new policy instruments in order to navigate the difficult terrain of policy making in the absence of diplomatic, popular, and interest group insulation. As in the three previous decades,[8] these responses took the form of regulations and directives issued by the Federal Council after consultation with the major vested interests. Largely circumventing the legislative arena, the Federal Council delegated the task of policy development to a string of consecutive expert commissions that, between 1989 and 1997, issued no fewer than five official reports. In the end, the Federal Council settled for the Three Circles Policy, which sought to reconcile the diplomatic imperative of free movement of European workers with the populist call for cultural closure.

The Policy Failure of the Global Ceiling

By the late 1980s, the continued viability of the global ceiling had come under fire from three different directions. Among the many challenges confronting Swiss policy makers during this period, the quick acceleration of European integration stands out as the most momentous and difficult. As the construction of a Single Market was becoming a reality within the European Union, members of the EFTA – including Switzerland – were invited to join a new EEA premised on the free movement of goods, persons, services, and capital for all EEA and EU member states. There was no question that the pursuit of strategic adjustment through EEA membership would yield significant economic benefits, providing Switzerland's export-oriented industries with open market access as well as dismantling barriers to the immigration of high-skilled European

---

[8] In the late 1970s and early 1980s there was a brief interlude of legislative activity when parliament passed a comprehensive new immigration law to replace the country's 1931 immigration law. The law sought to improve the rights of immigrants, while retaining the seasonal worker program and numerical controls. A year later, however, the law was defeated in a referendum called by the far-right (Skenderovic and D'Amato 2008).

workers. Yet policy makers clearly recognized that the global ceiling system with its immigration quotas was fundamentally incompatible with the principle of free movement on which EEA membership was premised. Not surprisingly, then, early negotiations quickly confirmed that the European Union – in particular its labor-exporting member states Portugal and Spain – was unwilling to tolerate the lesser legal status associated with the Swiss seasonal worker system. As early as 1989, BIGA director Klaus Hug argued that Switzerland had little choice but to accept the advancement of Europeanization and abolish its seasonal worker program (Mahnig and Piguet 2004).

The European Union's demand for freedom of movement for EU and EFTA nationals thus presented a fundamental challenge to the basic workings of Swiss immigration policy. Whereas the global ceiling system was designed to limit the number of economic migrants, the EEA was premised on just the opposite: to provide for an area of freedom of movement, unconstrained by state intervention. Thus, at the same time as Swiss policy makers remained committed to the overforeignization paradigm's principle of immigration control, they faced the potential loss of the very instruments they had relied on for the principle's implementation: worker rotation and recruitment caps. In an ironic twist of fate, Switzerland now found itself confronted with a ghost from the past: the realization of freedom of movement within the EEA bore close resemblance to Switzerland's open borders policy of the pre-World War I era – a legacy that the country had spent the last few decades seeking to leave behind.

A second challenge confronting policy makers was the lack of congruence between a longstanding recruitment policy benefiting low-skilled and labor-intensive sectors, on the one hand, and the rising economic paradigm of the "competition state" (Cerny 1997) situated in a global and knowledge-based economy, on the other. Free market economists within the newly established State Secretariat for Economics argued that Switzerland's longstanding policy of recruiting low-skilled foreign workers was harming the country's economic competitiveness and underscored that the country's comparative advantage needed to rest on its highly skilled workforce (Afonso 2007). These economic critiques of the policy status quo featured prominently in the media. The seasonal worker program in particular was criticized for propping up economically weak sectors, with several studies demonstrating the negative economic impact of unskilled immigration (Sheldon 2003). If immigration policy was to serve the interest of long-term growth and global competitiveness, these experts argued, it needed to favor high-skilled over low-skilled immigration.[9]

While the challenges of Europeanization and global economic competitiveness were principally the result of changes in the recruitment system's external environment, a third set of challenges that came to undermine the global ceiling system was endogenous to immigration policy itself: the large-scale settlement of noneconomic immigrants. While the economic boom of the 1980s had led to a notable increase in the number of foreign workers, immigration continued to rise even after the onset of a long period of economic stagnation in the early 1990s. Thus, whereas in 1970 only 30 percent of all permits were permanent (and thus no longer subject to government control), this proportion had increased to 75 percent by 1990 (Piguet 2006a, 79). To make matters worse for policy makers, by 1991 the majority of immigrants entering Switzerland were nonemployed (Piguet 2006a, 80).

Setting aside asylum applicants, the dual increase in the proportion of settled and economically inactive immigrants can be attributed to past policy choices. In particular, the introduction of compulsory unemployment insurance in 1978 meant that in marked contrast to the oil crisis of the mid-1970s, most immigrants who lost their jobs were now entitled to unemployment benefits, and instead of returning to their countries of origin they could wait out the recession in Switzerland. Most importantly, after labor shortages in the 1980s had once again created favorable negotiation conditions for sending countries, rules for family unification and permanent settlement for Italian workers were further liberalized and, several years later, extended to Portugal and Spain. Thus, while as late as the 1970s immigration still retained much of its cyclical character, declining diplomatic insulation led to a continual weakening of rotation until, by the 1990s, it had ceased to constitute a meaningful feature of the Swiss immigration system (Arbenz 1995, 31). Now Switzerland's foreign population was largely composed of permanently settled residents, rather than rotating guest workers. Combined with the government's decision to drastically reduce seasonal worker recruitment as a response to the pressures of Europeanization, the efficiency of the global ceiling policy was now fundamentally compromised. Immigration policy could no longer serve as a countercyclical labor market buffer.[10]

---

[9] For a more detailed account of the political influence of academic economists in the 1990s, see Afonso (2007).

[10] Parallel to these developments, starting in the 1980s Switzerland found itself confronted with steadily increasing numbers of asylum applicants. From a few thousand applications a year in the early 1980s the number of asylum seekers rose to over 41,000 in 1991 (Piguet 2006a, 80). Unlike the above processes of immigrant settlement, asylum

Policy Making under Diplomatic and Popular Pressure: The Three Circles Policy

Reform pressure continued to mount throughout the 1980s, but it was only with the onset of EFTA-EU[11] negotiations in 1989 that the Federal Council decided to move on the issue of immigration reform. As one of the basic freedoms of the EEA, the free movement of workers was fundamentally incompatible with the annual quotas on which the Swiss immigration system had been constructed. Initially the Federal Council had held out hope that it would be able to secure a permanent derogation to the free movement of workers, even reassuring the Swiss public that, given fears of overforeignization, it would not consider the abolition of annual quotas (*Tages Anzeiger* June 24, 1991). By late 1990, however, it had become clear that the European Commission treated access to the Single Market as a take-it-or-leave-it offer and at most was willing to grant a temporary derogation (Fischer et al. 2002). The Commission insisted that citizens of EEA states be able to work in Switzerland free of restriction and bring in their families without delay. For the Federal Council, this would require not only the lifting of immigration ceilings for EEA citizens, but also the abolition of Switzerland's longstanding seasonal worker program.

Given elite consensus that exclusion from the Single Market would seriously jeopardize Switzerland's economic competitiveness, the Federal Council did not consider recanting on EEA membership as a viable option. Yet because the treaty had to be approved by mandatory referendum, mounting popular opposition to EEA membership threatened to derail its ratification. This threat was all the more credible with the meteoric rise of the SVP – a formerly moderate conservative agrarian party that, under the leadership of Christoph Blocher, had transformed itself into a far-right anti-immigrant party with significant organizational and mobilizing capacities. Affirming the overforeignization paradigm and stating that "Switzerland is not a country of immigration," the SVP's xenophobic rhetoric justified its

---

migration was driven by political and economic developments in migrant-sending countries and was not subject to immigration quotas. While the Federal Council sought to reduce numbers through a series of asylum reforms, these efforts were largely ineffectual and could not prevent the populist exploitation of the asylum issue, and the politicization of immigration policy in general (Mahnig 2005).

[11] For simplicity's sake I use the term EU, even though the European Union was only established in 1993 as successor to the European Economic Community (EEC) (sometimes referred to as the European Community).

opposition to immigration by citing supposed cultural differences between immigrants and the Swiss. Accordingly, the SVP argued that immigrants belonged either to "culturally close" groups from Northern and Western Europe or, more commonly, to "culturally distant" groups from the rest of the world, who were allegedly incapable of integrating into Swiss society (Skenderovic and D'Amato 2008). In its principled opposition to Switzerland's EEA membership, the SVP focused its arguments on the loss of Swiss autonomy and the expected increase in immigration as a consequence of the free movement of workers.

As had been the case with previous bilateral negotiations over conditions governing the residence and family unification rights of guest workers, the lack of diplomatic and popular insulation once again placed the Federal Council between a rock and a hard place. Given the pressing need for reform, in 1989 the lower house asked the Federal Council to prepare a report that would consider the question of immigration reform within the legal and institutional context of Europeanization (Cerutti 2005). The government responded by establishing a commission spearheaded by BIGA, a collective actor well placed to develop policy proposals that are both administratively feasible and politically viable. In early 1991, with EFTA-EU negotiations still ongoing, BIGA issued its report that was to guide Swiss immigration policy for the better part of the 1990s. Its recommendations were framed as an answer to the fundamental dilemma confronting Swiss policy makers:

How can Switzerland achieve rapprochement with Europe in the face of the overforeignization fears of large segments of [its] population? ... The capacity to absorb foreigners and the will to do so are lessening at the same time that the free circulation of persons through Western Europe should be taking place.
(Bundesamt für Industrie, Gewerbe und Arbeit 1991, 177–8, my translation)

The proposed policy solution to this dilemma came in the form of the Three Circles model, which rested on two basic principles. First, in contrast to the government's earlier opposition to the free movement of workers in the EEA, BIGA now strategically embraced this freedom as fundamental to Switzerland's economic competitiveness:

We need foreign labor from countries with the same culture as ours, which is to say European countries. In the long term, such immigrants will only be interested in partaking in profitable economic activities in Switzerland if our labor market offers the same opportunities as comparable markets in other European countries. The free movement of persons proposed by the EC gives this issue additional importance.
(Bundesamt für Industrie, Gewerbe und Arbeit 1991, 177–8, my translation)

Second, BIGA reaffirmed Switzerland's longstanding overforeignization paradigm by reiterating the cultural threat posed by uncontrolled immigration: "Switzerland's national cohesion and national identity must not be endangered by too many foreigners" (Bundesamt für Industrie, Gewerbe und Arbeit 1991, 77, my translation). In order to resolve the tension between the external challenge of Europeanization and the continued prevention of overforeignization, then, the report shifted the overforeignization paradigm's traditional focus away from Switzerland's foreign population to its composition. Therefore, overforeignization was no longer exclusively the result of the number of immigrants, but hinged on their degree of "cultural distance" from the Swiss (Mahnig and Piguet 2004).

Immigration policy thus was to differentiate between three groups – or circles – of countries. The first circle, comprising citizens of the European Union and the EFTA, would enjoy freedom of movement in accordance with EU law. The second circle distinguished itself by the possibility of limited recruitment. Membership in this group was based on the notion of cultural proximity, defined by the Federal Council as "countries belonging ... to the same, European-influenced, culture, with living conditions comparable to those in Switzerland" (Eidgenössischer Bundesrat 1991, 303, my translation). Thus, economic immigration was to be limited to the "traditional recruitment regions" of the first-circle countries of Western Europe, together with the second-circle countries: Yugoslavia, the US, Canada, Australia, and New Zealand.[12] As formulated by the Federal Council,

[these] countries ... possess cultural, religious and societal values comparable to [the Swiss]. This will serve to protect Swiss identity and will increase the integration capacity [of immigrants]. The latter directly influences the degree to which the Swiss are willing to accept foreigners.

(Eidgenössischer Bundesrat 1991, 295, my translation)

Another important criterion for second-circle membership was the protection of human rights, which meant that citizens of countries with human rights violations could only enter Switzerland as asylum seekers, not as workers. Finally, the third circle was made up of countries marked by their "cultural distance" from Switzerland, a notion with strong

---

[12] The report mentions the possibility of adding Eastern European countries to the second circle.

ethnoracial undertones, as is evident in a later report by the Federal Council:

Swiss admissions policy in relation to foreign workers is based on the principle that the ethnic and national otherness of people from particular countries generally hinders their integration into our society. ... It is in fact the case that the criteria of integration capacity decisively impedes the admission of members of other ethnic and racial group because of their limited integration capacity.
(Eidgenössischer Bundesrat 1992, 29–30, my translation)

In other words, citizens of third-circle countries were generally excluded from economic admission, except for highly skilled experts who, under exceptional circumstances, would be admitted on a temporary basis.

When the Federal Council presented its report to parliament a few months later, it was largely based on BIGA's blueprint. The report received a mixed reception. Whereas all mainstream parties – excluding the far-right Swiss Democrats and the SVP – supported the principle of free movement for EEA citizens, there was no consensus on the Three Circles Policy.[13] While Christian Democrats and Social Democrats critiqued the distinction between the second and third circle as discriminatory and racist, the Liberals welcomed the shift from a "quantitative" to a "qualitative" mode of immigration control (Schweizer Bundesversammlung June 10, 1991, 1016). As the moral objections of the centrist parties indicate, what really marked the proposed policy was its *explicit* use of ethnic recruitment criteria, a rhetorical move that, by the 1990s, was no longer politically acceptable to much of the political mainstream (Mahnig and Piguet 2004). In important ways, of course, the use of ethnonational admission criteria constituted a continuation of Swiss immigration policy that had favored recruitment from Western Europe since its beginnings. The 1964 report of the Expert Commission on the Problem of Foreign Labor, for instance, stated in no uncertain terms that:

[t]he recruitment of foreign labor should be limited to countries with a way of life close to ours. While it is easy to recruit workers in faraway countries, it is necessary to reject their labor because they would experience great difficulties in adapting to our way of life, and it would be impossible for them to assimilate.
(Bundesamt für Industrie, Gewerbe und Arbeit 1964, 92, my translation)

---

[13] The report also addressed the question of asylum migration, without, however, suggesting any significant departures from the policy status quo. The lack of meaningful policy alternatives in this area came under strong attack in both houses.

There is little doubt that the prominence given to the notion of "cultural distance" in the Three Circles Policy was designed to placate the far-right in order to stave off the threat of a popular veto. Given the public concerns about increased immigration from the European Union, BIGA's report had explicitly warned about the unpredictability of a popular referendum on the question of EEA membership. Thus, the attribution of intrinsic cultural attributes to all members of a national group clearly echoes the arguments put forward by far-right groups, with the difference that BIGA and the Federal Council considered all citizens of EU member states – hence, also Southern and, potentially in the future, Eastern Europeans – as sharing a common "European" culture with the Swiss. By treating Europeans as a culturally homogenous group and by asserting that any future European immigration was going to be negligible in scope, the Federal Council aimed to assuage both "qualitative" and "quantitative" overforeignization fears among the public.

The significance of the Federal Council's populist strategy becomes apparent when we consider its willingness to defy business interests for the sake of populist pandering. In September 1991, the Federal Council decided to demote Yugoslavia – a longstanding and unpopular (Hainmueller and Hangartner 2013) recruitment country – from the second to the third circle, in response to mounting human rights violations. The decision had immediate and far-reaching labor market implications. As third-circle nationals, 44,000 Yugoslavs – a third of all seasonal workers – already working in Switzerland were to return home. Not surprisingly, trade unions and employers in the hospitality and construction sector were up in arms about this decision, calling it a "knife in the back" (Mahnig 2005, 181). Given the fierceness of business opposition, the Federal Council agreed to a transition period of two to three years. At the same time, it demanded that any future seasonal worker recruitment be limited to EU and EFTA countries and not include Yugoslav nationals. The government threatened that in the event of noncompliance, a quota for EEA immigrants would be imposed. Yugoslavia's banishment to the third circle had a palpable impact on recruitment. Whereas in 1990 over 55,000 Yugoslavs had entered Switzerland as seasonal workers, by 1996 this number had dropped to zero[14] (Mahnig and Piguet 2004, 99). As 1992, the year in which a popular referendum was to decide the fate of EEA membership, drew

---

[14] Some of the loss was offset by increased asylum immigration from the former Yugoslavia.

near, the Federal Council left no doubt that it was serious about limiting economic immigration to EEA nationals, even if this meant incurring the anger of employer associations.

In contrast to the referendums of the 1960s and 1970s, this time the Federal Council's populist gamble did not pay off. On December 6, 1992, with a record turnout of 79 percent – exceeding even that of the 1970 Schwarzenbach Initiative – 50.3 percent of Swiss voters rejected Switzerland's accession to the EEA. While the Federal Council had negotiated a five-year delay in the implementation of the agreement's free movement provisions, the concession had failed to detract from the fact that after the transition period Switzerland would no longer be able to control the entry of EU workers and their dependents. The "no" campaign, spearheaded by the populist group Campaign for an Independent and Neutral Switzerland (AUNS) under the leadership of Christoph Blocher, had argued that EEA membership, especially the abolition of the seasonal worker statute, would result in the mass immigration of workers and their dependents and impose significant fiscal and social costs on cantons and municipalities. The message clearly resonated with the public. A subsequent analysis of motivations for the "no" vote revealed widespread fears of an influx of foreign workers, alongside the loss of Swiss identity (Mahnig 2005). Once again, the institutions of direct democracy allowed for popular pressure to serve as a key driver of Swiss immigration politics. While in the past policy makers had been able to deflect popular opposition by means of major policy concessions, this time anti-immigration agitators were able to deliver on their veto threat and force the government to abandon its policy proposals.

POPULAR SOVEREIGNTY VERSUS EUROPEANIZATION: FROM THE 1998 TWO CIRCLES POLICY TO THE 2014 REFERENDUM ON MASS IMMIGRATION

After the referendum pressures for policy reform continued to build. In 1993 parliament passed a motion[15] charging the Federal Council with the development of a comprehensive immigration law that would put an end to decades of policy making via executive ordinance. The so-called Simmen Motion – named after its instigator, Christian Democratic member of the Council of States Rosemarie Simmen – marked the

---

[15] A motion passed by parliament requires the Federal Council to develop a policy proposal.

beginning of a sustained immigration debate that only came to a conclusion with the passage of the 2008 Immigration Act. Two policy milestones preceded the adoption of the new law. First, in 1998, the Three Circles Policy was replaced with a Two Circles model that shifted immigrant admissions from cultural to skill-based selection. In a second policy milestone the Federal Council, in 2000, ratified a bilateral treaty package (Bilaterals I) with the European Union, which provided for the free movement of European workers and their families.

The Two Circles Policy: The Paradigm of the Competition State

By the mid-1990s there was a broad elite consensus that the Three Circles Policy was no longer viable. First, economic critiques leveled against the earlier global ceiling system as impeding access to highly skilled labor were now directed with increasing force against the Three Circles Policy. With the ascendancy of the new economic paradigm of the "competition state" (Cerny 1997), economic experts considered global economic competitiveness to be the critical means for generating economic growth and rising standards of living at home (Palan et al. 1996). This new paradigm necessitated a shift in the framing of the national interest from satisfying the manpower demands of all economic sectors to privileging internationally competitive firms (Piguet 2006b). This ideational change was accompanied by a shift in political power from employer associations in labor-intensive, low-skilled, and domestically oriented sectors (i.e., agriculture, construction, and tourism) to business in high-skilled and globally oriented sectors. Given that under the Three Circles Policy many sending countries of globally mobile high-skilled labor were in the outer circle and thus were excluded from recruitment, Swiss multinational corporations and the high-tech sector demanded reforms that would ensure global access to a highly qualified workforce (Piguet 2006a).

In a second line of attack, normative pressures for reform mounted with the creation of the Federal Commission against Racism in 1995, which followed Switzerland's ratification of the UN Convention on the Elimination of Racial Discrimination. While the notion of "cultural distance" had been under fire right from the policy's inception – recall the arguments leveled against the differentiation between the Second and Third Circles in parliamentary debates – the Commission's decision to shine its spotlight on the Three Circles Policy returned normative questions into the public spotlight. The Commission's high-profile report, published in 1996, provided a damning critique of the policy status quo as "fundamentally racist," arguing that the Three Circles rested on "generalized judgments on group identities based on ethnicity, nationality, religion, rather than on individual characteristics, thus reflecting racially motivated prejudices" (Eidgenössische Kommission gegen Rassismus 1996, 7, my translation).

A third, contrasting, strand of criticism leveled against the Three Circles Policy came from socially conservative circles who continued to embrace the immigration paradigm of overforeignization, which now coexisted with the economic paradigm of the competition state. Concerned with the Three Circles Policy's inability to put an end to immigration from outside the EEA – in particular from the former Yugoslavia, whose nationals continued to arrive as family immigrants and asylum seekers – social conservatives demanded a fundamental reorientation of Swiss immigration policy to prevent overforeignization. Delegates of three bourgeois parties – the conservative-liberal Free Democratic Party (FDP), the far-right Swiss Democrats (SD), and the socially conservative Federal Democratic Union of Switzerland (EDU) – launched a popular initiative that came to be known as the 18 Percent Initiative because it demanded that the percentage of foreign residents, including asylum seekers and refugees, be capped at 18 percent (Skenderovic and D'Amato 2008).

While the Federal Council refuted many of the above criticisms – in particular the accusation of discrimination – it was not immune to the economic and normative pressures leveled against the Three Circles. At the same time, despite the people's rejection of the free movement of European labor at the polls, executive policy makers remained firmly committed to the pursuit of European market integration. In response to these economic, normative, and integration imperatives, in 1996 the Federal Council decided to establish a new expert commission,[16] this time under the leadership of past BIGA director Klaus Hug, who was charged with the development of a new policy blueprint. The Hug Commission's recommendations, which were published in 1997, would shape Swiss immigration policy for decades to come. The Commission's policy blueprint established the primacy of global competitiveness as the foundation of immigration policy: "[t]he admission of foreign workers must serve the

---

[16] In 1994 the Arbenz Commission's report had proposed the creation of an auction system for work permits where only the highest-bidding employers would be able to hire foreign workers (Afonso 2007). The report failed to win the support of political elites, and the commission's work ended up having little impact on government policy.

interests of the global economy" (Commission d'Experts en Migration 1997, 20, my translation). Arguing that the realization of the free movement of persons between Switzerland and the European Union was only a matter of time, the Commission emphasized the need to harmonize policy accordingly. Not only was the First Circle of European labor recruitment to be retained, but the number of seasonal workers was to be progressively reduced in preparation for Switzerland joining the European area of free movement.

Second, the distinction between the Second and Third Circles was to be removed, as cultural selection criteria not only lacked legitimacy but also compromised the country's economic interest. Further, the committee argued, "[t]he admission of foreign labor must not be influenced by some sectors or interest groups but in all cases must serve the long-term interests of the country" (Commission d'Experts en Migration 1997, 20, my translation). In order to move toward this goal, then, all non-European countries would become members of a Second Circle from which employers would select highly qualified workers on the basis of a human capital points system.

In 1998, the Federal Council officially abandoned the Three Circles model in favor of a Two Circles Policy. Admission for nationals of the Second (non-European) Circle countries would now be based exclusively on professional qualifications. While the Federal Council had clearly subordinated the interests of business to populist imperatives when drawing up the Three Circles Policy, the new policy clearly tilted the balance in favor of (high-skilled) business. The Two Circles Policy institutionalized Switzerland's departure from the old quota system, which had been in place since the 1950s. The new policy ushered in an era marked by the liberalization of admission procedures for EU workers, on the one hand, and the global pursuit of highly skilled labor, on the other. As a consequence, immigrant admissions quickly came to reflect the primacy of high-skilled immigration. Between 1996 and 2006 the proportion of economic immigrants increased from 19 percent to 37 percent of primary immigrants, with the proportion of the highly skilled within this group doubling.[17] The long-term viability of the new policy was based on the assumption that both streams would remain modest in size, which,

---

[17] http://cooperation.epfl.ch/webdav/site/cooperation/shared/diaspora/Presentation%20Fibbi%20-%20Swiss%20Immigration%20policy%20and%20the%20highly%20skilled.pdf, accessed September 28, 2014.

combined with a policy bias toward Europeans and the highly skilled, would deflect public backlash (Piguet 2006a).

Finally, with the adoption of the Two Circles model, the Federal Council adamantly refused to concede to the demands of the instigators of the 18 Percent Initiative. There was no question that a return to the era of immigration ceilings would preclude any further steps toward Europeanization. In parliament, Federal Councilor Jean-Pascal Delamuraz defended the government's proposed reforms by arguing that a sustainable balance between the native-born and the country's foreign-born population – or, in the words of social conservatives, the threshold for overforeignization – could not be adequately defined in numerical terms. Successful integration, Delamuraz argued, depended in large part on the *qualitative* characteristics of immigrants. In 1998, both houses of parliament followed the Federal Council in rejecting the initiative. During the National Assembly's deliberations, the Federal Council committed itself to a fundamental overhaul of the country's 1931 Immigration Act as an alternative to the 18 Percent Initiative. It assured parliament that it would submit its reform proposal after the popular vote was cast on the initiative (Wimmer 2001).

The Agreement on the Free Movement of Persons: Neutralizing the Referendum Threat

At the same time as the Federal Council found itself confronted with the 18 Percent initiative, it remained actively engaged in negotiations with the European Union. Despite its referendum defeat in 1992, the Federal Council remained firmly committed to the pursuit of European market integration, resuming negotiations with the European Union just months after voters had rejected EEA membership. Rather than revisiting the question of EEA membership, the Federal Council decided to opt for a bilateral treaty-based approach that would limit policy harmonization to discrete domains of cooperation, thereby posing a lesser threat to national autonomy (Linder 2011). By 1994 both sides had agreed on an agenda of seven issues, and formal negotiations commenced.

There was no question that the Federal Council could not afford another defeat on the path to European integration. Yet it found itself in the same kind of political bind that had made negotiations on EEA membership so challenging in the first place. The European Union once again was adamant that all issues under negotiation be treated as an indivisible package. Most importantly, the EU insisted that negotiations include the politically contentious issue of freedom of movement. Thus, Swiss access to the Single Market would be contingent on the abolition of immigration restrictions for EU and EFTA nationals, effectively removing this group from the jurisdiction of Swiss immigration law. The Federal Council knew that it could rely on parliamentary support for the treaty package as all major parties, except for the SVP, were unified in their support of regional economic integration. However, while the treaties' success was unlikely to be imperiled in the legislative arena, their fate was much more uncertain should the issue move into the popular arena. Given the seminal role played by the SVP in mobilizing the public to veto EEA membership in 1992, the Federal Council's domestic strategy had to focus on the referendum as a critical veto point.

Should the Swiss public make use of the optional referendum,[18] the main bone of contention was likely going to be the Agreement on the Free Movement of Persons. Given that the treaty package had to be either adopted or rejected as a whole, a popular rejection of freedom of movement would doom the entire project to failure and would put into question the long-term future of Switzerland's Single Market access. The Federal Council decided to pursue a two-pronged strategy in order to neutralize the referendum threat. First, it sought to co-opt the national leadership of the SVP, who was ambivalent about the Agreement after the Federal Council's decision to adopt a bilateral treaty-based approach had removed the issue of regional membership from the agenda.

Whereas the SVP's economically liberal wing – which represented the party's traditional clientele of employers in labor-intensive agriculture, construction, and hospitality – supported the agreement as a way of accessing new export markets and labor pools, its socially conservative wing – which relies on the support of blue-collar workers – opposed freedom of movement as a threat to immigration control. Despite the electoral appeals of its socially conservative campaigns, the party's parliamentary elite was dominated by business owners (Afonso 2013). Capitalizing on this ambivalence, the Federal Council managed to secure the support of the party's leader, Christoph Blocher – formerly one of Switzerland's most prominent industrialists – who took the position that the bilateral agreements would serve the country's financial and economic interests as long as Switzerland did not pursue EU membership (Mazzoleni 2013). Arguing that the bilateral treaties did not present a

---

[18] Unlike the EEA treaty, which was constitutionally subject to popular assent, for the bilateral treaties a referendum was optional, subject to popular initiation.

challenge to Switzerland's independence, neutrality, or security, Blocher advised his party not to oppose the treaties. Yet while the national party leadership came to officially support the agreements, the party's cantonal sections remained opposed, as were the majority of party members (Church 2004). In the final vote in the National Council the SVP remained divided, with fifteen delegates voting in favor and thirty-six against (Afonso 2013).

At the same time as the Federal Council courted the SVP's national leadership, it reached out to the left. Since the far-right SD had already declared their intention to call a referendum, all actors understood that the treaties only stood a chance of adoption if the trade unions refused to join forces with the far-right to oppose the free movement provisions. Whereas the business community had much to gain from the integration of Switzerland's export-dependent economy into the Single Market and therefore unreservedly supported the treaties, labor's position was more ambivalent. On the one hand, Swiss unions had traditionally held strong pro-European leanings. Moreover, many union members did not hold Swiss citizenship and stood to gain from freedom of movement (Fischer 2003a). On the other hand, the unions were concerned that the unregulated immigration of workers from lower-wage European countries would exert downward pressure on wages and work conditions. While the policy status quo partly compensated for Switzerland's loosely regulated labor market policy by requiring that the wages of foreign (but not Swiss) workers meet locally prevailing conditions (Fischer 2002), with the introduction of freedom of movement such one-sided compensatory measures would no longer be possible, as the EU considered any policy that did not equally apply to Swiss and EU workers to be discriminatory (Veuve 2001).

Well aware of their strategic advantage, the unions demanded far-reaching compensatory labor market measures that, given the dominance of Swiss business, at any other time would have been well beyond their reach. Importantly, the success of labor's strategy depended on employers taking seriously the possibility that unions would indeed exercise the referendum's veto power. Consequently, union leaders early on committed themselves to a referendum should employers and the Federal Council oppose their demands (Fischer 2003b). For labor, the decision to tie its hands early on in the negotiation process – which precluded any future backpedaling – reflected a process of strategic learning from the past. During EEA negotiations, unions had also called for flanking measures to protect the wages and working conditions of Swiss workers. These

demands, however, were quickly dismissed by both business and government officials because prominent union representatives had expressed
unconditional support for EEA membership early in the negotiation
process (Fischer 2003b). In the words of Social Democratic National
Assembly councilor Rudolf Strahm: "The Swiss Trade Union
Association supported the flanking measures but had decided early on
that it would support EEA membership even if their demands were not
met. The Federal Council was well aware of this and this is why it did not
take these demands seriously" (Strahm October 1, 1992, my translation).
Not surprisingly, then, this time the trade unions shifted their position on
European integration from unconditional to conditional support.

Faced with the union's veto threat and employers' opposition to the
unions' demands, the Federal Council decided to set up a special tripartite
taskforce in order to facilitate a compromise. In an unprecedented trade
union victory, the taskforce agreed on a set of far-reaching labor market
measures, ranging from the guarantee that newly hired immigrants would
receive no less than the "usual wages," to the extension of collective labor
agreements to entire sectors in cases of repeat noncompliance (Fischer
et al. 2002). This outcome, which closely corresponded to the unions'
initial demands, reflects the enormous veto power associated with the
institution of the popular referendum. Most business representatives were
convinced that the unions would follow through on their referendum
threat if their demands were not met (Fischer et al. 2002). In a similar
vein, a majority of business representatives believed that should the far-
right and trade unions form an alliance, a majority of the electorate would
vote against the bilateral treaties (Fischer et al. 2002). Significantly, the
union's veto threat remained credible throughout the policy process.
When the Council of States – the Assembly's upper house – and its foreign
affairs committee sought to water down the flanking measures agreed on
during the pre-parliamentary phase, the Swiss Trade Unions Federation
immediately announced that it had instructed its office to commence
preparations for a referendum. After the unions circulated a press release
draft that singled out individual councilors as having obstructed labor
market protections in the interest of big business, the Council of States
backed down (Fischer 2003b).

After the flanking measures' passage, the unions delivered on their
promise to oppose the referendum on the ratification of the bilateral
treaties, which had been organized by the far-right SD and a number of
smaller anti-immigrant groups. In the SVP, a minority of the party leadership – joined by several cantonal and regional SVP organizations –

actively opposed the treaties. The referendum took place in May 2000, followed in September by the vote on the 18 Percent Initiative. To the political establishment's great relief, a solid majority voted in favor of the bilateral treaties (67.2 percent) and against the 18 Percent Initiative (63.4 percent). After the September vote, Councilor Ruth Metzler announced that the people had sent a clear signal to the international community that Switzerland was ready to honor its international obligations (Skenderovic and D'Amato 2008). At the same time, she cautioned against interpreting the vote as an expression of popular support for a more liberalized admission of non-Europeans. The planned legislative reform, she asserted, must continue to exert strict control over immigration from outside of Europe.

With the ratification of the Bilaterals I, the Federal Council's progressive liberalization of immigration within the inner circle of the Three Circles and, later, Two Circles Policy had been affirmed. EU and EFTA citizens and their families now had the right to enter and reside in Switzerland as long as they possessed an offer of employment or sufficient financial means to live independently of state support. In effect, the Agreement on the Free Movement of Persons removed nationals of EU and EFTA countries from the jurisdiction of Swiss immigration law and conferred on this population a legal status in many ways comparable to that of Swiss citizens.[19] In the short term, the Federal Council had secured concessions on the speed of liberalization. Until 2004, Switzerland would be able to favor domestic over European workers, retain its regulations on the wages and work conditions of foreign workers, and impose quotas on immigration. Accordingly, the number of new residence permits issued to foreign workers was limited to 15,000 annually, and the number of short-term permits was capped at 115,500 (Piguet 2006b). The Federal Council had further negotiated the possibility of imposing overall immigration ceilings until 2007 and, in cases of excessive and unpredicted immigration inflows, until the year 2014. Only after 2014, 12 years after the Agreement on the Free Movement of Persons' coming into force, would the Federal Council no longer be able to unilaterally[20] impose limits on immigration from EU and EFTA countries.

---

[19] EU citizens were even privileged over Swiss citizens in relation to family sponsorship. Whereas an EU citizen could sponsor their parents for immigration, this was not possible for a (naturalized) Swiss citizen. I owe this point to Etienne Piguet.

[20] In cases of severe economic or social problems, Switzerland would be able to impose limits, but only with the EU's consent.

The Immigration Act of 2008: Policy Making in the Legislative Arena

Less than two months after the people's ratification of the bilateral treaties, the Federal Council submitted its draft legislation to the relevant societal interests for consultation and comment (*Vernehmlassung*). While the process of consulting with major sociopolitical stakeholders – parliamentary parties, cantons, the social partners, and nongovernmental organizations (NGOs), among others – had also been part and parcel of immigration policy making in the past, this was the first time since the failed immigration reform of 1982 (which would have improved the legal status of noncitizens)[21] that immigration policy was to move into the legislative arena. Even if its admissions provisions would largely amount to a writing into law of the policy status quo that had been established through regulations, ordinances, and bilateral treaties, the new law would constitute a major political milestone as it would serve to democratically legitimate the policy status quo and modernize Swiss immigration law by finally removing the country's archaic Immigration Act of 1931 from the books. Affirming the policy status quo, the Federal Council's proposed law would legally enshrine the Two Circle policy's principle of "dual admissions" by providing for freedom of movement for EU and EFTA nationals while pursuing a restrictive, labor market-driven admissions policy for third-country nationals. Significantly, this quota-based admissions policy for third-country nationals would be limited to highly skilled migrants and would effectively close the door to any further low-skilled recruitment from outside of the European Union and EFTA. Accordingly, the draft formalized the abolition of the seasonal worker program and replaced it with a temporary work visa program for highly skilled workers (*Kurzaufenthalter*[22]).

With the abolition of the seasonal workers program and a third-country selection policy limited to high-skilled workers, the government's draft marked a clear departure from decades of low-skilled labor recruitment that had defined Swiss postwar immigration policy until the early 1990s. The decision to institutionalize the new policy status by means of legislative immigration reform was driven by two mutually reinforcing considerations. First, policy makers were profoundly concerned about the

---

[21] The law was defeated at the referendum stage.
[22] *Kurzaufenthalter* would be admitted under one-year permits that were typically tied to specific time-limited projects. Permits could be renewed by one more year, after which workers would be required to leave.

continuing public unease with the absence of immigration controls over European workers. Despite the people's vote in favor of the Agreement on the Free Movement of Persons, the government was cognizant of the possibility of a future referendum defeat as transitional exemptions to the agreement expired and the European Union expanded eastwards in 2005. As the Federal Council already articulated in its rejection of the 18 Percent Initiative, policy liberalization in relation to European workers would only be politically viable if paired with policy restrictionism toward third-country nationals. Second, and reinforcing the populist imperative, the competition state paradigm clearly asserted that Switzerland's economic interest would be best served by the admission of highly skilled workers while framing low-skilled immigration as an impediment to economic modernization and a strain on the public purse. As the Federal Council stated,

admissions decisions should reflect long-term macro-economic interests ... and sustainable economic development ... and should neither serve to protect current economic structures by means of low-skilled and low-wage workers, nor support particularistic economic interests.

(Bundesrat 2002, 3725, my translation)

In particular, third-country admissions had to preempt the "mass immigration of low-skilled workers who would present heightened integration problems" (Bundesrat 2002, 3726, my translation). The government's draft thus expanded high-skilled admissions to self-employed entrepreneurs and granted all high-skilled workers – whether on temporary or renewable permits – the right to bring in their families for the sake of "the international competitiveness of Swiss firms" (Bundesrat 2002, 3726). At the same time, the Federal Council sought to reassure employers in labor-intensive sectors that any future low-skilled labor needs would be filled by European labor under freedom of movement provisions.

While the Federal Council's adoption of the Two Circles Policy's dual-admission system closely mirrored the 1998 proposals of the Hug Commission, it emphatically rejected the commission's proposal to establish a Canadian-style points system as the basis for the selection of third-country nationals. While the government's legislative draft did include considerations of professional adaptability and language skills when issuing renewable work permits, it explicitly rejected a formal points system in favor of an admissions system based on administrative discretion (Bundesrat 2002). In contrast to the transparency and standardization of decision-making associated with a human capital points system, immigration bureaucrats would retain wide discretion in deciding on whether or not an applicant's skills and characteristics would allow them to succeed in the Swiss labor market (Wimmer 2001). The Federal Council's draft thus reflected a fundamental tension between a policy realignment in favor of high-skilled immigration, on the one hand, and the influence of vested interests in labor- intensive sectors, on the other. The Federal Council's privileging of administrative discretion is best understood as a concession to the interests of employers and the cantons – key stakeholders whose autonomy would have been decidedly curtailed through the imposition of a points system. In the words of a political insider,[23]

the current system of distributing immigration quotas to the cantons, who in turn negotiate permit allocation with various interest groups and bureaucracies ... had the advantage for all involved that it was possible to consider special interests. In this way emerged a relatively stable network of relations between bureaucracies and especially those interest groups ... who were dependent on the mass import of unskilled labor. This network would have been destroyed by the introduction of a points system ... with its reliance on the demonstration of other, more transparent and collective, interests in order to influence the system.

(Wimmer 2001, 99–100, my translation)

After the legislative draft's publication for public comment, the Federal Council received 149 submissions, virtually all of which concurred that the 1931 Immigration Act had to be replaced with a more contemporary law. Beyond this cross-partisan consensus on the need for reform, three groups – the Liberals (FDP), Christian Democrats, and several employer associations – expressed basic support for the draft law. This substantive agreement with the Federal Council, however, did not extend to the majority of submissions, which shared little common ground on the direction that reform should take, with positions largely falling into two opposing camps. The first group, dominated by the left – the Social Democrats, the Greens, the Federal Commission against Racism, and women's and immigrants' rights organizations – claimed that the legal provisions governing the admission of third-country nationals were motivated by "overforeignization fears" and would institutionalize a two-class system that discriminated between privileged EU and EFTA nationals, on the one hand, and lesser-status third-country nationals, on

---

[23] Wimmer served as consultant to the commission that drafted the Federal Council's draft. He also served as director of the newly established Swiss Forum for Migration Studies – Switzerland's first academic migration research center.

the other. The Social Democrats in particular asserted that the 18 Percent Initiative had held undue sway over the Federal Council's proposals for the admission of third-country nationals (Eidgenössisches Justiz- und Polizeidepartement 2001).

A second group rejected the Federal Council's draft for just the opposite reason, arguing that it created too many rights for third-country nationals and would invite abuse of the system. The SVP, together with several cantons and the association of cantonal immigration directors, critiqued the draft for offering insufficient mechanisms to ward off the intense immigration pressure from non-European countries (Eidgenössisches Justiz- und Polizeidepartement 2001). The SVP further criticized the draft for not living up to the expectations raised by the Federal Council's promise of stricter immigration controls in return for the public's vote against the 18 Percent Initiative. Aside from fundamental disagreement on whether to liberalize or further restrict the admission of non-European migrants, there was strong disagreement on the qualitative nature of third-country admissions. While many supported the Federal Council's privileging of high-skilled migrants, others countered that the country's low-skilled labor needs could not be adequately met through European labor and warned of labor shortages in construction, agriculture, and the hospitality sector (Eidgenössisches Justiz- und Polizeidepartement 2001).

Despite sustained criticism in the *Vernehmlassung*, the Federal Council decided to retain the draft's basic admissions provisions. Warding off pressure to facilitate the recruitment of low-skilled workers, the government argued that it would only consider this option should the supply of EU and EFTA nationals be insufficient to meet labor market shortages in low-skilled sectors. The Federal Council further maintained that the EU's Eastern enlargement could provide an additional future source of low-skilled labor. The government emphatically rejected proposals for a new seasonal worker program, arguing that:

[e]xperience shows that sooner or later affected persons, employers, the social partners, and political parties demand settlement and family unification rights. . . . [A seasonal worker program] would also establish the basis for new amnesty demands and for humanitarian mobilization in favor of unskilled third-country nationals.

(Bundesrat 2002, 3773, my translation)

Finally, despite sustained criticism by the political right, the Federal Council retained the liberal family unification provisions that extended even to temporary third-country workers (*Kurzaufenthalter*). In March

2002, just months before the coming into force of the Agreement on the Free Movement of Persons, the government submitted its draft to parliament.

The Federal Council's draft was to undergo three readings in each house before, one-and-a-half years after the opening of plenary debate in the lower house, it was adopted in late 2005. As the lengthy legislative process indicates,[24] the legislature was deeply divided on key features of the law. The most controversial provision pertaining to immigrant admissions[25] was the exclusion from recruitment of low-skilled third-country nationals. The National Assembly's preparatory commission recommended adoption of the Federal Council's position to limit recruitment to highly skilled workers, but five different groups of parliamentarians suggested separate amendments, all of which were at odds with the preparatory commission's position. While the Social Democrats and Greens attacked the restrictive admission of third-country nationals as discriminatory and demanded entry for anyone with an offer of employment, the SVP demanded an opening of recruitment channels for low-skilled workers in particular.

In a rare development,[26] one of the SVP-sponsored amendments gained the vote of a majority of councilors and passed the lower house. The amendment relaxed the high-skilled clause for third-country nationals by allowing for the recruitment of "workers who are needed for specific jobs." Dubbed the "harvester clause," the amendment clearly bore the signature of the Swiss Farmers' Association (*Schweizer Bauernverband*), one of the biggest losers under the proposed law. The Association's submission to the lower house's preparatory commission had estimated a need for 5,000 to 6,000 harvesters beyond the available supply of EU and EFTA workers (*Amtliches Bulletin Nationalrat* May 6, 2004, AB 2004 N 717/BO 2004 N 716). The amendment was sponsored by a group of SVP delegates whose party had long been a mouthpiece of agricultural interests and small business owners and now constituted the largest faction in the National Council. Its lead sponsor, Ernst Schibli, himself member of the Board of Directors of the Swiss Farmers' Association, justified the amendment by arguing that without it, "entire

---

[24] Fewer than 10 percent of legislative proposals linger in the Swiss parliament beyond a second reading (Kriesi 2001).

[25] Other controversial provisions included the legalization of undocumented migrants as well as family unification and permanent residence rights.

[26] Ninety-five percent of the time, the Swiss parliamentary majority follows the majority view of their preparatory committees (Kriesi 2001, 63).

vocations would be hindered by or completely excluded from market-based economic development" (Schweizer Bundesversammlung May 6, 2004, AB 2004 N 711/BO 2004 N 711). In a similar vein, SVP Councilor Hansjörg Walter contended that:

[e]conomic sectors and regions that rely on the recruitment of low-skilled workers – such as hospitality, health care, construction, agriculture, and horticulture – also have a right to a sustainable future, to a sustainable economy. These branches fulfill to a large extent a general interest for the economy, especially in rural regions. . . . What is qualification? For me it is also hard work – and not only the distinction between manual labor and office labor. . . . I therefore ask you to agree to the request of the minority here, because it is important that the allocation of permits is not made alone according to qualification.
(Schweizer Bundesversammlung May 6, 2004, AB 2004 N711/BO 2004 N686, my translation)

The SVP's amendment passed by a margin of four votes, with the support of all SVP councilors and the majority of the liberal caucus, a group with many direct ties to interest groups in the low-skilled sector (*Neue Zürcher Zeitung* May 7, 2004).

In the upper house, the Council of States' preparatory commission expressed strong opposition to the amendment and called on the chamber to endorse the Federal Council's original clause. Speaking for the commission, liberal councilor Heberlein argued that the amendment constituted

a violation of the basic principle of high skilled immigration . . . The dual-admissions system cannot be watered down with exceptions that prioritize seasonal and sector-specific needs over formal qualifications. It is well known that the previous practice of granting work permits in sectors where they were needed resulted in the loss of immigration control. . . . The National Council's decision to allow for recruitment for "specific jobs" . . . represents a relapse into the era of seasonal worker recruitment.
(Schweizer Bundesversammlung March 16, 2005, 288, my translation)

The Council of States' preparatory commission's recommendations were widely endorsed and passed without any plenary debate. While the SVP held 28 percent of seats in the National Council, it only occupied 17 percent of seats in the Council of States. By contrast, the Christian Democrats, as the key supporter of the government's legislative draft, dominated the upper house with one-third of seats, while only holding 14 percent of seats in the lower house. As expected, the Council of States vetoed the National Council's amendment.

Before the National Council could return to the bill's second reading, two important developments took place in the popular arena that strengthened the government's position. After the Federal Council had negotiated a second set of bilateral treaties (Bilaterals II) with the European Union in 2004, the SVP and the AUNS forced a referendum on one of the treaties, the Schengen and Dublin Association Agreement. The agreement would put an end to systematic identity checks at the border, make Switzerland part of a passport-free zone, and allow the country to turn away asylum seekers who had already filed a request in another signatory country. In June 2005, after an intensive campaign, a majority of 54.6 percent of voters supported the ratification of the Schengen and Dublin Agreements. Just two months later, voters had to decide on one of the most controversial provisions of the treaties: the extension of the right to free movement to the ten largely Central and Eastern European accession countries. The referendum had been called by the right-wing SD and was supported by parts of the SVP. For the SVP, the party's internal divisions caused much consternation, with the party's two representatives in the Federal Council, Christoph Blocher and Samuel Schmid, firmly in favor of the agreement (Albertazzi and McDonnell 2015). In September 2005, 56 percent of voters voted in favor of the extension of the right to free movement.

These government victories were significant in that they legitimated the Federal Council's bilateral approach to policy harmonization with the European Union. Most importantly, they affirmed the Agreement on the Free Movement of Persons as a pillar of Swiss immigration policy. When the immigration bill returned to the National Council for its second reading, its preparatory commission returned discussion to the amended high-skilled immigration clause. The commission clearly recognized that the Council of States was unlikely to reconsider its position, given that the upper house's veto had been cast in the absence of any plenary debate, indicating a lack of dissent (Schweizer Bundesversammlung September 28, 2015, AB 2005 N 1225/BO 2005 N 1225). The commission sought to reassure the SVP, as the amendment's sponsor, that with the expansion of freedom of movement to the new member states there would be no shortage of available labor. In response, Councilor Schibli agreed to withdraw his amendment. In the plenary debate, SVP Councilor Hutter defended the reversal by arguing that:

[n]ow, after [the referendum of] September 25, the situation looks drastically different. The people have voted in favor of freedom of movement for the Eastern European countries, which means that Switzerland, and in particular the agricultural sector, will have access to 450 million people without special qualifications. This will be more than enough.
(Schweizer Bundesversammlung September 28, 2015, AB 2005 N 1225/ BO 2005 N 1225, my translation)

With the SVP supporting the position of the Federal Council and the Council of States, it was only the left that remained opposed. The National Council voted by a large margin to reject its previous amendment and to retain to the Federal Council's high-skilled immigration clause.

In December 2005, after a series of restrictionist amendments, the Federal Assembly voted the immigration bill into law. The Act was denounced by the left as discriminatory in its admission policy, hostile to immigrant integration, and marked by bureaucratic arbitrariness. The Social Democrats, Greens, and the Protestant People's Party called for a referendum to strike down the Act, together with the recently reformed asylum law. In September 2006, 68 percent of voters defied the left and voted in favor of the new Immigration Act, supporting federal policy by a significantly larger margin than had been characteristic of referendums organized by the right. The law came into force in January 2008, striking the 1931 Immigration Act from the books and affirming the government's dual strategy of openness toward Europe and closure toward third-country immigration.

The 2014 Referendum on Mass Immigration: The People Strike Back

The Europeanization of Swiss immigration policy in the 1990s and 2000s rested on the premise that the admission of European and highly skilled workers would not provoke the degree of populist backlash that had accompanied past liberalization of immigration policy. Until the mid-2000s, this strategy of depoliticization was remarkably successful. In the words of one political observer, "[t]he shift in immigration from non-European to European sending countries, from South to North, and from low-skilled to high-skilled migrants took place in the absence of any public immigration debate" (Imhof November 6, 2008, 1, my translation). With the institutionalization of freedom of movement for EU and EFTA nationals, however, the number of EU immigrants to Switzerland steadily increased after 2005. In the course of a decade, between 2006 and 2015, immigration to Switzerland increased by over 50 percent. Significantly, this was virtually entirely the result of freedom of movement, as EU immigration increased by close to 70 percent during this period (see Figure 3.1).

In the face of rapidly increasing immigration, Swiss public opinion soured even on "culturally similar" immigrants. Among EU immigrants, Germans comprised by far the largest single nationality, accounting for

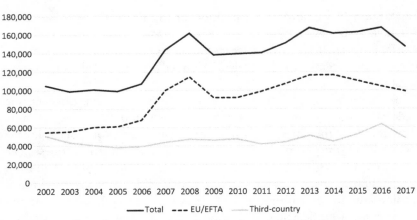

—Total   - - - EU/EFTA   ——— Third-country

FIGURE 3.1 EU and third-country immigration to Switzerland, 2002–17.

15 percent of all permanent residents and between 20 to 40 percent of all EU migrants after 2005. Anti-German sentiment soared as Germans elicited levels of hostility comparable to those expressed against black Africans and Tamils (Helbling 2011).[27] While these sentiments undoubtedly were triggered by rising immigration, they could also feed on Switzerland's long history of Germanophobia,[28] which has lent support to the argument that not only cultural difference, but also the absence of visible difference, can engender intergroup hostility (Jetten et al. 1998, Helbling 2011). The SVP was quick to exploit anti-German sentiment, and by 2006 German immigration had become the subject of a sustained, negatively framed media debate. In many circles, the steady inflow of highly skilled, High German speakers (as opposed to Swiss dialect speakers) came to be framed as an overforeignization threat. The bestselling newspaper *Blick* warned "In Plain Language: Switzerland is Becoming German!" (*Der Blick* February 10, 2007, my translation). In a four-part series titled "How Many Germans Can Switzerland Bear?"

[27] These findings are based on a survey conducted in Zürich in the mid-1990s, where respondents expressed low levels of hostility toward Italians, Spaniards, the Portuguese, and the French, high levels of hostility toward Yugoslavians, Arabs, and Turks, and intermediate levels of hostility toward black Africans, Tamils, and Germans (Helbling 2011). Note that the survey was conducted before the politicization of German immigration.

[28] Recall that the very term "overforeignization" was originally coined in relation to nineteenth-century immigrants from Germany.

the same paper published articles on topics including linguistic competition ("There is hardly anyone with whom I can still speak Swiss German") and labor market rivalry ("Job Fears: Do Germans Take Our Jobs Away?"). In December 2007, Germanophobia mounted after the president of the University of Zürich's student council protested, in a media interview, about the number of German professors at the university, arguing that their presence posed an obstacle to effective communication as well as a threat to Swiss employment (Helbling 2011). Criticism directed against German immigrants now became increasingly commonplace and was no longer confined to populist and socially conservative circles. Roger Schawinski, one of Switzerland's most prominent TV and radio personalities, who had long taken a socially liberal stance on immigration issues, now stated that "[i]t is a mistake that we speak High German with the Germans" and demanded that Germans should have to speak the local dialect (*Die tageszeitung* January 29, 2010, my translation).

The SVP stepped up its anti-immigration campaign after the 2011 election when, for the first time since 1991, the party failed to increase its vote share. Not only did the SVP fail to pick up seats in the upper house, it even lost seats in the lower house (Lachat et al. 2014). The party's losses in large part reflected rising electoral support for the moderate Conservative Democratic Party (BDP), a new party that was founded in 2008 after a split within the SVP. The BDP comprised most of the SVP's centrist-agrarian wing, leaving behind the party's far-right populist wing. Several months after their electoral setback, the SVP started to intensify its activism in the populist arena. Among their targets was the free movement of European nationals. In October 2011, the party announced that it had collected the signatures necessary to force a popular vote on its Initiative against Mass Immigration (*Masseneinwanderungsinitiative*). In its campaign, the initiative committee blamed rising immigration for a host of socioeconomic problems, ranging from higher unemployment and wage depression to overcrowded public transport and roads, rent increases, and the loss of arable land. "Uncontrolled immigration," so argued the initiative's sponsors, presented a threat to "Swiss freedom, security, full employment, natural beauty and Swiss prosperity" (World Elections 2015).

The SVP's Mass Immigration Initiative called for the introduction of immigration quotas and demanded that treaties in contradiction with these numerical limits be renegotiated within a three-year period. Anxious about the implications of a positive vote, the initiative was opposed by all federal actors other than the SVP. Policy makers were well aware that the initiative's mandate for an autonomous immigration policy would effectively end the free movement of persons for EU and EFTA nationals unless the European Union was willing to return to the negotiation table. Because the EU had repeatedly declared its categorical refusal to renegotiate the agreement's fundamental principle, however, the far more likely outcome would be the agreement's renunciation by either side, which, in turn, would lead to the automatic termination of the six other bilateral agreements and, likely, the Schengen–Dublin association agreement (Ackermann and Freitag 2015).

On February 9, 2014, in a watershed decision, a narrow popular majority of 50.3 percent and a solid majority of seventeen out of twenty-six cantons voted in favor of the Mass Immigration Initiative. The initiative's adoption triggered a political earthquake reminiscent of the domestic and international reactions that had followed the people's rejection of EEA membership in 1992 (Ackermann and Freitag 2015). Contrary to claims by policy losers, who were quick to attribute their defeat to voter ignorance, a post-ballot survey analysis revealed exceptionally high levels of issue-specific knowledge, with the initiative ranking sixth in the list of popular votes with the highest level of voter knowledge between 1981 and 2014. Accordingly, 77 percent of survey respondents were able to describe the initiative's contents in largely correct terms, with only 3 percent stating that they did not know what the proposal was about (Milic 2015, 54). However, while voters were aware of the initiative's potential to put at risk the country's bilateral approach, most supporters thought that the free movement principle would somehow be negotiable (Milic 2015, 58).

Implementing the Mass Immigration Initiative: The Primacy of Diplomatic Constraints

Only days after the initiative's adoption, the European Union made it clear that there was no option of renegotiating the Agreement on Free Movement. In the words of EU Commission President José Manuel Barroso: "Pact sunt servanda" ("Agreements must be kept") (Nuspliger February 17, 2014). Dispelling any doubt that the Union meant business, Barroso announced the exclusion of Switzerland from access to Horizon 2020 – the EU's prestigious research and innovation program – and the student exchange program Erasmus, after the Federal Council declared that it was unable to ratify the extension of freedom of movement rights to Croatia. Given that Swiss universities had been very successful in securing Horizon 2020 funding, it was feared that exclusion from the program would inflict significant damage on their competitiveness. Swiss officials managed to negotiate a temporary "partial association" that would restore access to research funding until late 2016 (Meyer June 20, 2016). Nonetheless, the continued insecurity about future access to EU funding led to a marked decline in funding applications, resulting in a halving of EU funding of Swiss research institutions from 4.2 to 2.2 percent in the course of one year (Donzé and Bühler September 18, 2016). Further decreasing the decision-making autonomy of Swiss policy makers was the decision of EU officials to make the reinstatement of "full association" status after 2016 dependent on Switzerland's signing of the Croatia Protocol. Any hopes for diplomatic accommodation was dealt a further blow with the United Kingdom's vote to leave the European Union in June 2016. There was little doubt that with the beginning of Brexit negotiations, the European Union was going to go to great lengths to avoid any precedent setting in its dealings with Switzerland, particularly in relation to freedom of movement.

In February 2015, the Federal Council made public its proposal for a new immigration system that would be based on annual quotas for all non-EU nationals. While the proposal paid lip service to the initiative's mandate of autonomous migration management, its provisions largely retained the policy status quo. Its quotas applied to all who were employed in Switzerland for longer than four months and, in a departure from previous policy, also to family dependents and refugees. As far as EU nationals were concerned, the Federal Council declared that "[t]he admission of EU citizens will be regulated by the AFMP [Agreement on Free Movement of Persons] as before, but the Agreement will have to be amended in line with the constitutional requirement" (The Federal Council February 11, 2015). The government's refusal to seriously consider the option of terminating the agreement was quickly criticized by the SVP (*Neue Zürcher Zeitung* February 2018, 2015). While the Mass Immigration Initiative had only demanded the agreement's renegotiation, the SVP was quick to threaten the introduction of an "enforcement initiative" (*Durchsetzungsinitiative*) to force the agreement's termination (Schweizerische Eidgenossenschaft February 11, 2015).

In December 2015, the Federal Council announced its intention to rely on the Free Movement Agreement's protection clause – which provides for the use of preventative measures in case of "serious economic or social problems" – to negotiate an upper limit to EU immigration once a critical threshold had been reached. According to the agreement, the protection clause could only be activated by a joint EU-Swiss committee. When the Federal Council announced that it would consider the option of unilateral activation, the new president of the EU Commission, Jean-Claude Juncker, responded that "a unilateral triggering of the protection clause is out of the question" (Maurer February 7, 2016, my translation). The EU declared both unilateral activation and the imposition of an immigration ceiling to be in violation of the agreement.

When the Federal Council's proposal moved into the legislative arena, the preparatory commissions of both houses distanced themselves from the government's idea of a quantitative limit. Instead, they argued, EU immigration should be reined in through labor market measures that favor the hiring of Swiss job seekers (Gmür and Gemperli April 16, 2016). The EU commissioner for employment and social affairs, Marianne Thyssen, promptly countered that any preferential treatment of Swiss workers would amount to discrimination among EU citizens, thereby violating the Free Movement Agreement (*Neue Zürcher Zeitung* June 11, 2016). Opposition also came from employer associations, who feared that stringent recruitment requirements would impose undue administrative burdens on firms. Except for the SVP, who continued to insist on a firm immigration ceiling, disagreement among parliamentarians centered on the questions of whether or not firms should have to justify rejections of Swiss job applicants and whether they should be required to interview all domestic applicants. In the end, legislators settled for a much watered down provision that required firms in regions and occupations with "above-average" unemployment – a threshold that remained undefined – to first post all new job openings with regional job agencies before advertising more widely (*Tages Anzeiger* December 13, 2016).

Predictably, the modest reforms were greeted with scathing criticism by the SVP, who denounced it as an "unprecedented breach of the constitution" (*Tages Anzeiger* December 13, 2016). Faced with the dilemma of either breaking Switzerland's bilateral treaties or disregarding popular sovereignty, the centrist parties decided to prioritize the country's bilateral treaties over the initiative's literal implementation. In doing so, policy makers appealed to the public that despite the Federal Council's best efforts, there had been no scope for negotiating any free movement concessions. As Federal Councilor Simonetta Sommaruga argued, Brexit was the "dagger" that had doomed Swiss-EU talks (*Neue Zürcher Zeitung* December 5, 2016). With bilateral negotiations paralyzed given that Switzerland's participation in Horizon 2020 required the prior ratification of the Croatia Protocol, which, in turn, could only proceed once the implementation of the Mass Immigration Initiative had been concluded, time pressure for a solution was mounting.

Among the case studies of this book, this policy episode stands out due to the remarkable weakness of diplomatic insulation stemming from Switzerland's strategic adjustment to European market integration. A repeal of the Free Movement Agreement was not a viable policy option as it would have nullified all bilateral treaties with the Union, which was out of the question as long as the government remained committed to full market access. In favoring a "flexible" response to the Mass Immigration Initiative, policy makers decided to evade the certain, significant, and long-lasting diplomatic costs of unilateral action and instead accepted the more uncertain risk of a popular veto. Given the issue's complexity, there was some basis for optimism that the public would not veto this policy choice. After all, in the past voters had supported the Free Movement Agreement. Moreover, as argued above, most voters who supported the Mass Immigration Initiative had done so assuming that the terms of the Free Movement Agreement would be negotiable (Milic 2015, 58) – an assumption that no longer held. Furthermore, the same year in which the Swiss electorate had voted in favor of the Mass Immigration Initiative, they had rejected an initiative organized by the environmental group Ecopop titled "Stop Overpopulation – Secure our Natural Livelihoods." The Ecopop Initiative had demanded a reduction of population growth to 0.2 percent, which would have required tight control over EU immigration.

More recently, in 2016 public opinion polls suggested that public restrictionism was lessening as the EU stood firm in its refusal to renegotiate the Free Movement Agreement. Importantly, Switzerland's temporary exclusion from the research funds of Horizon 2020 had served as a clear and highly public warning of the consequences of treaty violation. Now, over 80 percent of the Swiss public agreed that Horizon 2020 was important and that the Swiss economy was dependent on stable relations with the EU, with 61 percent favoring a flexible solution to the Mass Immigration Initiative (*Neue Zürcher Zeitung* May 23, 2016). Perhaps most significantly, 65 percent of the public – including one-third of SVP voters – favored the maintenance of the bilateral treaties over a literal implementation of the Mass Immigration Initiative (*Neue Zürcher Zeitung* May 4, 2016).

After the law's passage, the Mass Immigration Initiative and the new immigration reform continued to coexist as part of Switzerland's constitutional order. While the legislative reforms of 2016 succeeded in averting a Swiss version of Brexit, they did not amount to a broadly acceptable policy status quo. Progressive forces sought to remove the Mass Immigration Initiative from Switzerland's constitution by means of a new initiative titled "Get Out of the Dead End" (*Raus aus der Sackgasse*, or RASA) but were forced to withdraw due to a lack of political support. Whereas the Federal Council recognized the need for reconciling the constitution with the Free Movement Agreement, it was opposed to doing so by overruling an existing popular decision, for democratic reasons. The government decided against introducing an alternative proposal after the pre-parliamentary consultations on RASA made clear that neither legislators, nor cantons, nor interest groups were in support (*Neue Zürcher Zeitung* April 27, 2017). Meanwhile, several societal groups prepared for a referendum to challenge the Mass Immigration Initiative's legal implementation. In the end, its supporters failed to gather sufficient signatures to bring the question to a vote, in part because the various groups pursued divergent goals and the SVP decided not to sign off on the initiative (*Neue Zürcher Zeitung* March 2, 2017). Tolerated because of the absence of viable alternatives rather than its substantive merits, the policy status quo thus remains, rendering Swiss immigration policy acutely vulnerable to popular challenge.

Postscript

In 2018, the AUNS – the same group that, in 1992, had successfully defeated the Federal Council's proposal to join the EEA – announced its intention to submit a new immigration limitation initiative (*Begrenzungsinitiative*). Less constrained than the SVP, which did not want to alienate its liberal economic wing, AUNS's initiative called for the repeal of the Free Movement Agreement. Once the AUNS announced its intention, the SVP had little choice but to support it, given its prior sponsorship of the Mass Immigration Initiative and subsequent critique of the legislative implementation. At the time of writing, the initiative's outcome remains uncertain. Much appears to depend on the future development of EU immigration. For now, free movement immigration to Switzerland is on the decline (see Figure 3.1), largely due to strong German and Southern European economic performance. This change in circumstances has prompted a prominent SVP functionary to comment: "If immigration declines further, the initiative might become moot"

TABLE 3.1 *Swiss case studies summary*

Policy episode	Policy choice	Policy arenas	Popular insulation	Interest group insulation	Diplomatic insulation
Case study 1					
Postwar guest worker recruitment treaties	*Liberalization*	Executive arena	Intermediate	Low	High
Case study 2					
1960s Recruitment caps	*Selective restriction*	Executive arena	Low	Low	Intermediate
1964 Swiss-Italian recruitment treaty revision	*Selective liberalization*	Executive arena Legislative arena	Low	Intermediate	Low
1970 Global Ceiling system	*Selective restriction*	Executive arena Electoral arena	Low	Low	High
Case study 3					
1991 Three Circles Policy	*Selective liberalization*	Executive arena Electoral arena	Low	Intermediate	Low
Case Study 4					
1998 Two Circles Policy	*Paradigmatic liberalization*	Executive arena	Intermediate	Low	Low
2000 Agreement on Free Movement of Persons	*Selective liberalization*	Executive arena Legislative arena	Low	Low	Low
2008 Immigration Act	*Institutionalization of paradigmatic liberalization*	Executive arena Legislative arena	Intermediate	Low	Intermediate
Implementation of 2014 Mass Immigration Referendum	*Selective restriction*	Executive arena Legislative arena Electoral arena	Low	Intermediate	Low

(*Tages Anzeiger* November 27, 2018). At the earliest, voters will get to decide on the bilateral treaties in late 2020.

CONCLUSION

This chapter examined the dynamics of economic immigration policy making over the course of nearly seven decades of Swiss politics (see Table 3.1). It began in the late 1940s, when Switzerland responded to domestic labor shortages by establishing a closely regulated guest worker system designed to preempt guest worker settlement. The Swiss rotation system came under stress in the 1960s as a result of a decrease in guest worker supply, on the one hand, and the rise of anti-immigration populism, on the other. Rather than following its European neighbors and shut down recruitment completely, in 1970 Switzerland adopted a global ceiling that allowed for the flexible regulation of foreign worker recruitment by means of annual quotas. By the late 1980s, however, it had become clear that the days of low-skilled, rotation-based guest worker recruitment were numbered. The system came under challenge as the changing demands of economic competitiveness now required the recruitment of high-skilled, rather than low-skilled, workers at the same time as access to the European Union's common market required a liberalization of immigration from EU countries.

Faced with popular opposition, the Swiss government secured freedom of movement at the cost of a shutdown of "culturally distant" immigration under the Three Circles Policy in the 1990s. The 2000s witnessed a rapid succession of policy developments that reflected the intrinsic tension between the diplomatic imperatives of European freedom of movement and persistent popular calls for immigration control. The 2000s started out with the Federal Council's adoption of the Two Circles Policy, which replaced the principle of "cultural distance" with that of human capital, followed by the ratification of the Swiss-EU Free Movement Agreement. While all policy developments discussed to this point were passed in the form of either bilateral treaties or executive directives, the 2008 Immigration Act – the country's first immigration act since 1931 – institutionalized the developments of previous years through legislation. In 2014, the success of the Mass Immigration Initiative presented policy makers with an impossible choice between legislating the people's will or maintaining its bilateral treaties with the European Union. Policy makers decided in favor of the latter, passing policy that remains vulnerable to popular challenge.

In examining the regulation of foreign worker recruitment in Switzerland in comparative perspective, three patterns emerge. First, Swiss policy makers share with their German counterparts a remarkably low level of diplomatic insulation. Whereas German diplomatic vulnerability emerged from the need for postwar political rehabilitation, for Switzerland diplomatic pressure took the form of strategic adjustment to a rapidly changing geopolitical environment. Given Switzerland's status as a small, fiercely independent country surrounded by EU member states, its economic prosperity remains dependent on access to the European market. Since the late 1980s, adjusting to the project of economic and political regional integration has required that Switzerland sign the Free Movement Agreement and hence forgo the ability to close its borders to EU nationals. Given that immigration quotas had been the hallmark of the Swiss immigration regime since 1948, the decision to exempt EU citizens from immigration controls threatened the system's legitimacy and has since been challenged at the polls. As a result, Swiss immigration policy remains suspended between the popular mandate of immigration control and the diplomatic imperative of free movement.

A second characteristic of Swiss immigration politics is the pivotal role of popular referendums. Swiss policy makers – both in the executive and legislative arena – have little choice but to be continually mindful of the possibility of popular mobilization as they make immigration policy. With the unprecedented electoral success of the populist far-right SVP, which since 1999 has held the largest share of parliamentary seats, the politicization of immigration reforms has become institutionalized. In other words, Switzerland defies the well-entrenched scholarly expectation that immigration politics is defined by an "expansionary gap" between restrictionist public opinion and liberal immigration (Freeman 1994, 1995).

Lastly, Swiss policy makers are acutely vulnerable to business pressure. Because most parliamentarians also serve as representatives of interest groups (see Chapter 1, "Political Institutions"), economic interests feature prominently in the policy-making process. Unless the accommodation of business threatens policy defeat at a referendum – as was the case in the 1960s – Swiss policy makers have prioritized business demands over competing domestic interests. While throughout the postwar era, policy makers tended to confront opposing popular and business pressure, since the 1990s, as a result of rapid European market integration, business and diplomatic pressure have aligned against popular pressure, fueling an increasing polarization of Swiss immigration politics.

In sum, the case of Switzerland is unique in policy makers' lack of political insulation. Whereas the country's size and geopolitical positioning weakens the Federal Council's diplomatic insulation, the "double loyalties" of parliamentarians erase any meaningful interest group insulation. At the same time, both executive and legislative policy makers enjoy extraordinarily little popular insulation, given the ever present referendum threat. Being simultaneously exposed to powerful diplomatic, popular, and interest group pressures, the making of Swiss immigration policy resembles a tightrope walk accommodating these oftentimes contradictory pressures.

4

The Making of German Immigration Policy

Explaining Permanent and Temporary Economic Admissions

This chapter examines four episodes of foreign worker recruitment over the course of half a century of German[1] political history. We begin by investigating the factors that motivated the establishment of West Germany's legendary guest worker system in 1955, followed by its termination with the 1973 recruitment stop that institutionalized the country's non-immigration paradigm, thereby setting the path for future policy development. This first policy-making episode, which was confined to the executive arena, shows the significance of Germany's weak diplomatic insulation in accounting for the timing of its recruitment treaty with Italy. At the same time, the design and operation of the Federal Republic's recruitment system was shaped by the absence of learning from past policy failure. As a result, and unlike in Switzerland, guest worker recruitment did not accompany the enforcement of worker rotation and thus facilitated settlement processes very early on.

Our second case study examines the reopening of temporary recruitment channels in form of the project-tied program in the unified Germany in the early 1990s. Set once again in the executive arena, project-tied recruitment took place even though the recruitment stop of 1973 was still in force. Yet the program was successful in not challenging the prevailing non-immigration paradigm. Unlike the postwar guest worker program,

---

[1] The chapter exclusively focuses on the politics of economic immigration in the Federal Republic of Germany. Hence it does not examine the politics of guest worker recruitment in the socialist regime of the German Democratic Republic (1949–90). Unless noted otherwise, the terms West Germany, Germany, and Federal Republic are used interchangeably.

project-tied recruitment was firmly premised on worker rotation and was successful in preventing immigrant settlement. This policy episode thus demonstrates the importance of failure-induced policy learning in expanding the scope of executive-driven policy making within the ideational constraints of a prevailing (non)immigration paradigm.

Whereas the first two case studies involved the recruitment of low-skilled foreign workers, our third case study, the Green Card program of 2000, marks a clear departure from past policy by opening up Germany to high-skilled temporary worker recruitment. In this policy episode, executive actors took the unprecedented step of forgoing popular insulation by strategically moving liberalizing policy proposals into the electoral arena to gauge the public's receptiveness to a new pro-immigration paradigm. Even though worker recruitment continued to operate on a temporary basis, the political debate surrounding the Green Card program helped establish broad-based support for the desirability of high-skilled immigration, thereby challenging Germany's longstanding non-immigration paradigm. Lastly, the chapter's fourth case study examines the process of immigration reform from 2000 to 2004, which, while building on the paradigmatic shift facilitated by the Green Card program, ultimately failed in its attempt to usher in a new immigration paradigm that would have legitimized the large-scale and permanent immigration of highly skilled individuals. This final policy episode demonstrates the significance of the legislative and judicial arenas as veto points for partisan opponents of paradigmatic policy change.

THE POSTWAR GUEST WORKER SYSTEM (1955–1973)

When West German officials signed the first guest worker[2] recruitment treaty with Italy in 1955, they did not entertain the possibility that temporary foreign worker recruitment would result in large-scale settlement that would transform the Federal Republic into an ethnically diverse country of immigration. Whereas today's policy makers are cognizant of the fundamental tension between guest worker recruitment and immigration control, in the immediate postwar years the depth of this conflict was far from self-evident. Hailing from a fundamentally different political era, Prussia's and Weimar Germany's legacies of agricultural foreign worker recruitment did not expose the dynamics and irreversibility of immigrant settlement. Unlike Swiss policy makers, German

---

[2] I employ the term throughout the case study, even though historically it only entered the political vocabulary in the 1960s.

officials did not inherit a legacy of past policy failure which could have triggered a process of policy learning and reflection. Instead, the inception of Germany's guest worker system constituted a reactive and largely ill-conceived response to diplomatic pressures from abroad that fell on fertile ground with a government intent on rebuilding its severed diplomatic and economic relations with the West. These would soon be complemented by domestic labor market goals. Once domestic unemployment fell to economically acceptable levels, these diplomatic pressures, which dovetailed with the policy preferences of German foreign affairs and trade officials, led to the decision to recruit Italian workers in 1955. As a result, even when, in the 1960s, surging labor market demand ushered in a decade of largely unbridled recruitment, little thought was paid to the establishment of policy safeguards to ensure that recruitment would remain a temporary and reversible measure.

Prewar Legacies: Forced Rotation in Prussia and Weimar Germany

The policy legacies inherited by West German officials at the end of World War II date back to the late nineteenth century, when the country first experienced large-scale labor migration. Prussia – the German Empire's predominant state – was, similar to Switzerland, a traditional country of emigration that could not draw on significant domestic labor reserves when its economy expanded dramatically (Niederberger 1982). Notwithstanding, Prussian recruitment policy diverged from the open border policies pursued across much of Western and Central Europe in its strict regulation of entry and settlement. Initially, Prussia appeared to follow in the footsteps of the Swiss (Chapter 3) when, motivated by efforts to institutionalize industrial capitalism, it instituted visa- and passport-free travel across the North German Federation in 1867 (Torpey 2000). Yet the pursuit of economic liberalization conflicted with Bismarck's policy of "Germanization," which targeted East Prussia's large and intensely nationalistic Polish population (Brubaker 1992). This policy was now threatened by the arrival of large numbers of Russian-Polish agricultural workers whose presence risked, as the daily paper *Leipziger Tageblatt* asserted, the "Polonization of areas that had already been won over to Germanic customs, culture and language" (Bade 1982, 128, my translation).[3] Racially motivated concerns about

---

[3] Polish workers were also employed in the mining, steel, and construction industries in the Ruhr, a Western region of the Reich. However, because seasonal agricultural workers

Polish settlement were widespread even among Prussia's political elite, as reflected in Max Weber's warning that in the absence of immigration controls, Germany would be "threatened by a Slavic flood that would entail a cultural retrogression of several epochs" (cited in Torpey 2000, 109). In 1879, just over a decade after liberalizing cross-border movement, nationalist concerns prevailed over economic liberalization, and the Prussian-dominated Imperial government reinstituted passport requirements on travelers from Russia. This was followed, in 1885, by regulations that effectively closed the eastern border and allowed for the expulsion of 40,000 Polish workers (Herbert 2001).

Yet by 1890, Prussia's agricultural labor shortages had become sufficiently severe for the government to once again reform its course. Seeking to simultaneously cater to both economic lobbies that demanded the recruitment of agricultural workers and nationalist interests insisting on territorial closure, Bismarck decreed in 1890 a seasonal agricultural worker policy for Eastern Prussia that was based on forced rotation. In order to prevent settlement, employment was limited to unmarried workers, permits were tied to a given employer, and workers were required to leave at the end of each agricultural season. Bismarck's gamble paid off. Prussia's seasonal agricultural recruitment policy succeeded in accommodating the two dominant, yet contradictory, political impulses of economic liberalism and nationalist closure by means of state-enforced rotation. Between 1906 and 1913 – that is, until recruitment was abandoned with the outbreak of World War I – nine out of ten Polish migrant workers left Prussia each fall in order to return in the spring (Herbert 2001, 25).

World War I marked the momentous shift from voluntary to forced labor recruitment (*Zwangsarbeiter*). In order to meet labor shortages arising from war mobilization and production, over 300,000 Russian-Polish seasonal workers were forced to remain in Germany. As the war progressed, over half a million civilians from occupied regions to the east and 80,000 deported Belgians were conscripted into forced labor, alongside with 1.5 million prisoners of war (Herbert 2001, 89). Once the war was over, these workers were systematically pushed out of Germany; by 1924, the number of foreign nationals had dropped from over two million to 174,000 (Herbert 2001, 118).

were employed in the Reich's eastern region, parts of which had previously been Polish territory, they met with heightened fears of "Polonization."

In the Weimar Republic, like in 1920s Switzerland, foreign worker recruitment played a far less important role than in the prewar era. Yet, some important policy continuities remained. Even though initially enforcement of seasonal worker rotation came to a standstill for both logistical[4] and diplomatic[5] reasons, rotation was resumed in the mid-1920s. Unlike in Prussia, forced return in the Weimar Republic was focused not only on recent recruits but also on Polish agricultural workers who, as a result of the enforcement hiatus from the end of World War I to 1926, had settled in Germany. In 1923, for instance, two-thirds of all seasonal agricultural workers remained in Germany for the winter (Oltmer 2005, 354). Given the lack of secure residence status for non-citizens, Weimar officials were able to force the return of even long-term Polish residents, especially after the two countries had entered into a migration agreement that committed Poland to accepting the return of its nationals. Thus, in 1927, 91 percent of seasonal agricultural workers who had arrived the previous year returned to Poland, as did 47 percent of workers who had entered Germany between 1919 and 1925, and 19 percent of workers who had entered prior to 1918 (Oltmer 2005, 457). Through the return to a forced rotation policy, Weimar officials succeeded in both preempting and reversing the settlement of Polish agricultural workers.

Ideologically, the centrality of forced return (*Rückkehrzwang*) in Weimar Germany's migration policy reflected continuity with Prussia's use of rotation as a principally ethnonational, anti-Polish measure. In the mid-1920s, however, Weimar policy makers started to supplement ethnonational considerations with an active labor market policy. Starting in 1924, labor officials set annual recruitment targets that were coupled with the state of the economy. Reflecting the strength of the labor movement in the Weimar years, recruitment policy came to reflect two labor market principles that eventually would be carried over into the Federal Republic's recruitment policy. First, foreign workers were only to fill positions for which no native workers were available (*Inländerprimat*). Second, foreign workers were to be paid the same wages and benefits as their German counterparts (Herbert 2001). In important ways, and

---

[4] After World War I the legitimation cards that had been central to Prussia's rotation policy no longer existed (Oltmer 2005).

[5] Given Germany's weak international standing, Weimar officials were concerned that resuming its Polish-focused rotation policy would provoke the expulsion of ethnic Germans residing in territories lost to Poland in World War I (Oltmer 2005).

despite the relatively small size of the foreign worker population during the economically tumultuous Weimar years, the regulatory framework institutionalized in the 1920s left behind a social democratic policy legacy that would carry over into the postwar era.

With Hitler's rise to power and subsequent mobilization for war, Germany resumed its earlier practice of forced labor recruitment. While the Nazi elite deemed the employment of *Fremdarbeiter* (alien workers) as highly undesirable for racial reasons – Germany should remain a "racially pure" country – they considered labor importation as preferable over its alternative, the large-scale employment of German women (Herbert 2001). Thus, from 1939 to 1944 over seven million foreign nationals – three-quarters of whom were civilians – were forced to work in the Third Reich. What presented a historic departure from previous recruitment practice – in addition to its sheer scale and unparalleled brutality – was the fundamental racialization of employment policy, which placed Germans at the top of the employment hierarchy, followed by Italians and other "Western workers" (*Westarbeiter*), with Polish workers and "Eastern workers" (*Ostarbeiter*) from the Soviet Union at the bottom. With the end of the war, the vast majority of these laborers returned to their countries of origin, where many were subject to internment and harassment, especially in the Soviet Union.

The Postwar Recruitment Treaties: Executive Policy Making in the Absence of Diplomatic Insulation and Policy Learning

Only a few years after the end of World War II, the Federal Republic once again confronted the question of foreign worker recruitment when, in 1953, the Italian government approached the Adenauer government to enter in a labor recruitment agreement. At this time, West Germany had yet to experience significant labor shortages. The German economy still suffered from structural unemployment, in part because of the country's economic devastation during the war, in part because of the inflow of expellees from the former Eastern territories and, later, migrants from the German Democratic Republic. Hence, by 1950 alone an estimated twelve million expellees had settled in West Germany (Bethlehem 1982), boosting the country's workforce and adding to an already acute housing shortage resulting from the large-scale destruction of housing stock during the war (Larres and Panayi 2014). In the 1950s, an additional 3.8 million East Germans arrived (Fassmann and Münz 1994). Yet at the same time as policy makers were confronted with these domestic labor market and infrastructural challenges, the Federal Republic also faced the pressing need of diplomatic and economic reintegration into the West. Acutely aware of its lack of diplomatic insulation, the Adenauer cabinet was finely attuned to the diplomatic implications of its policy decisions.

While the cabinet initially declined Italy's request (Knortz 2008), a year later German diplomatic officials agreed to revisit the issue in the context of bilateral trade negotiations (*Rhein-Zeitung* December 14, 1954). The Adenauer cabinet itself was deeply divided on how to respond to Italy's request. Both the Ministry of Labor, as the key ministry on matters of recruitment, and the Federal Labor Agency[6] were unabashedly hostile to the idea of foreign worker recruitment. Whereas in Switzerland the biggest stumbling block to recruitment had been concerns about the possibility of immigrant settlement, in the Federal Republic opposition focused on the question of labor market impact. Speaking before the Bundestag – the lower house of parliament – Labor Minister Anton Storch stated that his ministry was willing to consider recruitment, but only "should a demand for workers arise that cannot be met from our own reserves" (Deutscher Bundestag February 17, 1955, 3388, my translation) and only once all possible rationalization measures had been exhausted (*Frankfurter Rundschau* December 20, 1954, *Süddeutsche Zeitung* December 21, 1954). The more diplomatically exposed economics and foreign affairs ministries, in contrast, welcomed recruitment as a means of facilitating the country's reintegration into European trade and diplomatic networks. Support for a recruitment treaty was spearheaded by Economics Minister Ludwig Erhard, the father of Germany's "economic miracle," who argued that Italy's growing trade deficit posed a threat to market liberalization and constituted a danger to the process of European economic cooperation. The only remedy to this dilemma, he asserted, was for Germany to recruit Italian workers. The Ministry of Foreign Affairs was equally invested in treaty ratification. Its senior officials concurred with Erhard's assessment that labor recruitment would have a highly beneficial impact on German–Italian economic relations. For both ministries, the recruitment of Italian workers was not a question of if, but rather of when.

Cabinet support for a recruitment treaty with Italy thus was driven by the preferences of diplomatically exposed foreign policy and trade officials, rather than by domestic labor market considerations. Yet given the

---

[6] *Bundesanstalt für Arbeitsvermittlung und Arbeitslosenversicherung*, the counterpart to the Swiss BIGA.

Labor Ministry's principled opposition, the anticipation of diplomatic and trade gains alone did not suffice for recruitment to commence. Guest worker employment became a possibility only once domestic unemployment was sufficiently low to assuage concerns that a treaty would threaten the jobs of native workers. This point was reached in 1955, when labor shortages emerged in low-skilled industrial sectors and in agriculture, which prompted the employers' peak association[7] to throw its weight behind calls for migrant worker recruitment (Knortz 2008). With declining unemployment, the Federation of Trade Unions[8] acquiesced to migrant recruitment on the condition that – like in the Weimar years – foreign workers would receive both equal pay and benefits and, in light of the continuing housing shortage, employer-provided accommodation (*Neue Zürcher Zeitung* December 22, 1955). While the horrors of the Holocaust and the massive exploitation of forced foreign labor during the war had thoroughly discredited the use of migration policy for ethnonational purposes,[9] the Weimar legacy of labor market-oriented recruitment was politically untainted and thus could carry over into the postwar era. In a cabinet meeting in October 1955, Chancellor Adenauer contended that a recruitment agreement with Italy would allow the Federal Republic to achieve its central economic and diplomatic goals simultaneously. He requested policy blueprints from the ministries of economics and labor, but owing to turf competition and conceptual disagreement neither report was deemed a suitable framework for a recruitment policy (Knortz 2008). By now, however, the speed of bilateral negotiations had overtaken the pace of interministerial discussions and, after nearly two years of negotiations, the German-Italian recruitment treaty was signed in December 1955.

With the onset of recruitment, German officials concurred with their Swiss colleagues that guest worker employment was to be a purely temporary labor market measure. Where they differed, however, was in their assessment of how to ensure the temporariness of migration. There is no evidence that German policy makers seriously grappled with the question of settlement prevention at the time when the recruitment system was established. Instead, officials put great faith in the self-regulatory power of the market and assumed that foreign workers would voluntarily return to their home countries should labor demand slow down. Looking

---

[7] *Bundesvereinigung der Deutschen Arbeitgeberverbände.*
[8] *Deutscher Gewerkschaftsbund.*
[9] This normative break is also reflected in the change in terminology from *Fremdarbeiter* (alien worker) to *Gastarbeiter* (guest worker) (Chin 2007).

at archival and newspaper records from the 1950s, it appears that the possibility that migrant workers might choose to remain, or that Germany might not be able to enforce the departure of those unwilling to leave, was not seriously entertained. As the *Frankfurter Allgemeine Zeitung* claimed, "in the event of unemployment in Germany, the foreign workers could be sent back home again" (cited in Herbert 1991, 211, my translation). In the words of one of Germany's foremost scholars of foreign labor history, policy makers "shared the firm conviction that this was a temporally limited phenomenon, a transitional development that would eventually disappear" (Herbert 1991, 213, my translation).

Policy makers' lack of concern with the question of settlement gave rise to two critical differences between Swiss and German recruitment policy. First, whereas the Swiss system included a large seasonal worker component, the overwhelming majority of guest workers in Germany were issued renewable, annual permits. Second, because Swiss policy makers were fully cognizant of the link between family unification and permanent settlement, they had placed tight restrictions on the issuance of family visas. In the Federal Republic, by contrast, there was a broad consensus that family unification was to be tolerated (Pagenstecher 1993). Many officials considered family migration to even be desirable, either for economic reasons – to lower the cost of worker turnover – or for reasons of public order and the preservation of family values (*Frankfurter Rundschau* February 27, 1961).

Accordingly, authorities accepted the recruitment of relatives and not infrequently hired married couples, thereby establishing recruitment practices that both facilitated and accelerated family immigration. By 1971 a third of all workers hired through the official recruitment commission were relatives of already employed guest workers (Pagenstecher 1993), with overall numbers probably much higher. Similarly, and in stark contrast to Swiss practice, the immigration of family dependents was largely handled in a laissez-faire manner. As a result, by 1968 a staggering 30 percent of the German adult foreign population had arrived as dependent spouses, rather than as recruits, resulting in a widening gap between the number of foreign workers and Germany's total foreign population (Figure 4.1). In Switzerland, by contrast, in the same year – and after a significantly longer recruitment period of twenty years – only 17 percent of adult migrants had entered as dependents,[10] reflecting a much smaller gap between the country's foreign working population and its total foreign population (Figure 4.1).

---

[10] Calculations by author, based on Pagenstecher (1993, 16).

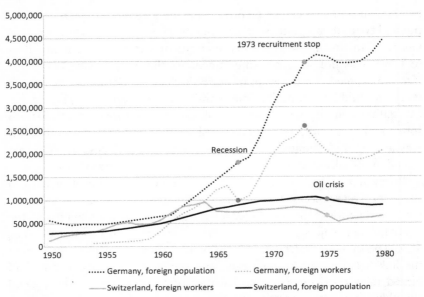

FIGURE 4.1   Foreign population and foreign workers, Switzerland and Germany, 1950–80.

For guest workers the incentives to remain were that much greater insofar as they were able to bring their families. In Germany, settlement processes were further facilitated by a highly permissive permit practice that entailed not only routine renewal of annual permits but also the issuing of indefinite permits (Deutscher Bundestag February 21, 1973). As a result, by 1968 – thirteen years into recruitment – 57 percent of male guest workers had resided in Germany for longer than four years (Auswärtiges Amt March 20, 1972). In Switzerland, by contrast, eleven years into (formal) recruitment only 25 percent of guest workers had been in the country for longer than three years (Buomberger 2004, Schweizerischer Metall- und Uhrenarbeiterverband 1962).

Why did German policy makers pay so little attention to the possibility of guest worker settlement? While the timing of recruitment was in large measure the result of the government's lack of diplomatic insulation, the nature of the recruitment system itself has to be understood in the context of the policy legacies left behind by the rotation systems of the late nineteenth and early twentieth centuries. Unlike in Swiss history, German policy legacies neither included the experience of large-scale immigrant settlement – at least not in relation to the most controversial group of foreign workers, Polish seasonal agricultural workers – nor the inability to reverse whatever limited settlement did occur. In other words, Germany's past management of Polish seasonal agricultural worker recruitment was marked by policy success, rather than failure. The absence of past policy failure, which preempted the possibility of policy learning, then, at least in part accounts for the relative naïveté of German policy makers when it come to the possibility of immigrant settlement. This contrasts with Switzerland's legacy of immigrant settlement, which provided both elites and the public with a basic understanding that, over time, uncontrolled temporary migration will turn into permanent immigration. This recognition of the long-term consequences of laissez-faire recruitment served to legitimate the concerns of those who sought to impose strict settlement controls. The significance of this last point becomes apparent when we consider one of only two instances where the German cabinet considered the question of immigration control: the negotiation of the 1964 German-Turkish recruitment agreement.[11]

Like comparable agreements with Greece, Spain, and Portugal that Germany ratified in the early 1960s, the 1964 agreement with Turkey was a response to heightened labor shortages after the Berlin Wall had cut off the East–West migration of German workers. Unlike the German-Italian agreement, however, it was entered into at a time when interior officials – charged with the mandate of immigration control – had become cognizant that a process of immigrant settlement was under way. Not only did the steady inflow of migrant workers show no sign of abating – in 1964, the number of foreign workers passed the one million mark (Figure 4.1) – but it had become clear that family unification and pro-longed residence were widespread. As a result, the Interior Ministry insisted that Turkish labor migration be strictly time limited and without the option of family migration. The labor and economics ministries strongly opposed these restrictions. The Foreign Affairs Ministry in 1961 brokered an agreement that limited employment to two years and did not include provisions for family unification (Hunn 2005). Yet less than a year later, the Economics Ministry and the Confederation of German Employers demanded that the two-year clause be dropped to lower worker turnover. The Interior Ministry was prepared to support

[11] The second instance was the attempt of the federal and *Länder* interior ministers to impose a three-year stay limit on guest workers during negotiations of the 1965 immigration law. Again, opposition by the economics and foreign affairs ministries led to the rejection of rotation (see Triadafilopoulos and Schönwälder 2006).

this revision in exchange for an amendment that explicitly ruled out the possibility of family unification. The Turkish government rejected this proposal, which would have denied its nationals the family unification rights available to guest workers from non-Turkish-sending countries. Other ministries concurred and warned that the proposed family unification amendment would set back the government's efforts to enhance Germany's image abroad (Triadafilopoulos and Schönwälder 2006). Realizing its political isolation, the Interior Ministry conceded, and the revised German-Turkish agreement of 1964 included neither a maximum stay clause nor special restrictions on family unification.

Even though interior officials had begun to recognize the long-term consequences of guest worker recruitment as early as 1961, the cabinet decided to subordinate emerging anxieties about immigration control to labor market and foreign policy imperatives, leaving the Interior Ministry isolated. The centrality of foreign policy considerations in the decision to extend family unification rights to Turkish nationals is a case par excellence of the government's lack of diplomatic insulation. For a young republic that could ill afford to incur reputational costs (Triadafilopoulos 2012), recruitment policy repeatedly constituted a "dramaturgical act" (Fitzgerald and Cook-Martín, 2014, 21) designed to reassure the international community of West Germany's commitment to liberal norms and the maintenance of good diplomatic relations. Whereas in Switzerland the fear of overforeignization loomed large from the beginning and motivated the construction of a system that not only assumed, but also enforced, rotation, there was no comparable dynamic in the Federal Republic (Schönwälder 2006). Because of the absence of policy learning, questions of immigration control received little attention at the point of policy inception. By the time when interior officials had recognized the risk of immigrant settlement, their concerns did not carry sufficient weight to prevail over the economic and diplomatic imperatives that had come to dominate policy making.

Had West German officials recognized the importance of rotation when the recruitment system was established, they would have been free to institutionalize rotation in bilateral treaties and in administrative practice. There is nothing to suggest that early, consistent enforcement of worker rotation would have been opposed by sending countries, who generally had as little interest in the permanent emigration of their nationals as did the Federal Republic. It was Turkey, after all, who insisted on the two-year stay clause in the original German-Turkish agreement (Hunn 2005, 32). In other words, rotation was not considered an inherently illiberal policy feature that was bound to elicit moral opposition. Rather, the question of rotation threatened to become the target of normative pressure if applied to some countries but not to others (analogous to the singling out of Turkey for the prohibition of family unification) or when implemented arbitrarily, as was the case in the early 1970s when some immigration authorities started to enforce rotation after years of laissez-faire (see Ellermann 2013).

In other words, diplomatic pressure does not operate indiscriminately. Not only are some policy questions more susceptible to international pressure than others, but political insulation also depends on the source of diplomatic pressure. Just as in the 1960s, when Canada's aspiration to become a global middle power made policy makers particularly vulnerable to accusations of moral hypocrisy from developing countries (see Chapter 5), the Federal Republic in the postwar years was least insulated from diplomatic pressures exerted by Western governments. This is reflected in Germany's decision to essentially limit recruitment to European states. After West Germany entered into additional recruitment treaties with Greece, Spain, and Turkey in the early 1960s, several non-European governments sought to follow suit, including Bolivia, the West Indies, Taiwan, India, Iran, Toto, and the Central African Federation. In an interministerial meeting in May 1962, policy makers decided against the recruitment of "Afro-Asian" workers, for reasons ranging from limiting the number of recruitment countries, to avoiding recruitment from overseas in order to facilitate return, to racism (Schönwälder 2004). Moreover, with the 1961 agreement with Turkey[12] the country had just opened up access to a vast supply of workers. While the Foreign Affairs Ministry expressed concern that the decision to refuse the

---

[12] It is important to bear in mind that in the postwar era Turkey was widely considered part of Europe, enjoying particularly close and longstanding diplomatic relations with Germany. In 1962 the German Foreign Affairs Ministry justified its decision to not expand the circle of recruitment countries by arguing that for the foreseeable future labor demand could be met "from existing labor reserves in Europe. This includes in particular the countries of Italy, Spain, Greece and Turkey" (Hunn 2005, 32). In a similar vein, with the signing of the EEC-Turkey Association Agreement in 1963, the EEC Commission's President matter-of-factly stated that Turkey belonged to Europe (Hunn 2005, 32). With the Association Agreement, Turkey was offered a clear prospect of eventual accession and was granted preferential trade conditions. Given its strategic importance, Turkey was also valued by other NATO members as a critical ally at the height of the Cold War. In other words, given the Federal Republic's Western orientation and its longstanding diplomatic and economic ties to Turkey, policy makers were susceptible to diplomatic pressure from Turkish officials.

recruitment requests of non-European states could open up the country to charges of racism, the Interior Ministry countered that West German recruitment policy rested on a politically defensible principle, as it differentiated between Europeans and non-Europeans, rather than between "races" (Schönwälder 2004). As a result, because the Federal Republic had no intrinsic interest in opening up recruitment to non-European states,[13] there were no compelling diplomatic reasons for overriding these preferences. What rendered West Germany so vulnerable to diplomatic pressure in the postwar years was its determination to reembed itself in close diplomatic and trade relations with the Western Bloc. By comparison, the stakes were much lower when it came to relations with states in the developing world.

Returning to the cabinet's decision to accede to Turkey's demands for equal family unification rights despite emerging apprehensions about immigrant settlement, the impact of Turkish pressure was not just based on the fact that German–Turkish relations – and Turkey's relations with the European Economic Community more broadly (see note 12) – were marked by diplomatic and economic closeness, but was also facilitated by the fact that policy making continued to be confined to the executive arena, where low levels of diplomatic, and high levels of popular, insulation gave a decisive advantage to diplomatic imperatives. Neither parliament nor the general public at the time paid much attention to questions of recruitment, prompting one scholar to comment that it is remarkable "that a policy with such potentially massive social consequences received virtually no sustained public questioning or debate" (Chin 2007, 47). Given the executive-centered nature of policy making, then, there were no countervailing popular pressures that could have buttressed the Interior Ministry's calls for stricter recruitment controls.

The Recession of 1966 and the Failure of Popular Mobilization

Two years later the era of popular insulation threatened to come to an end. The first politicization of guest worker recruitment was triggered by an article published in March 1966 in the mass tabloid *Bild*, titled "Are

[13] Germany eventually entered into recruitment treaties with three non-European states: Tunisia, Morocco, and South Korea. Importantly, these agreements differed from those struck with European states in that they were exclusively focused on small-scale recruitment of miners (and, from Korea, nurses) and included more stringent conditionalities for admission.

Guest Workers Harder Working Than Germans?" (*Bildzeitung* March 31, 1966, my translation). The article reported on a conference organized by the Confederation of German Employers that, ironically, was intended to shore up support for continued guest worker employment. This provocative challenge to the German work ethic sparked the Federal Republic's first major guest worker-related protests, as thousands of employees in the southwest of the country went on strike. In some firms, fights broke out between native and foreign workers. Even though the media widely condemned the *Bild* article, and worker protests quickly died down in response to trade union appeals, the event came to mark the beginning of the Federal Republic's first sustained public debate on migrant recruitment, including the social and fiscal implications of immigrant settlement. For the first time, recruitment was no longer exclusively framed as an issue of foreign affairs and labor market policy but instead came to be redefined as a matter of social and integration policy.

The debate was not without impact in governmental circles. The Interior Ministry took this opportunity to argue that Germany had "quite limited absorption and assimilation capacity" (Hunn 2005, 184, my translation) and demanded that residence permits and family unification be made contingent on occupational and behavioral assimilation. Even the Economics Ministry concluded that whereas the recruitment system continued to be economically beneficial, its noneconomic impacts – including the "irrational reaction of the German public" – spoke in favor of "stabilizing," rather than increasing, recruitment (Hunn 2005, 182, my translation). Instead of proposing measures to achieve this "stabilization," however, the ministry maintained that domestic rationalization, combined with modernization processes abroad, would automatically lead to a decrease in immigration.

Meanwhile, Germany experienced its first economic downturn. Even though unemployment remained modest by today's standards, the economic slowdown was widely perceived as a threat to the economic miracle that had come to define the young republic. Guest workers were now seen as competitors, rather than as facilitators of economic growth. In a 1967 public opinion survey, 62 percent of respondents supported laying off employees on the basis of immigration status, rather than on the basis of work performance (Allensbacher Institut, February 1966, cited in Schönwälder 2001, 174). Popular calls for the departure of guest workers were often tinged with xenophobic sentiments ("Foreigners out!"), and for the first time political elites felt the need to reassure the public that in contrast to Switzerland's much higher proportion of foreign nationals, Germany was *not* threatened by overforeignization (Süddeutsche Zeitung November 15, 1966, 252, *Neue Rhein-Ruhr-Zeitung* December 15, 1966, *Frankfurter Rundschau* December 29, 1966).

During the downturn, many guest workers decided to leave Germany. However, this process of return migration was not the result of coercive government action. In fact, unlike in Switzerland, the vast majority of workers – that is, all who had been employed for a minimum of six months – qualified for unemployment benefits and were entitled to reside in Germany for the duration of these benefits. In spite of this, many chose to receive their benefits in their home countries, and as a result around half a million guest workers – one-third of foreign workers – decided to leave (Hunn 2005, 188).

The economic downturn proved to be short-lived, and recruitment resumed quickly. Despite its brevity, the recession of 1966–7 had important political implications. First, it reassured many observers that guest worker recruitment was still responsive to labor market needs, even in the absence of forced rotation. Second, the recession put a premature end to the public immigration debate that had just gotten under way. Unlike in Switzerland, where the institution of the popular referendum not only provided a low threshold for public mobilization but also forced policy makers to be responsive to the anti-immigrant agendas of popular initiatives, no equivalent channels existed in Germany. The only potential mobilizing institution was the far-right National Democratic Party (NDP), which did see important electoral successes during this period. However, while the NDP did include the issue of guest worker recruitment in its platform – "[t]he German worker has a first-priority right to a guarantee of his job against foreign labor" (cited in Chin 2007, 60) – the party did not campaign on an anti-immigrant platform but focused instead on the much more radical demands of reestablishing the German Reich (Schönwälder 2001). Indeed, analyses of the party's electoral victories during this period[14] suggest that the far-right vote, rather than serving as a conduit for anti-immigration demands, is better understood as a protest vote against both the sociocultural changes embodied by the left-wing student movement and the political vacuum in the traditional right that resulted from the formation of the Grand Coalition (Deffner 2005, Kaltefleiter 1970).

---

[14] Between 1966 and 1968 the NDP gained seats in seven *Land* parliaments and in 1969 narrowly missed entry into the Bundestag.

The Recruitment Stop of 1973: The Oil Crisis as a Source of Diplomatic Insulation

With the end of the recession, recruitment resumed under a new coalition government of Social Democrats and Liberals, led by Chancellor Willy Brandt. However, politics did not fully return to its pre-recession status quo because the realities of permanent settlement could no longer be ignored. By 1969, the number of guest workers had passed the pre-recession mark of one million. Only one year later, numbers had nearly doubled to two million. In 1973, after three more years of market-driven recruitment, the foreign population reached the four million mark (Figure 4.1). In many industrial regions of the country, there was no denying that in the absence of public infrastructure investment, guest worker recruitment and family unification had led to overcrowded housing and schools.

As a result, an interministerial consensus emerged: one-and-a-half decades of unbridled recruitment had resulted in large-scale immigrant settlement. Whereas Swiss political elites had recognized this relationship before the commencement of recruitment in the late 1940s, it was only in the early 1970s that a comparable elite consensus was established in Germany. Once the government had acknowledged the reality of immigrant settlement, the cabinet had to decide how to deal with its unintended consequences. The ensuing debate, which drew in various societal interests, came to be framed as a choice between rotation, on the one hand, and immigrant integration, on the other. This was the first time that the possibility of state-enforced rotation was seriously considered, both within the cabinet and in public debates. Meanwhile, a number of local immigration authorities in the Länder Bavaria and Schleswig-Holstein had taken matters into their own hands and forcibly rotated some workers who had resided in Germany for several years (Deutscher Bundestag February 21, 1973, Evangelischer Pressedienst February 20, 1973, *Stuttgarter Zeitung* January 22, 1973).

In the rotation versus integration debate, the Confederation of German Employers strongly favored rotation as a tool for offsetting the fiscal and social costs of large-scale recruitment. Trade unions and the media, in contrast, argued that rotation was inhumane and would damage the country's image abroad (Schönwälder 2001). In the end the cabinet not only decided against rotation but equally rejected the option of ceiling controls – as instituted in Switzerland – on diplomatic grounds, once again demonstrating the country's vulnerability to reputational costs.

The Ministry of Labor expressed concerns that a ceiling system would require nationality contingents, a measure that would strain diplomatic relations with sending countries (Knortz 2008). More broadly, "inquiries abroad convinced Foreign Secretary Scheel that a recruitment stop and a noticeable reduction of the number of foreign employees would seriously disrupt the Federal Republic's relations with the main sending countries" (Schönwälder 2006, 259). At the same time as the cabinet rejected rotation and ceiling controls as politically viable policy measures, however, interministerial disagreements prevented the adoption of a coherent integration policy (Triadafilopoulos and Schönwälder 2006). Instead, in June 1973, the cabinet agreed on an "action program" designed to harmonize guest worker employment with the "absorption capacity" of social infrastructures. Accordingly, recruitment would no longer be possible in locales where foreign nationals accounted for more than 12 percent (in exceptional cases 6 percent) of the population.

When the government finally closed down recruitment it did so in ways strikingly different from those adopted by the Swiss Federal Council. In November 1973, only weeks after the beginning of the oil crisis, the Labor Ministry presented a much-anticipated appraisal of the country's labor market policy. The ministry's report contended that the fiscal and social costs of recruitment no longer justified its economic benefits and concluded that "it appears doubtful that further recruitment is sensible, both from a macroeconomic and a sociopolitical perspective" (cited in Knortz 2008, 175, my translation). On November 23 the cabinet decided, against the objections of employer associations, to stop all recruitment immediately. Diplomatic officials utilized the developing oil crisis to justify this measure to sending countries, thus preempting the imposition of reputational costs. Cabinet discussions of the preceding months, however, showed that a recruitment stop had become only a matter of time and that the oil crisis had provided the government with welcome political capital to mitigate its diplomatic costs. Significantly, the government's decision to end recruitment was not the result of popular pressure, as in the Swiss case, but rather was the result of a process of elite learning about the long-term implications of recruitment, paired with the strategic use of the oil crisis as a window of opportunity for stopping recruitment without incurring reputational costs.

Once the Brandt cabinet came to accept the fact of immigrant settlement and its concomitant social and infrastructural costs, the policy status quo was no longer tenable. Unable to make the kind of changes (such as rotation) that would have lowered the costs of recruitment while retaining its benefits, the only way forward was to shut down the entire system. The suspension of recruitment in 1973 thus stands in stark contrast to Swiss policy, where the Global Ceiling of 1970 constituted a regulatory instrument that could turn the supply of migrant workers on and off, depending on economic need (Figure 4.1). Even though the Swiss Federal Council was forced by popular pressure to scale down recruitment at a time of rapid economic growth, the tightrope walk between accommodating the needs of employers, on the one hand, and fighting economically disastrous overforeignization initiatives, on the other, had facilitated a policy compromise that, in the end, allowed the Swiss government to preserve flexibility on recruitment matters (see Chapter 3).

Looking at the politics of guest worker policy making in Germany from 1955 to 1973, two broad findings stand out. First, policy making throughout this era remained confined to the executive arena, and thus took place under conditions of high popular and low diplomatic insulation. The timing of recruitment reflected not only the foreign policy and trade priorities characteristic of cabinet agenda-setting, but also the lack of diplomatic insulation of cabinets in general, and the German executive in particular. Thus, and in contrast to classic political economy accounts of foreign worker recruitment that posit a political process propelled by the interests of employer lobbies, the Adenauer cabinet's decision to accede to Italy's request for a recruitment agreement was driven by the overarching agenda of reintegrating the Federal Republic into Western diplomatic and trade networks. While emerging labor shortages were necessary to secure the Labor Ministry's support for recruitment, it is unlikely that the treaty would have been signed as early as 1955 in the absence of foreign policy imperatives. The diplomatic benefits of entering into a recruitment agreement with Italy corresponded to the preferences of foreign and economic affairs officials, giving them the upper hand over recruitment skeptics within cabinet. At the same time, the government's 1964 decision to yield to Turkey on the question of family unification marks a case where the need to avoid reputational cost overrode the cabinet's substantive preferences. Finally, the Brandt cabinet's decision to shut down recruitment in 1973 reflected a recognition of the infrastructural costs incurred by large-scale settlement, rather than a lessening of labor demand, and was facilitated by the window of opportunity provided by the oil crisis, which allowed for the avoidance of reputational costs. After the oil crisis, the recruitment stop remained in place despite concerted lobbying by employer associations for sectoral exemptions. Thus, while internationally the Adenauer government was fundamentally constrained, domestically it enjoyed immense policy-making autonomy.

Insulated from popular pressure and impervious to the opposition of business, little stood in the way of its policy pursuits.

A second finding concerns the design of the guest worker system, which inadvertently facilitated settlement processes. We can only understand the naïveté of German policy makers on questions of immigrant settlement when we recognize the absence of policy learning from previous recruitment experiences. Whereas in Switzerland, failure-induced policy learning led to the creation of a strictly regulated rotation system with a large seasonal recruitment component and few rights to permanent residence or family unification, this was not the case in Germany. As a result, the postwar guest worker era left behind a legacy that associated immigration with costs rather than benefits, and declared Germany to be "a country of non-immigration."

THE NEW GUEST WORKER PROGRAMS OF THE 1990S

The post-recruitment stop politics of immigration in Germany is commonly considered to be "haunted by the mistakes, failures, and unforeseen consequences of the guest worker era" (Freeman 1995, 890). In the 1970s, the experience of unanticipated and, ultimately, unwanted mass immigration, alongside the social and political conflicts associated with the population increase of new ethnic minorities, gave rise to the conviction that "Germany is not a country of immigration." This (non)immigration ideology set the path along which migration policy was to travel until the end of the century, essentially precluding any further state-sponsored immigration.[15] There was a broad societal and elite consensus that guest worker recruitment was a "unique, non-recurrent event" that firmly belonged to the past (Joppke 1999, 82). With some minor exceptions, Germany ceased all attempts to recruit foreign workers until the 1990s, when the Conservative-Liberal government under Chancellor Helmut Kohl launched several temporary foreign worker programs.

While these "new guest worker programs" (Rudolph 1996) did not reach the scale of the postwar system (Castles 2006), they were far from insignificant (Figure 4.2).[16] During the first ten years of their operation, an annual average of 50,000 project-tied permits and 250,000 seasonal

---

[15] Setting aside the law of return for ethnic Germans, who were considered to be part of the German nation.

[16] Data from the *Bundesanstalt für Arbeit* cited in *Migrationsbericht 2014* (Bundesamt für Migration und Flüchtlinge 2015, 43, 56)

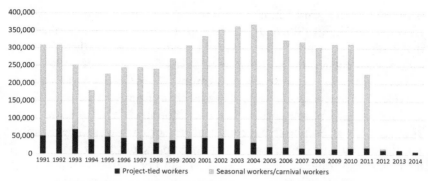

FIGURE 4.2 Guest worker recruitment in Germany, stacked, 1991–2014.

worker permits were issued (Bundesamt für Migration und Flüchtlinge 2010). This represented a total of three million permits issued over the course of a decade, equaling close to half the average number of work permits issued per decade in the postwar era. These programs would eventually be drastically scaled down in the 2010s, when freedom of movement was extended to the major Eastern European sending states of low-skilled labor (Romania, Bulgaria, and Croatia). However, the eventual absorption of these temporary foreign worker flows into intra-European migration did not amount to a legalization of uncontrolled flows. On the contrary, throughout its duration the new guest worker recruitment program was tightly controlled by the state, in terms of both rotation and overall numbers. We begin this second case study by asking: how can we account for this de facto departure from the 1973 recruitment stop by a government that continued to espouse the non-immigration ideology? We then examine one of these programs – the case of project-tied worker recruitment – in order to account for the new politics of temporary worker recruitment. Before further delving into these, it is important to identify some of the policy legacies confronting policy makers in the 1990s.

The Postwar Guest Worker System's Ideational Legacy: The Non-immigration Paradigm

After the recruitment stop, German immigration policy[17] officially became defined by the dual goals of immigration restriction

---

[17] While the German term *Ausländerpolitik* ("foreigner" or "aliens" policy) until very recently eschewed any reference to immigration, the English term "immigration policy"

(*Konsolidierung*) and immigrant integration. In 1977, the Social Democratic-Liberal (SPD/FDP) government outlined a policy blueprint that rested on four principles. First, and most importantly, the document officially articulated the non-immigration maxim: "the Federal Republic of Germany is not a country of immigration. West Germany is a country in which foreigners reside for varying lengths of time before they decide on their own accord to return to their home country" (cited in Katzenstein 1987b, 239–40). Second, the recruitment stop of 1973 was to be retained. Third, and building on the non-immigration principle, guest workers and their families should be encouraged – though not coerced – to return to their countries of origin. Finally, foreign workers who decided to stay were to receive secure immigration status, and the second generation's integration was to be supported (Meier-Braun 1988).

The blueprint thus reflected a tension between two divergent goals. On the one hand, the overall number of immigrants was to be reduced: all further immigration – including that of family dependents[18] – was to be discouraged and the departure of migrants already in the country to be promoted. On the other hand, the report called for the integration of those migrants who decided to stay in Germany. This tension was to remain unresolved well into the 1980s. In the years following the recruitment stop, the maxim that "Germany is not a country of immigration" was not solely a normative statement – asserting that mass immigration was to remain a thing of the past – but also reflected a lingering unwillingness to accept the fact that immigrant settlement had become an irreversible reality.

This reluctance to confront the fact of settlement was not confined to government circles. Even the German Trade Union Federation (DGB) – one of the most immigrant-friendly political actors – emphasized, in an internal 1978 position paper, that the recruitment stop must not be undermined by continued family unification. The document elaborated on the non-immigration paradigm:

[a]ccording to the German Trade Union Federation's understanding, Germany is not a country of immigration. The fact that up to 2.6 million foreign workers and

---

does not carry the same (prescriptive) connotations as in German (*Einwanderungspolitik*) and, in the interest of consistency, will be used throughout the book.

[18] Over time the non-Conservative parties would develop far more liberal preferences on family unification – in particular in relation to age limits for dependent children – than the Christian Democrats. We will briefly return to this partisan issue in the discussion of the 2004 Immigration Act.

about two million family dependents have lived and worked in Germany at various points in time does not make the Federal Republic a country of immigration. If that was the case, we would need a completely different immigration and integration policy. In our view, the Federal Republic is a country where large numbers of foreign workers have been present for more or less lengthy periods of time. From experience, most of these foreign workers will one day return to their native countries.

(Cited in Hunn 2005, 393, my translation)

Of course, there were also some that recognized the reality of permanent settlement early on. The Christian Democrats' "social committees" (*Sozialausschüsse*), a socially liberal association within the otherwise conservative party, stated as early as 1971 that Germany had become a country of immigration (Tietze 2008). Most famously, Fritz Kühn, the Social Democratic Federal Ombudsman for Foreigners' Affairs (*Ausländerbeauftragter der Bundesregierung*) declared in a government-commissioned memorandum that Germany had become a country of immigration and demanded far-reaching integration measures. Yet Kühn's demands were too radical for their times and fell on deaf ears with both the Social Democratic-Liberal government and the conservative opposition.

In early 1982, the Bundestag engaged in its first sustained debate on the fundamentals of migration policy. The debate took place in the context of rapidly increasing xenophobia, with two-thirds of Germans supporting the return of guest workers (Meier-Braun 1988, 24). In a climate of economic stagnation and decreasing employment rates of the foreign-born, guest workers and their families were now regarded as a fiscal drain. While class clearly played a role in shaping public attitudes toward guest workers, who were concentrated in the low-skilled sector, cultural concerns also featured prominently. The repeated singling out of Turks over other nationalities in integration debates in particular reflected both popular and elite fears that non-Judeo-Christian cultures constituted a threat to German social cohesion (Boswell and Hough 2008). Arguments that Germany had reached its "absorption capacity" were further fueled by continually increasing numbers of Turkish entrants, mostly through family unification, but also – following the 1980 Turkish coup d'état – as asylum applicants. The government, in a 1981 unpublished cabinet paper, expressed concern that "the uneasiness of much of the German population [with high numbers of foreigners] could turn into an openly defensive stance. The resultant social and political tensions would threaten peaceful coexistence (*gesellschaftlicher Friede*) in the Federal Republic" (cited in Meier-Braun 1988, 21, my translation).

In the ensuing debate, all parties reaffirmed the primacy of the recruitment stop and the non-immigration paradigm. The Social Democratic and Liberal parliamentary parties submitted a joint interpellation that called for the mobilization of "all political and legal means to continue to restrict the arrival of foreigners, in particular of their family members" as "the only way to achieve the integration of foreigners" (Deutscher Bundestag December 9, 1981, my translation). The government responded by affirming that:

in order to secure the German population's necessary support for the integration of foreigners, we need to pursue a consistent and effective policy of immigration restriction toward non-European Community countries. For this reason, the recruitment stop will remain in place. This also precludes the recruitment of seasonal migrant workers.

(Deutscher Bundestag May 5, 1982, my translation)

The Christian Democratic Union (CDU/CSU) opposition followed suit with an interpellation that demanded stricter immigration controls:

The Federal Republic of Germany is not a country of immigration. A circumvention of this principle by means of the uncontrolled influx of foreigners is to be prevented by all legal and humanely acceptable means. The recruitment stop is to remain in place. It must not be circumvented. .... As part of the divided Germany, the Federal Republic has historical and constitutional responsibility toward the German nation. Given its history and self-conception, Germany cannot become a country of immigration. .... The capacity of foreigners to return to their native lands (*Rückkehrfähigkeit*) as well as their willingness to do so has to be strengthened. .... Family unification should be achieved primarily by means of foreigners' return to their homeland.

(Deutscher Bundestag January 21, 1982, my translation)

On the Bundestag floor, all parties reiterated their programmatic commitment to the recruitment stop's continuation. At the same time, early partisan differences began to crystallize. Whereas the opposition Christian Democrats – in particular the Bavarian CSU – continued to categorically reject any recognition of Germany as a factual country of immigration, Social Democrats and Liberals now collectively acknowledged the fact that immigration had taken place. Federal Interior Minister Gerhard Baum (FDP) argued:

[W]e are not a country of immigration in the sense that we intentionally recruited with the aim of permanent settlement, or that we now pursue new recruitment of foreign workers. We are in favor of restricting entry. At the same time, we must recognize that for many foreign workers we have become a country of immigration. What matters now is what consequences we draw from this and what consequences those affected draw from it. Both sides are currently in a phase of transition.

(Deutscher Bundestag February 4, 1982, 4905, my translation)

Similarly, Social Democratic parliamentarian Hugo Brandt argued that, "it is certainly correct that we are not a country of immigration. But it is equally correct that for a period of time, we were a country of immigration. We have to face this problem. Generally, we can assume that the willingness to return will decrease with increasing length of residence" (Deutscher Bundestag February 4, 1982, 4911, my translation). In sum, the Federal Republic's first major parliamentary immigration debate demonstrated a cross-partisan consensus on the recruitment stop's continuation while at the same time reflecting a move toward the factual recognition of past guest worker immigration by the non-conservative parties.

Not long after the debate, the Social Democratic-Liberal government set out to establish return incentives for guest workers and their families (Hunn 2005). By the time the "law for the promotion of return" was passed, the Christian Democrats had returned to power by forming a coalition with the Liberals, ushering in Germany's "lost decade" of immigration policy, which was marked by the Kohl administration's (largely unsuccessful) pursuit of guest worker return and the prevention of further family and asylum immigration. Right up to the change in government in 1998, prominent Christian Democratic politicians, including successive interior ministers, continued to reiterate Germany's status as a country of non-immigration.

Germany's non-immigration ideology thus emerged as a response to the experience of unwanted large-scale immigrant settlement during the guest worker era and in the years following the recruitment stop. Significantly, while some of the integration challenges in the post-recruitment stop period can be partly attributed to the socioeconomic and religious demographics of the foreign-born population, public policy itself was instrumental in creating a vicious cycle that time and again reaffirmed the country's non-immigration ideology. Well into the 1980s, elite rhetoric and public policy sent clear signals that guest workers were expected to leave, thereby delaying the recognition of the finality of immigration by both German society and immigrants.

Policy Learning and the Construction of the Project-Tied System

The 1990s saw the first challenges to the non-immigration paradigm by parliamentary parties other than the Green Party, who since their entry into the Bundestag in 1983 had consistently challenged the prevailing paradigm. Between 1991 and 1997, Greens, Social Democrats, and Liberals all began to distance themselves from the non-immigration principle. The three parties in quick succession developed policy blueprints for a proactive, mostly economically driven, immigration policy (Tietze 2008). Yet this emergent paradigmatic shift was highly tenuous. Unlike the Greens, the Social Democrats' commitment to an active immigration policy was far from categorical. In fact, as we will see, the Social Democrats abandoned their proposal for a new immigration law when the party came to power in 1998. Furthermore, the debates driving these policy blueprints were limited to party elites – party leaders and parliamentary factions – and did not spill over into a broader, societal debate. Finally, the ruling Christian Democrats resisted any ideational change and continued to embrace the non-immigration paradigm as the foundation of German migration policy.

Despite the Christian Democrats' refusal to distance themselves from the non-immigration principle, in the late 1990s a significant but barely noticed policy change by the Christian Democratic-Liberal government led to the recruitment stop's gradual hollowing out. Passed as a governmental decree in the absence of public debate, the "regulation for exemptions from the recruitment stop" (*Anwerbestoppausnahmeverordnung*, ASAV) formalized already existing small-scale practices of the Federal Labor Agency by giving the executive discretion in deciding on possible exemptions from the recruitment ban (Velling 1995). As a result, recruitment came to cover diverse groups of foreign workers, ranging from project-tied workers working for subcontracted foreign construction firms, to seasonal workers in the agricultural and hospitality sectors, to cross-border commuters, trainees,[19] and certain high-skilled professionals.[20]

What allowed the government to pursue new foreign worker recruitment while continuing to assert the recruitment stop's primacy? The initiation of new recruitment, I argue, was contingent on a prior process of failure-induced policy learning. In recognizing that the postwar system's failure to enforce worker rotation was the root cause of unintended immigrant settlement, the Kohl government could credibly assert

---

[19] This group was officially referred to as "guest workers" (*Gastarbeiter*). The use of the term guest worker in this chapter, by contrast, refers to temporary foreign workers more generally.

[20] Only the first two categories, however, resulted in sizeable recruitment (Figure 4.2).

that the new policy's design would prevent the settlement of foreign workers and thus conform to the non-immigration paradigm. Accordingly, project-tied recruitment departed from previous policy in four fundamental ways. First, recruitment was firmly premised on rotation. Unlike the first guest worker system, where annual permits could be renewed indefinitely, permits now were tied to a (construction) project that was temporary in nature, and could not be extended beyond two years. Moreover, workers could only return to Germany after they had first resided in their country of origin for the same length of time that they had previously worked in Germany. Importantly, this provision not only served to ensure rotation but also meant that returning workers could not accrue a legal claim to permanent residence (which would have required five years of residence in an eight-year period) (Renner 1992). Second, worker recruitment was now subject to annual per-country quotas, which allowed for careful monitoring and ensured that the scope of recruitment would remain limited. Third, the new recruitment system categorically ruled out family unification – a provision that was supported by the strictly time-limited nature of employment. Fourth, project-tied employed was premised on the prevention of integration. Accordingly, foreign workers were integrated neither into German firms nor into the German labor market and social insurance system. Instead, as employees of subcontracted foreign firms, project-tied workers remained legally integrated into the labor regulations and social systems of their sending countries. Because project-tied workers did not pay into the German social insurance system, they could not accumulate claims against the German state that might give rise to future claims for legal residence (Kolb and Hunger 2003). Further, because project-tied workers were employed as members of foreign work crews, German employers did not have to invest in their training and bear the costs of their rotation. Similarly, project-tied workers were denied access to integration measures in areas of housing, language training, and housing assistance (Faist et al. 1999).

The project-tied system can thus be understood as a policy that was self-consciously designed to avoid the mistakes of the past.[21] Instead of

---

[21] While not the focus of this case study, the same can be said for Germany's seasonal worker program, which employed Eastern European workers predominantly in agriculture and hospitality. Not only did the prominence of seasonal employment among temporary foreign workers resemble the Swiss postwar strategy of favoring seasonal over annual permits, but worker rotation was effectively enforced. In the late 1990s, for

facilitating settlement processes by means of indefinite permit renewal, unlimited recruitment, family unification, and legal integration, foreign worker employment was now strictly premised on rotation (including a legally prescribed duty to return), annual ceilings, the prevention of family migration, and the preemption of integration. Importantly, it was these policy features that allowed for the renewed pursuit of guest worker recruitment within the ideational confines of the non-immigration paradigm. The significance of this claim becomes clear by looking at earlier demands for a reopening of recruitment channels in the mid-1970s, when – in the ban's immediate aftermath – employers were confronted with labor shortages and several employer associations and *Länder* governments demanded seasonal worker programs for affected sectors. Yet interior officials blocked these proposals, arguing that the implementation of a worker rotation system with sufficiently strict exit controls would prove too administratively demanding (Köppe 2002). Under the recruitment ban, then, foreign worker employment could not be considered a viable policy option so long as the possibility of permanent immigration remained. As long as the recruitment stop remained in place, guest worker recruitment could only be entertained if the return of workers could be ensured – a condition that was only considered administratively feasible years after the recruitment stop's passage.

What, then, motivated the government's decision to recruit project-tied workers? Already in the 1980s, policy makers started to experiment with small-scale and stringently regulated project-tied employment as a way of deepening economic cooperation with Central and Eastern European countries. In a parallel fashion to the postwar era, the beginnings of project-tied recruitment were driven less by labor market imperatives and more by trade and diplomatic considerations. Recruitment took the form of bilateral treaties[22] that imposed strict controls on worker and firm compliance, reflecting a broad cross-party consensus on the dual goals of immigration control and economic cooperation (Faist et al. 1999). Not surprisingly, then, recruitment gained momentum after the collapse of Communism. As Eastern Bloc countries began to transition toward market-based democracy, the government came to consider project-tied contracts – which provided sending states with much-needed

---

instance, a seasonal foreign worker in Germany was employed on average for fifty days per year (Faist 2003, 5).

[22] The first wave of treaties (1988–90) were with Yugoslavia, Hungary, Poland, and the Czech Republic.

foreign currency – as a means of supporting economic and political liberalization abroad. While the pursuit of project-tied recruitment was initially driven by Germany's foreign policy goals, labor market impera- tives gained prominence over time as unification triggered a construction boom that quickly came to rely on the comparatively cheap labor of project-tied workers, resulting in a high of 95,000 recruits in 1992 (Figure 4.2).

Recruitment under Fire: Interest Group Insulation in the Executive Arena

When, in the early 1990s, the increase in project-tied workers triggered intense political conflict it was not – as in the 1970s – the result of a failure of settlement control. Rather, domestic firms complained about unfair competition and wage dumping. While project-tied workers had to be paid at prevailing wage levels, the absence of a social wage – in conjunc- tion with prevalent illegal wage dumping – substantially reduced labor costs and rendered project-tied firms more competitive than German companies. These developments were further accelerated by noncompli- ance by Poland, the largest sending country, which substantially exceeded its annual quota (Faist et al. 1999). As a result, the German construction sector was inundated with highly competitive foreign construction com- panies and insolvencies among German small businesses grew rapidly.[23]

Employer associations and unions were quick to politicize the issue and appeal to legislators and the broader public for reform. The construc- tion employer association (*Zentralverband des Deutschen Baugewerbes*, ZDB) – representing the most negatively affected firms – and some unions (DGB and *Industriegewerkschaft Bauen-Agrar-Umwelt*, IG BAU) called for the program's termination and replacement with a new policy that would employ temporary foreign workers in German firms under the same conditions as domestic workers (Faist et al. 1999). In contrast, the federal umbrella association of employers (*Bundesvereinigung der Deutschen Arbeitgeberverbände*, BDA) did not support the demand for termination of project-tied employment, demanding instead a lowering of project-tied permit quotas. The Social Democrats, who led the opposition in the Bundestag and held the majority in the Bundesrat, quickly jumped on the bandwagon and used all parliamentary possibilities at their

---

[23] Between 1992 and 1995 insolvencies doubled in the former West Germany and increased twelvefold in the East (Faist et al. 1999, 192).

disposal to expose the program's adverse labor market impacts. The party supported the unions in calling for the termination of project-tied employment and demanded its substitution with work permits for 100,000 guest workers who would be employed in German firms for a period of six to eighteen months (Faist et al. 1999).

The government quickly conceded that the treaties had negatively impacted the competitiveness of small and medium-scale German businesses. Consequently it placed a hold on all Polish project-tied contracts to force Poland into contract compliance. Thus, the two governments engaged in lengthy negotiations that resulted in significantly lowered annual permit quotas as well as organizational reforms designed to improve implementation (Cyrus and Helias 1993). At home the German Labor Ministry set up a round table with the social partners. Yet while the ministry was willing to reform recruitment policy, it categorically rejected all demands by construction firms and trade unions for its termination. In 1992, as a result of the government's commitment to the program's continuation, negotiations soon came to an abrupt stop and were abandoned for good (Faist et al. 1999). A year later, the government did agree to permanently reduce the number of annual project-tied quotas, impose harsher sanctions for contract violations, and stop all recruitment in regions in which unemployment was at least 30 percent above the national average (see Figure 4.2). Beyond these remedial measures designed to protect domestic labor and firms, however, the government stood by its position to continue with project-tied recruitment, both to maintain good diplomatic and economic relations with Eastern European sending countries and to retain labor market flexibility at home (Faist et al. 1999).

Tellingly, the government rejected demands by the Social Democrats and the unions to allow for guest worker employment in German firms as a way of ensuring fair competition. Given that the legal framework underpinning project-tied recruitment was carefully designed to counteract settlement tendencies, a return to the postwar recruitment structures – which had placed guest workers directly with German employers – threatened to undercut the "temporariness" of foreign worker employment and ran counter to the government's (non-)immigration ideology. While a move away from the prevailing paradigm was already under way for the Social Democrats and Liberals and had long been completed by the Greens, Christian Democrats continued to hold on to the non-immigration principle, for both ideological and electoral reasons. The adherence to this paradigm precluded any foreign worker settlement, as

Christian Democratic parliamentarian Hans-Joachim Fuchtel argued in the Bundestag:

> The proposed solution of guest worker contracts is not as unproblematic as presented. Experience shows that these employees quickly become settled. If someone can stay in Germany for up to 18 months, they will likely want to remain for longer ... If we keep expanding their numbers, political pressure will mount to accept what happened in the 1970s.
>
> (Deutscher Bundestag, January 20, 1994, 17765, my translation)

For the next ten years annual recruitment numbers stabilized between 35,000 and 50,000 before dropping off to 30,000 by the end of the decade. After 2010 numbers dropped drastically, paralleling recruitment trends in the seasonal worker program (Figure 4.2). The decline in project-tied recruitment was the result of neither interest group nor popular pressure, but instead corresponded to the lifting of transitional labor market restrictions in 2011 and 2014 for the ten Eastern European member states who had joined the European Union seven years prior.[24] The opening up of the German labor market for all nationals of the new accession countries triggered a significant increase in "internal" (i.e., intra-European) labor migration from Eastern Europe (Figure 4.3),[25] marking an important break from decades of low levels of intra-EU mobility.[26] Importantly, as Eastern Europeans gained EU citizenship, and thus full access to the German labor markets, they were able to move out of temporary foreign worker programs into the regular labor market. However, given their skill profiles and the employment legacies of the new guest worker programs, many Eastern Europeans continued to work in low-skilled and precarious employment, a pattern that is also reflected in the high rate of circular migration for the new accession countries.

With the steep increase in the supply of Eastern European "internal" workers available to work in low-skilled jobs, Germany no longer needed

---

[24] That being said, many Eastern Europeans were able to secure work in Germany even before the official lifting of labor market restrictions – often as self-employed workers who were exempt from the transitional restrictions (see Figure 4.3).

[25] Because of low numbers there are no official data for Croatia between 2005 and 2011, and for Bulgaria between 2004 and 2006. Cross-national data for 2005 are estimates as there are no official data available.

[26] Throughout the 1990s, for instance, EU nationals accounted for just over a fifth of immigrants to Germany. At the same time more individuals left Germany for other EU member states than vice versa (Beauftragte der Bundesregierung für Ausländerfragen 1999, 18). By contrast, with eastern enlargement, Eastern European migrants alone accounted for 39 percent of *all* immigration to Germany in 2013, boosting the proportion of EU immigrants to over 60 percent (Bundesamt für Migration und Flüchtlinge 2015).

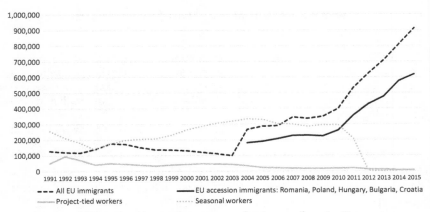

FIGURE 4.3 EU immigration and temporary foreign workers in Germany, 1991–2015.

to resort to large-scale temporary foreign worker recruitment. As a result, after three decades of pursuing these recruitment policies the guest worker programs of the 1990s began to fade into insignificance. It is important to recognize, however, that this turn away from guest worker recruitment was not the result of program failure. Rather, at least as far as the project-tied program was concerned, its demise reflected the success of regional economic integration as one of the program's primary goals. As the majority of sending countries of the 1990s joined the European Union, they came to enjoy full freedom of movement and services and could provide subcontracted labor free of the confines of the project-tied treaties. As a result, whatever project-tied employment remains is now limited to workers from Turkey, Serbia, Bosnia Herzegovina, and Macedonia, with no plans for further expansion (Bundesamt für Migration und Flüchtlinge 2013).

In many ways the return to guest worker recruitment in the 1990s was a puzzling development. The continued significance of the non-immigration paradigm, which emerged from the policy failures of the postwar recruitment system, clearly precluded the pursuit of permanent economic immigration by a Conservative government. Hence, the ability of policy makers to respond to diplomatic pressure and resume guest worker recruitment critically hinged on their ability to devise a recruitment system that could credibly commit to preempting all settlement processes. Policy makers succeeded in doing so by devising a system that – unlike past policy – was premised on worker rotation, annual ceilings, the preclusion of family unification, and the absence of labor market integration. These policy features reflected a process of failure-induced policy learning that sought to prevent the past from repeating itself. Thus, the availability of policy lessons from the past allowed for the pursuit of guest worker recruitment after a hiatus of twenty-five years – though critically, this time around recruitment design bore little resemblance to the system that had transformed postwar Germany into a country of immigration.

Finally, the government's decision to continue recruitment in the face of extensive and highly visible mobilization by the parliamentary opposition and the social partners reflects the executive's insulation from interest group pressure. Even though interest groups succeeded in moving the recruitment issue from the executive into the legislative arena – a case of agenda spillover – the cabinet was able to stay its course and continue with project-tied recruitment. Thus, with the demands of interest groups not resonating with its own preference, the government prioritized the pursuit of economic and diplomatic relations with Eastern Europe over interest group accommodation, even at the expense of abandoning its negotiations with social partners. The case of the new guest worker programs of the 1990s thus firmly continued along the path of executive-centered policy making that had come to mark the politics of foreign worker recruitment in the Federal Republic.

THE GREEN CARD PROGRAM OF 2000

The federal election of 1998 marked a watershed in German politics. With the coming to power of the Social Democratic-Green coalition, the Conservatives – for the first time in the Federal Republic's history – found themselves on the opposition benches. While the CDU (though not its sister party, the CSU) had taken the unprecedented step of removing from its electoral platform all reference to Germany as a "country of non-immigration," this programmatic change did not present a major ideational departure from the party's positioning during the preceding years. Rather, instead of indicating an endorsement of new immigration, the omission simply meant a collective recognition of past immigration. As before, the Conservatives' electoral platform called for the continued restriction of immigration.

With the departure from power of the last principled opponent of a more liberal immigration policy, a window of opportunity for paradigmatic immigration reform opened up. Throughout their electoral campaign, the Social Democrats had aggressively branded themselves as a modernizing and innovating force capable of leading the country into the twenty-first century's "New Economy." Even though the party's electoral campaign made no mention of its earlier endorsement of a more open immigration policy – the party instead articulated a vague goal of "managing and restricting immigration" – the change in government was accompanied by high expectations for an end to the country's *Reformstau* ("reform bottleneck"), which extended into the areas of immigration and citizenship.

Indeed, once in office the new government was quick to promise a "modern citizenship law" and "new immigration politics" (*neue Ausländerpolitik*) that would recognize – to cite the coalition treaty – "that an irreversible process of past immigration has taken place" (Hell 2005, 95, my translation). Yet when it came to the question of future immigration a rift quickly surfaced within the coalition government. In their coalition negotiations the two parties had quickly agreed to reform the country's early twenthith-century citizenship law, which had made the acquisition of citizenship contingent on descent rather than on territorial birth. Given that the non-immigration paradigm had shifted so that the reality of immigrant settlement was now universally acknowledged, integration had become the new policy imperative, including the need to put an end to the birth of third- and fourth-generation "foreigners."

However, while the Greens reiterated the need for a new immigration law, the Social Democrats warned that the simultaneous pursuit of citizenship and immigration reform would not be politically viable (Triadafilopoulos 2012). In a press interview, Social Democratic minister of the interior Otto Schily argued that the time was not right for a new immigration law, stating that "immigration already exceeds our load-bearing capacity" (Tagesspiegel November 15, 1998, 4, my translation). When Schily's comments came under fire from the left, Social Democratic Chancellor Gerhard Schröder affirmed that "any additional immigration to Germany is not manageable" and argued that the success of the coalition's citizenship reform hinged on the tabling of immigration reform (Die Woche November 26, 1998, 11, my translation). The senior coalition partner's volte face on the issue of immigration thus reflected the tenuousness of the party's ideological shift. Unlike the Greens, who had been unified in their support of a liberal immigration policy since the early 1980s, the Social Democrats' relatively recent commitment was far less principled. Now that the party was no longer in opposition, it was unwilling to take the political risks associated with the liberalization of immigration, especially considering the fact that they had not yet tested the waters of the electoral arena.

Thus, it came as a genuine surprise when just three months later, in February 2000, Chancellor Schröder, in his opening speech at the computer expo CeBIT, announced that Germany was "ready to issue the Card that is called 'Green' in America" (Hell 2005, 115, my translation). Even though – in reference to the coalition parties' colors – the originally named Red-Green Card was intended to offer temporary, rather than permanent, work visas to foreign computer specialists, the announcement dropped like a bombshell. What was so extraordinary about the chancellor's announcement was the fact that for the first time since the 1960s a prominent government official had sought out a public venue to proclaim the opening of new channels of labor migration.

Forgoing Popular Insulation: The Executive's Reframing of Immigration

Why did Chancellor Schröder initiate a new labor recruitment program at a time when the Social Democrats had decided against the pursuit of immigration reform? What motivated the chancellor's decision to depart from the well-tested practice of pursuing labor recruitment from within the safety of executive insulation? It is only when we explore these questions in tandem that we can begin to grasp the rationale driving the Green Card initiative. In the past, diplomatic pressure had been a critical trigger of guest worker recruitment. However, in 2000 policy makers faced no equivalent pressures to open up high-skilled recruitment. Analogous to previous guest worker programs, labor market demand was a necessary, but also insufficient, condition for the Green Card's pursuit. Instead, rather than conceiving of the program as simply yet another policy measure designed to address sectoral labor shortages, we should first and foremost understand it as an attempt to publicly reframe the issue of economic immigration.

To what extent was the Green Card initiative driven by domestic labor shortages? There is no question that governments are unlikely to pursue foreign worker recruitment in the absence of labor demand. Thus, Germany's information and communications technology (ICT) boom of the late 1990s, which was widely seen as the advent of a new knowledge-based economy built on information technology, had revealed significant shortages of domestic ICT workers. In 1998, BITKOM – Germany's information and telecommunications sector employer association – lobbied the new government to recruit 30,000 computer experts from Central and Eastern Europe, arguing that a lack of domestic labor was imperiling the country's economic growth (Ette 2003). However, instead of acceding to these demands for foreign worker recruitment, the government decided to pursue domestic labor market measures under the umbrella of the newly established Alliance for Labor, a roundtable made up of government representatives, employer associations, and trade unions.

Given the urgency of the matter, the alliance established an ICT-focused working group which by the fall of 1999 concluded that domestic policy measures such as enhanced training programs would be sufficient to remedy labor shortages at the occupational mid-level. However, in regard to upper-level professionals, the group concluded that because of low enrollment in university ICT programs domestic measures alone would not solve labor shortages in the short to medium term (Greifenstein 2001). The working group considered the adoption of a US-style Green Card, but there was disagreement within the Alliance for Labor about the desirability of this measure. Whereas the Green coalition partner, business, and the Ministry for Education and Research were in favor of recruiting abroad, the unions and the Labor Ministry voiced concerns about adverse labor market impacts (Greifenstein 2001). Meanwhile, labor shortages continued to intensify, and BITKOM, in anticipation of the computer expo CeBIT, stepped up its lobbying efforts, demanding the recruitment of 75,000 foreign ICT experts (Süddeutsche Zeitung February 23, 2000).

Yet the government remained unwilling to concede to these demands. In late January 2000 the Ministry of Labor's parliamentary state secretary responded to a question on the Bundestag floor concerning the desirability of foreign ICT worker recruitment, saying that:

at the present time the federal government is not of the view that we should liberalize the issuing of work permits to foreign ICT specialists. Like in other sectors, we need to deal with skilled labor shortages by means of domestic [labor market] measures. The recruitment of foreign workers would not solve the root causes of this shortage, it would only serve to conceal it in the short term.
(Deutscher Bundestag January 26, 2000, 7667, my translation)

Thus, despite significant labor market pressures and concerted business lobbying, less than a month before the Green Card announcement, economic considerations were not sufficient to sway the government to commence foreign worker recruitment.

When the chancellor announced the Green Card program he took everyone – including his closest allies – by surprise. It appears that Schröder had informed neither the Federal Chancellery nor his coalition partner of his decision to accede to the industry's demands for foreign ICT worker recruitment. In fact, the Green Card announcement had not even been included in the transcript of this speech that had been circulated to the press, leading some to argue that it was a spontaneous decision by the chancellor (Beck 2001, Westerhoff 2007). Even if the announcement itself was spontaneous – an assumption that is impossible to verify in the absence of Schröder's testimony – there is no question that given the substance of the working group's deliberations the chancellor must have already considered the measure prior to CeBIT. What, then, might have motivated Schröder to outmaneuver recruitment opponents within the Alliance for Labor by publicly announcing the Green Card, thereby creating a fait accompli?

To begin to understand what drove the Green Card initiative, we need to first examine whether, and to what extent, the program was driven by economic and labor market considerations. While the Green Card could not have come about in the absence of labor market demand, we cannot understand its inception with reference to economic considerations alone. First, the Green Card only weakly corresponded to substantive employer demands. In discussions about the program's regulatory details, both the federal umbrella and sector-specific employer associations argued that Germany could only be internationally competitive if, like its global competitors, it offered ICT recruits and their families the option of permanent, rather than temporary, residence (Angenendt 2002). While the Green coalition partner supported business demands to institute a US-style (H1 B) high-skill visa program with a road to permanent residence, the Social Democrats were unwilling to challenge the non-immigration paradigm and firmly resisted the conversion of temporary visas into permanent ones (Westerhoff 2007).

Consequently, the majority of German ICT firms stood to gain little from the Green Card program. In fact, the large multinational firms that dominated the sector preferred to utilize the existing option of filling domestic vacancies via international employee transfers. Not surprisingly, then, the Green Card was met with less demand than expected. Tellingly, despite their market dominance, the larger ICT firms accounted for only a quarter of all permits issued during the program's duration (Kolb 2003a). A second reason that attribution of the Green Card to interest group pressure is not plausible is the fact that the program was not necessary for the recruitment of foreign ICT experts. The government could have pursued ICT recruitment within the existing regulatory framework (ASAV), which, after all, had previously allowed for the recruitment of project-tied and seasonal workers (Kolb 2003a). In other words, the recruitment of computer specialists did not require additional regulatory or legislative measures, nor was the chancellor under political pressure to "go public" with the policy initiative.

What is most significant about the Green Card is its introduction with great fanfare, forgoing the executive arena's popular insulation. Schröder's Green Card announcement arose out of neither economic nor political necessity but instead presented a strategic attempt to reframe the issue of economic immigration. Borrowing from the US Green Card's charisma, Schröder's pronouncement that Germany was to issue its own ICT visas was a "dramaturgical act" (Fitzgerald and Cook-Martín 2014) that signaled to the domestic and international publics that under the leadership of a new government, the German "competition state" (see Chapter 3) was committed to being a player in the game for global talent and technological innovation. Accordingly, the Green Card was marketed as part of a larger public relations campaign under the slogan "Germany is spelled with .de" (Deutsche Bundesregierung 2000, my translation).

Beyond branding the country as ready to compete in the New Economy, the Green Card's announcement put into motion a fundamental reframing of the issue of immigration. Since the recruitment stop of 1973, immigration had come to be associated with the settlement of asylum seekers and family dependents, who were broadly associated with high levels of unemployment and reliance on public assistance. The image conjured up by the Green Card, in contrast, was that of human capital, in this case rich technology experts who would help Germany compete in the global economy. To quote the infamous words of Bavarian premier Günther Beckstein, the Green Card's introduction facilitated a shift in public and parliamentary debate from "immigrants who use us" to "immigrants who are useful to us." This new framing of immigration as an economic asset is clearly reflected in the report of the Independent Immigration Commission set up not long after the Green Card's announcement:

Immigration to Germany is supposed to enhance the competitiveness of the economy. No business enterprise should be forced to relocate to another country, to refrain from making investments or from availing themselves of growth potential due to labor shortages. It is particularly important to attract highly qualified immigrants to Germany, whose innovative abilities and technological skills can make a decisive contribution to securing the economic future.

(Unabhängige Kommission "Zuwanderung" 2001, 83, my translation)

In the extensive political debate that followed in the wake of the Green Card's announcement, trade unions and Christian Democrats initially opposed the measure. The DGB argued that the measure was misguided at a time when the unemployment rate stood at 10 percent. The government countered that the Green Card needed to be considered as part of a larger bundle of measures designed to fill labor shortages, lower domestic unemployment, and boost education and training. All too aware of the risks of popular backlash on matters of immigration, the government, after some initial wavering, stood firm in rejecting continued advances by industry to extend the program to other sectors (Jurgens 2010). While the government was confident in using the Green Card as a rhetorical device to conjure up a positive immigration frame, it was not (yet) prepared to realize its policy implications. The painful memories of the success of the Christian Democrats' previous year's petition drive against dual nationality – which had cost the Red-Green government a *Land* election, robbed them of their upper house majority, and forced them to considerably water down their proposed citizenship law – were all too fresh. The Social Democrats resolutely rejected any demands by employers and their Green coalition partner that Green Card holders be given access to permanent residence and instead insisted that the Green Card be a temporary labor market measure that was to remain in place only until enough domestic specialists were available (Westerhoff 2007).

While trade unions centered their opposition on the risk of adverse labor market impact, the Christian Democrats replicated the populist campaign strategy employed during the previous year's citizenship debate. Jürgen Rüttgers, the former federal technology minister and the Christian Democratic candidate for governor of North Rhine-Westphalia, made the opposition to the Green Card the linchpin of his gubernatorial electoral campaign. Arguing that better training at home should take the place of recruitment from abroad, he sent postcards to voters with the catchphrase "more training instead of more immigration" (Ette 2003). In another instance, Rüttgers stated that Germans prefer "children instead of Indians" (*Kinder statt Inder*) – a slogan derived from a media interview in which he argued that instead of recruiting foreigners to operate Germany's computers, the government should put German children in front of computers. Thus, he sought to exploit xenophobic attitudes by framing immigration as a threat to the future competitiveness of the nation's children.

This time, remarkably, the strategy of populism failed. Rüttgers' campaign came under sustained fire not only from the other political parties, the media, and the churches, but most importantly from the employer associations. Business – a longstanding supporter of the center-right – now publicly questioned the party's economic competency. In the end, the

Christian Democrats lost the election with the fourth-worst result in the party's history (Kolb 2003b). These considerations indicate that for the first time since the recruitment stop, the issue of immigration – what Schröder not long before had called "the loser topic ... a trap by the Christian Democrats" (Burgdorff June 12, 2000, my translation) – did not trigger widespread xenophobia, thus failing to produce the expected electoral gains. The fact that Rüttgers' arguments fell on barren ground was a clear indication of the government's success in framing high-skilled labor recruitment as a matter of economic competitiveness, establishing in the process a connection between immigrant recruitment and economic competency (Ette 2003). This link strengthened over time, as shown by the fact that visa demand was weaker than expected, to the extent that the government could not reach recruitment targets – something unprecedented in the Federal Republic's history of labor recruitment. While in the past, seemingly unlimited demand from abroad had eventually given rise to concerns about immigration control, this time around the relative absence of demand further heightened concerns about Germany's international competitiveness. As a result, whereas in the past Social Democratic support for the liberalization of immigrant admissions had constituted a political liability, the Green Card debate put an end to the longstanding dichotomy between immigration and economic growth – at least as far as high-skilled immigration was concerned.

After the fiasco of the North Rhine-Westphalian election, the Christian Democrats abandoned their opposition to the Green Card and openly supported the recruitment of highly skilled migrants. Thus, a paradigm shift – albeit partial insofar as it was limited to high-skilled immigration – appeared to have been completed. Germany was no longer a country of non-immigration but rather had become one of selective immigration. In the words of Cornelia Schmalz-Jacobson, former federal commissioner of foreigners, "[t]he very sudden swinging around of members of the government as well as numerous members of parliament was amusing and alarming at the same time. From one day to the next, prejudices that normally die hard, for instance, the slogan of the 'exceeded limit,' were not expressed anymore" (Schmalz-Jacobsen 2001, 41, my translation).

Despite the Green Card's minor labor market benefits, its political impact cannot be overstated. The extensive public debate triggered by the initiative firmly established high-skilled immigration to be in the national interest and resulted in broadly voiced demands for a new immigration law. The fact that all key stakeholders – employers, trade unions, and the churches – agreed on the need for comprehensive immigration reform sent a clear signal to the government that, despite the citizenship law's difficult passage, the pursuit of immigration reform was politically viable and supported by a rapidly evolving, broad-based paradigm shift. In April – barely two months after the chancellor's Green Card announcement – the Social Democrats relinquished their resistance, and the two coalition partners set up a working group to consider the prospects of immigration reform (Ette 2003). In June the government announced the creation of the Independent Immigration Commission, with the mandate to develop proposals for a new immigration law.

THE IMMIGRATION ACT OF 2004

When the Independent Immigration Commission (*Unabhängige Kommission* "Zuwanderung") began its work in July 2000, it did so under exceptionally favorable conditions. Not only was there a bipartisan consensus on the need for immigration reform, but the extensive public debate that had followed the Green Card announcement had been remarkably constructive, suggesting a rare window of opportunity for paradigmatic reform. In the words of Commission vice-chairman Hans-Jochen Vogel,

[without] a progressive change in attitudes we would have not received this [commission] assignment. This attitudinal change is reflected in the fact that ... Germany is now referred to as a country of immigration, and disagreements focus on the appropriate adjective, that is, on the question of whether we are a classical or a modern ... country of immigration.

(Cited in Krause 2004, 277, my translation)

The commission's work was accompanied by high expectations that it would serve as a catalyst for long-overdue immigration reform.

Paradigmatic Change in the Executive Arena: The Independent Immigration Commission

The government's decision to establish an Immigration Commission was far from obvious, as it meant that the coalition would have to shelve work on its immigration bill for close to a year. A delay of this magnitude was risky, given that parliament had already reached its halfway point and that it was in the government's interest to keep immigration reform insulated from the vicissitudes of electoral politics. Taking these risks into account, why did the government go ahead with its plan for an

Immigration Commission? The delegation of policy development to the commission can be attributed to two related strategic considerations, both of which reflect the Bundesrat's – Germany's upper house – significance as an institutional veto point. Because the Red-Green government had lost its majority in the upper house, the passage of immigration reform depended on the government's ability to secure some of the votes of the Conservative Länder in the Bundesrat. The choice of an Independent Commission to serve as the catalyst for paradigmatic policy change thus reflected the government's need to augment the legitimacy of its reform agenda and secure the support not only of societal elites, but also of the Christian Democratic opposition.

Looking at the imperative of public support, there is little doubt that the citizenship reform debacle of the previous year was fresh on policy makers' minds. The Christian Democrats' successful petition drive against dual nationality in 1999 had cost the Red-Green government their Bundesrat majority and turned what was supposed to be a case of historic citizenship reform into a watered down policy compromise. There was a sense that the strength of populist backlash was in part attributable to the government's decision to pursue radical policy change in the absence of broad-based public debate (Zinterer 2004). Now, faced once again with the challenge of radical reform, policy makers considered public support for immigration reform not only necessary, but also within the realm of possibility. In the words of one commission staffer:

[a]fter the Green Card, all of a sudden [public] discussions were marked by substantive expertise ... before, these kind of [well-informed] discussions were limited to expert circles. ... But all of a sudden they spilled over into the public sphere, and the representatives of industry added their support, and then there was a substantive discussion, and we thought, "finally."

(Cited in Zinterer 2004, 261, my translation)

Looking at public opinion data from 2000, there is clear evidence that restrictionism was weakening. In particular, there was strong support – 69 percent in November 2000 (Krause 2004, 275) – for the admission of highly skilled immigrants, whose presence was now considered necessary for Germany's continued economic competitiveness. Not only was there public support for high-skilled recruitment, but public opinion also favored the passage of an immigration law. Support peaked in the summer of 2000, when 70 percent of respondents were in favor of an immigration law that would admit a yearly quota of permanent immigrants. Finally, when asked more generally about their views on the introduction of new legislation to "regulate migration," 89 percent of the public was in favor (Cooper 2010, 420).

While the public climate seemed favorable for radical reform, the emergent paradigm shift had not yet been completed. Although the German public was willing to accept the admission and settlement of certain workers, support was limited to small numbers of human capital-rich workers whose recruitment would meet labor market needs. In other words, support for the selection of high-skilled workers did not translate into support for the kind of Canadian-style immigration policy envisaged by policy makers, which – given Germany's rapidly shrinking population – was driven not only by short-term economic but also by long-term demographic needs. The ideational distance between a demographically driven immigration policy and the preferences of the public is evident in public opinion polls. When asked whether a law on immigration should expand the number of immigrants, only 8 percent of respondents agreed, while 47 percent favored a reduction in numbers and 35 percent preferred the numerical status quo (Cooper 2010, 415).

While the commission was cognizant of the need for a sustained public debate – in particular on the question of demographically driven immigration – it nevertheless decided to conduct its deliberations behind closed doors. In order to facilitate internal consensus finding, the commission further chose to keep its engagement with the media to a minimum. Accordingly, only eight months into its work did the commission present its first resolutions to the public. While its tight-lipped public relations strategy was conducive to its own internal discussions, it prevented the commission from influencing public debate. Because the government had decided to shelve work on its immigration bill until after the commission report's publication, public debate during this period was instead dominated by the Christian Democratic opposition (Zinterer 2004).

In addition to securing the legitimacy of reform in the eyes of the public, the commission was intended to facilitate the building of a bipartisan consensus. Hence, Interior Minister Schily, concerned that the commission's deliberations would be hijacked by party political disputes, vigorously resisted all attempts to appoint frontline politicians (Green 2004). In his letters of appointment, Schily further emphasized that commission members were appointed as individuals, rather than as interest group or party representatives (Zinterer 2004). In other words, the Immigration Commission was composed of members who, while representing a broad range of societal interests, were also known to be independent thinkers removed from major partisan and ideological battles (Zinterer 2004). Most notably, the commission was chaired by a prominent Christian Democrat, former Speaker of the Bundestag Rita Süssmuth, who had long been a liberal voice within her party. Aside from including representatives of all the parliamentary parties – except for the CSU and the Party of Democratic Socialism – members were drawn from employer associations, trade unions, churches, local authorities, and the United Nations High Commissioner for Refugees.[27]

While the commission membership reflected an institutionally diverse body of individuals, it did exclude proponents of less centrist positions. Most importantly, not a single committee member belonged to the CSU, the Christian Democrats' culturally conservative Bavarian sister party and the only parliamentary group that still refused to refer to Germany as a country of immigration. Even among the Christian Democratic commission members there was no representation of those voices that were profoundly skeptical of a more open immigration policy. Clearly, partisan polarization had precluded the appointment of conservative members whose immigration views reflected the party line. Thus, the appointment of Süssmuth as commission chair was more indicative of the commission's political independence than of a substantive representation of the full range of policy positions. Unfortunately for Schily, Süssmuth's appointment was greeted with outright hostility by her party leaders, who felt sidelined by not having been consulted in this decision (Zinterer 2004). Consequently the CDU leadership demanded that Süssmuth resign from the commission, and when she refused to do so in a consequential move they set up their own commission under the chairmanship of party moderate Peter Müller.

Looking at the Independent Commission's nine months of deliberations, how close did its members move toward a policy consensus? Notably, preference convergence was strongest on issues of economic immigration. Because of Germany's lack of experience with a nontemporary economic immigration policy, expert assessments carried great weight with commission members, in particular demographic arguments in favor of the establishment of a labor market and human capital-oriented immigration system (Zinterer 2004). The commission quickly arrived at a consensus in favor of a multitrack, flexible immigration system designed to meet both short- and long-term needs. The system would create a permanent immigration track for in-demand highly skilled

---

[27] One societal group that was conspicuously absent was the immigrant community itself. This was attributed to the absence of centralized associations with large memberships that could have served as legitimate representatives of either Muslims or migrants more broadly (Zinterer, 2004).

foreign nationals in industry, science, and higher education – thereby widening the circle of current Green Card applicants and, notably, removing the time limit on their employment. The proposed policy would further create a temporary track for workers in areas of acute labor shortage. Longer-term demographic and economic needs would be met through the immigration of business entrepreneurs and foreign trainees, the employment of foreign graduates of German universities, and, most significantly, a Canadian-style human capital-based points system that would select new immigrants on the basis of their potential for social and labor market integration.

Initially there was disagreement within the commission as to whether to give points system entrants permanent residence from the onset or instead offer conversion from temporary to permanent status later on. Given that take-up of the (nonpermanent) Green Card continued to lag behind expectations, concerns about international competitiveness won out and facilitated a decision to grant immediate access to permanent residence. A final point of contention was the magnitude of immigration. Given the lack of policy experience, the commission agreed on low admission numbers for the first year of the system's operation: a maximum of 50,000 permits – 20,000 of which would be for points system entrants, 10,000 for foreign trainees, and 20,000 for temporary workers (Zinterer 2004). The commission's deliberations on economic immigration were marked by a remarkable degree of consensus finding. Of particular significance was the fact that industry and labor representatives quickly saw eye to eye, no doubt in part because the commission's nonpublic nature prevented any symbolic posturing (Zinterer 2004). Other areas of discussion were marked by far greater, more fundamental, internal conflict. This was especially the case in the area of refugee and asylum policy, where demands for greater human rights protections collided with calls for more effective immigration controls.

To what extent, then, does the Independent Immigration Commission's final report mark the conclusion of a paradigm shift? In relation to its recommendations on economic immigration, the report makes a clear case for the adoption of a new paradigm:

A paradigm shift from the recruitment stop to a managed labor-market oriented immigration is necessary. The existing regulations are insufficient to allow us to participate in the international competition for the highly qualified, and to tackle the demographically caused decline in young professionals.
(Unabhängige Kommission Zuwanderung 2001, 295, my translation)

The report clearly went well beyond the previously established bipartisan consensus, which had recognized the need for highly skilled foreign workers but could not resolve disagreements regarding their – temporary or permanent – immigration status. The call for the creation of a Canadian-style points system in particular marked the embracing of Germany as an immigration country where foreign nationals would be recruited as permanent immigrants and in recognition of their long-term contributions to Germany society.

In important ways, the Süssmuth Commission's work reflected the functions of government commissions more generally. It represented an attempt to serve as a catalyst for paradigmatic change by removing the discussion of fundamental policy principles from the vagaries of partisan politics and turning ideological battles into problem-focused discourses. Yet from the onset there were clear limits to the commission's capacity for paradigm shifting. At the same time as the commission's internal policy consensus augmented the legitimacy of the government's reform agenda, the Christian Democrats' refusal to recognize its legitimacy – demonstrated by the creation of its own commission – shows that the Süssmuth Commission's legitimation did not extend into socially conservative circles.

Paradigmatic Contestation in the Legislative and Electoral Arenas

In April 2001, three months before the Independent Immigration Commission published its recommendations, the CDU's Müller Commission issued its final report. The two reports marked the end of an extensive period of closed-door debate and signaled the beginning of the task of legislative majority-building. Given that the Social Democrats occupied a centrist position between the Greens to the left and the Christian Democrats to the right, Schily's reform project was contingent not only on securing Christian Democratic support in the Bundesrat, but also on forging a policy consensus with his more liberal Green coalition partner. Initially, bipartisan compromise seemed within reach. The Interior Ministry's draft was completed in August, and while it was clearly influenced by the Independent Commission's report it strategically incorporated key recommendations articulated by the Müller Commission.

On matters of economic immigration both commissions supported the introduction of a points system for high-skilled workers. However, the commissions differed in their rationale for recruitment. The Süssmuth Commission offered a dual demographic and labor market rationale for increased immigration and proposed that the points system be introduced without delay. The Müller Commission, by contrast, rejected demographic arguments and supported the creation of a points system only where necessary to meet labor market shortages. In the Interior Ministry's draft, Schily sided with the Müller Commission and proposed the introduction of a points system if deemed economically necessary. The government added that it did not expect to have to employ the system prior to 2010 (Meier-Braun 2002).

The most fundamental disagreement between the two commissions concerned questions of asylum policy and family unification. Whereas the Süssmuth Commission proposed a widening of asylum grounds to include persecution by nonstate agents as well as gender-related persecution, the Müller Commission was categorically opposed to any liberalization of asylum policy. Once again, the Interior Ministry's legislative draft sided with the Christian Democrats. Finally, while the Süssmuth Commission recommended raising the age of family unification from 16 to 18, the Müller Commission proposed an age limit of 6 and no higher than 10. Here the ministry adopted a compromise position, allowing for family unification up to age 12, except for the children of high-skilled workers, who would be able to immigrate up to age 18 (Green 2004).

The speed with which the ministry's draft was completed is indicative of the tight schedule Schily had set for the legislative process. With only one year left until the next federal election, passage of the bill in the Bundestag was to take place within three months (Reisslandt 2002). Schily faced the first stumbling block when, in a coalition meeting in early September, Social Democrats and Greens were unable to agree on a common policy blueprint (Krause 2004). Given the policy concessions the Interior Ministry had made to the Christian Democrats, the Greens refused to endorse the draft and threatened to bring down the government over it. Meanwhile, Schily's draft came under fire by the Christian Democrats and, in particular, the CSU, exposing longstanding internal divisions both within the CDU and between the two sister parties, especially on questions of economic immigration (Wüst 2009). In contrast to 2000, when the party's opposition to the Green Card program during the ICT boom had unexpectedly turned out to be a political liability, the economic landscape had since changed. Not only had the economy slowed down but – with the number of unemployed having crossed the four million mark – concerns about domestic unemployment loomed large. The Christian Democrats, and in particular the CSU, critiqued Schily's draft as promoting immigration at a time of rising domestic unemployment. Increasingly, even the CDU voiced positions that were at odds with the recommendations of its own immigration commission.

In the following months two critical events transpired that decisively tipped the balance of power between conservative moderates and hardliners in the latter's favor. First, the terrorist attacks on the World Trade Center on September 11, 2001 served as an exogenous shock that securitized the immigration debate overnight. As an agenda of internal security spilled over into questions of labor migration and integration, it threatened to derail the immigration law completely. Whereas the previous year's Green Card discussion had conjured up an image of immigrants as human capital-rich computer experts who would restore Germany's international competitiveness, after 9/11 this image became supplanted by one of sleeper agents who, unbeknownst to state authorities, conspired to attack Germany from within. Intent on taking the wind out of the Christian Democrats' sails, Schily put on hold immigration negotiations within the coalition and fast-tracked two emergency national security packages through the legislature. In order to win the support of the Greens, Schily took the critical step of conceding to the coalition partner's demands on questions of asylum policy and family unification in return for their votes on the anti-terror laws (Krause 2004). In early November, six weeks behind schedule, the cabinet signed off on the government's immigration bill.

A second event that jeopardized the future of immigration reform was the election of Bavarian premier Edmund Stoiber as the CDU/CSU's joint chancellor candidate. Stoiber's victory over centrist CDU candidate Angela Merkel marked a right turn in the Conservatives' impending electoral campaign. One of the party's most prominent immigration hardliners, Stoiber was known as a populist who did not shy away from exploiting immigration issues for electoral gain. The party leadership's ideological distance from the policy blueprint articulated by the Müller Commission could not have been bigger. From now on legislative debates clearly spilled over into the electoral arena.

The close to three months between the immigration bill's first reading in the government-controlled Bundestag and its passage on March 1, 2002 were marked by heated partisan disagreement. After the bill's first reading the Christian Democrats categorically rejected the bill, with only a few individual parliamentarians willing to compromise. Given that the government had already abandoned the Independent Commission's most far-reaching immigration proposal – a demographically driven points system whose operation did not rely on labor demand – there was no fundamental disagreement on the bill's basic goals. As the weekly news magazine *Die Zeit* commented, "most of the conflict is only about the technically and rhetorically important revisions of the relationship between rules and exceptions. Should one say: immigration is allowed, but only in quite a few cases? Or better: there is no immigration unless it is desperately needed?" (*Die Zeit* December 23, 2002, my translation).

For the most part disagreements on labor migration focused on the formal abolition of the recruitment stop, which, the opposition argued, would open the German labor market to foreign labor at a time of high unemployment (Kruse et al. 2003). The government replied that the proposed reform would only rationalize, rather than fundamentally alter, the legislative status quo. Not only were exceptions to the recruitment stop already commonplace, but admissions under the new points system would be small in size and would not apply to low-skilled labor, where domestic unemployment was highest. The Christian Democrats, however, continued to reject the bill on principle and argued that it would usher in a paradigmatic change they were not willing to support. In the words of CDU party whip Friedrich Merz in the debate leading up to the Bundestag vote, "Red-Green are not interested in limiting immigration, but in paradigmatic change. They want a multicultural nation of immigrants, we don't" (cited in Meier-Braun 2002, 132, my translation). Just a week before the Bundestag vote, the government made significant concessions in a last-ditch effort to gain the support of the Christian Democrats. Schily promised to delay the points system until 2010 and to make its implementation contingent on labor market demand. Furthermore, the new law's goal was to state "the management and limitation of immigration," rather than its pursuit. From the Conservatives' point of view, however, these concessions fell far short of the demand that the recruitment stop be retained and the points system deleted from the bill.

On the day of the Bundestag vote, chancellor candidate Stoiber reiterated his opposition to the points system and declared in a media interview: "Even today Germany is not a country of immigration. We do experience immigration, mainly for humanitarian reasons, but we are not a classical country of immigration" (cited in Meier-Braun 2002, 134, my translation). The same day, in a TV interview, former commission chair Müller vocalized the position of the moderate Conservative minority, "[o]bviously we need immigration, no one can refute this. And of course there is no denying that Germany is factually a country of immigration" (cited in Meier-Braun 2002, 134, my translation). On March 1, 2002, the immigration bill passed the Bundestag with the support of the Social Democrats and Greens. The CDU and CSU over-whelmingly opposed the bill, except for a handful of defectors, while the Liberals and Socialists abstained.

The Legislative and Judicial Arenas as Veto Points: The Bundesrat and the Federal Constitutional Court

After having successfully moved the bill through the Bundestag at break-neck speed, the government was still no closer to having secured the necessary Bundesrat majority. The coalition needed to move quickly given that elections in the *Land* of Saxony-Anhalt, which the incumbent Social Democratic government were expected to lose, were only weeks away. With the prospect of a further reduced Bundesrat voting bloc, the coali-tion partners decided to pursue the necessary Bundesrat majority by breaking one *Land* away from the Conservative voting bloc. Their target was Brandenburg, a *Land* which not only had the four votes necessary to pass the bill but was also governed by a grand coalition of SPD and CDU. Jörg Schönbohm, Brandenburg's interior minister and most senior Christian Democrat in the cabinet, had indicated that he might support the immigration bill, provided certain conditions were met (Green 2004). In late February the government acceded to his request and lowered the age ceiling for family unification. Meanwhile, the Christian Democratic leadership exerted immense pressure on Schönbohm to vote against the immigration bill. According to uncorroborated news reports, Stoiber went as far as to threaten to resign as chancellor candidate should Brandenburg vote in favor of the law. Regardless of whether or not this was the case, there is no question that a successful passage of the govern-ment's bill through the Bundesrat would have gotten Stoiber's federal election campaign off to the worst possible start.

The Bundesrat vote of March 22, 2002 turned out to be one of the most memorable votes in German parliamentary history. When, after five hours of debate, Brandenburg cast its vote, Interior Minister Jörg Schönbohm (CDU) voted against the bill, while Minister for Social Affairs Alwin Ziel (SPD) voted in favor. The speaker of the house reminded the delegates that votes had to be cast unanimously and turned to Brandenburg's premier, Manfred Stolpe (SPD), to clarify the *Land*'s vote. Stolpe confirmed that Brandenburg had voted in favor. A scandal erupted in the house as the opposition accused Stolpe of violating the constitution. Yet with Brandenburg's vote having been registered as in favor, the immigration bill had reached the critical vote threshold and passed the Bundesrat.

The Bundesrat commotion highlights the upper house's role as veto point in German federal politics. Given the frequency of *Land*-level elections – sixteen *Länder* governments are elected for mostly five-year terms – Bundesrat majorities are liable to change between federal elections. *Länder* voting patterns typically reflect partisan divisions at the federal level, and *Länder* coalition governments typically abstain if one of the partners is in opposition in the Bundestag. Since most *Länder* governments are coalitions, the threshold for legislative blockage can be surprisingly low. In the case of the immigration bill, had Brandenburg's vote been counted as an abstention – as the Constitutional Court later ruled it should have been – the veto threshold would have been just 25 percent of votes cast, with fewer "no" votes cast than "yes" votes and abstentions combined (Green 2004).

After the bill's Bundesrat passage, the opposition appealed to Federal President Johannes Rau not to sign the law. After having reviewed the bill for two months, and despite sustained protest by the opposition, Rau signed the bill into law. However, the government's victory was short-lived. Arguing that the law should be struck down on procedural grounds, the Conservative-ruled *Länder* initiated proceedings for abstract review with Germany's Federal Constitutional Court. In December, just two weeks before the law was scheduled to come into force, the court ruled in a split vote that Brandenburg's vote had not been cast unanimously, as required by the constitution, thereby striking down the immigration law. The parliamentary opposition had succeeded in using the Constitutional Court as a veto point to repeal the passage of an immigration law they had opposed for partisan reasons.

In May 2003, the Red-Green coalition – which had won a narrow electoral victory the previous fall – voted the unchanged bill through the Bundestag. The Christian Democrats, who were now in full control of the upper house, asked for a further 128 changes to be made, including the cancelation of the points system, which the government refused to agree to (Schmid-Drüner 2006). As expected, the bill was defeated in the Bundesrat and referred to the parliament's Mediation Committee. Negotiations dragged on for over a year, with labor migration as the main point of contention. Whereas the coalition partners, particularly the Greens, continued to push for the points system, the Christian Democrats insisted that visas for high-skilled immigrants be made contingent on an existing job offer. The bill was dealt a further blow with the Madrid train bombings in March 2004, which returned issues of national security to the top of the political agenda. The Christian Democrats now demanded that the immigration bill allow for expulsion based merely on suspicion of terrorist activities – a provision opposed by the Greens (Schmid-Drüner 2006).

After the exogenous shock of the Madrid terrorist attacks, the Social Democrats finally conceded to the opposition's demand to abandon the points system. The Greens responded by declaring the negotiations as failed, triggering a coalition crisis. In an unprecedented procedure, which came to be called the "Grand Immigration Coalition" (*Grosse Einwanderungskoalition*) (Busch 2007, 412), Schily formulated the disputed sections of the bill jointly with the leaders of the opposition, after assuring his coalition partner that each formulation would be jointly discussed afterwards. Delegating the negotiation process to a small circle of parliamentary leaders turned out to be successful, as Schily and the Christian Democrats obtained a settlement. In July 2004 – four years after the Independent Immigration Commission had begun its work – the new bill passed both houses of parliament.

As suggested by its title, the "2004 Act on the Residence, Economic Activity and Integration of Foreigners" bore little resemblance to the Interior Ministry's initial draft bill, not to mention the Independent Immigration Commission's report. While the law did provide for a long-overdue simplification of residency policies and formulated a more coherent approach to integration (see Triadafilopoulos 2012), with the elimination of the points system the main feature of the law had been lost. What had started out as a bill to open up Germany to high-skilled immigration resulted in a law that retained the 1973 recruitment stop, while adding three new exceptions, each of which was contingent on an actual job offer. First, the Green Card program was now folded into the new law, albeit with some important changes. Any high-skilled individual with a matching job offer in any sector can qualify and, if accepted, will be placed on a track to permanent residence.[28] Second, self-employed individuals can qualify for a temporary residence permit if their business is considered beneficial for the regional economy. If their business succeeds, they qualify for permanent residence after a three-year period. Third – and arguably the most innovative feature of the new law – foreign

---

[28] In addition, dependent spouses now have the immediate right to work. Under the old Green Card program, dependent spouses had to wait one year before gaining access to the labor market.

graduates of German universities can now have their resident permits extended by one year in order to find employment.

What accounts for the failure of what had promised to be a case of historic immigration reform? The pursuit of immigration reform in the 2000s was motivated by an evolving shift in immigration paradigms that had gained unexpected momentum with the Green Card debate, followed by the rise to power of the Federal Republic's first center-left Red-Green government. While the Greens had long supported a more open immigration policy, the Social Democrats, concerned about the possibility of popular backlash, had come to endorse the new paradigm much later and more tentatively. By contrast, the opposition Christian Democrats were, beyond the highly selective admission of small numbers of high-skilled workers, internally divided over the pursuit of immigration. The CSU in particular – holding on fast to its social conservatism and unwilling to forgo populist strategies to gain votes at the expense of policy liberalization – refused to endorse the new immigration paradigm. Thus, with a paradigm shift underway but still incomplete, the government's successful pursuit of immigration reform critically hinged on the absence of institutional veto points that would allow the Conservative opposition to obstruct reform. While the government was in firm control of the Bundestag, over time the Bundesrat came to constitute a formidable veto point in the legislative arena. Not only did *Land*-level elections deliver disproportionate gains for the opposition, but – with the immigration bill lagging behind schedule and in anticipation of the upcoming federal election – political debates spilled over from the legislative to the electoral arena. After the opposition failed at blocking reform in the Bundesrat, it turned to the judicial arena as the last viable veto point.

The failure of the Independent Immigration Commission to facilitate a bipartisan consensus on immigration reform was clearly rooted in the ideological opposition of social conservatives among the Christian Democrats. Over time, the party's conservative wing gained in power as Edmund Stoiber won the CDU/CSU's chancellor candidacy and immigration debates became securitized in the aftermath of 9/11 and the Madrid train bombings. As a result, starting in the fall of 2001, constant election-eering turned the initially modest partisan disagreement over labor migration into an unbridgeable gulf, resulting in an immigration law that had been gutted of its original features. Far from being a historic milestone, the Immigration Act of 2004 reiterated the centrality of the decades-old recruitment stop and continued the long-established (and much reviled) practice of admitting immigrants on the basis of regulatory exemptions.

Postscript

Since the 2004 Immigration Act, the admission of high-skilled immigrants to Germany has undergone some legislative updating in response to policy developments at the European level. Passed under a Grand Coalition government led by Christian Democratic moderate Angela Merkel, a first change came with the 2007 Act to Implement Migration and Asylum Directives of the European Union, which liberalized the admission of self-employed immigrants by lowering both minimum investment and job creation requirements.[29] As a result, the immigration of self-employed third-country nationals nearly doubled to a (still modest) average of 1,400 entrants per year (Bundesamt für Migration und Flüchtlinge 2015, 2016). In a second development, the 2012 Act to Implement the Highly Qualified Professionals Directive of the EU instituted the Blue Card as a replacement for the Immigration Act's highly skilled immigration category. The EU Blue Card is of particular significance as it constitutes the first directive on third-country labor immigration to be adopted by the European Union (Cerna 2013). With the passage of the Blue Card Directive, the European Union for the first time features as a policy arena in the politics of economic immigration policy making (see Chapter 7).

With the size and conditions attached to Blue Card admissions left at the discretion of the member states, Germany opted for a liberal interpretation of the directive. Whereas the 2004 Immigration Act limited high-skilled immigration to in-demand occupations, the Blue Card opened up immigration to any high-skilled worker with a job offer above a certain salary threshold. Moreover, for high-skilled workers from in-demand occupations, salary thresholds were lowered further and the requirement that German and EU workers enjoyed hiring priority removed. As had been the case with the treatment of high-skilled workers under the 2004 Act, Blue Card holders were offered favorable residence and family reunification conditions.[30] These liberalizations quickly showed their intended effect. Prior to the Blue Card program, annual admissions of high-skilled workers remained below 370. With the Blue Card program, admissions climbed to 6,800 by 2015, representing an

---

[29] Self-employed immigrants now are required to invest €500,000 rather than €1,000,000, and to create five, rather than ten, new positions.

[30] Blue Card holders can transition to permanent residency after only three years (and two years if they demonstrate strong German skills). Accompanying spouses do not have to pass the pre-entry language tests required of most family immigrants.

eighteenfold increase in high-skilled admissions in the course of four years (Bundesamt für Migration und Flüchtlinge 2016).

These increases in immigration took place in an overwhelmingly depoliticized context, supported by a new elite discourse of Germany's "welcome culture" (*Willkommenskultur*). Intended to make Germany a more attractive destination for high-skilled workers, the term "welcome culture refers chiefly to qualified immigrants, who are welcome today as a result of demographic and economic needs. It decidedly does not refer to those who are unwelcome, yet we are obliged to accept for reasons of EU law" (Bade 2014, cited in Taunert and Turton 2017, 36). Thus, until the refugee crisis of 2015, public restrictionism was on the wane, with only 21 percent of Germans in 2014 agreeing that there were "too many immigrants" (The German Marshall Fund of the United States September 10, 2014, 9). As numbers of asylum seekers skyrocketed in 2015, however, popular backlash followed, fueling the electoral success of the far-right Alternative for Germany (*Alternative für Deutschland*), which entered the Bundestag in 2017 with close to 13 percent of the popular vote. While Chancellor Angela Merkel had sought to expand the concept of "welcome culture" to include refugees, the discourse could not withstand the popular concerns triggered by the arrival of historic number of asylum seekers.

In 2019 the Grand Coalition government passed the Skilled Worker Immigration Act (*Fachkräfteeinwanderungsgesetz*), which extended many of the preferential conditions attached to the immigration of highly skilled workers to that of skilled workers. Thus, third-country nationals with a recognized qualification in any occupation could now enter and work in Germany, provided they either had a job offer or were able to secure a job offer within six months. Additionally, Germans and EU nationals would no longer receive hiring priority over qualified third-country nationals. The passage of the Skilled Worker Immigration Act was the result of drawn out negotiations between the coalition partners – interrupted by the 2015 refugee crisis – of legislation that could respond to sustained employer demand for foreign skilled labor (in particular in health care, the care industry, and the trades) while securing the support of both coalition partners. On the one hand, the bill accommodated the demand of Christian Democrats to separate labor migration from asylum migration. Access to a two-year work permit for certain rejected asylum seekers with occupational qualifications would be regulated under a separate Employment Toleration Law (*Beschäftigungsduldungsgesetz*). Social Democrats, on the other hand, won a symbolic battle over legal terminology. Instead of the original term *Zuwanderung*, the law's name was changed to *Einwanderung*, signaling an acceptance that Germany is and will remain a country of immigration. As SPD parliamentarian Lars Castelluci declared during the bill's final debate: "Today is a day that will enter history. Germany openly admits for all to see: 'We are a country of immigration'" (Stratmann-Mertens July 6, 2019, my translation).

While the bill's title suggests that the paradigmatic shift that began with the Green Card program but was never embraced by social conservatives might finally be completed, the actual impact of the new law is likely to be modest. Government officials estimated that the law would increase skilled worker admissions from 28,000 to 53,000[31] annually (Stratmann-Mertens July 6, 2019). Because only workers whose foreign credentials are recognized by German authorities – a notoriously high hurdle – will be able to work and remain, its impact on immigration is likely to remain small. More importantly, until Germany passes a new comprehensive immigration act that embraces the new paradigm, the gradual opening up of high-skilled – and, more recently, skilled – immigration continues to take place in a context of legal exceptionality. Because the 2004 Immigration Act's recruitment stop continues to frame permanent economic immigration as an exception to the rule, the paradigmatic embrace of Germany as a country of immigration remains incomplete.

CONCLUSION

This chapter has examined Germany's politics of economic immigration policy making over the course of six decades. Whereas the 1950s and 1960s were defined by a reopening and historically unparalleled expansion of temporary foreign worker recruitment, the 1970s and 1980s were marked by a recruitment hiatus under the now officially articulated "non-immigration" paradigm. Temporary recruitment channels were reopened in the 1990s, but with important caveats. In contrast to the postwar decades, recruitment policies were firmly premised on rotation and ensured that worker recruitment would remain reversible and operate within the confines of the non-immigration paradigm. It was only in the 2000s that the non-immigration paradigm came under fundamental challenge, when policy makers sought – with limited success – to shift

---

[31] In addition to 25,000 family members.

economic recruitment from temporary to permanent immigration. In examining the paradigmatic tension between temporary and permanent economic immigration policy in the Federal Republic, three patterns stand out.

First, among the countries examined in this book, Germany shares with Switzerland a comparatively low level of diplomatic insulation (Table 4.1). Given the historical legacies of the Holocaust and Nazi Germany's military aggression, the Federal Republic's political survival depended on its successful diplomatic reintegration into the postwar Western community. The creation of the postwar guest worker system was in significant measure driven by pressure from European states who favored labor emigration as a solution to domestic unemployment. Diplomatic pressure not only served as a trigger for Germany's first recruitment treaty in 1955, it also shaped subsequent negotiations – in particular the 1964 recruitment treaty with Turkey, where the lack of diplomatic insulation prevented the imposition of restrictive conditions despite emerging anxieties about immigrant settlement. Finally, diplomatic pressure played a critical role in the recruitment of project-tied workers in the 1990s. This time, however, it was not so much Germany's international reputation that was at stake but rather the preservation of regional stability at the end of the Cold War.

A second characteristic of German economic immigration policy until the early 2000s is its depoliticized nature and locus in the executive arena (Table 4.1). Until the 2004 Immigration Act, economic admissions took the form of bilateral treaties and regulations that constitutionally were not required to pass through the legislative arena. Executive-centered policy making not only amplified policy makers' lack of diplomatic insulation, it also reinforced their popular insulation. Until the 1990s, German immigration politics was marked by a degree of depoliticization only rivaled by that enjoyed by Canadian policy makers. Depoliticization was a reflection of postwar German politics more broadly, as the urgency of postwar reconstruction, paired with the destruction of democratic civil society under totalitarianism, did not allow for popular mobilization on a wide range of policy issues. By the 1990s, however, political parties had adopted distinct issue positions on immigration policy, and public debate on immigration had become a staple of German political life. Thus, by the time the left sought to institutionalize a new immigration paradigm with the 2004 Immigration Act, German immigration politics was marked by a degree of partisan politicization that drastically reduced the popular insulation of policy makers and turned the legislative and electoral arenas into viable veto points.

TABLE 4.1 *German case studies summary*

Policy episode	Policy choice	Policy arenas	Popular insulation	Interest group insulation	Diplomatic insulation
Case study 1					
Postwar guest worker recruitment treaties	*Liberalization*	Executive arena	High	Intermediate	Low
1973 recruitment stop	*Paradigmatic restriction*	Executive arena	Intermediate	High	High
Case study 2					
New guest worker programs of the 1990s	*Selective liberalization*	Executive arena	High	Medium	Low
Protectionist reforms in mid-1990s	*Selective restriction*	Executive arena Legislative arena	Intermediate	Intermediate	Low
Case study 3					
2000 Green Card Program	*Selective liberalization*	Executive arena Popular arena	Intermediate	Intermediate	Intermediate
Case study 4					
2004 Immigration Act	*Failed paradigmatic liberalization*	Executive arena Legislative arena Judicial arena	Low	Medium	High

Finally, the case of the 2004 Immigration Act illustrates the challenge of paradigmatic policy liberalization in contexts where a longstanding paradigm opposes, rather than embraces, immigrant settlement. Whereas paradigmatic liberalization in the settler colonial states grappled with the question of *who* to admit, policy makers in guest worker states faced the question of *whether* to admit immigrants. When elite support for a pro-immigration paradigm had finally begun to crystallize, the window for depoliticized, executive-driven policy making had closed. Consequently, policy debates were marked by partisan electioneering and, ultimately, policy spillover into the legislative, electoral, and judicial arenas. While the recruitment stop remains part of German immigration law, subsequent policy developments, in particular the incorporation of the EU Blue Card into German law, have progressively expanded the range of policy exemptions. Importantly, these high-skilled exemptions have institutionalized de facto permanent economic immigration and thus continue to challenge and undermine Germany's non-immigration paradigm.

5

The Making of Canadian Immigration Policy

Explaining Economic and Family Admissions

This chapter examines the evolution of Canadian economic and family immigration policy through three case studies starting from the 1960s to the 2010s.[1] We begin our analysis with the period of 1962–1976, which marks the progressive replacement of Canada's race-based immigration system with an admissions policy premised on skills and family ties.[2] This paradigmatic shift was propelled by the government's lack of diplomatic insulation while at the same time being facilitated by its popular insulation. First enacted in the form of executive regulations in 1962 and 1967, the new skills-based immigration paradigm became institutionalized and legitimized in the legislative arena with the passage of the 1976 Immigration Act.

The chapter's second case study examines a succession of policy reforms from the mid-1980s to the early 2000s that changed the size and composition of Canadian immigrant admissions. First, the reforms shifted the logic of economic admissions from the principle of occupational demand to that of human capital. In a second development, a politically insulated executive shifted the balance from family to economic admissions, establishing an immigration system fundamentally defined by high-skilled immigrant selection. Once again, these policy shifts were passed largely unnoticed by the Canadian public within the safety of the

---

[1] The chapter focuses exclusively on policy making at the federal level. It therefore does not examine Quebec's policy regime, which operates with a significant degree of autonomy from the rest of Canada.

[2] It also provided for humanitarian admissions – an immigration stream that is excluded from this analysis.

executive arena in the form of regulatory reform. Only after a subsequent process of elite consultation and debate did these changes become more broadly legitimized with the passage of the 2001 Immigration and Refugee Protection Act.

Our third case study covers the years of neoconservative rule from 2006 to 2015, when a newly constituted Conservative Party enacted a series of far-reaching changes to Canadian economic and family immigration policy. Reflecting the Conservatives' market-liberal agenda, the government shifted the balance of immigration from permanent to temporary economic admissions and changed the logic of points system admissions from human capital to employer demand. Not long after, policy makers sought to rein in family immigration by inflicting drastic cuts to parent and grandparent sponsorship. While previous cases of legislative reform were based on extensive elite consultation and consensus building, in this third case study policy makers scaled down the process of elite consultation and instead focused on reshaping Canada's immigration system through the strategic exploitation of its executive policy-making powers.

FROM RACE-BASED TO SKILLS- AND FAMILY TIE-BASED IMMIGRATION: 1962–1976

In the early 1960s Canada became the first settler colonial state to turn its back on the principle of race-based immigrant admissions. The 1962 Regulations sounded the death knell for the White Canada policy and ushered in an immigration regime that was to be premised on the principle of skills-based and family tie-based immigrant selection. Canada's embrace of source country universalism came as a response to sustained diplomatic pressure to end ethnoracial discrimination. Driven by low diplomatic insulation, policy reform was facilitated by the government's high popular insulation. Yet as long as the pursuit of paradigmatic reform took the form of executive regulation only, it could not garner the broad-based legitimacy necessary for its institutionalization. It was only after the new immigration paradigm was affirmed in the legislative arena with the passage of the 1976 Immigration Act that Canada's new skills-based immigration regime could become politically embedded.

The 1962 Immigration Regulations: Policy Liberalization under Diplomatic Pressure

When Liberal Prime Minister Mackenzie King delivered his keynote speech on immigration in the House of Commons in 1947 (see

Chapter 1), he affirmed the basic principles that had guided Canadian policy since its inception. While immigration was integral to the country's continued economic and demographic development, King argued, immigrant selection had to preserve the basic character of Canadian society. Accordingly, the reopening of immigration channels after the hiatus of World War II would necessitate the continued exclusion of Asian immigrants, as "[l]arge-scale immigration from the Orient would change the fundamental composition of the Canadian population" (Parai 1975, 452). Some years later, King's Secretary, J. W. Pickersgill, in his role as Minister of Citizenship and Immigration, elaborated on this race-based immigration paradigm:

> We tried to select as immigrants those who will have to change their ways least in order to adapt themselves to Canadian life and to contribute to the development of the Canadian nation. This is why entry into Canada is virtually free to citizens of the United Kingdom, the United States, and France, so long as they have good health and good character. ... That is why a deliberate preference is shown for immigrants from countries with political and social institutions similar to our own.
>
> (Parliament of Canada 1955, 1254)

The principle of ethnic stratification was reflected in an admissions policy that distinguished between three classes of immigrants. Formalized with the 1952 Immigration Act, the policy actively recruited as "preferred immigrants" citizens of the United States, Britain, and Northern Europe. Below this group, in the "nonpreferred" category, were immigrants from Southern and Eastern Europe, who were to be admitted only during times of economic growth. Finally, in the bottom category, "excluded" non-white immigrants from outside of Europe were categorically denied admission (Triadafilopoulos 2013a).

While Mackenzie King's immigration speech heralded a comfortable return to the pre-World War II status quo, few could have anticipated that just a decade after the 1952 Immigration Act's passage, Canadian immigration policy would change in ways so fundamental that it would bear little resemblance to the race-based system of old. By moving from the principle of race-based to skills-based selection, the 1962 Immigration Regulations came to mark a paradigmatic watershed in Canada's immigration history. What facilitated this radical, and unprecedented, departure from a policy regime that had been institutionalized for seventy-five years? Why were Canada's reforms more far reaching than those of the United States, even when the latter followed suit soon thereafter in rejecting the principle of race-based immigrant selection (see

Chapter 6)? Following Fitzgerald and Cook-Martín (2014) and, with some modifications, Triadafilopoulos[3] (2013a), I argue that the government's decision to abandon the national origins principle was first and foremost the result of Canada's lack of diplomatic insulation. The rejection of overt ethnoracial discrimination reflected the diplomatic imperatives of a country that was aspiring to become a global middle power in a world in which the horrors of the Holocaust, the rapid spread of decolonization, and the emergence of a global human rights regime had delegitimized the practice of racial and ethnic discrimination. Because Canadian policy makers operated in a context of low diplomatic insulation, the government's continued reliance on racial criteria for immigrant selection threatened to undermine its ambitions in the area of foreign relations. At the same time that diplomatic pressure to end racial selection created a powerful impetus for abandoning the White Canada policy, popular insulation served as a necessary condition for liberalization to be politically feasible.

Policy Making under Low Diplomatic Insulation

With the end of World War II, Canada stepped out of Britain's shadow to emerge onto the international stage as a global middle power. Its foreign policy quickly came to be defined by humanitarian and peacekeeping interventions abroad, a commitment held firm across a succession of Liberal and Conservative governments and embodied in the country's unwavering support for the United Nations. Canada quickly came to play a central part in the United Nations' peacekeeping program, which was proposed in 1957 by prominent diplomat Lester Pearson, and was given a nonpermanent seat in the UN Security Council in 1948–9 and again in 1958–9.[4] Besides its active involvement in UN diplomacy, Canadian foreign policy was also profoundly influenced by its membership in the British Commonwealth, which witnessed the rapid progression of decolonization as most of the empire's nonwhite colonies gained independence between 1947 and 1964.

---

[3] Triadafilopoulos attributes the decision to a combination of international and domestic normative pressures. This analysis, in contrast, considers international pressure as the primary impetus for policy reform in the 1960s.

[4] At the time, Lester Pearson was secretary of state for external affairs and the president of the UN General Assembly. His proposal for peacekeeping forces was an attempt to deal with the Suez crisis – an effort for which he was recognized with the Nobel Peace Prize. A firm believer in diplomacy and multilateralism, Pearson would later become prime minister of Canada.

From the late 1940s into the early 1960s, the two pillars of Canadian foreign policy – Canada's rise as a global middle power with a commitment to peacekeeping and multilateralism, and its membership in the British Commonwealth – came under increasing conflict with the principle of race-based immigrant selection. Canada's diplomatic corps bore the brunt of this clash as the newly independent Commonwealth members openly castigated Canada for its racially discriminatory immigration policies. For example, after gaining independence in 1947, India, among the Asian Commonwealth countries, made its membership in the Commonwealth contingent on other members revoking their anti-Indian immigration exclusions. In 1948, Indian Prime Minister Nehru visited Canada to lobby for the creation of small quotas for Indian nationals. The Canadian government responded by establishing annual quotas for a total of 290 Indians, Pakistanis, and Ceylonese, and, in 1957, doubled the Indian quota from 150 to 300 and provided quota exemptions to immediate family members of Canadian citizens from India (Fitzgerald and Cook-Martín 2014, 173).

These exemptions were clearly motivated by a concern for Canada's bilateral and multilateral relations. As expressed in an unpublished report from the Department of External Affairs:

There can be little doubt that friendly relations between Canada and these three countries [India, Pakistan, and Ceylon] as well as China and Japan have been hampered considerably in light of its new international obligations ... As a member of the United Nations, Canada has assumed an unqualified obligation to eliminate racial discrimination in its legislation. It can be argued that racial restriction in immigration violates this United Nations commitment.

(Lauren 1996, 242)

Similarly, Canada faced sustained pressure to end discrimination from the Caribbean Commonwealth countries. Canadian consular officials in the Caribbean conveyed their complaints to the Department of External Affairs, which in turn lobbied the Department of Citizenship and Immigration to open up immigration channels to West Indian nationals (Triadafilopoulos 2013a). Throughout the 1950s and into the 1960s, Canadian diplomats warned that the government's progressive positioning in foreign affairs would be used by foreign observers to shame Canada for its racist immigration policy (Triadafilopoulos 2013a). In 1961, for instance, Progressive Conservative Prime Minister Diefenbaker's principled anti-racist stance on the question of South Africa's Commonwealth membership further threatened to expose Canada's moral duplicity. As the only white Commonwealth country to do so, Canada had joined nonwhite members at the Commonwealth Prime

Minister's Conference in opposing South African membership because of its apartheid system[5] (Freeman 1997).

We can thus sum up with Fitzgerald and Cook-Martín that "[i]t is clear from both public and private statements of leading policymakers from the late 1940s to the 1960s that ethnic selection would have to be sacrificed due to Canada's place in the Commonwealth and the United Nations" (Fitzgerald and Cook-Martín 2014, 184). Because Canada's aspirations as a new global middle power were based on its role in multilateral institutions such as the Commonwealth and the United Nations, successive Progressive Conservative and Liberal governments were deeply susceptible to diplomatic pressure. Importantly, Canada's lack of diplomatic insulation occurred in an international environment where the geopolitical standing of non-Western countries of emigration was on the rise – by 1961, Asian, African, and Latin American countries accounted for two-thirds of the UN General Assembly – and where multilateral organizations espoused principles of nondiscrimination and global human rights, discrediting the ideological foundations of Canada's immigration policy.

In 1961, the same year that Diefenbaker made his principled stance on the question of South Africa's Commonwealth membership, parliament passed the Canadian Bill of Rights, which spelled out basic human rights to be held by all without regard to race, national origin, religion, or language. Just months later, the cabinet ended formal racial discrimination in immigrant selection (Fitzgerald and Cook-Martín 2014, 176). This decision was formalized in 1962 with an Order-in-Council. For the first time in Canadian history, immigration policy would be based on skill, rather than race or national origin. The 1962 Regulations radically broke with the past by abolishing the provision of preferred countries of immigration and opening up economic immigration to anyone with the necessary skills. As Minister of Immigration and Citizenship Ellen Fairclough remarked to parliament, under the new policy

any suitably qualified person from any part of the world can be considered for immigration to Canada entirely on his own merits without regard to his [*sic*] race, colour, national origin or the country from which he comes. This is a substantial advance over the former regulations in that the selection of immigrants, insofar as selection on the basis of skills is concerned, will be done without discrimination of any kind.

(Parliament of Canada January 19, 1962, 9)

---

[5] When it became clear that South Africa's application would be rejected, Prime Minister Verwoerd withdrew the application.

Despite this radical liberalization of economic recruitment policy, however, the government did not fully eliminate racial discrimination in family admissions. Even though the class of relatives eligible for sponsorship now covered nationals of all countries, the preferred country principle was abolished only for immediate family members. In other words, Canadians' right to sponsor *extended* family members[6] continued to be based on racial criteria and was extended only to relatives originating from Europe and other established sending countries in the western hemisphere.

Policy Making under High Popular Insulation

The substance of the 1962 Regulations, as well as the way in which they were brought about, is instructive of the constraints facing Canadian policy makers in the postwar decades. One of the most significant features of the 1962 immigration reforms is the fact that they took the form of an executive Order-in-Council rather than, as broadly expected, statutory legislation. Ever since the Immigration Act of 1869, which delegated extensive authority to the cabinet (Triadafilopoulos 2012), Canadian immigration has been primarily regulated through Orders-in-Council.[7] These are issued by the cabinet, are approved by the governor general, and do not require full parliamentary assent.[8] As past immigration minister, Jack Pickersgill, stated after Minister of Immigration and Citizenship Fairclough tabled the 1962 Regulations in the House of Commons:

> The reason why such a fundamental change of policy could be made without parliament's approval is that the real control over immigration has always been at the Cabinet's discretion. The Immigration Act in practice leaves the government free to do almost anything it wants.
> (Parliament of Canada February 27, 1962, 1332)

As a result, Canada's longstanding tradition of executive dominance in immigration policy making had engendered a politics of immigration that rarely engaged the legislative arena. Parliamentary debate on questions of immigration was rare, a pattern that was further reinforced by executive

---

[6] Children over the age of 21, married children, siblings, and unmarried orphaned nieces and nephews.

[7] Order-in-Council can take the form of notices of appointments, regulations, or legislative orders authorized by existing legislation.

[8] Even to date there have been only five major immigration acts, passed in 1869, 1919, 1952, 1976, and 2001. While occasionally amended in parliament, these acts typically function for long periods of time by being regularly updated through Orders-in-Council (Simmons 2010).

strategy. For instance, the Department of Immigration for many years produced annual immigration figures on the last day of the parliamentary session in order to avoid parliamentary debate (Kelley and Trebilcock 1998).

Yet despite longstanding executive dominance on matters of immigration, in his campaign leading up to the Progressive Conservatives' 1957 electoral victory Diefenbaker had promised that "[t]he Immigration Act would be overhauled – Canada must populate or perish" (Hawkins 1988, 127). In 1959, Fairclough assured parliament of the government's commitment to a new immigration act. Two years later her department decided to split reform into two stages: Citizenship and Immigration would issue a new set of regulations, to be followed by a new immigration bill. Yet work on a legislative draft was quickly abandoned, and the department settled for regulatory reform instead (Hawkins 1988). Unsurprisingly the cabinet's decision to adjourn legislative reform came under biting criticism from parliament. After Fairclough had tabled the new regulations in the House, Liberal member of parliament Leon Crestohl chastised the government for reneging on its commitment to legislative reform:

I find no precedent for a government dealing so evasively with such a serious matter when a different course had been promised not only to parliament but to the people of Canada. The production of a new set of immigration regulations instead of the revision of the Immigration Act is, I consider, an affront to the rights of Parliament, to the press of Canada and indeed to the people of the entire country.

(Parliament of Canada February 27, 1962, 1327)

Why did the Diefenbaker government commit to rewriting the 1952 Immigration Act only to renege on its promise once drafting had gotten under way? There is little reason to doubt that the government's commitment to reform was genuine, given that the policy status quo threatened to compromise Canada's foreign policy goals. As we saw earlier, government officials were acutely aware that the White Canada policy defied the interests of immigrant-sending states in the Global South, who now held a majority of seats in prominent multilateral organizations. Given that the elimination of overt discrimination from its immigration policy would amount to a rejection of Canada's longstanding paradigm of race-based immigration, a new immigration act clearly constituted the most appropriate mode of reform.

At the same time, however, the pursuit of immigration reform in the legislative arena stood to compromise the government's ability to retain full control over the reform process and fast-track policy change to deflect mounting international pressure. The biggest threat posed by legislative reform was the mobilization of the Canadian public, who held deeply ambivalent, if not unequivocally racist, attitudes toward the admission of non-European immigrants. Ambivalence toward universal admissions even extended to organized interests. For instance, a survey of interest groups conducted by the Royal Commission on Canada's Economic Prospects in 1953 and 1955 revealed a lack of consensus among domestic interests on the criteria by which to select immigrants. While some trade unions supported an anti-discriminatory policy, several unions from British Columbia – a longstanding hotbed of anti-Asian agitation – argued that "[i]f we are to maintain our cultural heritage it is essential that the present racial composition be maintained" (Fitzgerald and Cook-Martín 2014, 175). The Canadian Manufacturers' Association similarly demanded that "steps should be taken to assure that a responsible proportion of future immigrants shall be of British or Northern and Western European stock" (Fitzgerald and Cook-Martín 2014, 175). Similarly, even though the Canadian Council of Churches and the Canadian Jewish Congress supported the principle of nondiscrimination (Triadafilopoulos 2013a), the United Church of Canada remained ambivalent on the issue of racial selection, arguing that while "there should not be a colour bar," Canada nevertheless must steer clear of the problems associated with Puerto Ricans in New York City (Fitzgerald and Cook-Martín 2014, 175).

Concern about the possibility of a restrictionist turn is clearly reflected in the justification of the cabinet's decision to end racial selection through an Order-in-Council, rather than legislation, given by Minister Fairclough:

It is much easier to be more restrictive in drawing legislation than it is to be more flexible, and that was partially the problem which confronted us. . . . I should have liked to bring in a new act complete with regulations at one time, but it became evident very soon in our study of the act that this was probably not a wise course. Therefore we took the alternative, and we have brought in regulations, which I submit to this house are workable, flexible and will permit the entry of many persons who were heretofore denied entry to Canada.

(Parliament of Canada February 27, 1962, 1334–5)

This assessment was affirmed by David Corbett, one of Canada's most prominent immigration experts at the time, who congratulated Fairclough for placing "immigration policy in its proper context as part of foreign policy" and welcomed the new regulations as a strategically wise move that had allowed for policy reform that was more progressive than public opinion, and that therefore could not have been achieved with a new immigration act (Knowles 2007, 188).

Canada's longstanding tradition of immigration policy making through Orders-in-Council allowed the Diefenbaker government to circumvent the legislative arena and enact paradigmatic reform through regulation alone. Aided by the reform's initial limited impact, policy makers were thus able to ensure that the end of White Canada would attract little public attention. This top-down enactment of paradigmatic policy change was conditioned on the popular insulation of a government that, with its low diplomatic insulation, was under intense international pressure to liberalize its immigration policy. While members of parliament objected to the government's reneging on its earlier promise of statutory reform, the substance of the new regulations – the rejection of racial selection – was broadly welcomed by legislators of all partisan stripes for the message it sent to the international community. In the words of New Democrat Harold Winch:

We welcome anything, whether it be by legislative enactment or regulatory change, that is going to mean the placing of the citizenship and immigration laws of Canada on a basis which will better demonstrate what democracy means to our country, our peoples, our governments and legislative bodies. We welcome anything that will demonstrate to the world that we are completely honest in our position on immigration; that it should be on a non-discriminatory basis not influenced by colour, sex, creed or the country from which these people come.
(Parliament of Canada January 19, 1962, 12)

Moving from procedure to substance, it is instructive to look at the Order-in-Council's substantive limitations. While policy makers struck all racially discriminatory provisions from economic admissions, they retained a preference for European family immigrants. This incongruence reflected a compromise between the diplomatic imperative of nondiscrimination, on the one hand, and the widespread view that an influx of non-European and largely unskilled immigrants would harm Canada's domestic interests, on the other. An internal memorandum from Deputy Minister Davidson, written just two weeks before the new regulations were introduced to the House, stated:

Our prime objective in the proposed revision is to eliminate all discrimination based on colour, race, or creed. This means that, if we continue to allow Greeks, Poles, Italians, Portuguese and other Europeans to bring in the wide range of relatives presently admissible, we will have to do the same for Japanese, Chinese, Indians, Pakistanis, Africans, persons from the Arab world, the West Indies and so forth. The only possible result of this would be a substantially larger number of unskilled close relatives from these parts of the world to add to the influx of unskilled close relatives from Europe.

(Hawkins 1988, 130)

The memo continues by justifying the department's decision, outlined in the draft regulations, to curtail family unification rights for all – including Europeans – as a necessary compromise between the principle of non-discrimination, on the one hand, and the imperative to limit the entry of unskilled non-European immigrants, on the other. However, when Fairclough announced the new regulations just two weeks later, it became apparent that the department had retreated from its decision to universally curtail sponsorship rights. Instead, concerned with the political fallout of depriving European immigrants of sponsorship rights, the new policy retained racially stratified family sponsorship provisions.

The government's concern with preempting political backlash reflects the lessons learned from a sponsorship scandal just three years earlier, when the Diefenbaker cabinet had issued an Order-in-Council to restrict family sponsorship to immediate family members (Hawkins 1988). The 1959 Order had been driven by a mounting backlog of sponsorship applications at a time when high unemployment coincided with rapidly increasing family immigration from Southern Europe. The cabinet no doubt was aware that drastic curtailment of family sponsorship rights that had long been institutionalized for European immigrants would not be met with popular support. Thus, the cabinet issued the order without advance notice, even neglecting to mention it in the parliamentary debate on the department's immigration estimates (Hawkins 1988). However, the strategy misfired and all hell broke loose as both the Liberal opposition and the Progressive Conservative Ontario government, joined by some ethnic groups, criticized the department for this "unnecessary and cruel act" against the Italian community (Parliament of Canada April 15, 1959, 2710–15). Recognizing her strategic error, Minister of Immigration and Citizenship Fairclough rescinded the order almost immediately.

What conclusions can we draw from this instance of failed executive policy making? First and foremost, the sponsorship scandal stands out as an exception to the rule of remarkably unconstrained immigration policy making by the Canadian executive. Freda Hawkins, a close observer of Canada's postwar immigration politics, observes that the Canadian cabinet has typically confronted few domestic pressures pertaining to immigration, with two exceptions: advocacy efforts in individual immigration cases, and, on matters of policy, sponsorship rights (Hawkins 1988). The issue of family unification stands out in that it directly impinges on the interests of all immigrant communities and thus allowed ethnic groups in Canada who – especially when compared to their US counterparts – at the time were still too heterogeneous, poorly organized, and lacking in government access to pool their resources and collectively act as interest groups (Hawkins 1988). Thus, the government's otherwise relatively high interest group insulation was weakened on questions of family sponsorship.

Yet the sponsorship controversies of the late 1950s and, as we are about to see, the mid-1960s cannot be solely attributed to interest group mobilization, which, in comparative perspective, remained modest. Instead much of the Immigration Department's political vulnerability resulted from the intersection of two contextual factors unrelated to interest group lobbying that reflected the lack of institutionalization of immigration politics at the time. First, the immigration portfolio's lack of stature in cabinet meant that immigration ministers received little political backup during times of scandal or controversy. Second, the department's relationship to parliament was marked by deeply entrenched mutual hostility. Until the late 1960s parliament took little interest in immigration policy, and regular communication between senior immigration officials and parliament was close to nonexistent. When members of the two branches interacted it typically concerned individual cases, which made for highly acrimonious relations (Hawkins 1988). Constitutionally empowered to circumvent the legislative arena yet politically vulnerable to parliamentary opposition because of the absence of cabinet support, immigration ministers throughout the 1950s and 1960s continued to stumble over the issue of family sponsorship.

The 1967 Points System and the Principle of Skills-Based Admission

When the Liberals came to power in 1963, Prime Minister Lester Pearson was quickly confronted with the shortcomings of the 1962 Regulations. Most pressingly, the continued use of national origin as the basis for family sponsorship continued to attract criticism both at home and abroad. Notably, beyond the question of family immigration the regulatory changes had not resulted in any apparent shift toward non-European immigration, even for the economic stream. Not only were economic admissions tightly controlled, but the absence of consular offices in many parts of the world presented nearly insurmountable hurdles for visa applicants from the Global South (Triadafilopoulos 2012). Diplomatic pressures for the full elimination of racial discrimination in immigrant admission weighed particularly heavily on Pearson, a career diplomat with high ambitions in the area of foreign affairs. Speaking to the press during a visit to Jamaica in late 1965, Pearson committed to removing any remaining racial discrimination from Canadian immigration policy "in fact as well as in theory" (Triadafilopoulos 2013a, 28). Yet while Pearson could be confident that the elimination of the remaining vestiges of racism could be achieved within the safety of popular insulation through regulatory reform, doing so would still require the government to grapple with the longstanding challenge of family sponsorship – an issue that Immigration Minister John Robert Nicholson, speaking to the Cabinet Committee on Immigration, declared to be the most problematic aspect of immigration policy (Suyama 1994). There was no question that the elimination of racial discrimination from the 1962 Regulations would require a return to the drawing board on the question of how to devise sponsorship rules that were both nondiscriminatory and politically acceptable.

Despite policy makers' preference for keeping family sponsorship out of the legislative arena, the lessons taught by the Progressive Conservatives' sponsorship scandal suggested that the success of sponsorship reform hinged on the government's ability to persuade parliament and attentive publics of its merits. Thus, Prime Minister Pearson's first step toward reforming the 1962 Regulations was to commission a policy document from the Department of Citizenship and Immigration (soon to be reorganized into the Department of Manpower and Immigration) for consideration by a Special Joint Committee of the Senate and House of Commons on Immigration. The resultant White Paper on Immigration, tabled in parliament in 1966 by Minister of Manpower and Immigration Jean Marchand, clearly articulated the case for an immigration policy that "must involve no discrimination by reason of race, colour or religion" (Canada Department of Manpower and Immigration October 1966, 5–6). The document reiterated that ethnic selection "creates strong resentments in international relations" (Canada Department of Manpower and Immigration October 1966, 17) and affirmed the 1962 Regulations in their emphasis on the need to recruit skilled immigrants. The White Paper argued in favor of integrating immigration and labor market policy with a view to long-term economic development: "A selective immigration policy today must be planned as a steady policy of recruitment based on long-term considerations of economic growth" (Canada Department of Manpower and Immigration October 1966, 12).

Deputy Minister Tom Kent was determined to reform the sponsorship system in order to preempt an expansion of the unskilled labor force, and to do so "without inciting political controversy" (Kelley and Trebilcock 1998, 353). Instead of discriminating on the basis of national origin, the White Paper proposed to limit family immigration by differentiating on the basis of Canadian citizenship. While both Canadian citizens and permanent residents would be able to sponsor immediate family members, extended sponsorship rights would only be reserved for the former.[9] By denying permanent residents the right to sponsor extended family members, policy makers sought to slow down the pace of family immigration that, as the White Paper stated, not only imposed significant economic costs but also threatened social cohesion because of increasing residential concentration. More broadly, the White Paper affirmed the 1962 Regulations in their emphasis on the need to recruit skilled immigrants. However, upon reviewing the White Paper the Special Joint Committee joined ethnic groups in expressing sharp criticism of the department's proposal to prioritize economic interests over family admissions. In particular, the committee was skeptical of the desirability of high-skilled recruitment in the absence of clearly specified selection criteria. In the end, the only societal actor who unequivocally endorsed the White Paper was the business community (Kelley and Trebilcock 1998).

After the Joint Committee's harsh assessment, the department returned to the drawing board. After several months a departmental taskforce led by Deputy Minister Kent presented a new approach to family and economic admissions. Kent proposed to simultaneously solve the sponsorship problem and establish transparency in economic admissions through a nondiscriminatory policy that would distinguish between sponsored, nominated, and independent immigrants. While all would have the right to sponsor immediate family members, the selection of extended ("nominated") family members and economic ("independent") immigrants would be based on "the various factors affecting a person's ability to settle successfully in Canada" (Kent 1988, 409–10). The proposed points system would assign a score mostly based on human capital factors: age, education, training, occupational skill in demand, personal qualities,

---

[9] Immediate family members were spouses, unmarried children under the age of 21, orphaned relatives under the age of 16, and parents and grandparents who would not be allowed to work. Extended sponsorship rights could be given to all children, regardless of age, and accompanying spouses and unmarried children under 21, brothers or sisters, with their spouses and unmarried children, unmarried nephews and nieces under the age of 21, and parents or grandparents who would be permitted to work. These extended sponsorship rights were subject to the requirement of primary education and in-demand labor-market skills.

knowledge of English or French, presence of relatives in Canada, employment offers, and employment opportunities in the area of destination (Kelley and Trebilcock 1998). While immigration officers would still enjoy some discretion in evaluating the personal qualities of applicants, there was no question that the proposed points system would be a major step toward curtailing administrative discretion in immigrant selection. Equally important was the fact that the new category of nominated relatives would allow for family unification regardless of national origin or citizenship while also establishing numerical control over extended family admissions. Thus, while nominated relatives would receive a significant boost based on family ties, their admission would be contingent on skills and labor market conditions. In other words, with the 1967 Regulations, Canadian immigration policy would come to be firmly premised on the principles of skill and family ties.

When speaking to the Parliamentary Committee on Immigration, Minister Marchand declared that, with the new regulations, "[b]oth the efficiency and the humanity of the selection process will be increased *and be seen to be increased*" (Triadafilopoulos 2013a, 32). Marchand's assessment was vindicated as the department's draft regulations were met with immediate approval by both the Special Joint Committee and the press. With the 1967 points system, Canadian immigration policy "[was] placed on a progressive footing, in line with the image Canadian officials wished to project both domestically and internationally" (Triadafilopoulos 2013a, 32). Not only did the 1967 Regulations eradicate all remnants of explicit ethnoracial discrimination, but with the introduction of the points system labor market considerations – in particular a preference for highly skilled immigrants – became a foundational principle of Canadian immigration policy.

Comparatively speaking, then, what renders the policy changes of 1962 and 1967 so remarkable is that in both cases Progressive Conservative and Liberal governments passed nonincremental policy change in the form of executive regulation. The regulations that laid the foundation for Canada's contemporary immigration regime emerged from a political context marked by low diplomatic and high popular insulation. Moreover, on the issue of family sponsorship policy makers were faced with significant interest group pressure. The 1967 points system differed from the 1962 reforms in that it did not skirt the controversial sponsorship issue but instead was able to defuse the opposition of ethnic lobbies by basing extended family admissions in part on human capital and labor market considerations, rather than on national origin or citizenship status. With the creation of the points system, then, cabinet not only retained control over economic admissions but also was able to regulate the entry of extended family members.

The 1976 Immigration Act: Institutionalizing Paradigmatic Reform in the Legislative Arena

The 1967 Regulations accomplished the goal of mending diplomatic relations with the immigrant-sending states of the Global South. Domestically, however, they lived an uneasy coexistence with the 1952 Immigration Act. Not only did the 1952 statute contain sections that provided a legal basis for a racially stratified immigration policy – in particular exclusions based on unsuitability for the Canadian climate – but unlike the 1967 Regulations, the Immigration Act did not specify the principles on which Canadian immigration policy was to be based. Throughout the 1960s, as the regulatory reforms threw into stark relief the Immigration Act's anachronism, members of parliament called on the government to finally tackle legislative reform. At the same time, public concern with the rapid increase in non-European immigration mounted and coincided with the economic stagnation of the late 1960s and the economic shock following the oil crisis in the mid-1970s (Nord 1980). The unprecedented upsurge in non-European immigration was driven not only by the abolition of ethnoracial immigration restrictions, but also by the curtailment of Commonwealth immigration by the British government (Wood 1978). Thus, while as late as 1968 immigration from the Global South accounted for 20 percent of Canadian admissions, by 1974 half of all admissions originated from the Global South (Wright and Maxim 1993, 341). Despite a number of regulatory interventions – such as the withdrawal of the right of visitors to apply for permanent residence from within Canada – by the early 1970s immigration was "near-chaotic" (Wood 1978, 550). With the 1952 Immigration Act unable to provide any direction for how to respond to these pressures, calls for a new immigration act intensified.

Parliamentarians' demands for legislative reform fell onto fertile ground with Prime Minister Pierre Trudeau's appointment of Robert Andras as Minister of Manpower and Immigration after the Liberals' reelection in 1972. The Liberals had performed dismally at the polls and only managed to hold on to power by forming a minority government. When Trudeau announced his decision to stay, he promised to take steps to deal with immigration and to tackle the challenge of economic recovery

(CBC October 31, 1972). Andras was a strong player in cabinet, having held a range of ministerial positions during the previous four years, and was determined to accomplish a new immigration act. Given the contested nature of immigration policy, Andras was convinced that meaningful statutory reform would only be possible if a consensus could be reached on a basic question: "Why do we have immigration to this country?" (Knowles 2007, 204). Supported by all parliamentary parties, the minister charged his department with the preparation of a Green Paper and, in an unprecedented step, invited the provinces and organized interests to submit position briefs.[10] The document was to present a range of reform options in order to facilitate a consensus on the substance of a new immigration act (Kelley and Trebilcock 1998). After the 1974 elections, which restored the Liberals to a majority government, Andras presented the paper to the House of Commons:

The Green Paper acknowledges what we all know, the difficulties in reaching consensus in this field. On the subject of immigration there exist many and often conflicting views about the right line of policy to adopt. Nevertheless, there are several key elements in the present Canadian policy which the Green Paper assumes Canada's future approach should safeguard. Canadians will want, I believe, an immigration policy that meets our social, economic and cultural needs, that respects the family, that is free from discrimination, and that keeps the door open to refugees. Our approach to the immigration policy review has been inspired by the conviction that the subject of immigration to Canada needs to be examined in an extremely wide framework.

(Parliament of Canada February 3, 1975, 2820)

Despite its formal neutrality, the 1974 Green Paper's underlying tone toward immigration was decidedly more negative than that of the 1966 White Paper, which, written at a time of economic growth, had unequivocally praised the benefits of immigration. The Green Paper, by contrast, coincided with the oil crisis and, while recognizing the importance of immigration for Canada's continued population growth, spent much of its discussion on the social problems associated with population growth, such as "congested metropolitan areas, housing shortages, pressures on arable land, damage to the environment" (Minister of Manpower and Immigration 1974, 5). Not only were immigrants held responsible for many of the problems associated with urbanization, but

---

[10] In contrast to a White Paper, which is intended to present the government's position on a given issue, a Green Paper is designed to facilitate informed discussion. Both involve consultation with societal elites.

the increasing ethnic diversity of Canada's population was identified as the cause of increased racial tensions. In the end, however, the Green Paper endorsed continued immigration on the condition that it was firmly tied to labor market needs. This condition extended to the category of nominated relatives, for which the Green Paper recommended that ten (out of a maximum of thirty) points awarded for family ties be made conditional on a prearranged job offer – a proposal that was expected to cut nominated class immigration by 40 percent (Triadafilopoulos 2012, 108).

Given the Green Paper's skepticism of policy liberalization, departmental officials advised the minister to forgo public debate, not only to speed up the legislative process but also to avert anti-immigration backlash at this time of economic turmoil (Hawkins 1977, Wood 1978, Kelley and Trebilcock 1998). These concerns were not unfounded. In 1973, even among university-educated Canadians, support for immigration had fallen to a low of 39 percent, down from 57 percent in 1959 (Kelley and Trebilcock 1998, 373). Yet not only did the Liberal caucus call for parliament to be involved in the reform process, but the minister himself was committed to a nationwide debate on immigration. Advocating for public hearings across the country, Andras declared, "[W]e're going to have a dog and pony show. We will take this across the country and talk it out" (Parliament of Canada February 3, 1975, 2815–20). In the end the minister's position won out with the vocal support of the Liberal caucus and the parliamentary opposition, and a Special Joint Committee of the Senate and the House of Commons was formed.

The Special Joint Committee, consisting of members of the House of Commons and the Senate, interpreted its mandate widely as "facilitating a focus to a national debate on future immigration to Canada" (Hawkins 1977, 55). The committee thus served as a catalyst for Canada's first national immigration debate and held close to fifty public hearings in twenty-one cities across the country. While the process did not significantly engage the general public, a wide range of organized groups (and some individuals) made over 1,800 submissions that ranged from the categorical rejection of nonwhite immigration to demands for an open borders policy (Hawkins 1977). Many submissions were openly critical of the Green Paper. In particular, ethnic groups disapproved of the Green Paper as encouraging racially motivated opposition to immigration, and critiqued its pessimistic tone (Kelley and Trebilcock 1998). As Wood's study of the mobilization of East Indian associations shows, immigrant groups sought to prevent a return to ethnoracial immigrant selection and lobbied for a liberalization of family sponsorship. Their demands did not always fall on sympathetic ears, however. Committee members often appeared dismissive, commenting that "'there were too many in proportion to the numbers of East Indians in Canada'; 'the speakers were mostly elite types'; ... and 'many misunderstood what the Committee was after, and just concentrated on the glories of Indian cultural traditions'" (Wood 1978, 556).

Nevertheless, the committee's report – which would serve as the basis for the 1976 Immigration Act – made a case for continued immigration on the basis of demographic, economic, family, and humanitarian reasons.[11] The report categorically endorsed the principle of nondiscrimination and explicitly distanced itself from the Green Paper's association of immigration with social problems, arguing instead that the latter were the result of the socioeconomic and cultural dynamism of urbanization more generally (Kelley and Trebilcock 1998). The committee proposed that while the points system should be retained, it should be subject to an annual immigration target that would be set by the minister in consultation with the provinces, and be subject to parliamentary scrutiny. Immigrants who met the points requirements would thus continue to be admitted on a first-come, first-served basis, until – and here the committee departed from the 1967 Regulations – the quota for a given year was reached. Finally, on the contentious issue of family sponsorship, the committee charted a middle path by proposing the abolition of the nominated class in return for the inclusion of parents (regardless of age) in the list of immediate family members (Kelley and Trebilcock 1998).[12]

All the evidence suggests that the committee hearings were mainly an exercise in public relations intended to "lend an appearance of grassroots consensus" to immigration reform (Wood 1978, 555). In fact, as the hearings commenced immigration officials were already drafting the legislation's framework. Nonetheless, the hearings quickly showed that there was no "grassroots consensus" on the question of immigrant admissions. Whereas over 80 percent of individual submissions demanded tight controls – including a stop to either all or all nonwhite immigration – this was the case for fewer than 20 percent of organizational submissions (Wood 1978, 558). While the committee chose to ignore restrictionist public demands, the persistent communication of anti-immigration attitudes by

---

[11] Demographic arguments at the time focused on Canada's relatively small population, rather than on a decreasing birthrate.

[12] Other significant proposals included the creation of a separate policy regime for refugees.

the Canadian public helped sensitize legislators to the need for depoliti-cized policy making (Wood 1978). At the same time the committee was impressed with the vote-mobilizing capacity of immigrant lobbies, which accounted for close to one-third of all presentations. According to Wood, at least four cabinet ministers justified the need for a liberal immigration policy by arguing that their electoral success depended on the ethnic minority vote (Wood 1978, 559).

Unlike its 1966 predecessor, which did not even produce a final report, the 1975 Joint Committee's work was positively received by parliament. Quite remarkably, sixty out of its sixty-five recommendations would find their way into the 1976 Immigration Act. At a time when parliament was demanding more influence over the direction of immigration policy, the Special Joint Committee was able to fulfill the role of "middleman" (Nord 1980) by allowing for the reciprocal communication of policy preferences between the government, parliament, and the organized public. Committee members skillfully carved out a role for parliament as a competent actor in the making of immigration policy and took great care not to be perceived as rubberstamping executive preferences on immigra-tion (Nord 1980). In its hearings, the committee strategically occupied a middle ground between the range of articulated policy positions and was careful not to fully endorse the position of any one of the key actors. Affirming the minister's vision, the committee strove to depoliticize the issue of immigration and to broker a consensus on the fundamentals of immigration policy rather than adopt an adversarial position – a strategy undoubtedly aided by a basic partisan consensus on immigration as well as the community of interest between a majority government and its parliamentary caucus. As a result, the work of the Special Joint Committee served to establish legislators as competent policy makers on matters of immigration, weakening the longstanding executive monopoly over immigration policy making.

When the government introduced its immigration bill in the House of Commons, it received near unanimous support from all parties as well as from the major interest groups, academics, and the media (Kelley and Trebilcock 1998). The Immigration Act of 1976, which was to serve as the cornerstone of immigration policy until the passage of the Immigration and Refugee Protection Act of 2001, spelled out for the first time in Canadian history the primary objectives of its immigration policy, namely the promotion of the country's economic, demographic, social, and cultural goals, the principle of nondiscrimination, the importance of family reunion, and a commitment to refugee protection. Reflecting these principles, the Act established three distinct classes of immigrants who could be admitted to Canada: the economic class, to be admitted through the points system; the family class; and the refugee class. Closely following the recommendations of the Special Joint Committee, the Act modified the 1967 Regulations by establishing an annual immigration target. Thus, in an important innovation, the Act imposed on the government the mandate to plan for the future by annually consulting with the provinces on desirable immigration levels and to present these in annual reports to parliament (Knowles 2007).

At the same time the Act affirmed the basic principles underlying the 1967 Regulations. Designed as a piece of framework legislation – a point to which we will return in our discussion of the 2001 Immigration and Refugee Protection Act – the Act spelled out the broad principles of Canadian immigration policy while leaving most operational questions to the regulatory process. Thus, the 1976 Act firmly shut the door on race-based admissions and institutionalized an immigration policy that, together with the principle of family ties, was in significant part driven by human capital and labor market considerations. As developed in the 1978 Regulations, the points system provided policy makers with a flexible instrument for accommodating shifting views on whether economic admissions should be determined by short-term labor market considerations (the tap-on, tap-off approach) or instead treat skilled immigration as integral to long-term economic growth (the human capital model).

For some time the points system would continue to reflect the tap-on, tap-off approach by awarding points for job offers or in-demand qualifications, and by adjusting immigration levels on the basis of projected unemployment figures. Hence the 1978 Regulations prioritized practical training and experience over formal education. With the passage of time, however, policy makers would tilt the balance toward human capital considerations. On the question of family immigration, the government took a relatively expansive view, legislating "with one eye fixed on the voting strength of the increasing number of [new] Canadians" (Wood 1978, 564).[13] Thus, not only would the nominated class be retained, but all parents would now be eligible for sponsorship under the family class.

The passage of the 1976 Immigration Act marked the conclusion of a fourteen-year-long reform process that transformed Canada's racially stratified immigration system into a policy regime where the principles

[13] In 1976, for instance, nearly half of the forty-six marginal seats held by the Liberal Party had strong ethnic minority concentrations (Wood 1978).

of skills- and family tie-based admissions had come to displace ethno-racial discrimination. With the passage of the 1962 and 1967 Regulations the cabinet responded to diplomatic pressures to end Canada's national origins policy. In doing so, policy makers were able to usher in paradigmatic reform because they operated from within the safety of the executive arena. Yet while the popular insulation of the executive constituted a critical condition for rapid liberalization, the regulations' break with the past was too radical for it to remain confined to the executive arena. Because paradigmatic reform challenges fundamental policy principles, its legitimation requires widespread support. This condition cannot be met where policy is made by a small circle of bureaucrats in the absence of public debate. As a case of paradigmatic reform, then, the shift from an ethnoracial to a skills- and nondiscriminatory family tie-based immigration paradigm lacked legitimacy as long as policy makers continued to circumvent the legislative arena. As pressure for legislative reform and public debate mounted, immigration officials had to learn the hard way that the pursuit of paradigmatic policy reform in the legislative arena required widespread consultation and consensus building, even at the cost of making concessions to representatives of large immigrant constituencies on questions of family immigration in exchange for electoral support. Once executive actors had learned this lesson, statutory reform progressed smoothly, undoubtedly aided by partisan agreement and, most importantly, the fact that at this time of majority government the legislative arena did not constitute a formal veto point. The 1976 Act thus came to mark the end of a policy-making tradition where immigration policy was exclusively developed by bureaucrats behind closed doors, insulated not only from societal interests but also from the interference of legislative actors. While the decision to move reform into the legislative arena meant that immigration officials had to surrender any hopes of a speedy reform process, it allowed for the emergence of an elite consensus in favor of an active, comparatively liberal immigration policy – a commitment that still defines Canadian immigration policy to this day.

TILTING THE BALANCE FROM FAMILY TO ECONOMIC ADMISSIONS: THE RISE OF HUMAN CAPITAL-BASED IMMIGRATION, 1985–2002

From the mid-1980s until the early 2000s, Canada experienced a succession of reforms that would profoundly alter the size and composition of immigrant admissions. As had already been the case with the shift from race- to skills- and family ties-based immigrant admissions, policy change first took the form of regulatory reform before becoming institutionalized several years later in the form of a new immigration act. Collectively these changes effected two momentous policy shifts. First, without abandoning the points system, the reforms marked the end of Canada's tap-on, tap-off approach that had coupled economic admissions to the state of the economy. This signified a change in the logic of economic admissions from filling short-term labor market shortages to meeting the structural demands of a globally competitive knowledge economy. As economic admissions became uncoupled from labor market fluctuations, immigration levels came to be set and maintained at historic highs. In a second policy shift the immigration reforms enacted between the mid-1980s and the early 2000s profoundly altered the balance between economic and family immigration. Whereas the family stream had dominated Canadian immigrant admissions since the 1976 Act, the reforms of the 1990s expanded economic admissions while curtailing family sponsorship, thereby paving the way for a policy regime that to this day is defined by economic immigration. Just as had been the case in the 1960s, the reforms of the 1990s were passed from within the safety of the executive arena.

Yet unlike the 1960s, the impetus for reform did not stem from diplomatic pressure but rather reflected policy makers' dissatisfaction with the workings of the 1976 Act. Even though policy reform was shielded from popular and interest group pressure, policy makers strategically reached out to domestic elites through extensive consultation in order to legitimate their reform project. This process of societal legitimation was concluded in the early 2000s when the government decided to institutionalize the incremental regulatory reforms of the 1980s and 1990s in the legislative arena. With the coming into force of the Immigration and Refugee Protection Act and its regulations, the paradigmatic shift toward a human capital-based immigration system was complete.

The Failure of Economic Selectivity under the 1976 Immigration Act

In the early 1980s Canada's immigration policy came under increasing criticism for failing to fulfill the points system's promise of economic selection. Since the late 1970s the majority of immigrants had arrived in Canada not through the points system but via the family and humanitarian streams. The rising significance of the family class in particular was singled out as a criticism of the 1976 Immigration Act. In 1981, the government's Annual Report to Parliament on Immigration Levels stated:

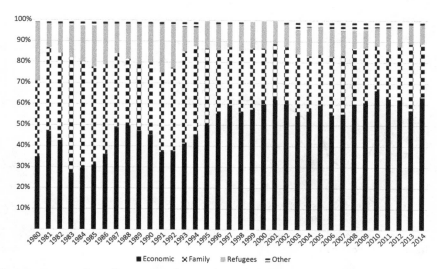

FIGURE 5.1 Canadian permanent resident admissions by category, 100 percent stacked columns, 1980–2014.

"The family class is now the predominant part of the immigration movement" (Hawkins 1991, 86). In less than a decade, from 1975 to 1983, the proportion of family class entrants had increased from 34 percent to a high of 55 percent.[14] By contrast, the proportion of economic entrants had dropped from 73 percent in 1971 to a low of 31 percent in 1983 (Knowles 2007, 230, Citizenship and Immigration Canada 2003). Thus, throughout the 1980s and well into the 1990s points system entrants accounted for a minority of admissions (Figure 5.1); it was only in the mid-1990s that economic admissions regained the upper hand over family and humanitarian immigration (Figure 5.2).

What accounted for the comparatively residual role of economic selection in immigrant admissions from the late 1970s into the early 1990s? Looking at the development of family immigration, the relatively expansive sponsorship provisions of the 1976 Immigration Act clearly facilitated a steady inflow of spouses and fiancé(e)s, unmarried children under 21, as well as elderly or disabled parents and grandparents. Moreover, the assisted relatives provision (formerly the nominated relatives class)

[14] When the entry of immediate family members through non-family streams is added to family-class entries, immediate family members accounted for 75 percent of all admissions in the mid-1980s (Hawkins 1991, 87).

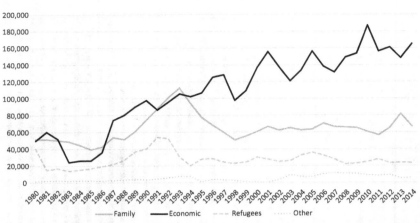

FIGURE 5.2 Canadian permanent resident admissions by category, absolute numbers, 1980–2014.

allowed for more distant relatives to enter through the points system. While officially situated in the economic stream, the admission of assisted relatives was nevertheless criticized as being insufficiently economically selective, given that a substantial number of points were awarded on the basis of family ties. In 1987 assisted relatives accounted for 14 percent of all economic admissions.

Yet while policy makers were able to manipulate the entry of assisted relatives fairly painlessly by changing the weight given to family ties under the points system, reining in the immigration of immediate family members was a much more delicate matter. In the lead-up to the 1988 federal election – a period of weakened popular insulation – the incumbent Progressive Conservative Mulroney government even decided to lift the age requirement for dependent children (Kelley and Trebilcock 1998). This "J88" regulation, which was rescinded in 1992, was a clear nod to ethnic minority voters, and was predicted to increase the proportion of family immigrants by 3–4 percent (Chuenyan Lai 1988, 111). It expanded family size across most immigrant categories, in particular in the Parent and Grandparent Program (Kustec 2006). The challenge of reining in family immigration is succinctly articulated by Freda Hawkins:

In all countries of immigration ... family reunion has become a sacred subject which can only be handled with extreme care. Hardly any Canadian politician fails to do homage to it at the appropriate moment, and every Canadian bureaucrat puts some soothing reference to it in any ministerial speech concerns with immigration. Although it is an official objective of Canadian immigration policy, family reunion is and always has been a problematical area of immigration management.

(Hawkins 1991, 85)

It was not only the stickiness of family immigration that threatened to marginalize economic immigration but also Canada's tap-on, tap-off approach to labor recruitment. Because intake levels were regularly adjusted to reflect fluctuations in unemployment, economic admissions were scaled back during times of economic downturn. The coupling of immigration levels to unemployment rates throughout the postwar period was particularly strong between 1979 – when governments started to set annual immigration targets – and 1989, before petering out in the early 1990s (Veugelers and Klassen 1994, 364). This relationship had important consequences when the Canadian economy went into steep recession in the early 1980s. As unemployment surged from 7.6 to 12 percent in the course of just two years (1981–3), policy makers slashed economic admission levels by nearly two-thirds, from 60,200 to 24,200 (Figure 5.2).[15] Moreover, points system admissions were now no longer based solely on labor market demand but required a concrete pre-entry job offer. Unless a government was willing to impose steep cuts on family sponsorship, as long as economic immigration levels remained tied to labor market fluctuations the economic class would not be able to regain its former preeminence.

Shifting the Balance from Family to Economic Admissions in the Executive Arena: The 1980s and 1990s

The 1980s

In the 1984 federal election, the Progressive Conservatives under Brian Mulroney won the largest governing majority in Canadian history. Mulroney's victory brought to a close two decades of Liberal rule.[16] As Canada's "natural governing party" (Carty 2015), the Liberals had laid the foundations of the country's postwar immigration system and opened up immigration to all parts of the world. The Liberals' policy activism that engendered the 1967 points system and the 1976 Immigration Act,

---

[15] www.statcan.gc.ca/pub/71-222-x/2008001/c-g/desc/desc-a2-eng.htm, accessed June 28, 2016

[16] The Liberals were in power from 1963 to 1984, interrupted by ten months of minority Progressive Conservative rule under the leadership of Joe Clark from 1979 to 1980.

together with the launch of state-sponsored multiculturalism under Pierre Trudeau, had sealed the Liberals' reputation as the party of immigrants and solidified the link between foreign-born Canadians and the Liberal Party. Yet even though it was the Liberal Party that was most closely associated with pro-immigration activism, all parliamentary parties, including the Progressive Conservatives, were broadly supportive of immigration. After all, it had been a Progressive Conservative prime minister, John Diefenbaker, who first sealed the fate of White Canada. More generally, the Progressive Conservatives had long considered immigration to be a critical component of Canada's economic development. After Mulroney's victory, prominent party functionaries pushed for the strategic adoption of an expansive immigration policy in order to weaken Liberal dominance and make inroads among ethnic voters (Veugelers 2000).

Once in power the Progressive Conservatives quickly put into action their programmatic commitment to strengthening Canada's global competitiveness by means of a pro-business agenda that included free trade and deregulation. Mulroney's economic reforms quickly spilled over into the area of immigration and set into motion a decade of top-down, executive-driven regulatory reform that was to expand immigration and shift the balance of admissions in favor of the economic stream. A day after taking office, Mulroney established a Ministerial Task Force, chaired by maverick Deputy Prime Minister Erik Nielson, to review a wide range of government programs (Savoie 1994). A year later the Nielsen report's immigration recommendations, released auspiciously after the onset of economic recovery, set the tone for the immigration reforms of the coming years. Reflecting the growing ideational influence of the notion of positive immigrant selection among economists, the report warned of the declining economic selectivity of Canadian immigration policy:

The acceptability of a reasonable and sustained immigration level is highly dependent on its being seen to consist of people who readily adapt and contribute to Canada's economic and social life. This is less and less the case. ... Selected immigrants have now declined from 30 to 14 percent of the annual movement, which in itself has dropped to 88,000 from its 10-year average of 122,000. Half of the movement is now made up of the sponsored family class, one-third of which also enters the labour market, but with no prior selection-based assessment of the impact. Except for some 6,000 self-employed and entrepreneur groups, much of the remaining 26,000 consists of people admitted for humanitarian reasons. ... The problem is that many in this growing group could never have met Canada's immigrant selection standards and are, indeed, a major source of dependency and welfare and settlement resources at increasing cost. ... It is essential to strike a better balance in the immigration movement if Canada is to avoid serious longer term economic and social problems. This can only be done by insisting on positive selection abroad of immigrants who will make a real contribution to our economic and social development.

(Task Force on Program Review 1986, 136–7)

In order to facilitate economic selection, the Task Force called for "a somewhat higher level of immigration, expanding with the economy" (Veugelers 2000, 100). The report further recommended the abolition of the prearranged employment requirement for points system entrants, in addition to measures designed to reduce the size of the humanitarian class by limiting admissions to Convention refugees and those fleeing Communist regimes.

While the Task Force was still deliberating, the government conducted a general review of immigration policy and published its conclusions in a special report to parliament and the Annual Report to Parliament on Future Immigration Levels (Green and Green 1999). The reports echoed the Task Force's view that economic immigration should be strengthened, advising on a "moderate, controlled increase" in order to avert a population decline below thirty million by the year 2000 (Veugelers 2000, 101). At the same time, policy makers took a more cautious stance on noneconomic admissions by arguing that "the increase in the economic stream must not ... be at the expense of the social [family] and humanitarian streams" (cited in Green and Green 1999, 434). In a departure from previous justifications of economic immigration that had relied exclusively on short-term labor market considerations, the reports signified an important shift in utilizing economic immigration for long-term, structural purposes. The articulation of a demographic rationale for immigration had already been introduced in 1984, shortly before the Liberal government's electoral defeat, in a background paper tabled with the Annual Report to Parliament on Immigration Levels (Hawkins 1988). The Mulroney government continued to explore potential solutions to population decline by conducting several demographic analyses. While the focus on demographic goals in immigration policy was to prove short-lived – in 1989 a government review established that immigration policy was not an effective tool for reversing population decline (Green and Green 1999) – it nevertheless paved the way for placing immigration planning on a long-term footing.

After these policy deliberations the government raised economic immigration levels and expanded the business component of economic

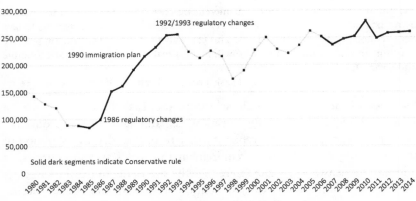

FIGURE 5.3 Canadian permanent resident admissions, 1980–2014.

admissions. In 1986 the investor class was added as a third stream to the existing two business classes of self-employed workers and entrepreneurs. The same year the arranged employment prerequisite for points system entrants was dropped. The impact of these incremental regulatory reforms, passed within the political insulation of the executive arena, were quickly felt. Between 1985 and 1989 the number of economic entrants tripled, expanding the economic class' relative significance from 31 to 47 percent of total admissions. Family immigration, on the other hand, declined from 47 to 32 percent of admissions, despite increasing in absolute terms (Figure 5.2). Given the government's reluctance to make deep cuts to the noneconomic streams, total immigration more than doubled in the course of just four years to 191,500 in 1989 (Figure 5.3). It would only be in the 1990s that the expansion of family immigration would come to an end.

The first signs of an emerging commitment to rein in family admissions was the immigration minister's decision, in 1987, to freeze the proportion of family class entrants at 30 percent. At the same time administrative resources were diverted from the processing of applications from family immigrants to those of business entrepreneurs (Parliament of Canada March 24, 1987). As is typical of regulatory measures, these policy changes did not attract much public notice. As a result the Mulroney government was free to experiment with shifting the predominant logic of immigration from family to economic admissions. The Conservatives' attempts to change the composition of immigration flows was vocally opposed by the Liberal opposition in the House of Commons. Given their longstanding appeal to immigrant voters, the Liberals demanded that the family class be expanded to include siblings and that, under the points system, family ties be accorded the same weight as education, language, and job skills. In a lengthy House of Commons debate in March 1987, Liberal immigration critic Sergio Marchi denounced the government's immigration reforms for their impact on family unification:

[U]nder the Tory regime the priority for the family class designation has been lowered substantially. .... [T]he Conservatives doubled the number of entrepreneur immigrants permitted into Canada. While we all welcome and recognize the economic benefits of business class immigrants, this category should not develop into the predominant one and create a situation whereby those immigrants, able to pay their way into the country, would be the only or principal benefactors of our system. In addition, our immigration officers abroad have reported to me personally that as a result of the ambitious entrepreneurship targets posed by Ottawa and the extensive work required to review and approve each single business proposal, financial and personnel resources are being shifted away from the family class sector into the business immigration class. The net effect, of course, of the family reunification applications processed is both fewer and slower.

(Parliament of Canada, March 24, 1987, 4485–6)

While the Liberal Party had traditionally been more sympathetic to the principle of family reunification than the Progressive Conservatives, the Liberals' demands for an expanded family class are best understood as a reflection of the legislative arena's constituency-focused logic, rather than as an expression of ideological principles. When the Liberals were back in power they would eventually oppose the very same measures they had demanded while in opposition (see the discussion of the Immigration and Refugee Protection Act). Most importantly, the Liberals' demands were of no consequence for Immigration Minister Benoît Bouchard. Not only did the government command a solid parliamentary majority – the Progressive Conservatives held 75 percent of seats in the House of Commons – but the government's attacks on family immigration were pursued within the purview of ministerial discretion.

While there was no question that the Conservatives were committed to an immigration policy anchored in economic selection, the strength of the Canadian economy during the latter half of the 1980s masked the significance of Mulroney's economic immigration liberalism. It was only when the economy plummeted in the early 1990s that the government's programmatic break with the country's longstanding tap-on, tap-off approach became evident. By means of regulatory measures alone, the Mulroney government in the early 1990s enacted immigration reforms that not only would decouple economic immigration from the business cycle, but also break the dominance of family immigration.

The 1990s

In 1990 the Mulroney government's departure from the practice of short-term and business cycle-driven immigration planning was signaled by Immigration Minister Barbara McDougall's announcement of a five-year immigration plan. In an unprecedented move, and despite the severe recession at the time, the 1990 plan provided for an increase in immigration from 200,000 to 250,000 within two years – at a level to be maintained until 1995 (Kelley and Trebilcock 1998, 386). The government's rejection of the old tap-on, tap-off approach was evident not only in its decision to increase immigration at a time of economic contraction, but also in its adoption of the five-year plan, which effectively tied the hands of policy makers and did not allow for annual levels adjustments based on transitory labor market conditions. Finally, of at least equal significance to these economic immigration reforms was the government's disclosure of further plans to change the balance between the family and economic streams in favor of the latter (Knowles 2007). By 1995, when the policy changes started to show their effect, the percentage of family immigrants had dropped from 50 percent in 1984, when Mulroney took office, to 36 percent of admissions.

The 1990 immigration plan was preceded by extensive Canada-wide consultations with business, labor, and a broad range of civil society leaders. Ultimately the consultations allowed the government to argue that its plan to increase immigrant admissions independent of year-by-year labor market conditions reflected a liberalizing consensus among societal elites and federal political parties. In its final report the government concluded that there was "solid support for some increase in immigration over the next five years" (Employment and Immigration Canada 1990, 6). A closer review of the 1990 levels consultations, however, reveals a political process that was a far cry from one of democratic deliberation, despite the fact immigration officials had reached out to a much broader range of actors than in the past (Simmons and Keohane 1992). In the end the consultations proved to be less an exercise in soliciting the substantive input of interest representatives than in gauging the state of elite opinion in order to preempt the need for damage control. Most importantly, despite the government's constitutional powers to go it alone, the levels consultations served to publicly legitimate executive-driven regulatory reform. As observers of the consultations, Simmons and Keohane describe the process as follows:

The Minister's introduction suggested that the government was open, within reason, to responding to various interests and agendas ... As no strong stance was taken on what future policy might look like, it was difficult for anyone to raise major criticisms. As subsequent events unfolded, it became equally clear that the new ideas were not to be developed in open debate, nor was any opportunity given to groups who might want to lobby in the plenary meeting around a particular issue, with the result that again it was difficult for anyone to raise major criticisms. ... EIC [Employment and Immigration Canada] achieved its joint objective of avoiding dissent while assessing current views and potential reactions to different policy options by a particular structuring of the afternoon working groups. These were organized so that individuals were encouraged to express diverse views, but the format was one which limited the possibility of organized opposition and confrontation. Within the afternoon workshops, it often seemed to participants that discussion on a particular theme was just underway when the Chair (an EIC appointee or staff member) would point to the need to pass on to the next agenda item. In consequence, debate and the mobilization of dissent among those with similar views was made difficult.

(Simmons and Keohane 1992, 439–40)

These observations vividly describe a dynamic where policy makers reach out to societal interests in order to test the waters of elite opinion while retaining tight control over the process – at times even manipulating procedures – to undercut dissent.

For two years after the consultations immigration officials continued work on a new policy blueprint. Published in 1992 under the title *Managing Immigration: A Framework for the 1990s* (Employment and Immigration Canada 1992), the report marked a clear shift in the goals of economic immigration from the recruitment of skilled industrial workers to the pursuit of highly skilled knowledge workers. The report justified the immigration minister's decision to raise immigration levels independent of labor market conditions with Canada's transition to a "globalized, highly competitive, knowledge-based economy" where, even at times of high unemployment, highly skilled jobs continued to go unfilled (Employment and Immigration Canada 1992, 14). From now on immigration policy was to facilitate the admission of immigrants who would raise the skills profile of the Canadian workforce. High levels of immigration would, undoubtedly, also help the Conservatives appeal to immigrant and ethnic constituencies. The report's proposed immigration levels exceeded even those of the 1990 immigration plan: admissions would continue to be raised by 50,000 annually between 1992 and 1995. In a controversial move, the report proposed to shift the balance between economic and family immigration. During the 1990 levels consultation, the government's proposal to curtail family immigration by narrowing the definition of family had been opposed by most groups (Kelley and Trebilcock 1998). Now, two years later, *Managing Immigration* proposed to raise the average skill level of immigrants not only by increasing economic admissions and imposing more stringent educational requirements for points system entrants, but also by reining in immigration through the family and assisted relative classes (Simmons 2010).

After the report's publication, the Mulroney government enacted a series of regulatory reforms aimed at curtailing family immigration. In 1992 policy makers tightened the definition of immediate family by lowering the age limit for sponsored children from 21 to 19. The following year the assisted relatives program was effectively abolished by fully moving it into the points system and reducing the points awarded for family ties. The program had allowed for the sponsoring of extended family members, provided that the applicant scored enough points under the points system and that the sponsor met the financial requirements.

Not surprisingly, these decisions quickly came under fire from immigrant advocates. The Canadian Association of Social Workers criticized the changes to the family class as discriminating against immigrant groups with more extensive understandings of family (Kelley and Trebilcock 1998). David Matas, a prominent Winnipeg immigration lawyer and commentator, argued that these changes would "have a traumatically restrictive effect on family unification" (Knowles 2007, 237). In a similar vein, Howard Greenberg, national chairman of the Canadian Bar Association's immigration section, critiqued that "the use of family relationship as a factor in obtaining immigrant status is reduced considerably" (Knowles 2007, 242).

Given past experience with attempts to curtail family sponsorship as well as the objections aired by interest representatives during the 1990 levels consultation, the Mulroney government was fully cognizant of the unpopularity of its reform measures. Yet having significantly raised overall levels of immigration helped shield the government from accusations of being anti-immigration, and the protests of immigrant advocates remained without political repercussions for the minister. Passed within the institutional safety of the executive arena and bolstered by the extensive consultation process of previous years, the Mulroney government was able to adopt regulatory measures that not only were to remain in place after the Liberals returned to power in late 1993, but also succeeded in inflicting deep and lasting cuts to family immigration. As Figure 5.1 illustrates, the number of family immigrants contracted by more than half between 1993 and 1999 – from a high of 112,600 to 51,000 – before stabilizing at an average of about 65,000 in the 2000s. Through regulatory reform alone the Mulroney government succeeded in permanently

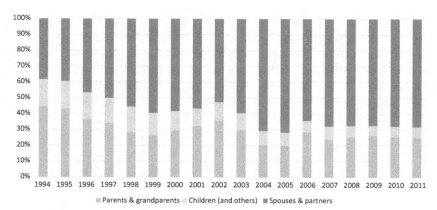

FIGURE 5.4 Family immigration to Canada, 1994–2011.

shifting the balance between economic and family immigration – a policy aspiration that has proven elusive to US policy makers (see Chapter 6). As a result the proportion of family immigrants, which had stood at an average of 45 percent from 1980 to 1984, fell to 38 percent from 1985 to 1994 and, after the 1992–3 reforms started to show their desired effect, dropped to 31 percent from 1995 to 1999. Under Mulroney the proportion of family immigrants thus contracted from half to a third of admissions.

This trend would accelerate after the Liberals came to power in late 1993. Despite the Liberals' vocal support for expanding the family class while in opposition, now that the party had moved into the executive arena its policy goals closely resembled those of its Conservative predecessors. For the Liberals, continuing Mulroney's policy of high levels of immigration equally opened up new room for maneuver on questions of family immigration. Prime Minister Jean Chrétien sought to rein in extended family sponsorship by reducing immigration targets for the Parent and Grandparent Program. As a result the number of parent and grandparent admissions fell rather precipitously from over 40,000 in 1994 to less than 15,000 in 1999. While parents and grandparents accounted for 45 percent of all family entrants when the Liberals came to power, by the late 1990s they made up as little as 26 percent of family immigrants (see Figure 5.4).

The Populist Interlude: The Reform Party and the Federal Election of 1993

Before turning our attention to the passage of the 2001 Immigration and Refugee Protection Act, we will briefly revisit the early 1990s when the spectacular (but short-lived) rise of the populist, western-based Reform Party threatened to disrupt the modus operandi of depoliticized immigration policy making. The Reform Party began as a western-based political protest movement seeking to represent western interests in federal politics. In addition to a commitment to free trade and direct democracy, the party's platform focused on reducing the size of the federal government, retrenchment of the welfare state, and an end to English–French bilingualism and multiculturalism. Initially the party paid little attention to immigration. After the Reform Party's early endorsement of a White Canada policy was widely denounced, its leader, Preston Manning, moderated the party's position on immigration. In the lead-up to the 1993 federal election, Reform called for a reduction in immigrant admissions and a curtailment of noneconomic immigration. While not part of its central platform, the party's positions on immigration quickly became the focus of media attention after the *Toronto Star* and the *Globe and Mail* called immigration the election's "phantom issue," in articles titled "Immigration: Too Hot to Handle" and "Immigration Goes Undiscussed." This opened the door to an emotionally charged media debate, with Canada's six major English-language newspapers publishing over 200 articles linking the Reform Party and immigration in the course of forty-five days (Soberman 1999, 281). Public opinion polls confirmed that Reform supporters held significantly more restrictionist views on immigration than other partisans, with 67 percent of Reform supporters agreeing that there are "too many immigrants" – compared to the national average of 53 percent (Soberman 1999, 268).

While newspapers varied in their assessment of the Reform Party's platform, there was broad agreement that the time had come to break the silence on questions of immigration and multiculturalism. Yet "scared stiff of white, mainstream backlash" (*Montreal Gazette* October 6, 1993), neither Progressive Conservatives nor Liberals were willing to engage the electoral arena on the volatile issue of immigration; instead mainstream politicians sought to discredit Reform candidates as racists and bigots. Only late into the campaign did the Progressive Conservatives decide to appeal to potential Reform defectors when hinting at possible immigration reforms, should they be returned to power (Soberman 1999). In the end the 1993 elections marked the beginning of thirteen years of Liberal rule. The Progressive Conservatives under their new leader, Kim Campbell, lost spectacularly, having their seats slashed from 169 to two. The Reform Party, by contrast, won 52 seats and 19 percent of the overall vote (26 percent outside of Quebec) (Cairns 1994). After the election, however, immigration politics quickly returned to its previous status quo, as public attention was diverted to other issues and the Reform Party struggled to build a base beyond western Canada. By the time that parliament started to work on a new immigration act, the Reform Party had disbanded.

Institutionalizing Human Capital-Based Immigration in the Legislative Arena: The Immigration and Refugee Protection Act of 2001 and Its Regulations

The passage of the Immigration and Refugee Protection Act and its accompanying regulations in the early 2000s marked the institutionalization of Canada's human capital-based immigration regime.[17] More than twenty-five years after the passage of the 1976 Immigration Act and over thirty amendments later there was a widely shared consensus that a new immigration act was overdue. Yet despite being hailed as "legislation for the new millennium" (Elinor Caplan, Parliament of Canada June 13, 2001, 1515–20), in most matters of family and economic admissions the new immigration act did little more than to "[bring] the letter of the law in line with trends in bureaucratic practice under previous discretionary provisions" (Dauvergne 2003, 727). However, the new Act's limited departure from the policy status quo was not the result of legislative stonewalling. On the contrary, most of its features survived the legislative process intact. Rather than marking a break with existing policy, the Act's primary purpose was the legal integration and legitimation of existing administrative practice within the legislative arena. Like its 1976 predecessor, the Act took the form of framework legislation, continuing the longstanding Canadian practice of delegating key aspects of policy making to the regulatory process and, thus, the executive arena. The new immigration act thus remained silent on key policy questions, including the setting of immigration levels, the balance between family and economic immigration, provisions for family sponsorship, and the selection of economic immigrants through the points system. Instead these decisions once again were delegated to the regulatory and administrative process, ensuring that Canadian immigration policy making would continue to be concentrated in the executive arena, well insulated from popular and interest group pressure.

---

[17] It also marked the move to a more restrictionist asylum policy, a policy area not examined here.

"Not Just Numbers" and the Human Capital Paradigm of Immigrant Selection

The coming into force of the Immigration and Refugee Protection Act and its regulations in June 2002 marked the conclusion of nearly a decade of public consultation and debate on the future of Canadian immigration policy. We begin our discussion with one of the most seminal documents of the 1990s: the Legislative Review Advisory Group's report *Not Just Numbers: A Canadian Framework for Future Immigration* (1997). The Legislative Review was convened by Minister of Citizenship and Immigration Lucienne Robillard but operated at arm's length from the ministry (Dauvergne 2003). *Not Just Numbers* is important not only because the new immigration act closely followed its recommendations on economic and family immigration, but also because, informed by extensive public consultations, it gave expression to the views of societal and political elites at the turn of the twenty-first century.[18]

Not Just Numbers forcefully articulated a human capital paradigm as the foundation of future immigrant selection. "The truth is that Canada is competing with other industrialized countries to attract the best human capital, that we are not always on the winning side of this competition, and that something needs to be done to change that" (Legislative Review Advisory Group 1997, 3). Decrying the points system's occupational demand-driven operation, the report criticized the heavy weighting of occupational qualifications as disregarding the fluidity of labor markets and argued that occupation-based selection did not prepare applicants well for establishing a life in Canada. *Not Just Numbers* demanded far-reaching changes to the points system that would base immigrant selection on transferrable skills such as education, work experience, and language competency – attributes that would give immigrants "the flexibility to work in several different occupations during their working life" (Legislative Review Advisory Group 1997, 56). In other words, with the rise of a global knowledge-based economy the economic benefits of immigration would only be maintained with a shift toward human capital-based immigration.

On matters of family immigration *Not Just Numbers* adopted a two-pronged approach. While the report's recommendations on economic

---

[18] This was not true for all recommendations. For instance, policy makers did not adopt the report's proposal to split immigration legislation into two separate acts to reflect its multiple logics: one dealing with immigration policy and citizenship, the other with refugee policy.

admissions reflected a widely shared consensus, this was not a viable option for the discussion of family sponsorship. The review team's consultations had revealed deep divisions between those who wanted to see the right to family sponsorship remain limited to the nuclear family, and others who advocated multicultural understandings of family that would extend sponsorship rights to more distant relatives. In this debate the Legislative Review positioned itself closer to the restrictive camp. Repeatedly emphasizing the importance of family immigration, it emphatically limited its proposals for policy liberalization to members of the nuclear family. Given the cultural shift toward the embrace of same-sex relationships, the report argued, spousal sponsorship should be redefined to include both common-law and same-sex partners. Similarly, in recognition of the oftentimes delayed onset of children's independence, the report recommended raising the maximum sponsorship age for dependent children from 19 to 22. The report further proposed to exempt spouses and dependent children from medical inadmissibility provisions and to reduce sponsors' obligations of financial support from ten to three years.[19] Finally, in response to widespread criticism of the length of the sponsorship process – in 80 percent of cases spousal sponsorship took longer than eleven months (Legislative Review Advisory Group 1997, 49) – the Legislative Review proposed to allow in-Canada applications for spouses and dependent children.

While all of these provisions eventually would find their way into the Immigration and Refugee Protection Act, not all constituted departures from existing administrative practice. As far as the sponsorship of same-sex partners and the possibility of in-Canada applications for nuclear family members was concerned, policy liberalization simply institutionalized and rendered transparent already existing administrative practices under the highly discretionary "humanitarian and compassionate" decision-making criterion of the 1976 Act (Dauvergne 2003, LaViolette 2004). Moreover, as we will see, while these liberalizing provisions would facilitate modest increases in the number of immediate family admissions, these increases would be more than offset by cuts in the admission of extended relatives.

Whereas the Legislative Review affirmed the nuclear family as "the focal point of emotional, economic and cultural dependency" (Legislative

---

[19] In cases where the immigrant would impose "excessive costs on health or social services." For more details, see www.cic.gc.ca/english/resources/tools/medic/admiss/excessive.asp, accessed January 18, 2017.

Review Advisory Group 1997, 42), it took a much less sanguine view of the sponsorship of parents and grandparents:

We view the situation for parents and grandparents very differently. There is rarely the sort of primary emotional dependency between independent adults living in Canada and their parents living abroad that one finds between a husband and wife, or a parent and a young child. Few countries accord such an extraordinary privilege to the parents of adult residents. Most countries are far more restrictive than Canada, if they grant permanent status to parents at all.

(Legislative Review Advisory Group 1997, 49–50)

The report not only minimized the benefits of sponsoring extended family members but also discussed at length the problem of sponsorship breakdown. It noted that despite sponsors' legal obligation to financially support their relatives for a period of ten years, about 20 percent of sponsored parents and grandparents were already on welfare three years after arrival. More broadly, the use of welfare by sponsored parents and grandparents was close to four times that of the general population and was increasing (Legislative Review Advisory Group 1997, 45–6). While the Legislative Review did not propose the abolition of parent and grandparent sponsorship altogether, it did suggest "limitations on the sponsoring of grandparents" (Legislative Review Advisory Group 1997, 46) and held that there are "no compelling grounds – either of a public interest or of a humanitarian nature" (Legislative Review Advisory Group 1997, 50) – to extend the proposed liberalizing provisions for nuclear family members to this group.[20]

The Immigration and Refugee Protection Act as Framework Legislation: Preserving Executive-Dominated Policy Making

The 1976 Immigration Act had been designed as a piece of framework legislation based on the premise that there "would be much advantage if a new immigration act devoted itself chiefly to a clear statement of essential principles of policy and to creating the statutory basis on which the necessary administrative apparatus is erected" (Citizenship and Immigration Canada 2001, 1). The Immigration and Refugee Protection Act was to follow this pattern. First introduced in the House of Commons in April 2000, Bill C-31 died in committee when the Liberal Chrétien government called an early election. After the Liberal Party's

---

[20] The report included one liberalization pertaining to non-nuclear family members: the sponsorship of a relative or close personal acquaintance of the sponsor's choice, subject to them being proficient in English or French and having completed secondary school. This recommendation did not make its way into the Immigration and Refugee Protection Act.

consolidation of its parliamentary majority, the immigration bill was reintroduced as Bill C-11 in February 2001, once again in the form of framework legislation. As Liberal parliamentary secretary to the minister for human resources, Raymonde Folco, elaborated:

> What kind of legislation will serve Canada best in the very volatile world of immigration and refugee protection? Events have already shown us that we need a flexible, responsive piece of legislation, not a cumbersome, rigid law. To answer that question, I want to turn to the very structure of the act, which this bill would enshrine in law. This is framework legislation. In other words, it sets out the general principles and policies on which our efforts in the area of immigration and refugee protection must be based. It says clearly that the procedures for the application of these principles and policies will be generally found in regulations. ... If we want usable and responsive legislation that can be understood, we have to put into law what ought to be in law. We should leave to regulation what is properly left to the regulatory process. We will therefore be able to adjust rapidly to meet the needs of Canadians while ensuring that those rights and principles are duly respected.
>
> (Parliament of Canada May 1, 2000b, 1555–600)

Consistent with the nature of framework legislation, Bill C-11 entailed remarkably few details about the selection of family and economic immigrants. Under "selection of permanent residents," the legislation simply stipulated that:

> 12(1) A foreign national may be selected as a member of the family class on the basis of their relationship as the spouse, common-law partner, child, parent or other prescribed family member of a Canadian citizen or permanent resident.
>
> 12 (2) A foreign national may be selected as a member of the economic class on the basis of their ability to become economically established in Canada.

Economic selection criteria and their weight, details of family sponsorship, and admission numbers for the various streams would all continue to be determined through regulation. In fact, the range of policy decisions that immigration ministers can make without full parliamentary approval is quite astounding, especially when compared to the United States, where something as simple as increasing the number of visas for skilled workers is subject to congressional approval (Woroby 2015).

In the parliamentary debates that ensued, one of the key criticisms leveled against the bill's provisions for economic and family immigration was precisely the fact that virtually all questions of substance were delegated to regulation.[21]

---

[21] On questions of refugee policy and immigration control, the bill included more extensive substantive provisions.

The following statement by Canadian Alliance MP Leon Benoit is representative of the arguments advanced by the parliamentary opposition:

I find it of great concern that the single most important and valuable component of Canadian immigration, the economic category, is only dealt with by a single sentence in the bill. It is hard to believe that there is only one sentence. The single sentence in clause 12(1) would be the guiding principle on which countless regulations would be developed. The law in fact would be created through regulation. It is not in the bill. This is a real concern to me. How can we hold departmental officials, the minister and the cabinet accountable if there is no assurance that changes will be made by passing them through parliament? I fully understand and accept that certain aspects of any legislation have to be left to regulation, but the balance in this legislation is way out of line. ... As with the economic class, there are a few guiding principles regarding the family, which are laid out pretty much in one sentence in the legislation. Subsequently everything else would be left to the interpretation of the bureaucrats, the minister and the cabinet of the day.

(Parliament of Canada February 27, 2001, 1305–10)

Despite Minister of Citizenship and Immigration Caplan's repeated assurance that the "regulations ... will be developed in as an open and consultative manner as this bill has been developed" (Parliament of Canada February 26, 2001, 1535–40), criticism did not abate. While there would be opportunity for public comment after the proposed regulations' publication in the *Canada Gazette*, there was no question that the delegation of such substantial policy making to the regulatory process would minimize parliamentary input and debate. When the New Democrats insisted that parliament should be given the opportunity to scrutinize the regulations at the bill's committee stage, the Liberals agreed to present the draft regulations to the Standing Committee on Citizenship and Immigration. The Liberals' willingness to compromise, however, did not extend beyond reviewing the new regulations. Confronted with parliamentary demands that any subsequent regulatory amendments be put before parliament for approval, the Liberals refused to concede ground. In the end the Immigration and Refugee Protection Act stated that while new regulations must be presented to each House of Parliament, this would not be required for subsequent amendments.[22]

Because the immigration bill included few substantive details on economic and family immigration policy, the parliamentary opposition had few targets for substantive criticism, at least prior to the regulations' submission to the Standing Committee on Citizenship and Immigration.

[22] Sections 5(2) and (3).

The move toward a human capital model of immigrant selection in particular – however vaguely conveyed in the immigration bill but clearly articulated by Minister Caplan – elicited very little debate in the House of Commons. In her introduction of the proposed legislation Caplan identified the human capital paradigm as the foundation of Canada's future economic immigration policy. In comments reminiscent of the arguments advanced in *Not Just Numbers*, she affirmed:

The new century will belong to those who are best able to develop and expand their collective human capital. The knowledge based economy has become a reality. If Canada is to compete and succeed, we must continue to attract skilled workers from across the globe, to share their knowledge and their skills and to build bridges with the rest of the world.

(Parliament of Canada February 26, 2001, 1520–5)

The absence of parliamentary debate on the human capital paradigm as the guiding principle of immigrant selection was not exactly surprising. Not only was it shared by economists, who exerted influence both as civil servants within the immigration bureaucracy and as external experts providing testimony before the Standing Committee on Immigration and Citizenship, but it was also the case that consultations throughout the 1990s had confirmed widespread societal elite support. In other words, there was bipartisan support not only for the principle of human capital-based immigrant selection but also for the maintenance of high immigration levels. The still weakened Progressive Conservatives welcomed the move from an occupation-based to a human capital-based economic selection system, even demanding an "exponential ... increase" in immigration in recognition of its "economic necessity" (Parliament of Canada February 26, 2001, 1730–5). Only the right-wing Canadian Alliance – the Reform Party's successor, whose efforts to "unite the right" had been rebuffed by the Progressive Conservatives – as the official opposition party made a brief pitch for an occupation-based selection (Parliament of Canada June 13, 2001, 1545–50).

It was only when the government submitted its draft regulations to the Standing Committee on Citizenship and Immigration that parliamentary discussion could turn to the thornier details of immigration reform. In its deliberations the committee closely considered the views expressed by organized interests during its hearings. In contrast to the near unanimous endorsement of the *principle* of human capital-based immigration – as articulated in the framework legislation – the proposed regulatory changes to the points system's *operation* elicited intense criticism. The majority of the 1,700 comments submitted during the open period alone were directed at the points system reforms. Supported by some Liberal backbenchers as well as the New Democrats, opposition was ultimately driven by the business community, who was concerned that the heavy weighting of formal education, the points system's high pass mark, and its retroactivity provisions would impede labor recruitment. The CEO of Canadian Manufacturers and Exporters protested that "the proposed immigration regulations would slam the door on skilled workers seeking to come to Canada" (Canada News Wire March 22, 2002), while the chairman of the Canadian Association of Management Consultants warned that "if they leave the points system they've devised in place, nobody will get through, the thresholds are so high" (Ramsay April 15, 2002). The Standing Committee on Citizenship and Immigration was persuaded by the merits of these concerns, as expressed in its final report:

> The vast majority of the skilled workers needed by this country will not be able to qualify for permanent residence either as a result of the point distribution in the grid or because the proposed pass mark of 80 is simply too high. Numerous examples were provided of highly educated technology professionals, fluent in an official language, who would not have a successful application. And skilled trades people would fare even worse.
>
> (Standing Committee on Citizenship and Immigration 2002, 6)

Among the recommendations by the Standing Committee were changes to points allocation in favor of the skilled trades and applicants with second undergraduate degrees, a lowering of the pass mark from 80 to 70, and stricter limits on retroactivity.[23]

The Standing Committee's report was not without effect. The final regulations, announced by newly appointed Immigration Minister Denis Coderre in June 2002, contained several revisions in line with the Standing Committee's recommendations. On virtually all of the above points, the government met the committee halfway. It even went beyond the committee's recommendations in increasing the point allocation for skilled trades credentials. Perhaps most importantly, the points system's new pass mark of seventy-five most clearly reflected a compromise between the government's proposed score of eighty and the Standing Committee's recommendation of seventy points. Unlike parliament at large, the Standing Committee was able to exert policy influence because not only was it able to grapple with the operational details of immigration

---

[23] "All skilled worker applications received before December 31, 2001 should be processed under the existing selection criteria until March 31, 2003" (Standing Committee on Citizenship and Immigration 2002, 4).

reform, but it also provided institutional access for interest groups – above all business. At the same time it is easy to overstate the significance of the government's concessions. The retroactivity changes, for instance, would become moot as soon as the application backlog was cleared. Most importantly, both the allocation of points and the pass mark could be changed again through regulatory amendment alone, thereby bypassing the legislative arena.

Just as had been the case with human capital-based immigration, the parliamentary debate on the bill's family immigration provisions quickly established a bipartisan consensus. Family unification, all parties affirmed, should continue to serve as a fundamental principle of Canadian immigration policy. The immigration minister herself declared that "[t]he family class, the parents, grandparents and dependent children who come together to create families and communities and contribute today but also in the future to the building of the country, is the reason why family reunification is such an important cornerstone of our immigration policy" (Parliament of Canada May 1, 2000a, 1535–40). Yet it quickly became apparent that the government's endorsement of the principle of family unification did not translate into an equivalent commitment to enlarge the family stream. While the government did respond to demands by the New Democrats to include parents in the legislation's definition of family class, this step was largely symbolic. Not only did existing regulations already allow for the sponsorship of parents, but the ability to sponsor parents was first and foremost a function of annual immigration targets – a measure unaffected by legislative reform. It is telling that the most significant regulatory changes to the sponsorship of core family members – the inclusion of same-sex partners and the raising of the age of dependent children from 19 to 22 – would not significantly increase the number of sponsorship applications. Even if we set aside the fact that same-sex partners had already been able to immigrate (albeit without legal certainty) under the 1976 Act's "humanitarian and compassionate" provisions (Dauvergne 2003), the relatively small number of same-sex unions would serve to keep demand in check.[24] Similarly, while children between the ages of 19 and 22 had been excluded from sponsorship since 1992, raising the age ceiling would affect a relatively small

---

[24] In 2011, same-sex couples accounted for 0.8 percent of all couples in Canada. If we assume a comparable gender breakdown for sponsored partners, of the 38,541 spouses and common-law partners entering Canada in 2011 only 308 would have been same-sex couples (Statistics Canada 2015).

number of cases.[25] It was only when the New Democratic members of the Standing Committee sought to add brothers and sisters to the family class – something that, as the case of the US shows (see Chapter 6), would drastically increase demand for family visas – that the Liberal committee members blocked the proposal.

By formalizing existing administrative practices and expanding sponsorship rights within the confines of the core family, the Liberal government was able to claim credit for championing family unification without having to compromise its commitment to a human capital-based immigration system. Tellingly, the Immigration and Refugee Protection Act did not disrupt the shift from family to economic admissions that had begun in the late 1980s and had come to define administrative practice in the 1990s (Figure 5.2). Throughout the 2000s successive governments were able to contain family immigration because they compensated for increased demand for core family sponsorship by squeezing out the admission of extended family members (i.e., parents and grandparents) (Figure 5.4). Unlike the admission of spouses and dependent children, which is based on demand, the number of parent and grandparent visas is politically determined. As immigration levels are annually decided by government – rather than being determined through legislation or regulation – the flow of noncore family members can be easily slowed by lowering target ceilings and slowing processing times. In other words, the remarkable containment of family immigration to Canada is the result of continued executive-dominated policy making.

With the passage of Canada's Immigration and Refugee Protection Act and its regulations in the early 2000s, the paradigmatic shift that was set in motion in the 1980s was finally concluded. Canada's immigration policy was now firmly premised on the primacy of human capital-based immigration, having decoupled economic admissions from the state of the economy while at the same time prioritizing economic over family admissions. Given Chrétien's solid parliamentary majority, the legislative institutionalization of human capital-based immigration took place in the absence of veto points. The structure of framework legislation effectively prevented substantive debate in the legislative arena; it was only after the

---

[25] In 2012, approximately 1,800 children older than 19 were sponsored under the family class (most accompanied sponsored immigrants within the parent and grandparent category, see www.gazette.gc.ca/rp-pr/p1/2013/2013-05-18/html/reg1-eng.html#REFa10, accessed February 17, 2017). Family sponsorship data show no increase in the total number of sponsored children after the age ceiling was raised in 2002.

draft regulations were submitted to the Standing Committee on Citizenship and Immigration that legislators were able to meaningfully engage with the immigration bill. In a manner akin to the Special Joint Committee's role in the lead-up to the 1976 Immigration Act, the Standing Committee allowed for the reciprocal communication of policy preferences between the government, parliament, and interest groups. Given the strength of employer opposition to the increased points threshold and the undervaluing of the skilled trades, the Chrétien government decided to compromise on both counts, allowing for the Immigration and Refugee Protection Act and its regulations to pass with broad bipartisan support. However, it is important to note the limited scope of the government's concessions. Most importantly, the government rejected legislators' demands to make subsequent regulatory amendments subject to parliamentary approval. Future immigration policy making – including changes to the points threshold or points allocation – would thus continue to be contained within the executive arena and remain relatively insulated from popular and interest group pressure.

The institutionalization of paradigmatic change, as argued in Chapter 2, is conditional upon the absence of veto points. Paradigmatic shifts are typically accompanied by broad-based political contestation about competing paradigms, as elites seek to select a new paradigm to replace a failed one. The case of the Canadian Immigration and Refugee Protection Act, however, does not fully conform to these expectations. Instead of paradigmatic competition, we observe a broad elite consensus in favor of a human capital-based immigration system. Had the legislative arena constituted a viable veto point – that is, had Chrétien not commanded a parliamentary majority – the economic and family immigration provisions of the Act would have likely still been adopted. While the Canadian Alliance – the largest opposition party – did not endorse the new paradigm with the same enthusiasm as the Liberals and Progressive Conservatives, they did not mount any principled opposition either, focusing restrictionist demands on family and humanitarian immigration instead. What can account for this – in comparative perspective remarkable – policy consensus not only among parties of all stripes but also among societal elites more broadly?

The shift from occupational demand- to human capital-based economic admissions in Canada occurred within the larger nation-building paradigm of the settler colonial state (see Chapter 1). This paradigm not only embraces immigration as serving the national interest, but, unlike guest worker states, takes for granted the link between immigration and permanent settlement. In contrast to German policy makers who confronted fundamental opposition to the pursuit of human capital-based immigration in the 2000s (see Chapter 4), the Chrétien government did not have to persuade anyone of the desirability of (permanent) immigration. In other words, in Canada the scope of potential conflict over immigration is limited to the size and composition of immigration flows. Yet even within those comparatively narrow parameters, the policy making dynamics of the Immigration and Refugee Protection Act demonstrate a remarkable cross-partisan consensus not only about the ideal size of immigration flows, but also about the primacy of the economic stream. This pattern is reflected in the 2004 Canadian Candidate Survey, where candidates from all parties – by then the Canadian Alliance and the Progressive Conservatives had merged to form the Conservative Party of Canada – resoundingly support high levels of immigration. The percentages of candidates supporting either current or higher levels of immigration range from 100 percent of Bloc Quebecois candidates, to 94 percent of New Democrats and 91 percent of Liberals, to 77 percent of Conservatives[26] (Black and Hicks 2008, 260).[27]

Turning to candidate preferences on the composition of immigration flows, we observe a solid cross-partisan consensus in favor of the primacy of points system admissions, with Liberal and Conservative candidates taking virtually indistinguishable positions; 89 percent of Conservatives, 88 percent of Liberals, 84 percent of New Democrats, and 76 percent of the Bloc Quebecois support an increase in skills-based immigration, with no candidate preferring a decrease (Black and Hicks 2008, 261). However, this consensus weakens – though does not disappear – when considering the family stream. All parties express much lower support for an increase in family admissions, with support strongest among the New Democrats and the Bloc (64 percent and 52 percent respectively favor an increase), whereas Liberals and Conservatives tend to favor the policy status quo (52 and 42 percent respectively). The difference between Liberals and Conservatives becomes more pronounced when turning to cuts in family admissions: 30 percent of Conservatives but only 11 percent of Liberal candidates favor a reduction in family immigration (Black and

---

[26] Among Liberals, 46 percent favor higher and 45 percent current levels of immigration; equivalent figures for the Conservatives are 40 and 37 percent; 67 and 27 percent for the New Democrats, and 48 and 52 percent for the Bloc Quebecois (Black and Hicks 2008, 260)

[27] Conversely, no Bloc Quebecois candidates, 1 percent of Liberals, 3 percent of New Democrats, and 14 percent of Conservatives favor a reduction in immigration.

Hicks 2008, 261).[28] In sum, while the positioning of Liberal and Conservative candidates on the size and composition of immigration flows is roughly comparable, there is a restrictionist streak among Conservative candidates pertaining to overall levels in general and family immigration in particular that is absent among Liberals.

Comparatively speaking, then, the breadth and depth of Canada's cross-partisan support for immigration is remarkable. As Triadafilopoulos observes, "Canada is unique among major immigration countries in the degree to which immigration policy is depoliticized and immigration itself is not only accepted but also enthusiastically embraced by political parties" (2013b, 6–7). Canadian cross-party support for immigration flourishes in a political environment where, most of the time, immigration does not feature prominently on party platforms or in electoral campaigns.[29] Given the electoral clout of immigrant voters in Canada – resulting from the large size of Canada's foreign-born population, its urban concentration, electoral institutions that favor geographically concentrated groups, and citizenship rules that have produced one of the highest naturalization rates in the world (Triadafilopoulos 2013b) – parties stand to gain much from appealing to immigrant voters. Importantly, cross-party support for immigration – including the absence of a viable anti-immigrant party at the federal level – prevents the mobilization of anti-immigrant attitudes.

This "Canadian exceptionalism" (Bloemraad 2012) of favorable public attitudes toward immigration (excepting asylum immigration), however, is a relatively recent phenomenon. From the passage of the 1976 Act until the late 1990s, between 60 and 70 percent of Canadians agreed that "there is too much immigration to Canada" (Reitz 2011, 9) – a percentage not that dissimilar to popular views expressed in other countries. It is only in 1997 that we observe a marked decline in anti-immigration attitudes. By the 2000s only 30–40 percent agree that immigration levels are too high. In another, more positively framed poll, anti-immigration attitudes are weaker but still follow the same intertemporal pattern.[30] Accordingly, from the 1970s until 1997, 40 to 55 percent

---

[28] Thirty-seven percent of Liberals and 29 percent of Conservatives favor an increase in family admissions.

[29] At least until the mid-2000s (and with the exception of the Reform Party in 1993).

[30] The first, Environics Institute, poll only allows for ("strong" or "somewhat") agreement or disagreement with the statement that Canada receives too much immigration. There is no "just right" option. The second, Gallup, poll asks: "In your opinion, do you feel there are too many, too few, or about the right number of immigrants coming to Canada?"

of Canadians favor a decrease in immigration. This changes between 1997 and 2001, when the percentage drops to 30 to 35 percent, and falls to 20 percent in 2005 (Reitz 2011, 9). The decline in anti-immigration attitudes since the late 1990s cannot be accounted for by any of the nonvariable factors that have been theorized to account for Canadian exceptionalism, such as the country's geographical isolation, which protects against spontaneous migrant arrivals. Neither is this attitudinal change driven by the growing proportion of immigrants among Canada's population. Public opinion research has shown that the foreign-born are no more supportive of immigration per se than native-born Canadians (Reitz 2011).[31]

Instead it is likely that the weakening of popular restrictionism since the late 1990s can in part be attributed to the success of the economic framing and management of immigration policy since Mulroney. Canadian public opinion data show that a third of variation in attitudes toward immigration can be accounted for by perceptions of the economic impact of immigration (Reitz 2011, 13–14).[32] Significantly, these perceptions are overwhelmingly positive: 82 percent of Canadians agree that immigration has a positive economic impact, while only 25 percent believe that immigrants "take away jobs." It is plausible to assume that the shift from the tap-on, tap-off approach to a human capital model has shaped how Canadians conceive of the economic impact of immigration. For over two decades the political decision to maintain high immigration levels even during recessionary times has sent a strong signal that immigration provides economic benefits independent of the state of the labor market. Accordingly, popular support for immigration increased in the early 1990s, despite a peak in unemployment (Reitz 2011). To the extent that pro-immigration attitudes are driven by the perception that immigration is in Canada's economic interest, popular support for noneconomic immigration will be weaker. Mirroring attitudes of parliamentarians, Liberal and Conservative voters will likely be less supportive of family, and in particular asylum, immigration than of high-skilled immigration.[33]

---

[31] In a 2010 Environics Institute poll, 58.4 Canadian-born respondents and 57.1 percent of immigrants expressed support for immigration (Reitz 2011, 11).

[32] Based on the 2010 Environics Focus Canada survey.

[33] Candidate support for higher levels of immigration is at 88 percent (Liberal) and 89 percent (Conservative) for the points-system entrants, 37 percent (Liberal) and 89 percent (Conservative) for family immigrants, and 29 percent (Liberal) and 29 percent (Conservative) for resettled refugees. The drop in support is far less pronounced among NDP and Bloc voters (Black and Hicks 2008, 261).

Popular support for immigration is thus likely contingent on first, the selection of immigrants on the basis of their perceived economic contributions, and second, the ability of policy makers to tightly manage and control immigration. Whereas policy makers have close to perfect control over economic admissions, control over nuclear family admissions is weaker, and control over asylum flows weaker yet. Had we focused our analysis on the politics of asylum reform under the Immigration and Refugee Protection Act, elite preferences likely would have been more restrictionist and the policy-making process more politicized than is the case with economic and family immigration reform (see Chapter 7).

During the Mulroney era, Canadian immigration policy underwent two profound shifts. First, the nature of immigrant admissions changed from being dominated by family immigration to becoming defined by economic immigration. Second, immigration levels shifted upward and became permanently uncoupled from labor market fluctuations. Remarkably, despite its far-reaching implications for immigrant constituencies, the reversal of fortunes between the economic and family classes took place through a series of incremental reforms within the executive arena and was passed largely unnoticed by the Canadian public. The wide scope for executive discretion that had long marked Canadian immigration policy allowed policy makers to enact far-reaching regulatory reforms without having to engage the legislative arena. While immigration officials made a concerted effort to reach out to societal elites in order to democratically legitimate their reforms, they were able to do so in ways that allowed for complete agenda control and that preempted the mobilization of opposition voices. The shift toward an immigration system firmly premised on economic selection thus transpired within the safety of popular and, to a slightly lesser extent, interest group insulation.

Unlike the politics surrounding the reforms of the 1960s and 1970s, diplomatic pressure played no discernible role in the shift from family to economic immigration. Given that the change in visa mix took place in a context of increasing overall admissions, sending states stood to benefit from greater immigration opportunities through the receipt of remittances. In the end the dynamics described here produced a set of immigration policies that, as we will see in Chapter 6, came to differ starkly from US immigration policy. Eventually, in a manner akin to the regulatory reforms of the 1960s, these momentous policy shifts would become institutionalized in the form of a new immigration act. However, reflecting Canada's executive-dominated policy making regime, the 2001 Immigration and Refugee Protection Act and its regulations did not so much change as affirm the regulatory status quo. While at the committee stage the opposition did win some policy concessions, at a fundamental level the Act legitimated over a decade of executive policy making, firmly institutionalizing an immigration system defined by human capital-based immigrant selection.

THE TURN TO MARKET-DRIVEN IMMIGRATION: 2006–2015

From 2006 to 2015, with the newly constituted Conservative Party coming into power, Canada's immigration system underwent a series of rapid and far-reaching reforms that left virtually no area of immigration and integration policy untouched.[34] The new government broke with the previous policy-making modus operandi in two consequential ways. First, ideologically the Harper Conservatives were located much further to the right than any previous postwar Canadian government. Whereas in the past both Progressive Conservatives and Liberals had pursued largely indistinguishable and centrist immigration agendas, the merger of the Progressive Conservatives with the socially conservative Canadian Alliance/Reform Party introduced a new element of partisanship into Canadian immigration politics. While the Party's social conservatism was somewhat held in check by political calculus, its economic agenda of market liberalism and a scaled back state had a profound impact on immigration reform.

In a second, related break with the past, the Harper government eschewed the consensus-oriented policy-making style that had marked Canadian immigration politics for the past decades. Having won the election on the basis of a minimal winning coalition, the Conservatives governed by appealing to their socially conservative base while also reaching out to immigrant constituencies in oftentimes symbolic ways. Under the policy entrepreneurship of Citizenship and Immigration Minister Jason Kenney, the government strategically exploited and increased its already significant immigration policy-making autonomy. As a result the Conservatives enacted far-reaching immigration reforms from within the political insulation of the executive arena. Through ministerial fiat alone, the government shifted the balance of immigration from permanent to temporary economic admissions and fundamentally reshaped the points system by changing its admissions logic from human capital to employer demand. In the area of family immigration,

---

[34] Changes to asylum and refugee policy, citizenship policy, and integration policy are beyond the scope of this chapter.

(margin note: balance of power resides in executive branch)

restrictionist policy reform did move into the legislative arena, although this did not weaken the government's insulation. Not only did the Conservative Party control parliament, but policy makers strategically buried politically delicate amendments to the Immigration and Refugee Protection Act – such as changes to parent and grandparent sponsorship – in omnibus bills in order to deflect debate and interest group mobilization. As a result, when the Liberals returned to power in 2015 they inherited an immigration system much different from the one they had left behind a decade earlier.

The Failure of Human Capital-Based Immigration under the Immigration and Refugee Protection Act

The period from 2006 to 2015 marked a critical interlude in Canadian politics as the newly formed Conservative Party of Canada won two minority governments before attaining majority rule in 2011. The founding of the Conservative Party in 2003 marked the conclusion of a decade of vote splitting between the ailing centrist Progressive Conservatives and the populist, neoconservative, and western-based Reform Party, which rebranded itself as the Canadian Alliance in 2000. While the Alliance had shed the populist ideals and moderated the social conservatism of the Reform Party, its commitments to fiscal conservatism, limited government, and a law-and-order agenda became key pillars of Conservative rule under Prime Minister Stephen Harper. A founding member of the Reform Party, Harper had been instrumental in moving the Reform Party's immigration platform away from the far-right positions of its base that had included demands to return to race-based immigrant selection, slash immigration (especially family immigration) and abolish multiculturalism, and use referendums to decide on questions of immigration policy (Dyson 1994).

While the party had moderated its positioning in order to widen its electoral appeal, the unification of the right produced a Conservative Party that held significantly less centrist views than the Progressive Conservatives under Mulroney. While the Harper Conservatives made a concerted – and in many places successful – effort to break the Liberals' traditional stronghold on ethnic minority and immigrant voters and to brand the Conservative Party as pro-immigration (Marwah et al. 2013), to a much greater degree than any previous government they also viewed immigration in strictly economic terms. Immigration was to be welcomed to the extent to which it provided tangible economic and fiscal benefits.

This economic utilitarianism crowded out other longstanding goals of Canadian immigration policy such as nation building, demographic growth, family unity, and humanitarianism. As a result the party held a less than sanguine view of family immigration, which was associated with sponsorship breakdown and fiscal costs, while being outright hostile toward asylum immigration, which the government repeatedly linked to fraud, criminality, and terrorism.

While the political challenges of family immigration – its noneconomic logic and expansive drift – had been confronted by previous governments, the Harper Conservatives under Citizenship and Immigration Minister Jason Kenney were the first to problematize human capital-based immigration.[35] Most fundamentally, they questioned the points system's premise that human capital – in particular formal education – was the engine of successful economic integration. Thus, while critiques of the 1976 Immigration Act had focused on its lack of economic selectivity – the dominance of family over points system admissions – not long after the passage of the 2001 Immigration and Refugee Protection Act, the points system itself came under attack. The Conservatives argued that workers who had entered through the Federal Skilled Worker Program had insufficiently high employment rates and earnings.

The government's questioning of the economic efficacy of human capital-based immigration was supported by a receptive bureaucracy, given that its critique was based on a growing body of research which showed that rising educational attainment since the 1990s had not been able to arrest the downward trend in employment rates and earnings of immigrants since the 1970s (Frenette and Morissette 2003, Hiebert 2006, Reitz 2014). Because the economic benefits of immigration depended upon high wages, economists argued, declining immigrant earnings – with its associated risk of poverty – not only increased the costs of immigration but also reduced its benefits (Dungan et al. 2012). Importantly, not only did immigrant earnings continue to decline during recessionary periods – a finding that contradicted the notion that human capital would provide a buffer from the vicissitudes of the market – but several studies showed that this decline extended across several business cycles, including during times of economic growth (Reitz 2014, 105). Most troublingly, since the 1990s immigrant earnings had declined relative to the earnings of native-born Canadians (Green and Worswick 2012). Challenging the economic

---

[35] The challenges of humanitarian immigration remain outside the scope of this chapter.

optimism reflected in the human capital debates of the 1980s and 1990s, one of the most influential studies of the early 2000s concluded that "compared to earlier cohorts, recent immigrant cohorts will – at least in the near future – be more likely to have difficulty making ends meet and will also be more financially vulnerable to shocks such as job loss" (Frenette and Morissette 2003, 15–16).

A second line of critique targeted the points system's lack of labor market responsiveness. On the one hand this critique was driven by market-liberal ideology. Thus, the Conservatives criticized that not only was a human capital-based points system ill-suited to fill short-term labor shortages, but its operation was premised on state intervention in the free play of the market. On the other hand there was, for solely pragmatic reasons, bipartisan agreement that the points system was in need of reform because of its mounting backlogs. Because the Federal Skilled Worker Program operated on a first-come, first-served logic, high application numbers had resulted in backlogs at times exceeding half a million applications, which translated into wait times of several years. Not surprisingly employers complained that the points system did not allow for the timely filling of permanent positions. While many businesses in high-skilled sectors could partially compensate for these rigidities by accessing temporary high-skilled labor, this was rarely the case for employers in low-skilled sectors. Not only did high-skilled admissions dominate the permanent economic stream, where they accounted for 85 percent of admissions, but a comparable skills bias characterized temporary foreign worker recruitment.[36] During the last ten years of Liberal rule – a period in which temporary worker admissions rose steadily (Figure 5.5) – 61 percent of temporary foreign workers were high-skilled.[37] As a result, despite an increasing supply of temporary foreign workers employer demand for low-skilled labor remained largely unmet.

---

[36] In 2004, 85 percent of all admissions (including dependents) through the economic stream were through the Federal Skilled Worker program. The remainder were made up of business immigrants (7 percent), provincial nominees (5 percent), and live-in caregivers (3 percent) (Citizenship and Immigration Canada 2005, 22).

[37] High-skilled workers are categorized as occupational skill level O (managerial), level A (professional), and level B (skilled and technical), low-skilled workers as occupational skill level C (intermediate and clerical) and D (elemental and laborers). Using data by Kustec (2012), I excluded all admissions where skill level was "not stated."

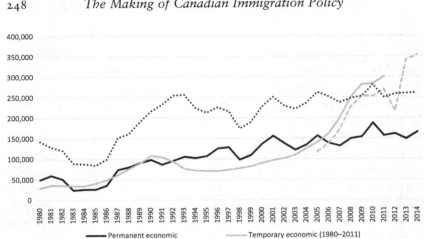

FIGURE 5.5 Canadian permanent and temporary economic admissions, 1980–2014.

Market Liberalism and the Pursuit of Economic Immigration Reform

The Rise of Temporary Foreign Worker Recruitment

In contrast to European guest worker states, in Canada – as in other settler colonial states – temporary foreign worker recruitment has traditionally played a subordinate role in immigrant admissions. This pattern, however, came under fundamental challenge after 2006 as the Conservatives sought to retool economic admissions in the name of labor market responsiveness. While temporary foreign worker admissions had already been on the increase since the mid-1990s, the Conservative Party's coming to power marks a clear acceleration of this trend (Figure 5.5[38]). Starting in 2008, in a historically unprecedented

---

[38] In 2013, Citizenship and Immigration Canada (CIC) changed the way it reported temporary immigration data. It started to distinguish between permit Temporary Foreign Worker program permit holders and International Mobility Program permit holders. The Temporary Foreign Worker Program (TFWP) is intended to fill short-term labor shortages and requires a Labor Market Opinion, with permits tied to particular employer. Arrivals under the International Mobility Program (IMP) do not require a Labor Market Opinion and hold an open work permit. Many IMP entrants arrive under NAFTA or through international exchange programs. The temporary economic data for 2005–14 presented here include both TFWP and IMP entrants. These figures do not perfectly map on to previous CIC data, hence the two separate lines for temporary economic admissions.

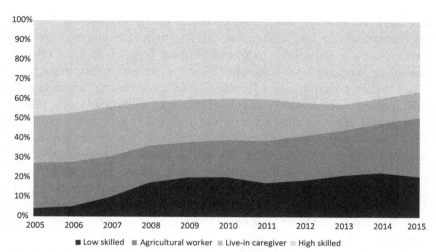

FIGURE 5.6 Canadian temporary foreign work program permit holders, stacked by program, 2005–15.

development, temporary foreign worker admissions started to surpass not only economic stream admissions but all three permanent – economic, family, and humanitarian – immigration streams combined. For the first time in Canadian history more foreign nationals were admitted as guest workers than as residents and future citizens, prompting some to pronounce "the end of settler societ[y]" (Dauvergne 2016). In a second development, after 2006 temporary worker admissions underwent drastic quantitative and qualitative changes, signaling a partial break not only with Canada's nation-building paradigm, but also with its human capital-based immigration regime. Whereas in 2005 half of all workers arriving through the Temporary Foreign Worker Program were classified as high skilled, by 2015 high-skilled workers accounted for just over a third of temporary worker admissions (Figure 5.6).

Of particular interest here is the Low-Skill Pilot Project, which drove the expansion of low-skilled recruitment. The program burgeoned from just over 2,000 admissions in 2005 to over 40,000 admissions in 2014, a twentyfold increase. The Low-Skill Pilot Project was quietly launched as a policy initiative by the Chrétien government in 2002 in response to employer demand in the oil and gas industry (in northern Alberta) and in construction (especially in Vancouver and Toronto) (Fudge and MacPhail 2009). Like most subsequent reform initiatives the program did not require any statutory basis as it fell within the parameters of executive action set by the Immigration and Refugee Protection Act and its regulations. In line with other existing temporary foreign worker programs – the Seasonal Agricultural Worker Program and the Live-in Caregiver Program – the Low-Skill Pilot Project was tightly regulated. The Chrétien government made little effort to promote the program, and the average annual number of recruits never exceeded 2,000 under Liberal rule. This all changed with the electoral victory of the market-liberal and western-based Harper Conservatives. Western employers in the construction and hospitality sectors in particular stepped up their demands for more low-skilled temporary foreign labor, arguing that the government had to act to fill labor shortages while the economic boom lasted (Fudge and MacPhail 2009).

Just months after being sworn into office the Conservative government announced a number of new initiatives designed to make it "easier, faster, and less costly for employers to hire temporary foreign workers" (Cragg 2011, 20). Among the most significant changes was the introduction of lists of "regional occupations under pressure," which relaxed the requirement for employers to demonstrate efforts to recruit domestic workers. Far from the restraint historically associated with the operation of Canada's Temporary Foreign Worker Program, the number of listed occupations proliferated rapidly. In the course of less than a year the regional list for British Columbia had expanded to over 230 occupations, ranging from taxi drivers, babysitters, cleaners, dancers, and actors to engineers (Fudge and MacPhail 2009). Other reforms followed in quick succession. In 2007 the requirement for a "labor market opinion" – an assessment of the need to recruit abroad – was significantly scaled back while the duration of work permits was extended from one to two years. In 2011 another consequential policy change allowed employers to pay temporary foreign workers 15 percent below the prevailing wage. Collectively these changes amounted to an unprecedented break with Canada's longstanding tradition of tight state management of immigration in favor of market-based deregulation.

The speed with which these reforms materialized was remarkable, although not entirely unprecedented. Given the enormous policy-making latitude on matters of immigration enjoyed by the Canadian executive, the government was able to pursue these policy initiatives within the existing statutory framework without broader societal consultation or legislative involvement. As long as the Conservatives lacked a parliamentary majority (2006–11), policy makers faced particularly strong incentives to exhaust whatever policy-making authority could be exercised within the confines of the executive arena and to avoid spillover into the legislative arena. At the same time the rapid expansion of guest worker recruitment indicated not only the executive's popular insulation, but also a decline in interest group insulation. As Rheault's study of corporate lobbying in Canada (2013) has shown, unlike permanent economic immigration levels, temporary worker inflows tend to correlate with the intensity of employer lobbying. In contrast to the points system, temporary foreign worker programs tend to be sectoral and hence provide concentrated economic benefits to employers with equivalent policy preferences (Rheault 2013). As a result, guest worker programs provide fertile conditions for interest group lobbying, a pattern we repeatedly observe in the politics of guest worker recruitment in Switzerland (see Chapter 3). Likewise, in Canada employer lobbies were instrumental in the creation of the Low-Skill Pilot Project in 2002 (Fudge and MacPhail 2009, Cragg 2011).

Interest group insulation varies not only by recruitment program but also by partisanship. Liberal governments in Canada have been less likely to make policy concessions in response to employer lobbying than Conservative administrations (Rheault 2013), a pattern that likely reflects both ideological leanings and the Liberals' lesser reliance on business as a source of political support. Accordingly, even though the Low-Skill Pilot Program was established under the Chrétien Liberals the Liberal government subsequently showed little enthusiasm for the program and kept tight control over its size. It was only with the coming to power of the Conservatives that employer lobbies in low-skilled sectors – oil and gas, hospitality, and construction – gained significant policy concessions (Cragg 2011). Employer lobbying was focused on the length of the labor market opinion process and the prevailing wage rate requirement, and policy reforms accommodated employers on both counts. Policy makers responded to interest group pressure not only reactively but also proactively by soliciting employer feedback and input into policy development (Cragg 2011). The Harper government's employer-friendly policies thus likely reflected both the lesser interest group insulation of a Conservative government and the fact that ideologically the Harper Conservatives were particularly closely aligned with employer preferences.

In deciding to drastically deregulate and grow Canada's Temporary Foreign Worker Program, the Conservatives' policy reforms broke with two paradigms that together had underpinned Canadian economic immigration policy from the mid-1980s until the 2001 Immigration and Refugee Protection Act. First, under the settler colonial state's nation-building paradigm immigrants have usually been admitted as permanent residents, rather than as temporary workers. Second, as policy makers progressively embraced the human capital paradigm, economic immigration policy came to be defined by high-skilled admissions. In departing from these paradigms the Conservatives not only undercut the elite consensus that had underpinned Canada's immigration regime for over two decades but also challenged the basic premise on which popular support for immigration rested. In contrast to relatively strong and stable popular support for the policy status quo under the points system, public support for temporary worker recruitment was both weaker and contingent on sustained economic growth. In 2008 – before the Conservatives' most controversial reform provisions were passed – a minority (44 percent) of Canadians supported the temporary worker program. Tellingly, there was significant subnational variation based on regional economic performance: support ranged from a high of 58 percent in Alberta (Canada's booming oil sands province) to 39 percent in Ontario (Keung April 25, 2008). By 2014, support for the Temporary Foreign Worker Program had dropped to 30 percent nationwide[39] and to 41 and 22 percent in Alberta and Ontario respectively (*Angus Reid Global* May 30, 2014). Support was lowest among unemployed Canadians (20 percent), reflecting a perception of temporary foreign workers as labor market competitors during economically precarious times.

It was not long before the Conservatives' deregulation of the Temporary Foreign Worker Program became a political liability and threatened to undercut its popular insulation. In 2013 the news media revealed evidence that the Royal Bank of Canada and HD Mining had used the temporary foreign worker programs to dismiss hundreds of Canadian workers and replace them with lower-paid temporary foreign workers. Public backlash was swift and vocal and dominated media coverage for close to a year. Given the immigration bureaucracy's structural attunement to shifts in public opinion and public debate – its director general of communication ensures that all senior officials receive a newsfeed every morning – the government decided to correct its course and reinstate the prevailing wage requirement, increase financial and administrative hiring requirements, and tighten the labor market opinion process (Woroby 2015).

---

[39] Thirty-eight percent of the public opposed the program and 32 percent were neither opposed nor in favor.

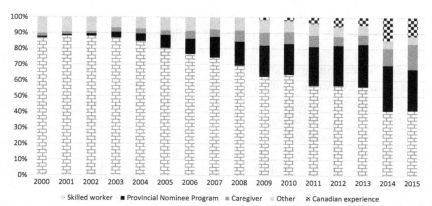

FIGURE 5.7 Economic class, by program, 2000–15.

The Shift to Employer-Driven Immigrant Selection

Between 2008 and 2015 the Canadian government progressively shifted the logic of permanent economic admissions from a human capital to an occupational demand-based model. Accompanying this change was a shift in the selection of economic immigrants from the state to employers, reflecting the conviction that in the words of Immigration Minister Jason Kenney, "[e]mployers are going to do a much better job at selection than a passive bureaucracy" (Paperny April 5, 2012). These changes had profound implications for the Federal Skilled Worker Program (i.e., the points system), which since 1967 had been the main catalyst for economic immigration. First, the program's significance diminished in both absolute and relative terms as the proportion of economic immigrants admitted through the points system was cut in half in the course of a decade. Whereas in 2005 points system entrants accounted for roughly 80 percent of permanent economic admissions, by 2015 this was the case for just over 40 percent of economic immigrants (see Figure 5.7).

Second, selection through the Federal Skilled Worker Program shifted from the first-come, first-served admission of applicants who met a certain human capital threshold to a system where in-hand job offers and priority occupations replaced education as key criteria for selection. In stark contrast to the previous paradigmatic shift from occupational demand-based to human capital-based immigrant selection in the 1990s, the Conservatives' pursuit of market-liberal immigration reforms transpired unilaterally, without the customary consultation of societal elites beyond business. Instead, under the capable leadership of Immigration Minister Jason Kenney, the Conservatives strategically exploited the government's discretionary powers under framework legislation and unilaterally enacted far-reaching market-liberal policy reforms, both within the confines of the executive arena and through legislative amendments to the Immigration and Refugee Protection Act. Under Kenney's skillful policy entrepreneurship, the unpopular and unglamorous immigration portfolio moved into the inner circle of cabinet politics, providing the immigration minister with the kind of agenda-setting influence that would have been the envy of previous immigration ministers (recall Ellen Fairclough's frustrations with her lack of cabinet support). Thus, "over the course of a decade in office, [the Harper government] undertook a sweeping overhaul of policies, rules, regulations, systems and process, all without tabling a new Immigration Act .... The name, the IRPA [Immigration and Refugee Protection Act], is merely the skin of the old system. Inside is a very different beast" (Omidvar 2016, 179).

As a first step, in 2008 parliament passed the omnibus budget Bill C-50, which amended the Immigration and Refugee Protection Act in ways that augmented the already significant policy-making autonomy of the executive. First, the bill eliminated the immigration minister's obligation to process all submitted immigration applications and authorized the retroactive application of immigration regulations. Immediately, in an unprecedented and highly controversial move, Kenney used this provision to eliminate the vast visa processing backlog for the Federal Skilled Worker Program and tossed out the application files of 280,000 foreign skilled workers and their families, many of whom had been waiting for a decision for years. In a second amendment to the Act, Bill C-50 empowered the immigration minister to issue binding instructions concerning the processing of immigration applications. During his seven-year tenure as Minister of Immigration and Citizenship, Kenney, who was widely acknowledged as Prime Minister Harper's right hand (Castonguay February 2, 2013), made extensive use of his new powers, issuing nine sets of Ministerial Instructions, most of which concerned the Federal Skilled Worker Program (Satzewich 2015). In the 2008 *Action Plan for Faster Immigration*, Kenney issued instructions that limited points system admission to applicants from specified in-demand occupations and to those with preexisting employment offers.[40] In 2010 he

---

[40] Alternatively, applicants had to have been legally resident in Canada for at least a year as a temporary foreign worker or international student.

refined the occupation list and capped the number of applications without employment offers at 20,000, followed by a further reduction to 10,000 in 2011.

The policy significance of these reforms, all effected through ministerial fiat, was immense. Passed with the express goal of reducing application backlogs, speeding up processing, and improving labor market responsiveness, these changes ultimately gutted the human capital system by shrinking the Federal Skilled Worker Program and tying admissions to labor market demand and in-hand job offers. Thus, whereas in 2005 130,000 workers (many of whom did not have job offers in hand) were admitted to Canada through the points system, by 2014 this number had been cut in half, with the vast majority of applicants holding "Arranged Employment Offers." With the contraction of the Federal Skilled Worker System from over 80 percent to just over 40 percent of permanent economic admissions, other recruitment programs gained in prominence, most notably the Provincial Nominee Program (PNP) (Figure 5.7).

The PNP, established under the Liberals in 1995, allows provinces with low levels of immigration to nominate immigrants on the condition that they fill a specified job in the province. By 2007 all provinces (except for Quebec) and two northern territories had enacted PNP agreements with the federal government. In a parallel fashion to the Low-Skill Pilot temporary worker project, which had remained small in size under Liberal rule, the PNP rapidly expanded under Harper's immigration agenda of labor market and employer responsiveness, especially after the Conservative government removed the cap on PNP admissions in 2008. As a result, while from 2000 to 2005 an annual average of fewer than 5,000 immigrants were admitted through the PNP, this number grew to 33,000 per annum between 2006 and 2015.

With the expansion of the PNP Canadian immigration policy not only moved further toward the goal of labor market responsiveness by being receptive to regionally specific, short-term labor market needs, but also increased the influence of employers over immigrant selection. To a greater extent than is the case federally, interest group insulation is much lower at the provincial level, where "employers typically set the terms for their provincial government" (Triadafilopoulos 2013b, 14), and the Harper reforms augmented this influence further. The same pattern holds for the Canadian Experience Class (CEC) established by the Conservatives in 2009 to allow international students – whose enrollment more than doubled over the 2000s – and high-skilled temporary foreign workers with Canadian work experience to adjust their status to that of permanent resident. By 2014, admissions through the CEC peaked at close to 24,000 immigrants, accounting for about 15 percent of economic stream admissions (Figure 5.7).

The rise of the PNP and CEC at the expense of the Federal Skilled Worker Program marks a critical change in Canadian immigration policy as it constitutes a shift from "one-step" to "two-step" immigration. Thus, whereas the Federal Skilled Worker Program grants permanent residence upon entry, two-step immigration programs such as the PNP and CEC instead admit applicants on a temporary basis before offering some the option of applying for permanent residence, subject to labor market conditionalities. In doing so Canada followed New Zealand and Australia in erecting higher hurdles to permanent residence while simultaneously creating legal pathways for some temporary employer-sponsored migrants to become permanent residents. While the developments discussed here certainly reflected the Conservatives' ideological commitments, they likely were also influenced by policy reforms in New Zealand and Australia, reflecting the close relationship between the two prime ministers as well as frequent trips to Australia by Immigration Minister Kenney. Thus, Australia and New Zealand intensified temporary foreign worker recruitment before Canada did. Similarly, Canada's adoption of Express Entry (see below) followed Australia's example, who in turn had copied the program from New Zealand. In this instance, diplomatic influence did not take the form of diplomatic pressure but rather reflected a case of policy learning from abroad.

From a theoretical perspective, the significance of the 2008 Immigration and Refugee Protection Act amendments – in particular the enactment of Ministerial Instructions – lies in the fact that they were passed as part of an omnibus budget bill. Throughout its tenure the Harper government used omnibus bills to pass far-reaching legislative amendments in a range of policy areas, including immigration, in order to deny the parliamentary opposition the opportunity for policy input (Wilson 2016). Thus, between 2005 and 2015 not only did the length – and hence the "omnibus-ness" – of Budget Implementation Bills expand from an average of 66.5 pages to 305.5 pages (Wilson 2016, 40), but their number doubled as well. Budget and other kinds of omnibus bills provide governments with tight control over the policy process as they lump together multiple unrelated issues that are voted on in their entirety. This means specific proposals attract little attention and, even when they do, they are unlikely to be opposed because voting against the bill can threaten to bring down the government. This is particularly true in times of minority rule and hence can account for the success of the Harper Conservatives in effecting significant immigration reforms through legislative amendment even during minority rule. Where legislative amendments are included in omnibus bills, "it is almost impossible for individual members of Parliament, both government and opposition, to properly understand the myriad provisions in such bills, nor does any single parliamentary standing committee, such as the Finance Committee, which would normally review budget bills, have sufficient expertise to analyse provisions ranging across the spectrum of government policy" (Wilson 2016, 41). Recall the central role played by the Standing Committee on Citizenship and Immigration in providing both majority party parliamentarians and the opposition with an opportunity for policy input leading up to the passage of the 2001 Immigration and Refugee Protection Act. By contrast, because omnibus bills seek to preempt legislative and public debate on proposed policy reforms, they afford the executive immense political – and in particular popular – insulation.

In 2015 new Immigration Minister Chris Alexander announced, by means of Ministerial Instructions, the creation of the Express Entry system as the "biggest watershed in Canadian immigration" since the points system's inception (Sevastopulo and Doyle June 21, 2015). With the institution of Express Entry the Conservatives' points system reforms that began in 2008 came to their logical conclusion. Instead of admitting applicants on a first-come, first-served basis, the new system created an electronic interface between potential immigrants and potential employers. It presented employers with a pool of applicants whose desirability is measured relative to other applicants, rather than determined by a prior specified points threshold.

Most importantly, the new system evaluated applicants on the basis of their employability rather than their human capital, with the highest points being awarded to those with existing job offers. Out of a maximum of 1,200 points, 600 could be awarded for a job offer alone, with the remaining points largely based on work experience, age, language fluency, and education. Importantly, unlike the old points system, under Express Entry no formal backlog is created, as the files of unsuccessful applicants expire after twelve months. In the program's first year of operation only about 5 percent of applicants were successful, and Express Entry accounted for as few as 20 percent of permanent economic admissions. All successful applicants had in-hand job offers and, in stark departure from previous admission patterns, 80 percent of selected applicants had applied from within Canada, mainly as temporary foreign workers, intracompany transfer workers, or, less commonly, international students (Chiose March 31, 2016).[41]

Express Entry thus signifies a major departure from past practices of skilled immigrant selection. By delegating critical aspects of immigrant selection to employers and by elevating jobs and work experience over broader conceptions of human capital as the basis for recruitment, Express Entry no longer bears much resemblance to the points system of the 1990s and 2000s. Unlike the move from occupational demand-based to human capital-based immigration that evolved from the late 1980s onward, Express Entry was created in the absence of widespread elite consultation, with the important exception of employers. Institutionally empowered through Ministerial Instructions, the government and senior bureaucrats pushed their executive policy-making power to its limits, even enacting the kind of retroactivity provisions that had been struck down by the Standing Committee on Citizenship and Immigration when scrutinizing the Immigration and Refugee Protection Act's regulations. Instead the Conservatives adopted a new modus operandi of unilateral, top-down policy making that, while institutionally facilitated by Canada's executive-dominated political system, nevertheless carried with it – as we saw in the case of temporary foreign worker recruitment – the risk of future policy reversal. While at the time of writing it is too early to declare the program's fate, recent policy adjustments under the Trudeau Liberals suggest that its ideological underpinnings will likely not become fully institutionalized.

Market Liberalism and the Pursuit of Family Immigration Reform

With the 2011 federal election, Stephen Harper led the Conservative Party not only to its third consecutive victory, but also to its first parliamentary majority. Emboldened by their new majority status, the Conservatives quickly moved to tackle one of the riskiest areas of immigration reform: the curtailment of family sponsorship. Given that the government's embrace of immigration was largely premised on its economic utility, family sponsorship was an obvious candidate for reform. In November 2011, Citizenship and Immigration Minister Kenney

---

[41] Express Entry quickly came under fire for impeding the settlement of graduating international students because of its heavy reliance on job offers and work experience. In 2015, of 8,000 applicants who had studied in Canada only 1 percent had enough points to qualify (Chiose March 31, 2016).

announced Phase I of the government's *Action Plan for Faster Family Reunification*, which singled out the Parent and Grandparent Program (PGP) as in need of reform. At a news conference Kenney decried the backlog of 165,000 PGP applications that had led to average wait times of six years as a "problem of math. ... When the number of applications exceeds the number of people admitted to Canada over time, we end up with long and growing backlogs" (cited in Chen and Thorpe 2015, 87). What Kenney failed to mention was the fact that the PGP backlog was not primarily the result of increasing PGP applications but of decreasing PGP admissions. The backlog was the logical conclusion of an immigration policy that since the 1990s had prioritized the entry of immediate family members over that of extended relatives in order to curtail family immigration. As consecutive governments restricted the entry of elderly relatives through administrative delays and drastically lowered admission ceilings, the number of visas available for parents and grandparents progressively shrank both over time and in relation to those available to other family class immigrants, resulting in mounting backlogs.

Through Ministerial Instructions, Kenney announced a significant increase in the PGP quota for 2012 and 2013 in order to reduce the existing backlog (see Figure 5.2) and then declared a two-year moratorium on any new PGP applications. In order to deflect the moratorium's impact, the minister announced the creation of a new Super Visa that would admit parents and grandparents as visitors for a period of up to two years, for a maximum of ten years in total. In 2013 the government's *Action Plan* entered Phase II. The PGP program would resume in 2014, but annual admissions would be slashed from a previous annual average of 17,500 in the 2000s to 5,000 visas per annum. Kenney further announced a drastic tightening of sponsorship requirements for parents and grandparents by increasing the minimum income necessary for sponsorship by 30 percent, requiring that sponsors demonstrate this income level for three years (as opposed to one) and extending sponsorship obligations for a period of twenty (instead of ten) years. Lastly, Phase II of the *Action Plan* institutionalized the Super Visa as a permanent feature of Canadian family immigration policy.

The Conservatives' changes to family sponsorship between 2012 and 2014 reflected both continuity and discontinuity with past family immigration policy. On the one hand, the slashing of PGP visas followed a two-decades-old pattern of seeking to contain family immigration by curtailing the entry of extended relatives. The targeting of parents and grandparents in particular was motivated by a deeply entrenched conception of elderly family members as "human liabilities" (Chen and Thorpe 2015, 90). With the rise of the human capital paradigm in the late 1980s, points system entrants were pursued for their human capital while elderly family members became problematized as a social burden based on their assumed lack of human capital. Under Harper's neoconservative government, the fiscal costs of family immigration took on a new urgency, given the embrace of economic utilitarianism as the key rationale for immigration. In 2013 Kenney justified the sponsorship changes to the PGP program by forcefully articulating parents and grandparents as a fiscal burden on Canadian society:

If you think your parents may need to go on welfare in Canada, please don't sponsor them. We're not looking for more people on welfare, we're not looking to add people as a social burden to Canada. If their expectation is that they need the support of the state then they should stay in their country of origin, not come to Canada.

(CBC News May 10, 2013)

Where past attempts to cut the immigration of extended family members had been held in check by the risk of alienating immigrant constituencies, the Conservatives' creation of the Super Visa was a political masterstroke. While the government was careful not to outright abolish the PGP program, the political fallout from its initial suspension and subsequent contraction was successfully contained by the Super Visa's introduction. The Super Visa was enthusiastically embraced by immigrant communities because it allowed those with sufficient financial resources to bring in their elderly relatives without the delays associated with the PGP program – no small consideration given the realities of old age.[42] Thus, in March 2013 the government prided itself on having issued 1,000 Super Visas per month, with an approval rate of 86 percent (Citizenship and Immigration Canada March 6, 2013).

The creation of the Super Visa marks a radical break with decades of Canadian family immigration policy because it introduces temporariness into a historically permanent immigration stream. As "continuous visitors" (Chen and Thorpe 2015, 91), Super Visa holders have to return to their home countries at the end of every two years in order to apply for visa renewal, a requirement that renders family reunification contingent

---

[42] The Super Visa is designed to privatize all associated costs by denying visa holders access to public health care and social benefits; sponsors have to meet minimum income conditions and are required to pay high annual premiums for private health insurance, even for short visits.

on the health status of elderly relatives and stable family income, as well as the continued willingness of private insurance companies to extend coverage (Chen and Thorpe 2015).[43] Most importantly, the Super Visa can only be extended to a maximum of ten years, which means that in the absence of policy reform, visa holders will never be able to permanently join their families, hence calling into question the very notion of family reunification. In the words of a critic, "[t]his isn't family reunification; families aren't tourists in one another's lives" (Omidvar May 20, 2013). Unlike with previous reforms, the government engaged stakeholder consultation after announcing its *Action Plan*. However, even though its proposals received mixed responses and did not meet with broad-based elite and public support, the government charged ahead with its proposed reforms and effected radical changes to parent and grandparent sponsorship through ministerial fiat.

The Conservatives' determination to reduce all immigration that did not directly provide economic benefits for Canada also extended beyond the PGP program. In 2014, the government reduced the age of dependent children eligible for family sponsorship from 22 to 19. While the Mulroney Progressive Conservatives had done the same in 1992, the Harper Conservatives' discursive justification of this change broke new ground in its utilitarian application of market liberalism to the immigration of dependent children. In its Regulatory Impact Analysis Statement, the Department of Citizenship and Immigration justified its decision on the basis of the lower economic payoffs of the admission of older dependent children:

Statistics demonstrate that older dependent children (those who arrive between the ages of 19 and 21) have lower economic outcomes than those who arrive in Canada at a younger age (between 15 and 18 years old). ... In other words, the current definition of a dependent child for immigration purposes is out of step with the Government of Canada's objective of selecting migrants who contribute best to Canada's economic growth and sustainability. ... Reducing the age of dependent children would support Canada's immigration priorities by placing more emphasis on younger immigrants, who integrate more rapidly into the labor market and who would spend a greater number of years contributing to the economy.

(Citizenship and Immigration Canada May 18, 2013)

In a statement that vividly reflected the scope of the Conservatives' market-liberal agenda, the immigration department went on to emphasize that older children now excluded from family sponsorship might

[43] See note 42.

nevertheless be admitted into Canada "on their own merit" through the economic stream after having acquired "the skills and experience required to contribute to Canada's overall economic growth" (Citizenship and Immigration Canada May 18, 2013).

From 2006 to 2015, Canadian immigration policy thus underwent a series of reforms that were unprecedented in their speed and scope, and perhaps most importantly in the manner in which they came about. In the course of less than a decade the points system's human capital logic had become sidelined by the principle of employer demand, the centrality of permanent immigration had become undercut by the exponential rise of temporary foreign worker recruitment, and the sponsorship of extended family members had become drastically curtailed through the shift from family reunification to temporary visitation. Most of these changes were passed through ministerial fiat, with the immigration minister strategically exploiting the executive's policy-making autonomy. Even when policy moved into the legislative arena, the government did not adopt the consensus-oriented policy-making style that had characterized past episodes of immigration reform. Instead of using the legislative process to identify points of contention and offer some policy concessions for the sake of broader political support, the Harper government decided to bury immigration amendments in vast omnibus bills, effectively preempting any legislative debate on its proposals. As a result policy reform was marked by high popular and interest group insulation,[44] except on the issue of temporary foreign worker recruitment, where western-based employer associations were quick to mobilize and exploit their links to the Conservative Party at the same time as the government's deregulation overreach triggered popular backlash. Despite the Conservatives' overall success in implementing their policy agenda, the speed of reform came at the cost of policy legitimacy. Given that despite their paradigmatic nature, the reforms had not been institutionalized through consultation with societal elites and through parliamentary debate, when the Conservatives were voted out of power in 2015 they left behind a policy legacy vulnerable to reversal.

Postscript

After having campaigned on a pro-immigration, pro-multiculturalism platform, the Liberal Party under the leadership of Justin Trudeau swept

---

[44] On the question of diplomatic insulation, foreign governments did not mobilize on the reform proposals.

into power in late 2015. While the Trudeau government's most politically salient migration policy change was the admission of 40,000 Syrian refugees in its first year of office, the Liberals also reversed several family and economic immigration reforms enacted by the Conservatives. In 2016 the Liberals doubled the number of parent and grandparent visas to 10,000 while leaving the Super Visa program intact. Immigration Minister John McCallum further announced a budget increase of $75 million over the course of four years in order to speed up family class processing (Mas January 8, 2016). Parent and grandparent visas were once more doubled to 20,000 in 2017, allowing for a backlog reduction of 84 percent relative to 2001 and a shortening of processing times from seven to two years (Immigration, Refugees and Citizenship Canada January 11, 2019).

In contrast to the Conservative Party, who had framed the immigration of nonworking-age family members as a drain on fiscal resources, the Liberals argued that a generous family immigration policy was desirable not only for the sake of family unity, but also because it promoted economic growth. Rejecting former Citizenship and Immigration Minister Kenney's neoliberal justification for slashing parent and grandparent admissions, Trudeau, likely seeking to appeal to immigrant constituencies, framed family immigration as "an important help and driver to the middle class" and argued that older relatives fulfilled a critical economic function as providers of childcare to working parents (CBC News September 25, 2015). In another reversal of Conservative policy reform, the Liberals restored the age ceiling for dependent children to 22, arguing that "increasing the age limit will also help to enhance Canada's economy by making it a destination of choice for skilled immigrants who want to keep their families together" (CBC News September 25, 2015).

Turning to economic immigration policy, the Liberals retained the framework of Express Entry while at the same time weakening its labor market rationale. In 2016 the government slashed the value of in-hand job offers from 600 to 200 points[45] – representing a drop from 50 to 17 percent of the maximum total score – in addition to lifting the requirement of mandatory job bank registration. While job offers still carried significant weight – slightly more than educational credentials and official language proficiency – a job offer was now no longer a precondition for Express Entry selection. The government further reintroduced a family

---

[45] Except for provincial or territorial nominations, which were awarded 600 points.

unification rationale into economic immigration by awarding fifteen points to Express Entry applicants with siblings in Canada.[46] In sum, the Liberals lessened the significance of short-term labor demand as a basis for points system admission without, however, fully restoring the old human capital-based model. While it is too early to say whether economic integration has improved under Express Entry, there is no question that retaining the system has its political merits. Because it renders any backlogs administratively invisible – unsuccessful applications are not retained, forcing unselected applicants to reapply the following year – it allows the immigration minister to claim credit for running an efficient immigrant selection system.

Finally, turning to the question of temporary foreign worker recruitment, the Trudeau government's most significant policy reversal was the abolition of the "four-in, four-out" rule – requiring certain temporary foreign workers to leave Canada after four years – which had been put in place by the Conservatives to prevent temporary foreign worker settlement. Arguing that the rule's abolition would "prevent unnecessary hardship and instability for both workers and employers," the Liberals emphasized a commitment to permanent immigration pathways, invoking the longstanding nation-building paradigm that had come under challenge by the Harper Conservatives. The Liberals further tightened labor market regulations by requiring employers in low-wage sectors to advertise to at least two underrepresented groups – youth, persons with disabilities, Indigenous persons or recent immigrants – before hiring temporary foreign workers. While recruitment under the Temporary Foreign Workers Program has largely stagnated under the Liberals, admissions under the International Mobility Program – which provide Labor Market Opinion-exempt access to the labor market, mostly under the North American Free Trade Agreement or international exchange programs – have increased by 45 percent under the Liberal government, to 255,000 permits in 2018. While it is still too early to fully assess the Liberals' policy legacy, these developments suggest that at the same time as large-scale temporary foreign worker recruitment is likely to remain an integral part of Canada's economic migration policy, permanent immigration appears to have regained some of its former preeminence. Most prominently, annual admissions of permanent residents are

---

[46] "Express Entry Improvements: Spring 2017," June 5, 2017. www.canada.ca/en/immigra tion-refugees-citizenship/news/2017/03/express_entry_improvementsspring2017.html.

now at a historic high, having increased from 260,400 in 2015 to a target of 340,000 admissions in 2020.

CONCLUSION

In comparative perspective Canada's politics of economic and family immigration policy making are set apart in important ways from the three other country cases examined in this book. First, unlike in any other country, the executive arena has been and continues to be the locus of immigration policy making (Table 5.1). In part, the executive arena's centrality in policy making is a feature of policy making in Westminster-style systems more generally. Yet executive dominance in Canadian immigration policy making has also been the result of a longstanding pattern of immigration acts taking the form of framework legislation, leaving many of the most important policy decisions to regulation and other types of executive Orders-in-Council. A second characteristic of Canadian immigration policy making is the tendency of governments to pursue, despite their enormous policy autonomy, consensual-style policy making through consultations with a wide circle of social elites. At least, this has been the case for our first two case studies, with the reforms of the Harper years being a partial exception to the rule. In cases of paradigmatic reform, even though policy change is conceived of and largely decided on in the executive arena, Canadian policy makers have generally been careful to subsequently legitimize their project – if necessary by means of minor policy concessions – by engaging with societal and parliamentary elites. As a result, with the short-lived exception of the 1993 federal election, Canadian immigration politics has lacked the partisan polarization that characterizes contemporary immigration policies in the other countries. As the joint result of the executive's popular insulation and its commitment to securing elite support for major reform projects, Canadian immigration politics – at least in the area of economic and family admissions – exhibits remarkably little politicization, with public opinion being largely supportive of the policy status quo.

Substantively speaking, the politics of economic and family immigration policy in Canada produced relatively frequent paradigmatic reforms that moved economic admissions toward liberalization and family sponsorship toward restriction (Table 5.1). These paradigmatic shifts – from race-based to skills-based admissions, from occupational demand to human capital immigrant selection, from a family-dominated immigration system to one defined by economic immigration – have been

TABLE 5.1 *Canadian case studies summary*

Policy episode	Policy choice	Policy arenas	Popular insulation	Interest group insulation	Diplomatic insulation
Case study 1					
1962 Regulations and 1967 points system	*Paradigmatic liberalization*	Executive arena	High	Intermediate	Low
1976 Immigration Act and Regulations	*Institutionalizing paradigmatic liberalization*	Executive arena Legislative arena	High	Intermediate	Low
Case study 2					
1980s and 1990s: Multiple Orders-in-Council	*Paradigmatic liberalization* (human capital-based economic immigration)	Executive arena	High	Intermediate	High
2001 IRPA and Regulations	*Selective restriction* (family immigration) *Institutionalizing paradigmatic liberalization*	Executive arena Legislative arena	High	Intermediate	High
Case study 3					
2006–2015: Multiple Ministerial Instructions and Immigration and Refugee Protection Act amendments	*Paradigmatic liberalization* (temporary economic immigration) *Paradigmatic restriction* (family immigration)	Executive arena Legislative arena	Intermediate	Intermediate	High

facilitated through the institutional and strategic factors identified above. The lack of policy gridlock in particular is made possible by the relatively high popular and interest group insulation of the Canadian executive, in addition to the lack of legislative veto points. In a similar vein, the overall trend toward policy liberalization can be accounted for by the centrality of the executive arena, which is marked by low diplomatic and high popular insulation. The executive's high degree of interest group insulation, on the other hand, can account for the success of restrictive family sponsorship reform, especially when compared to equivalent but unsuccessful efforts in the United States. While the restriction of family immigration did not always proceed as planned, over time Canadian policy makers developed strategies that rendered restriction less visible (e.g., by slowing processing times and decreasing visa allotments, rather than abolishing entire programs) and shielded reformers from the electoral costs of alienating immigrant voters (by simultaneously raising overall admissions or creating the Super Visa to compensate for sponsorship restrictions).

While diplomatic pressure was instrumental in effecting policy liberalization in the 1960s and 1970s, the policy reforms of the 1990s and 2000s reflected technocratic attempts to correct the shortcomings of the policy status quo. In other words, the safety of the executive arena allowed policy makers to "puzzle" (Heclo 1974) and experiment in search for policy solutions, subsequently reaching out to elites on their own terms for the sake of policy legitimation. In both case studies, policy spillover into the legislative arena was carefully engineered to affirm, rather than undermine, executive policy making.

In contrast, our third case study – the years of Conservative rule from 2006 to 2015 – stands out as an exception in many ways. Ideologically to the right of Canada's traditional bipartisan consensus on immigration, the Harper government used its institutional powers to reshape and in important ways restrict both human capital-based economic and family immigration without engaging in broad-based elite consultation and legislative debate. At the same time, with the exception of temporary foreign worker recruitment, the reforms followed a familiar pattern of high popular and high interest group insulation, and were passed in a context marked by the absence of diplomatic pressure. Given their lack of legislative institutionalization, however, it remains to be seen whether this latest round of reforms will turn out to be a brief aberration or whether it will lastingly shape the substance and nature of Canadian immigration policy making.

6

The Making of US Immigration Policy

Explaining Economic and Family Admissions

This chapter examines the making of US economic and family immigration policy from the 1950s to the mid-2010s. Following in broad strokes the pursuit of nondiscriminatory immigration admissions in Canada, the first case study examines the development of a US policy regime anchored in family ties and occupational skill. Driven by the diplomatic imperative to forge a global anti-Communist coalition, efforts to end the exclusion of immigrants from the Global South in the early 1950s quickly moved into the legislative arena where, however, reform was repeatedly blocked by powerful congressional restrictionists. While reformers eventually secured a historic victory with the passage of the 1965 Immigration and Nationality Act, the abolition of the national origins system was secured at the cost of major concessions to restrictionist legislators. As a result, policy liberalization was less far reaching than in Canada.

The chapter's second case study again mirrors Canadian reform initiatives that sought to tilt the balance of immigrant admissions from family-based to economic admissions. Once again, the locus of US immigration reform was in the legislative arena, where the need to accommodate societal interests thwarted efforts to curtail family immigration. Instead, the 1990 Immigration Act attained an increase in high-skilled admissions only by raising overall levels of immigration. The chapter's third case study examines the failure of Comprehensive Immigration Reform – the combined pursuit of legal immigration reform, immigrant legalization, and immigration enforcement – under the Bush and Obama presidencies. Spanning over a decade, efforts at Comprehensive Immigration Reform were repeatedly thwarted by legislators' weak popular insulation as a newly empowered restrictionist wing within the Republican Party pursued an anti-immigration agenda for electoral gain. Even though the growing electoral strength of ethnic minority voters propelled the pursuit of policy liberalization on the political agenda, minority electoral clout and interest group lobbying could not neutralize the political risks attached to a pro-immigration agenda at this time of heightened anti-immigration populism.

FROM RACE-BASED TO FAMILY-BASED IMMIGRATION: 1952–1965

With the passage of the 1965 Immigration and Nationality Act, the United States joined Canada in rejecting the age-old paradigm of race-based immigration and instead embraced a new policy regime that, at least formally, was to be anchored in family ties and occupational skill, rather than national origin. Similar to the Canadian case, the initial impetus for reform came in the form of diplomatic pressure. With the Cold War spreading across the globe, if the US was to augment its new superpower status it could no longer afford to blithely disregard diplomatic pressures for policy liberalization as it had done throughout the era of international isolationism. Criticism of the national origins quotas by governments across Southern Europe and the Global South left little doubt that the policy status quo threatened to undermine US efforts at building a worldwide anti-Communist coalition.

Yet in contrast to Canadian policy makers, who were able to neutralize diplomatic pressure by enacting paradigmatic reform through executive Orders-in-Council, the longstanding congressional dominance of US policy making required that reform pass through the legislative arena. Even though attempts to repeal the US national origins quotas preceded reform initiatives in Canada, American immigration reform ended up lagging behind Canadian policy developments, as Congress served as a formidable veto point throughout the 1950s and early 1960s. With public opinion on immigration reform ambivalent at best, there were few electoral incentives for liberalizing immigrant admissions. As a result, key conservative legislators who continued to embrace the old race-based paradigm were able to veto policy liberalization by virtue of their leadership positions on congressional committees. Even when, with the 1964 congressional and presidential elections, reformers scored a victory sufficiently large to push open a window of opportunity for paradigmatic legislative reform, they remained constrained by the need to make major concessions to congressional restrictionists. Thus, the new immigration act, while repealing the race-based system of old, fell short of the original vision of the executive–legislative reform coalition in important ways. In the end, the Act amounted to a case of selective, rather than comprehensive, policy liberalization.

The 1952 McCarran–Walter Act: The Hegemony of the Race-Based Immigration Paradigm

The path of paradigmatic immigration reform that led to the 1965 Immigration and Nationality Act started out with the passage of the 1952 McCarran–Walter Act, which affirmed the longstanding race-based system established by the 1924 Johnson–Reed Act. Encompassing both the National Origins Act and the Asian Exclusion Act, the 1924 Act had laid the foundation of an immigration policy designed, to cite a congressional committee report, "to preserve ... the racial status quo in the United States" (Hutchinson 1981, 485). The Act had lowered overall immigrant admissions while favoring the admission of Northern and Western European immigrants by means of nationality-based admission quotas that sought to stem the flow of "races from southern and eastern Europe" (Hutchinson 1981, 484), that is, Italians, Slavs, and Eastern European Jews. Under the quotas the admission of immigrants from any non-Asian country outside of the western hemisphere was capped at 2 percent of the number of co-nationals present in the United States in 1890.[1] These nationality-based restrictions were supplemented by a categorical ban on Asian immigration.[2] Signed into law by President Coolidge, 83 percent of Republicans and 81 percent of Democrats – virtually all legislators except those representing Southern and Eastern European constituencies in the urban centers of the northeast – had voted in favor of the 1924 Act (Gimpel and Edwards 1999). The principled opposition of Southern legislators in particular, which was to continue well into the 1950s, reflected not only the deep-seated racial divisions of the South, but also a tradition of immigration restrictionism that took hold in the South during the Progressive Era after attempts to recruit Western European immigrants to boost the region's white population and its economic development had failed (Higham 1955).

---

[1] In 1927 the "two percent rule" was replaced with an annual global cap of 150,000.
[2] Except for the Philippines which, as a US colony, remained exempt from quotas until 1934.

The 1952 McCarran–Walter Act left the 1924 Act's national origins provisions intact and replaced its Asian exclusions with a symbolic annual quota of a total of 2,000 for all countries of the "Asia Pacific Triangle." It was passed over the veto of President Truman, who objected that:

the quota system ... discriminates, deliberately and intentionally, against many of the peoples of the world. ... It is incredible to me that, in this year of 1952, we should again be enacting into law such a slur on the patriotism, the capacity, and the decency of a large part of our citizenry.

(Truman June 25, 1952)

Passed at a time when the US had long abandoned its isolationist foreign policy, and race-based discrimination was becoming globally discredited, the McCarran–Walter Act – like its 1952 Canadian counterpart – was deeply anachronistic: it was more reflective of the exigencies of the inter-war period than of a new postwar era. However, unlike Canada's 1952 Immigration Act, whose racist provisions were supported by both executive and legislative policy makers (see Chapter 5), the McCarran–Walter Act revealed a schism between executive and congressional pref-erences. Importantly, the Act reflected the dominance of the legislative arena in US immigration policy making, a pattern with far-reaching implications for the way in which the country would eventually turn its back on race-based immigrant admissions in 1965. While the reforms ushered in with the 1965 Immigration Act did constitute a watershed in the history of US immigration policy, its break with the past was not as clean as that enacted by Canadian policy makers in the 1960s and 1970s. In order to understand the nature of US policy liberalization in the 1960s, we need to first examine the reaffirmation of race-based restrictionism in the early 1950s.

Why, despite President Truman's vocal opposition, did the 1952 Act perpetuate the prewar immigration policy of ethnoracial discrimination? Like the Canadian government, the US executive faced strong diplomatic pressure to put an end to race-based admissions (Fitzgerald and Cook-Martín 2014). Whereas the country's disengagement from European politics in the interwar period had sheltered US presidents from the objections of European states that were negatively affected by the national origins quotas, the 1940s ushered in a period of lowered diplomatic insulation. As the United States came to embrace a globally pivotal role in World War II and, subsequently, the Cold War, US presidents became increasingly concerned that the country's race-based immigration policy would compromise its foreign policy pursuits. In contrast to Canada, where an executive-centered politics of immigration allows for regulatory reform to be passed quickly within a well-insulated executive arena, US immigration policy making has always been marked by greater congressional dominance. Given the continued societal embeddedness of racism, in particular in the American South, as well as the political and ideological strength of McCarthyism, presidential calls for policy liberalization in the early 1950s fell on deaf congressional ears, reflecting the legislative arena's greater diplomatic and weaker popular insulation. Whereas Truman's internationalism made him deeply attuned to the intersection of immigration policy and foreign affairs, congressional restrictionists viewed immigration as a matter of domestic policy that intersected with foreign policy only insofar as it was wielded as a weapon against Communism.

Executive Policy Making under Decreasing Diplomatic Insulation

The United States' entry into World War II in 1941 marked the end of an era of US foreign policy of nonentanglement in international politics. During the interwar period the United States had progressively withdrawn from military and diplomatic involvement in Europe and Asia while reorienting its foreign relations with Latin America from a focus on military intervention to economic penetration. While the US government could safely ignore the opposition of Asian and European governments to its national quota system, it was much more cognizant of the risks of restricting immigration from the Americas, a region that at the time accounted for over 70 percent of US foreign investment (Fitzgerald and Cook-Martín 2014, 102). While most members of Congress supported the imposition of national origins quotas on Latin American countries, the US State Department and the president, supported by Senator David Reed, co-sponsor of the 1924 Immigration Act, raised strong objections. In 1928, then Secretary of State Frank Kellogg warned the Senate Immigration Subcommittee that western hemisphere quotas "would adversely affect the present good relations of the United States with Latin America and Canada" and "would be apt to have an adverse effect upon the prosperity of American business interest in those countries" (Fitzgerald and Cook-Martín 2014, 106). It was the State Department's sustained opposition in a context of weak diplomatic insulation that can account for the western hemisphere's quota exemption (Divine 1957, Fitzgerald and Cook-Martín 2014).

The weakening of diplomatic insulation in the 1940s can also account for the incremental lifting of Chinese exclusions as China became incorporated into the war effort. President Franklin D. Roosevelt himself called for a repeal of Chinese exclusion by emphasizing its importance "in the cause of winning the war and of establishing a secure peace" and in "silenc[ing] the distorted Japanese propaganda" (Fitzgerald and Cook-Martín 2014, 110). In 1943, the Magnuson Act substituted Chinese exclusion with small, symbolic quotas and opened up naturalization to persons of Chinese descent. From the late 1940s onward, diplomatic pressure to put an end to racial discrimination was in large part driven by Cold War imperatives. Soviet media systematically called out the United States for its race-based immigration policy. Secretary of State Dean Acheson wrote to President Truman that "our failure to remove racial barriers provides the Kremlin with unlimited political and propaganda capital for use against us in Japan and the entire Far East" (Fitzgerald and Cook-Martín 2014, 112). Pressure to lift Asian exclusions led to the elimination of racial restrictions on naturalization and the end to the categorical ban on Asian immigration in favor of symbolic quotas for countries of the "Asia Pacific Triangle."

Yet diplomatically motivated liberalization came to a standstill when confronted with the national origins system. Even though it abolished racial restrictions on naturalization, the 1952 McCarran–Walter Act retained the 1924 Act's national origins provisions, despite presidential calls for their abolition. While the 1952 Act's failure to abolish the quotas was largely the result of congressional politics, it was also the case that the executive branch itself was not yet unified in its opposition to the quotas. On the one hand, President Truman in his veto of the 1952 Immigration Act underscored the quota's diplomatic costs:

Today, we have entered into an alliance, the North Atlantic Treaty, with Italy, Greece, and Turkey against one of the most terrible threats [Communism] mankind has ever faced ... But, through this bill we say to their people: You are less worthy to come to this country than Englishmen or Irishmen. ... In no other realm of our national life are we so hampered and stultified by the dead hand of the past, as we are in this field of immigration. ... The time to develop a decent policy of immigration – a fitting instrument for our foreign policy and a true reflection of the ideals we stand for, at home and abroad – is now.

(Truman June 25, 1952)

On the other hand, many officials in the State Department favored the quotas. In the early 1950s the paradigm of race-based immigration was still well entrenched within the department – in particular in its Visa and Passport Office[3] (Wolgin 2011) – and the department's concern with

---

[3] Robert Alexander, assistant director of the Visa Office, even authored some of the most restrictive provisions of the 1952 Act.

warding off the threat of Communism dovetailed with the quota system's limitation of Southern and Eastern European immigration. It would only be in the late 1950s that the State Department would become one of the strongest opponents of the national origins quotas.

Legislative Policy Making under the Race-Based Immigration Paradigm

From the 1920s until the early 1960s congressional immigration politics was dominated by legislators of the Southern Democrat–Northern Republican alliance who represented districts with few immigrants and held firmly restrictionist immigration preferences. Throughout the 1950s two resolutely restrictionist members of Congress were able to dominate the legislative process and, ultimately, ensure that Truman's calls for the abolition of the quotas would go unheeded: Francis Walter, chairman of the House Immigration Subcommittee, and Pat McCarran, chairman of the Senate Subcommittee on Immigration and Naturalization. Walter (D-PA) represented a district with a large population of "old stock Americans" and held close ties to patriotic organizations and Southern Democrats (Zolberg 2006). A stalwart defender of the national origins system, "from the onset of his protected tenure Walter insisted that maintenance of the national origins quotas system was nonnegotiable" (Zolberg 2006, 303). Senator McCarran (D-NV), a fervent anti-Communist and vocal critic of Truman's internationalist position on immigration, shared with Walter a long and distinguished political career and a commitment to preserving the quota system. As a senior senator and chair of the Judiciary Committee, the Immigration Subcommittee, the Appropriations Subcommittee, and the Subcommittee on Foreign Aid, McCarran controlled much of the legislation considered in Congress (Marinari 2016). According to one historian, "[t]he power of these two individuals [Walter and McCarran] was so great that from the end of World War II until early 1960s, they, more than anyone else, shaped policymaking" (Wolgin 2011, 33).

In the late 1940s McCarran commissioned a Senate report on immigration, the first comprehensive immigration review since 1911. Published in 1950, the report made it clear that McCarran "wanted to wrestle the reform process away from liberal reformers in Congress and shape the final bill with little consultation with the stakeholders involved" (Marinari 2016, 10). Arguing in favor of preserving the national origins system, the report would ultimately serve as the blueprint for the 1952 Act. However, unlike the discursive justifications underpinning the

1924 Immigration Act, which had asserted eugenic theories of biological differences between the "races," the report's defense of national quotas was grounded in notions of cultural, rather than biological, difference. Echoing Canadian Prime Minister Mackenzie King's 1947 statement (see Chapter 5), the report stated that:

[w]ithout giving credence to any theory of Nordic superiority, the subcommittee believes that the adoption of the national origins quota formula was a rational and logical method of numerically restricting immigration *in such a manner as to best preserve the sociological and cultural balance in the population of the US*. There is no doubt that it favored the peoples of northern and western Europe over those of southern and eastern Europe, but the subcommittee holds that the peoples who made the greatest contribution to the development of this country were fully justified in determining that the country was no longer a field for further colonization and, henceforth, further immigration would not only be restricted but directed to admit immigrants considered to be more readily assimilable because of the similarity of their cultural background to those of the principal components of our population.

(Bennett 1966, 129–30, emphasis added)

Whereas Truman's views on immigration were informed by a global context, McCarran's coalition of conservative Republicans and Southern Democrats viewed immigration as a matter of domestic policy that would preserve the ethnic order of the 1920s and ward off the external threat of Communism (Marinari 2016). While the globally declining legitimacy of race-based immigration policy prompted congressional restrictionists to shift their rhetoric from one of "racial fitness" to cultural assimilation, their diplomatic insulation shielded them from pressure to dismantle the national origins system. Instead, they agreed to support largely symbolic policy concessions, which allowed legislators to claim credit for dismantling blatantly racist provisions without having to take the more consequential, electorally risky step of abolishing the national origins system. Ultimately, in blocking the abolition of the quotas congressional restrictionists could count on the persistence of anti-immigrant and racist attitudes among the American public. In polls conducted throughout the late 1940s and 1950s, a plurality – at times even a majority – of Americans opposed the admission of immigrants even from Europe (Wolgin 2011), reflecting a continued race-based bias against Eastern European and Jewish refugees.

In order to preempt any efforts at liberalizing and internationalizing immigration policy, McCarran utilized his position as chairman of the Senate Judiciary Committee to propose an omnibus immigration bill that relied on anti-Communist rhetoric to argue in favor of preserving the national origins quotas, in addition to tightening national security screening, exclusions, and deportations. The bill included the symbolic liberalization of abolishing Asian exclusion in favor of a minimal quota of one hundred from countries in the Asia Pacific Triangle, in addition to removing all remaining race, nationality, and gender barriers to citizenship.[4] Representative Walter followed suit by introducing a similar immigration bill in the House, which included slightly more liberal provisions by allowing for the reallocation of unused quotas.

On the other side of the debate were legislators who represented districts with large immigrant populations, most notably Senator Herbert Lehman (D-NY) and Representative Emmanuel Celler (D-NY), both of whom would end up playing a critical role in the passage of the 1965 Act. In February 1951, Representative Celler, one of Congress' most outspoken critics of the national origins quotas, responded by introducing a moderately liberal bill that provided for the reallocation of unused national quotas – that is, quotas from Northern and Western European countries that held two-thirds of all visa slots (Reimers 1999) – to oversubscribed quotas among European allies, especially Italy. He also persuaded Herbert Lehman (D-NY) to sponsor an equivalent bill in the Senate. In order to open up immigration to Southern and Eastern Europeans, Lehman's bill also changed the base year on which visa allocation was to be based from 1920 to 1950 (Wolgin 2011).

In order to undermine these efforts, in a highly unorthodox move McCarran and Walter called for immediate joint hearings on their bills, which allowed for the exclusion of Celler's bill from consideration, thereby weakening his influence as the new chairman of the House Judiciary Committee (Marinari 2016). In an attempt to showcase widespread support for the quotas, McCarran and Walter packed the committee hearings with prominent witnesses supportive of their cause, including patriotic groups such as the American Legion, Daughters of the American Revolution, and Veterans of Foreign Wars, as well as the American Federation of Labor (AFL), a longtime supporter of immigration restriction. When asking the American Legion to support his bill, McCarran urged that "unless the patriotic organizations express themselves promptly and forthrightly to the members of the Senate, we shall shortly be faced with destruction of our protective immigration barriers"

---

[4] Moreover, persons of one half or more Asian ancestry born and living outside the Triangle were counted against the Asian nation of their parents' birth, thereby further reducing the number of available visas for any given country within the Triangle.

(Marinari 2016, 15). The senator even secured the support of the Japanese American Citizens League who spoke out in favor of the bill because it promised to eliminate the bars to Asian immigration and naturalization (Campi 2004). While removing the bar to naturalization was an important step toward greater racial equality, opening up immigration for Japanese nationals was to be purely symbolic: under the new "Asia Pacific Triangle" provision, annual immigration from any Asian country would be capped at one hundred.

By contrast to immigration reform in the 1920s, employers were largely silent on the bill, reflecting the fact that "European immigration was no longer relevant to the American economy" (Zolberg 2006, 311), as employers could freely draw on cheap Mexican workers, who, under the western hemisphere rule, were exempt from the quotas. In a similar vein, although historically a supporter of immigration restrictions, trade unions remained on the sidelines because of internal divisions. While the AFL continued its longstanding support of the quota system and expressed its support for the McCarran–Walter bill, the Congress of Industrial Organizations (CIO) opposed the bill, as did other unions whose membership included the descendants of Southern and Eastern European immigrants.

Lobbying efforts against the 1952 Act was led by a host of Jewish organizations and included representatives of other religious and ethnic groups, the Association of Immigration and Nationality Lawyers, the CIO, the International Ladies' Garment Workers' Union, and several civil rights associations. With the exception of the American Jewish Congress, who condemned the quota system as racist, these groups pursued pragmatic strategies and proposed modest changes to the quota system, rather than its outright abolition. Catholic groups in particular sought to increase the number of visas for Catholic-majority countries such as Italy (Wolgin 2011). Behind closed doors, the American Jewish Congress conceded that the quotas "had become an untouchable 'sacred cow' that legislators refused to reform because they believed it had worked" (Marinari 2016, 16).

Recognizing McCarran's and Walter's tight grip on the legislative process, congressional liberals decided to focus their bill on moderately revising, rather than repealing, the quota system. In response to a more radical proposal by Senator Jacob Javits (R-NY) – one of the future sponsors of the 1965 Immigration Act – Lehman responded that the quota system was "so ingrained in our laws that it is, perhaps, unrealistic to try to root it out completely. What we can and should do is to modify it to take the racist taint away" (Marinari 2016, 18). Writing to a fellow liberal, he maintained that "as desirable as it is to establish a grand new design in our immigration program we must recognize that we face the danger today of having even the present amount of immigration – as inadequate as it may be – choked off by such measures as the McCarran bill" (Marinari 2016, 18). Lehman, whose Senate bill provided for the pooling of unused visas to allow for some redistribution from Northern and Western to Southern and Eastern Europe, equally expressed concern that, in the absence of presidential or international pressure, fundamental immigration reform was out of reach (Marinari 2016).

Given the grip that McCarthyism, with its virulent anti-internationalism, held on much of the Congress, even moderate reform proposals were met with immediate backlash. So pervasive was congressional hostility to the abolition of the national origins quotas that only two members of Congress – Hubert Humphrey (D-MN) and Franklin D. Roosevelt, Jr. (D-NY) – were willing to sponsor Lehman's moderately liberal bill in the House (Marinari 2016). Representative Emmanuel Celler, the immigration liberal par excellence, decided not to support Lehman's bill and instead endorsed Walter's House bill in the hope that he would be able to amend it, thereby winning out over the more restrictive McCarran Senate bill. Celler's support of Walter's bill was a striking admission of defeat by congressional immigration liberals. As historian Maddalena Marinari argues, "[t]hat a longtime critic of restriction like Celler had relented demonstrated the hold that the restrictionist coalition in Congress had over the legislative process and the limits of liberal reformers' influence" (2016, 22).

In the end McCarran's version won out over Walter's more moderately restrictionist bill, and McCarran deflected all attempts for all but the most minor amendments to his bill. As a result, the quota system itself survived unscathed, without allowing for the option of pooling unused quotas. In a similar vein, while Asian exclusions were repealed, McCarran blocked all attempts to allocate the small Asian quotas by country of birth rather than by ancestry. In addition to preserving the national origins quotas, the bill also introduced a new set of admission preferences. The first preference, which was to account for 50 percent of each country's quota, was to go to skilled or in-demand labor, 30 percent to the parents of citizens, and 20 percent to the spouses and minor children of permanent residents. Unused visas were to partly go to a fourth preference: siblings of US citizens. While McCarran defended the heavy emphasis on skilled selection as a way of ensuring "that the admission of aliens ... will serve the national interest" (Wolgin 2011, 38), the heavy weighting of this economic preference in effect ensured the continued restriction of immigration from Southern and Eastern Europe, with their largely unskilled labor markets.

The bill passed both chambers of Congress by a large margin, reflecting the well-entrenched alliance between conservative Republicans and Southern Democrats that had dominated policy making since the 1920s. Truman now had to decide whether to sign or veto the bill. From the State Department's point of view, the abolition of the bars on Asian immigration and naturalization was a sufficient improvement to support the Act (Zolberg 2006). Records show that in a private memorandum, Secretary of State Dean Acheson urged Truman not to veto the McCarran–Walter bill because the rescinding of Asian exclusion would serve US Cold War interests (Marinari 2016, 28). However, other executive actors opposed. In particular, the Mutual Security Administration – charged with strengthening America's allies in Europe through military and economic assistance, most importantly through the Marshall Plan (Zolberg 2006) – supported a presidential veto. In the end President Truman vetoed the Act, only to have Congress override the veto by a vote of 278–113 in the House and 57–26 in the Senate.

Looking at the politics of immigration reform from 1950 to 1952, several dynamics stand out. First, despite the presence of a liberal caucus – made up of Northern Democrats and New York Republicans – the majority of legislators held restrictionist views on immigration. As late as the mid-1950s, even among Northern Democrats only 36 percent favored increasing immigration, with Republicans being half as likely to support policy liberalization as Northern Democrats (Zolberg 2006, 302). In the early 1950s, unabashed racism and immigration restrictionism were still firmly entrenched in American public opinion. In fact, on no other issue did the preferences of liberal Democratic Party elites differ more strongly from those of their constituents than on immigration: Northern Democratic Party elites were four times more strongly in favor of liberalizing immigration than their supporters (Zolberg 2006, 302). Yet to understand the 1952 Act simply as a reflection of legislators' lack of popular insulation is to disregard the fact that the majority of Congress favored the policy status quo not only for electoral reasons but also for ideological ones, reflecting the sociocultural embeddedness of notions of race-based hierarchy, especially in (but not limited to) the American South. The pervasiveness of immigration restrictionism even among congressional elites was magnified by the power which Senator McCarran and Representative Walter held over the legislative process. Had it not been for these two senior and deeply restrictionist legislators, it is likely that the 1952 Act would have included some policy concessions to congressional immigration liberals (such as the pooling of unused quotas).

Interest groups played a negligible role in the reform process leading up to the 1952 Act. The groups opposed to the McCarran–Walter bill – ethnic and religious lobbies, together with civil rights groups – were, in addition to being internally divided, simply too weak to hold any leverage over the policy process. Similarly, despite the prominence of restrictionist lobbies in the hearings process, it was clear that McCarran had no intention of incorporating feedback from witnesses into the final draft of his bill (Marinari 2016). Given the continued domestic hegemony of the paradigm of race-based immigrant admissions, the only clear impetus for policy liberalization could come from abroad. Truman's principled support for the abolition of the national origins quotas thus reflected his diplomatic responsibilities and the salience of foreign policy in the executive arena. However, like pro-immigration lobbies, the executive branch itself was divided on the future of the national origins system. In the early 1950s the quotas still enjoyed the support of many State Department officials, undoubtedly amplified by McCarthyism. In contrast to the presidency, Congress had few institutional incentives to heed diplomatic considerations, except where they impinged on national security and the fight against Communism. Given the centrality of the legislative arena in the American separation-of-powers system, presidential demands for policy liberalization by themselves were of little consequence as long as a diplomatically insulated Congress was dominated by immigration restrictionists.

The Policy Failure of the National Origins System: 1953–1960

Despite the resounding override of Truman's veto, the passage of the McCarran–Walter Act did not put the quota question to rest. On the contrary, the Act's affirmation of the national origins system continued to serve as a thorn in the side of immigration liberals and remained a target of reform efforts throughout the 1950s. In every year between 1953 and 1965, legislators introduced bills to revise or abolish the quotas. Most of these efforts were blocked by Representative Walter – by now opposed to all quota pooling – and Senator James Eastland (D-MS), the new chairman of the Judiciary Committee. The institutionally entrenched power of Southern Democrats thus continued to prevent several comprehensive immigration reform bills proposed by Northern legislators from making it beyond the committee stage (Tichenor 2002). Despite these setbacks, some reform efforts did succeed and managed to incrementally liberalize the preference categories and chip away at the quota system (Wolgin 2011). Hence, in 1957 a moderate reform act sponsored by Senator John F. Kennedy (D-MA) sought to reduce the backlog of oversubscribed quotas by granting nonquota visas to anyone in the first three preferences whose petition had already been approved. While minor by itself, this attempt to clear the family preference backlogs constituted a significant step toward reform of the quota system itself, as it opened the door to future backlog clearing.

Truman himself, before leaving office in 1953, helped lay the groundwork for immigration reform by convincing the 1952 Democratic National Convention to endorse a call for revising the McCarran–Walter Act. In a consequential decision, Truman established the Commission on Immigration and Naturalization and staffed it with immigration liberals. The commission's report, *Whom We Shall Welcome*, largely relied on foreign policy arguments to make the case for the abolition of the quota system (Fitzgerald and Cook-Martín 2014) and would come to play an important role in shaping the 1965 Hart–Celler Act. Arguing that the 1924 Immigration Act's Japanese exclusion clause had fueled the growth of Japan's militarism and anti-Americanism in Japan – developments that had culminated in the attack on Pearl Harbor – the report asserted that "American immigration policy and law must be formulated in awareness of their international impact and must be designed to advance our foreign policy" (Fitzgerald and Cook-Martín 2014, 46). Echoing Truman's veto message, the commission declared that:

[i]mmigration is part of foreign policy. ... American immigration policies have frustrated and handicapped the aims and programs of American foreign policy throughout the period since 1924. The interference is acute today. ... The major disruptive influence in our immigration law is the racial and national discrimination caused by the national origins system.
(US President's Commission on Immigration and Naturalization 1953, 47, 52)

The report's timing was opportune as, starting in the mid-1950s, the political context of immigration policy making underwent important changes that would usher in a new era of policy making, which would eventually isolate, both in Congress and in the executive branch, the supporters of race-based immigration policy. Starting in the mid-1950s, the restrictionist front in Congress and the State Department started to weaken as a result of generational turnover and the decline of McCarthyism. In 1954, Senator McCarren died, and Representative Walter was left to carry the restrictionist torch without his longtime ally. Reelected in 1954 to a Democratic Congress, Walter hinted that he was no longer categorically opposed to reforming the quota system "if something fairer can be devised" (Zolberg 2006, 323). The year 1954 also marked the censure of Senator McCarthy, leading to the demise of McCarthyism. The weakening of militant anti-Communism – which throughout the reform process in the early 1950s had intersected with support for the national origins quotas – was a consequential development as it chipped away at whatever support the national origins system still enjoyed within the executive branch, in particular within the State Department. Moreover, while security concerns continued to feature prominently in the department, by 1957 many of the most restrictionist senior bureaucrats had either retired or left (Wolgin 2011). In fact, with the appointment of internationally renowned immigration liberal Abba Schwartz as Assistant Secretary of State for Security and Consular Affairs, the State Department would come to play a prominent role in the drafting the 1965 Act and its abolition of the quota system.

In a second momentous change, the 1955 merger of the AFL and the CIO into the United States' largest union federation, the AFL-CIO, shifted organized labor to a pro-immigration position. Prior to their merger, the AFL had endorsed reforming, but not dismantling, the quota system, whereas the CIO had demanded its abolition. Within two years of the merger the AFL-CIO Executive Committee informed the federation's new legislative office that one of its top priorities was to raise immigrant admissions to 250,000 and to secure the "abolishment of the national origins quota system entirely" (Tichenor 2002, 204). The pro-immigration stance of organized labor was a serious blow to restrictionist groups, who now fully relied on influential supporters in congressional committees to protect the policy status quo from a growing cross-party coalition in favor of policy liberalization (Tichenor 2002). Importantly, the anti-quota stance of organized labor was not an isolated incident but signaled a much broader realignment of interest group positioning on matters of immigration in the latter half of the 1950s, as more and more groups shifted their advocacy positions from one of partial to comprehensive immigration reform. Thus, by the time John F. Kennedy was elected president the basic parameters that would define US immigration policy making over the coming decades had been put in place.

Finally, the increasing clout of reform interests in Congress and civil society was supported and legitimized by a growing recognition that the 1952 McCarran–Walter Act had outlived its usefulness – even among those who endorsed its basic principles. Quite remarkably, by the early 1960s two-thirds of all immigrant admissions did not take place through the national origins system but via alternative legal pathways for the admission of Displaced Persons and Cold War refugees (Joppke 1998a). At the same time as the quota system was losing its status as the main gateway to US immigration, its inequities were becoming ever more brazen as the modest reform efforts of the 1950s proved powerless in stemming the mounting backlog of immigration quotas for disadvantaged countries – in particular Greece, Italy, Portugal, and Poland. By 1963, Greece with its annual quota of 308 had accumulated a backlog of 97,577 at the same time as the underuse of visas by Northern European countries continued, with Britain and Ireland having used up only 25,000 of 65,361, and 5,500 of 17,756 allocated visas, respectively (Joppke 1998a, 26).

The 1965 Immigration and Nationality Act: The Shift from Race-Based to Family-Based Immigration

The passage of the 1965 Immigration and Nationality Act – commonly referred to as the Hart–Celler Act – marked the conclusion of a period of incremental reform to the national origins system that gained momentum in the 1950s. The circuitous path that led to this policy watershed is indicative of the challenges not only of paradigmatic reform per se, but also of policy reform in the US system of checks and balances in particular, a system where policy spillover from the executive into the legislative arena is the norm and where congressional institutional fragmentation turns the legislative arena into a formidable veto point. Even in the rare instances where the stars align in favor of paradigmatic reform, the requirement for policy to travel through an intricate committee system means that reform bills will often bear only a faint resemblance to the reformers' original vision.

Congressional Veto Points and the Defeat of Paradigmatic Reform

The 1958 midterm elections delivered a blow to the conservative congressional coalition as Republicans suffered heavy losses and the rank of Northern Democrats swelled. The shifting congressional balance of power was augmented by John F. Kennedy's 1960 presidential victory, which, despite its narrow margin, was widely interpreted as a symbol of a new age of social progressivism. Kennedy's election campaign had courted ethnic and immigrant voting blocs with the promise of abolishing the national origins system, a commitment lent credibility by his Catholic background:

We shall adjust our immigration, nationality and refugee policies to eliminate discrimination ... The national-origins quota system of limiting immigration contradicts the rounding principles of this nation. It is inconsistent with our belief in the rights of man. This system was instituted after World War I as a policy of deliberate discrimination by a Republican Administration and Congress. The revision of immigration and nationality laws we seek will implement our belief that enlightened immigration, naturalization and refugee policies and humane administration of them are important aspects of our foreign policy.
(The American Presidency Project July 11, 1960)

Invigorated by Kennedy's victory, the Democratic Study Group, a caucus of liberal Democrats, narrowly won a vote to increase seats on the House Rules Committee, a strategic move that provided liberal representatives with a working majority on the committee (Tichenor 2002).[5] Since the late 1930s the Rules Committee had been notorious in blocking the flow of progressive legislation, especially under chairman and leader of the Southern Democrats Howard W. Smith (D-VA), who was described as "the second most powerful man in the House."[6] As the *New York Times* commented, "Smith has killed, watered down or postponed more progressive legislation than any other Congressman in modern times" (*New York Times* January 12, 1964).

Yet, despite these victories, Kennedy was politically constrained by the continued dominance of Southern Democrats and Republicans as chairmen of key committees, most importantly Senator James Eastland, chair of the Senate Judiciary Committee, and Representative Francis Walter, chair of the House Subcommittee on Immigration. Recognizing that any attempt to abolish the national origins system would incur the wrath of these committee chairs, who could rely on widespread restrictionist immigration attitudes, Kennedy decided to stay clear of directly challenging the

---

[5] In 1959, liberal Northern and Western Democrats formed the Democratic Study Group – a caucus that lobbied the Democratic leadership to appoint liberals to influential committees, demanded procedural reforms that would weaken committee chairmen, and pursued legislative initiatives. The group was remarkably effective, largely due to strategic procedural and legislative initiatives that were supported by its own whip system (Zelizer January 22, 2015).

[6] Second only to the speaker of the House.

Walter–McCarran Act. Instead, the White House continued the incremental reform strategies of the 1950s by liberalizing admissions outside the quota system and granting quotas to the newly independent states of the Caribbean (Triadafilopoulos 2010).

In May 1963, Representative Francis Walter, one of the most ardent supporters of the national origins quotas, died in office. Already in the process of moving on civil rights legislation, Kennedy saw a window of opportunity for linking civil rights and immigration reform and decided to move beyond reform incrementalism and draft legislation to replace the McCarran–Walter Act. In his message to Congress, Kennedy decried the national origins system as

without basis in either logic or reason. It neither satisfies a national need nor accomplishes an international purpose. In an age of interdependence among nations, such a system is an anachronism, for it discriminates among applicants for admission into the United States on the basis of the accident of birth.

(Kennedy 1966, 139)

The following day, Senator Philip Hart (D-MI) introduced corresponding legislation that was co-sponsored by a bipartisan group of twenty-six senators, including seven members of the Senate Judiciary Committee. In the House, Representative Emmanuel Celler (D-NY), chairman of the House Judiciary Committee, followed suit by introducing a companion bill. In subsequent weeks fifty-five House members introduced identical bills.

The Hart–Celler bill included sweeping changes to the policy status quo, most importantly the immediate elimination of the Asia Pacific Triangle and the phasing out of the quota system, to be replaced with a "first-come, first-served" preference system based on work-related skills and family ties. The abolition of the quotas was to take place over a five-year-period because, as Kennedy argued, "too rapid a change might ... so drastically curtail immigration in some countries the only effect might be to shift the unfairness from one group of nations to another" (Wolgin 2011, 98). The bill rejected any limits on western hemisphere immigration and proposed the creation of an immigration pathway for refugees. Importantly, the reform would entail only a minimal increase in immigrant admissions – from 157,000 quota immigrants to 165,000. In fact, reformers did not tire of assuring the public that while immigration reform would change the principles of selection, it would not increase overall immigration.

The reform bill enjoyed broad-based support among interest groups, including civil rights groups, religious organizations, organized labor, ethnic groups, and refugee support groups. Prominent members of the Kennedy administration, in particular Secretary of State Dean Rusk, strongly endorsed the bill. Speaking before a subcommittee of the House Judiciary Committee, Rusk reiterated the by now familiar pro-reform arguments: the policy failure of the national origins system and the harm it inflicted on American foreign policy (Triadafilopoulos 2010). Yet despite significant bipartisan support in both chambers of Congress, the Hart–Celler bill quickly became mired in congressional gridlock and was held up in committee throughout 1963 and 1964. Its key opponents included Senator James Eastland (D-MS), chairman of the Senate Judiciary Committee and principled supporter of race-based quotas, and Michael Feighan (D-OH), Walter's successor as chair of the House Immigration Subcommittee, who opposed the bill not only for ideological reasons but also because of a personal feud with Emmanuel Celler, head of the parent House Judiciary Committee (Gillon 2000). As a result, by the time of Kennedy's assassination on November 22, 1963, neither Immigration Subcommittee had held hearings on the bill (Tichenor 2002).

With Kennedy's assassination and Lyndon B. Johnson's swearing in, immigration liberals once again feared for the future of immigration reform. In contrast to Kennedy, who had entered the White House with a record of legislative activism on immigration reform, Johnson had famously voted in favor of the Walter–McCarran Act and subsequently either opposed policy liberalization or remained silent on the issue (Tichenor 2002). When former Kennedy advisors implored the new president to stay Kennedy's course on immigration, Johnson countered that the pursuit of immigration reform would jeopardize other reform endeavors. In conversations with his close advisor Jack Valenti, Johnson expressed reservations about pushing for a reform package that enjoyed so little public support (Tichenor 2002). Johnson's pragmatic stance on the matter was not surprising, given his reputation as one of the most politically shrewd and strategic of legislators. Johnson continued to proceed cautiously, briefly referencing immigration reform in his 1964 State of the Union address: "We must lift by legislation the bar of discrimination against those who seek entry into our country, particularly those with much-needed skills and those joining their families" (Johnson January 8, 1964). Barely a week later the president convened the major immigration reform players in the White House to endorse the Kennedy proposal, which was still pending before Congress, all the while insisting that civil rights legislation was to take precedence over immigration reform. Hearings commenced in the Senate and House immigration subcommittees, though with significant delay in the latter, because of Representative Feighan's obstructionism. In the end no further action was taken and the immigration bill was allowed to expire with the adjournment of Congress (Kennedy 1966).

Power Consolidation and the Navigation of Congressional Veto Points: The Passage of Paradigmatic Reform

In November 1964 Johnson won a landslide election victory, getting a record 61 percent of the popular vote and carrying forty-four states at the same time as the Democrats secured overwhelming majorities in both the House (295–140) and the Senate (68–32). Running against Barry Goldwater, Johnson's campaign had championed the passage of the 1964 Civil Rights Act and espoused the Great Society anti-poverty programs. Most importantly, he was able to capitalize on his opponent's support of aggressive military action, including the use of nuclear weapons in Vietnam, by portraying Goldwater as a threat to national security. Johnson's triumphant electoral victory cemented his reputation as a skilled political leader, which he had cultivated over the past years by virtue of his legislative successes. The passage of the Civil Rights Act of 1964 in particular was testament to his ability for astute political manipulation, as Johnson took advantage of the fact that civil rights legislation was seen as a cornerstone of Kennedy's legislative legacy and, with a mixture of aggressive lobbying and outmaneuvering of the conservative congressional coalition, secured the passage of the Civil Rights Act. As Sidney Milkis comments co Johnson's legislative victory "continued – even accelerated – developments of the Kennedy era that accentuated the power and independence of the executive; arguably his administration marked the height of modern presidential leadership" (Milkis 1993, 171).

With the 1964 election the window for paradigmatic immigration reform was thus pushed wide open, as "no administration since Franklin Roosevelt's first had operated subject to fewer political constraints than President Johnson's" (Aaron 2010, 3). At the same time, immigration liberals worried that the opening would be short-lived. As one pro-reform lobbyist recalls,

a recognition ... spread like wildfire among Liberal and labour organizations – that the back of the old conservative-Dixiecrat coalition had been broken, but that it might amend again as soon as the next election [and that] we must get everything through in the next 2 years that we need in the next 10.

(Cited in Tichenor 2002, 214)

Johnson's legendary "politics of haste" (Kearns Goodwin 1991) – reflected in the passage of eighty of his legislative proposals in 1965 alone – attests to fact that the president shared in this assessment. On his legislative agenda, immigration reform was now one of the most pressing items, and days after the new Congress convened the president announced to Congress his commitment to repealing the national origins quotas and to doing whatever was necessary to break the reform gridlock. In fact, Johnson left no doubt that he would be willing to endorse *any* bill that abolished the quotas (Marinari 2014).

Decreasing Diplomatic Insulation in the Legislative Arena

Predictably, the argumentative frames employed by executive officials closely echoed those of previous administrations, emphasizing the quotas' deleterious foreign policy consequences. Thus, speaking before Congress, Secretary of State Dean Rusk stressed that:

[w]hat other peoples think about us plays an important role in the achievement of all foreign policies. . . . More than a dozen foreign ministers have spoken to me in the last year alone, not about the practicalities of immigration from their country to ours, but about the principle which they interpret as discrimination against their particular countries. . . . [E]ven those (countries) who do not use the quotas . . . resent the fact that the quotas are there as a discriminatory measure.
(Cited in Fitzgerald and Cook-Martín 2014, 118)

Similarly, Attorney General Nicholas Katzenbach warned the legislature that the "[n]ational origins system harms the United States in still another way: it creates an image of hypocrisy which can be exploited by those who seek to discredit our professions of democracy" (cited in Fitzgerald and Cook-Martín 2014, 118). Other administration officials likewise emphasized the "hypocrisy costs" (Greenhill 2011) incurred by the national origins system and impressed upon Congress "the urgency" of immigration reform

in terms of our self-interest abroad. In the present ideological conflict between freedom and fear, we proclaim to the world that our central precept is that we are all born equal . . . yet under present law, we choose among immigrants on the basis of where they are.
(Cited in Tichenor 2002, 215)

While executive officials had long warned of the diplomatic and reputational costs of the quota system, these arguments could now also be heard in the legislative arena. Given the political salience of the Vietnam

War, foreign policy featured prominently on the congressional agenda, and as a result concerns about the diplomatic repercussions of immigration policy. More broadly, by the early 1960s the Cold War between the United States and the Soviet Union had spread to Asia and Africa, the countries most affected by the quota system (Gillon 2000). Moreover, diplomatic pressure for policy liberalization reflected not only Cold War imperatives but also the much broader normative and institutional changes that followed in the wake of decolonization in Asia and Africa (see Chapter 5). As the newly independent countries of the Global South gained diplomatic leverage in bodies such as the United Nations, US officials increasingly struggled to maintain American credibility abroad, especially in the lead-up to the ratification of the International Convention on the Elimination of All Forms of Racial Discrimination in 1965 (Graham 2005). With the end of isolationism, "the global ambitions of the United States made it slowly but inexorably susceptible to 30 years of diplomatic leverage" (Fitzgerald and Cook-Martín 2014, 139).

The following arguments reflect the spillover of foreign-policy-based arguments from the executive into the legislative arena, a process that had been under way since the late 1950s. In the House, John Lindsay (R-NY) was one of several members who warned of the quota system's harmful impact on foreign relations:

[T]his nation has committed itself to the defense of the independence of South Vietnam. Yet the quota for that country of 15 million is exactly 100. Apparently we are willing to risk a major war for the right of the Vietnamese people to live in freedom at the same time our quota system makes it clear that we do not want very great numbers of them to live with us.

(Cited in Chin 1996, 299)

Senator William Proxmire (D-WI), an outspoken critic of the Vietnam War, argued that the McCarran–Walter Act "is very bad foreign policy in a day when the attitudes and actions of people other than northern and western Europeans are increasingly important to our future" (cited in Shanks 2001, 165). In a similar vein, Senator Hiram Fong warned that the quotas

hurt America's image as the leader of the free world. Many countries of Asia and the Pacific have traditionally sought more than a token of immigration to the United States. These are the countries that will play a large and vital role in determining the future of world events.

(Cited in Chin 1996, 299)

Representative Ogden Reid (D-NY) likewise warned of the quota's impact on decolonization: "It must be remembered that our immigration policies often make up the first and only personal contact that people of other countries have with the United States" (cited in Shanks 2001, 165). Senator Leverett Saltonstall (R-MA) cautioned that "[f]ailure to act would in the long run [will] result in a weakening of our foreign relations and a decline in our domestic, economic, and social wellbeing" (cited in Shanks 2001, 165). Even Michael Feighan (D-OH), chairman of the House Judiciary Immigration Subcommittee and one of the fiercest opponents of immigration reform, eventually had to concede that "our Secretary of State and two Attorney Generals have testified that the quota system has made problems in the conduct of our relations with certain foreign countries" (cited in Chin 1996, 299).

Awareness of the reputational costs of the policy status quo also began to filter down to the public. In a 1963 Harris Poll, 78 percent of white Americans agreed that race discrimination in the United States harmed its standing abroad (Fitzgerald and Cook-Martín 2014, 117). Yet public concern about the reputational costs of racist policy did not translate into support for *increasing* immigration. A 1965 Harris poll published in the *Washington Post* found that 58 percent of Americans were "strongly opposed to the easing of immigration laws" (Wagner 1986, 421). Concerned about restrictionist popular attitudes, the Johnson administration sponsored its own Gallup poll, which confirmed overwhelming public opposition to increasing immigration while at the same time affirming that half of Americans supported repealing the national origins quotas (Zolberg 2006).

Safeguarding Popular Insulation

With these findings in hand, the White House issued the "Blue Book," a thick briefing book that prepared administration officials for the hearings process in early 1965. The book advised officials testifying before Congress to stress that the immigration bill "leaves the present authorized level of immigration substantially unchanged" (cited in Gillon 2000, 168). This line was faithfully followed by White House officials with the result that, when Attorney General Nicholas Katzenbach testified before the Senate against a western hemisphere ceiling, he disregarded demographic evidence to the contrary when asserting that "there is not much pressure to come to the United States from those [Latin American] countries" (Graham 2005, 5). The debate also surfaced in the Senate, where Senator Ervin pushed administration witnesses on the question of anticipated changes in the size and composition of immigration. Executive officials predicted that the majority of new immigrants would come from Southern (Italy, Greece) and Eastern (Poland) Europe and that annual numbers would increase by only 50,000 to 75,000 (Graham 2005, 5). The same strategy was adopted by congressional reformers such as Emmanuel Celler, who instructed his colleagues to assure the public that "the effect of the bill on our population [in numbers] would be quite insignificant." In the Senate, Edward Kennedy followed suit by assuring his colleagues that "[o]ur cities will not be flooded with a million immigrants annually" (cited in Gillon 2000, 168).

These assurances were clearly more a product of political necessity than of evidence-based analysis. As historian Steven Gillon argues, "neither Congress nor the White House had carefully analyzed the potential impact of the family preference system" (Gillon February 2, 2018). Congressional debate grappled not only with the question of quota repeal and (as we are about to see) the capping of western hemisphere immigration, but also with the consequences of lifting restrictions on Asian immigration. President Gerald Ford, then House minority leader, recalls that "it was anticipated that the 1965 amendments would substantially increase the number of Asian immigrants" (Chin 1996, 306). Similarly, Representative Peter Rodino argued that the increase in Asian immigration "could be substantial" (cited in Chin 1996, 307), as did several members of the Immigration Subcommittee – though it appears that nobody foresaw the level that actually occurred (Chin 1996). Others anticipated only modest increases in immigration from Asia. Most famously, House Judiciary Committee chairman Emmanuel Celler reassured his colleagues that the

claim has been made that the bill would bring in hordes of Africans and Asians. This is the answer to that false charge: Persons from African and Asian countries would continue to come in as heretofore, but would be treated like everyone else. With the end of discrimination due to place of birth, there will be shifts to countries other than those of northern and western Europe. Immigrants from Asia and Africa will have to compete and qualify in order to get in, quantitatively and qualitatively, which, itself, will hold the numbers down. There will not be, comparatively, many Asians or Africans entering this country. ... Mr. Chairman, since the peoples of Africa and Asia have very few relatives here, comparatively few could immigrate from those countries, because they have no family ties in the United States ... There is no danger whatsoever of an influx from the countries of Asia and Africa.

(Cited in Chin 1996, 331–2)

In the end the congressional record remains inconclusive on the question of how much immigration from Asia was actually anticipated, as it is on the question of what "particular countries" policy makers had in mind when they devised the per-country limits which were to guard against, in the words of Senator Dirksen, "opening up the gates to a vast flood from some particular country" (cited in Chin 1996, 326). Whereas some comments suggest that it was directed against Asian countries, other evidence suggests that legislators targeted Southern and Eastern European countries (Chin 1996). Whatever the case may be, there is little doubt that progressive reformers did their best to seek to reassure congressional restrictionists and the American public that the proposed changes would not lead to fundamental changes in the demographic composition of the nation, nor would they lead to unprecedented levels of immigration.

In pursuing this strategy of depoliticization, reformers had time on their side. Given the Hart–Celler bill's expiration the previous year, reformers had an immigration bill ready to go and could capitalize on the political momentum of Johnson's landslide victory. With the next campaign season still in the distant future and the waning legitimacy of race-based discrimination, reformers faced little risk of electoral mobilization against a quota repeal. In striking contrast to the lead-up to the 1952 McCarran–Walter Act, for instance, patriotic societies made no concerted effort to mobilize in favor of the national origins quotas. Senator Edward Kennedy, the bill's floor manager, commented that in his meetings with patriotic society representatives they "expressed little overt defense of the national origins system" and signaled their willingness to accept reforms as long as immigration did not increase (Kennedy 1966, 142). Furthermore, as Daniel Tichenor (2002) has argued, while the public was clearly opposed to increasing immigration, immigration reform itself held little political salience for most voters, especially compared to other legislative initiatives of the civil rights era. As an American Jewish Committee lobbyist in Washington observed, "there is no great public demand for immigration reform," which "is a very minor issue" (Graham 2005, 2). In a 1965 Gallup poll, 20 percent of Americans expressed no opinion on the question of immigration levels (compared to 2 percent in the early 1990s), while 39 percent supported maintaining current immigration levels and 33 percent favored a decrease (Shanks 2001, 234).

Finally, after close to fifteen years of stalled reform, there was a widely shared acceptance of the need for immigration reform, especially given the failure of the national origins quotas in effectively regulating admissions.

Mounting pressure for legislative action was reflected in the electoral challenges faced by one of Congress' most strident reform opponents, Representative Feighan, who in 1964 nearly lost the primary against a pro-reform contender of Czech descent who threatened a rematch should Feighan continue to stall on immigration reform (Gillon 2000). With trade unions – a chief sponsor of immigration restrictions in the past – having entirely abandoned their support for the quota system, the rank of interest groups opposed to policy liberalization had drastically thinned, and there was a general sense of the inevitability of quota reform.

Navigating Congressional Veto Points

Thus, when the hearing process began in early 1965, congressional reformers found themselves in a decidedly favorable position. Not only were strategic and normative arguments against the national origins quotas broadly accepted by congressional elites and increasingly also the public, but with the 1964 elections progressive Democrats were institutionally empowered to break the longstanding stranglehold of the Rules Committee and the Southern-dominated seniority system. Three immigration reformers were added to the Immigration Subcommittee after President Johnson had pressured House Democrats to increase its size (Zolberg 2006), thereby limiting the ability of its restrictionist chair, Michael Feighan, to block the bill's progression. Johnson had also succeeded into persuading Senator James Eastland – who in the past had refused to hold hearings on any bill designed to abolish the quota system – to temporarily relinquish his chairmanship of the Senate Judicial Committee to freshman senator and immigration liberal Edward Kennedy (D-MA). This remarkable strategic coup was the result of a series of Oval Office meetings between Johnson and Eastland that involved a mix of "horse-trading, presidential intimidation, and assurance that [Feighan] could save face by ultimately voting against the measure" (Tichenor 2002, 214).

When Senate hearings began in February, Senator Kennedy underscored that despite its repeal of the national origins quotas, the administration's proposal was far from radical. In terms of immigration numbers, Kennedy assured Congress and the public that "the present level of immigration remains substantially the same," as the proposal "merely updates our present law to conform more fully with our actual practice" (cited in Zolberg 2006, 330). The bill, introduced by Philip Hart and co-sponsored by a bipartisan group of thirty-three senators, closely reflected President Johnson's recommendations, which largely mirrored John F. Kennedy's bill. The proposal retained a preference for skills-based immigration, while making some concessions to congressional skeptics by increasing the proportion of family immigrants and the share of visas going to immigrants from northwestern Europe, at the expense of refugee admissions (Zolberg 2006, 330). Senate hearings on the immigration bill were interrupted from late March until the end of May while the Voting Rights Act was in front of the Judiciary Committee. The hearing process proceeded relatively uneventfully, with the overwhelming majority of witnesses supporting the bill's basic principles (Kennedy 1966).

Meanwhile, the legislative process in the House got off to a rocky start. The fact that the newly constituted House Immigration Subcommittee prevented its chair from holding the bill hostage did not mean that Feighan was going to endorse it. In the words of Assistant Attorney General Norbert Schlei, one of the bill's principal authors, Feighan considered "the traditional supporters of the national origins system" to be his most important constituents (cited in Marinari 2014, 225) and, aside from his longstanding opposition to the repeal of the quotas, objected to both the western hemisphere exemption and the exemption of newly independent countries in the West Indies, out of opposition to nonwhite immigration. At the same time, as discussed above, "the primary challenge suggested that [Feighan's] political survival required him to support some form of immigration reform, but he also wanted to appease his conservative followers and, perhaps most of all, deny Celler the legislative victory he desired" (Gillon 2000, 170). Thus, prior to the beginning of the House subcommittee hearings, Feighan sent up a trial balloon for his new vision of immigration reform in a speech to the American Coalition of Patriotic Societies. For the first time he publicly expressed a willingness to abolish the national origins quotas though, in contrast to the White House's denunciation of race-based admissions, Feighan decried the quota's ineffectiveness (Gillon 2000). At the same time he made it clear that his support for the quota repeal would be contingent on the ending of nonquota status for the western hemisphere through the creation of a worldwide immigration ceiling (Marinari 2014).

Despite the administration's repeated assurances that the reform bill would not increase immigration, Feighan used the committee hearings to challenge these claims. In a heated exchange with Attorney General Katzenbach on the western hemisphere provisions, he contended: "Well, I am sure you are not suggesting – or are you – that Congress wait until nonquota immigration from Latin American reaches floodgate proportions before acting?" (Marinari 2014, 229). Feighan remained immune to the appeals of White House officials to relent on the question of a worldwide ceiling. President Johnson, in a personal meeting with Feighan, offered significant concessions, most importantly a change in the preference system to favor family reunification over skills-based admissions. Yet these concessions could not break the impasse over the bill. Johnson was prepared to defer to Secretary of State Rusk on the question of the global ceiling, but Rusk was resolutely opposed to the proposition, arguing that this would "vex and dumbfound our Latin American friends, who will now be sure we are in final retreat from Pan Americanism" (cited in Marinari 2014, 230). Instead, he suggested an amendment stating that should total immigration ever exceed 350,000, the president would make a recommendation for congressional intervention. In a memorandum to Johnson, presidential advisor Jack Valenti reasoned that "[w]hat this will do is keep non-quota status for Latin Americans, but allow Feighan to tell his right-wing friends that the Congress and the President will act if immigration looks like it is getting out of hand" (cited in Marinari 2014, 230). Concerned about the foreign policy implications of capping western hemisphere immigration, Valenti counseled delaying passage of the bill.

In June, Feighan caught backers of the Celler bill unawares by introducing his own immigration bill. Like the administration's proposal, Feighan's bill repealed the national origins quotas and ended the Asia Pacific Triangle provisions. While it retained nonquota status for the western hemisphere, it also set a global ceiling of 325,000 immigrants. Feighan's and the White House's reform proposals differed in two important respects, both of which reflected the influence of organized labor on Feighan. First, Feighan's bill stipulated that applicants for work visas had to receive Department of Labor certification to ensure that there were no American workers available. This provision was one of the few clear indications of direct interest group influence on the legislative process, with organized labor lobbying for strict controls on skilled and semi-skilled immigration in order to ward off labor market competition with union members (Triadafilopoulos 2010, Reimers 1983). Second, and more importantly, Feighan insisted on reversing the administration's preference structure by giving first priority to family reunification, in an attempt to favor immigration from Western Europe and preventing cultural and ethnic change (Bon Tempo 2008). Feighan's bill thus reserved 74 percent of all visas for family unification and established four preference categories for family immigration and only two – 20 percent of all visas – for immigrants with needed skills. Strikingly, the largest preference category, with 24 percent of visas, was for the brothers and sisters (and their spouses and children) of US citizens – pushed for by Representative Peter Rodino (D-NJ) on behalf of his family-oriented Italian constituents and their ethnic associations, which gave the 1965 Act the nickname the "Brothers and Sisters Act" (Joppke 1999).

The shift from skills-based to family-based immigration policy was quietly accepted by the White House, "thus transforming an immigration reform bill into a family unification measure." Aside from corresponding to the demands of both organized labor and ethnic lobbies, the change also made the bill more palatable to conservatives, who believed that a policy based on family ties would be even more restrictive than the old national origins system (Gillon 2000, 173). For instance, infamous nativist Senator Strom Thurmond (R-SC) argued that:

The preferences which would be established by this proposal are based, I believe, on sound reasoning and meritorious considerations, not entirely dissimilar in effect from those which underlie the national origins quotas of existing law. Blood relationships and family ties stem from the sense of identity and preference, and it is most desirable that unification of families be a major consideration in our immigration formula.

(Cited in Lee 2015, 542)

Virtually overnight Feighan had hijacked the legislative process, as his bill managed to replace, in the words of staffer Abba Schwartz, "the Administration's proposal as the pending bill on immigration reform" (cited in Marinari 2014, 231). As its key concession, the bill refrained from imposing a ceiling on the western hemisphere. The bill that was sent to the House floor thus reversed the administration's admission priorities by prioritizing family ties-based over skills-based admissions and imposing a global ceiling on immigration, as well as reducing refugee admissions. As Edward Kennedy recalled,

It was felt in many quarters, of both the private and public sectors, that the Administration perhaps paid a needlessly heavy price in getting this cooperation. But, given its attitude in this matter, little could be done to salvage many reasonable provisions in the original bill.

(Kennedy 1966, 145)

While in hindsight (and in comparison with Canada) the shift from skills-based to family-based immigration reform would mark a historic moment in US immigration history, reformers at the time only shared a clear commitment to ending race-based immigration, rather than a vision of what a nondiscriminatory system might look like. In other words, arguments in favor of paradigmatic reform focused on the repeal of the old, rather than the embrace of a new, paradigm. Thus, descriptions of policy alternatives often more closely resembled a smorgasbord of admission criteria than a coherent reform vision. To quote Senator Hart,

[w]e need a careful selection of immigrants. We should discriminate – but not with irrational concepts founded on the theories of ethnic superiority. Congress must enact a statute that will be discriminatory in the best meaning of the word – on the grounds of security and economic and scientific benefit; on the principles of family unity and asylum to the homeless and the oppressed.

(Kennedy 1966, 141)

As a result, the question of what a desirable balance between economic and family admissions was to look like received far less attention than restrictionist concerns with maintaining current immigration levels. The question of the western hemisphere ceiling in particular became a major object of contention in the ensuing debate. Opponents of the quotas' repeal made their support for the bill contingent on the capping of western hemisphere immigration. Representative Clark MacGregor (R-MN) proposed an amendment that would impose an annual ceiling of 115,000 on western hemisphere immigration, arguing that the population explosion in Latin America would trigger sharp increases in immigration, including nonwhite immigration from the newly independent countries of the Caribbean.[7] Progressive reformers, in turn, echoed the Johnson administration's position that US immigration law should continue to reflect the special relationship between the United States and its neighbors. Eventually, despite having first been accepted by a 156–4 teller vote, the MacGregor amendment was rejected by a 189–218 roll call vote. Instead of controlling western hemisphere immigration by means of a ceiling, the House bill provided for indirect controls by requiring labor certification of all but the immediate family of citizens and permanent residents.

After the passage of the Voting Rights Act, the Senate resumed work on the immigration bill. Despite the administration's success in replacing Immigration Subcommittee chair Eastland with Ted Kennedy, immigration reform quickly came to a halt because of the obstructionism of Senator Samuel Ervin (D-NC) and Senate Minority Leader Everett Dirksen (R-IL), both staunchly restrictionist members of the Immigration Subcommittee. Ervin was opposed to the repeal of the national origins

---

[7] Spouses, parents, and minor children of US citizens would be exempt from the ceiling.

quota but realized its political inevitability. Instead, supported by Dirksen, he introduced an amendment to the bill that, among other measures, provided for a 120,000 ceiling on the western hemisphere, which was to go into effect in July 1968 unless a presidential commission recommended otherwise and Congress adopted its recommendation. While Senator Ervin and Representative Feighan both agreed "strongly about placing the Western Hemisphere on a quota footing with the rest of the world," Ervin was much better placed to get his way as a majority on the Senate subcommittee shared his view that "a threatened avalanche" of immigration from the western hemisphere "would become unmanageable unless we place realistic limitations" (cited in Marinari 2014, 233).

Concerned that Ervin's refusal to endorse an immigration bill that did not include a western hemisphere ceiling would jeopardize the entire reform package, the Johnson administration was

unwilling to wage a battle for this cause. It was believed that, given the general parliamentary situation and the strong support voiced by Senator Dirksen for a curb in Western Hemisphere immigration, the inclusion of the Ervin amendment ... was necessary to get the bill out of committee and to the Senate floor.

(Kennedy 1966, 147)

At this point, even the Department of State, as the last remaining executive opponent of the Ervin amendment, relented and accepted the president's decision to concede on the question of western hemisphere immigration. Likely reflecting executive concerns about the endorsement's diplomatic costs, presidential support for the Ervin amendment was to be played, in the words of Johnson's advisor Valenti, "as a Committee sponsored thing, not as something the Administration has consented to" (cited in Marinari 2014, 235). After the full Senate had passed the bill with a majority of 76 to 18, it was referred to Conference Committee to reconcile the two differing versions. Bolstered by their success in the Senate, House supporters of the MacGregor amendment joined forces with Senate restrictionists to ensure that the final bill would include a ceiling on western hemisphere immigration.

As signed into law by President Johnson, the 1965 Immigration and Nationality Act provided for the immediate repeal of the Asia Pacific Triangle and the abolition of the national origins system as of July 1, 1968. Until then, any unused quota slots would be reassigned to countries with visa backlogs. Instead of governing immigration on the basis of national origins quotas, the new immigration regime would be based on a preference system that provided for a total of 170,000 eastern hemispheric and 120,000 western hemispheric immigrant visas on a first-come, first-served basis, subject to a 20,000 limit for any single country and exempting spouses, children, and parents of US citizens. Of the seven preference categories governing admissions, four were based on family unification, two were for admission of professional, skilled, and unskilled workers, and one was for refugees. Collectively the family-based preferences allocated 74 percent of quota admissions to family reunion – including 24 percent for brothers and sisters of citizens – not counting those family members (children, parents, and spouses of US citizens) admitted outside the quotas. In contrast, only 20 percent of quota entries were reserved for economic immigrants (10 percent for high-skilled immigrants, 10 percent for skilled and unskilled workers in short supply) and 6 percent for refugees (Zolberg 2006).

At the Immigration Act's signing ceremony at the Statue of Liberty, Johnson declared:

This bill that we will sign today is not a revolutionary bill. It does not affect the lives of millions. It will not reshape the structure of our daily lives, or really add importantly to either our wealth or our power. Yet it is still one of the most important acts of this Congress and of this administration. For it does repair a very deep and painful flaw in the fabric of American justice ... This bill says simply that from this day forth those wishing to emigrate to America shall be admitted on the basis of their skills and their close relationship to those already here ... The days of unlimited immigration are past. But those who do come will come because of what they are, and not because of the land from which they sprung.

(Johnson October 3, 1965)

Johnson, like other reformers, expected further changes to the 1965 Act after the Select Commission on Western Hemisphere Immigration would finish its work in 1968. By then, however, the White House had moved on to other policy agendas, and the obstructionism of congressional restrictionists prevented the adoption of the commission's modest recommendation to delay the ceiling's enactment. In particular, Senator Eastland, who served as chair of the Senate Subcommittee on Immigration until 1978, blocked any efforts at reforming the 1965 Act (Marinari 2014). Instead, in 1978 the separate hemispheric limits were replaced by a global ceiling, with identical country limits for all western hemisphere countries, including Mexico. Thus, a frustrated Abba Schwartz commented:

The Immigration Act of 1965 eliminated the national origins quota system, which was our major objective, but in so doing, the Act established an immigration system whose parochial framework stands in sharp contrast to the more flexible

and internationally oriented provisions of the proposal recommended so strongly
by President Kennedy.

(Marinari 2014, 98)

Thus, even at the time of its passage commentators had no illusions about
the vast gap between the reformers' vision, on the one hand, and the 1965
Act, on the other. As the *New York Times* stated, although "under the
House protocol, the bill bears the name of the chairman of the House
Judiciary Committee, Emanuel Celler ... in a very real sense it is the bill of
Michael Aloysius Feighan [who] largely shaped it and guided it through
more than 12 weeks of labor" (Marinari 2014, 238).

The passage of the 1965 Immigration Act marked the conclusion of well
over a decade of reform incrementalism that followed in the wake of the
1952 McCarran–Walter Act's failure to liberalize the country's racially
stratified immigration system. As the country moved away from its longstanding international isolationism and embraced its new position of Cold
War superpower, its diplomatic insulation weakened and pressure for
repealing the national origins quotas mounted. Yet in contrast to Canada,
US executives – who bore the brunt of diplomatic pressure – did not have
the luxury of promptly repealing the national origins quotas through
regulatory reform. Instead, with no choice but to pursue legislative change,
reformers faced a hostile legislative arena where restrictionist Southern
Democrats dominated policy making through control of key committees.
It was only after the 1964 elections handed President Johnson a landslide
victory and decisively weakened the restrictionist congressional coalition
that paradigmatic reform seemed possible. Thus, with the reputational costs
of the national origins quotas having become sufficiently large to also
register in the legislative arena, there was little opposition to their repeal.

Still, while restrictionists had become sufficiently weakened to no
longer veto immigration reform per se, key restrictionist legislators continued their stranglehold over the House and Senate Immigration
Subcommittees and forced reformers to make painful concessions. By
appealing to public opposition when any increases in immigration were
put forth, and being less constrained diplomatically than the White
House, congressional restrictionists secured a consequential victory in
imposing a first ever ceiling on western hemisphere immigration.
Likewise, appealing to public opposition to a demographic change in
immigration flows while simultaneously responding to demands by
organized labor to curtail economic immigration, restrictionist legislators
succeeded in shifting the proposed immigration preferences from a labor
market-based to a family-based admissions regime. Thus, while the

1965 Act remained true to reformers' commitment to abolish the national origins quotas, paradigmatic liberalization came at the costs of major concessions that would come to haunt US immigration politics to the present day. First, by institutionalizing an immigration regime dominated by family reunification, policy makers inadvertently closed the door to a skills-based immigration policy. Second, by capping western hemisphere immigration and extending the eastern hemisphere's per-country limits to the Americas, US immigration policy, for the first time in its history, became detached from the realities of longstanding patterns of regional labor mobility. As western hemisphere visa demand far exceeded supply, the 1965 Act set the scene for large-scale undocumented immigration from Mexico.

TILTING THE BALANCE FROM FAMILY TO ECONOMIC ADMISSIONS: THE 1990 IMMIGRATION ACT AND THE FAILURE OF HUMAN CAPITAL-BASED REFORM

Even though the authors of the 1965 Immigration Act had envisaged the legislation as the beginning of a series of progressive immigration reforms, by the time the Select Commission on Western Hemisphere Immigration had finished its work in 1968, neither executive nor congressional reformers were willing to take on congressional restrictionists over the question of the western hemisphere ceiling. Immigration reform was effectively taken off the legislative agenda, and a period of political stalemate settled in. By the early 1980s the political climate had become decidedly hostile to policy liberalization: the US economy was in recession, undocumented immigration was on the rise, and the 1964 Act's demographic impact had become plain to see. Between 1960 and 1980, the proportion of European immigrants shrank from 75 percent to less than 40 percent of admissions, while the proportion of Hispanic and Asian immigrants expanded from 25 percent to nearly 60 percent of admissions (Chishti et al. October 15, 2015). Meanwhile public opinion was decidedly hostile to policy liberalization. Convinced that the country had lost control over its borders, the American public favored significant reductions in both legal immigrant and refugee admissions and a crackdown on undocumented immigrants (Tichenor 2002).

Not surprisingly, neither Republican nor Democratic policy makers were optimistic about the prospects of policy liberalization. In 1980, Republican Senator Alan Simpson, who was to play a seminal role in immigration reform, privately reminded colleagues that Americans were "offended" by immigration policies that make them "the sugar daddies of the world" (cited in Tichenor 2002, 243). Yet, if the conventional wisdom among policy makers in the early 1980s was "that immigration reform was certain to fall under the spell of either inertial or restrictionist forces" (Tichenor 2002, 243), then conventional wisdom was to be proven wrong. With the passage of the 1990 Immigration Act, US policy makers endorsed an immigration policy that would allow for historically unprecedented levels of immigrant admissions.

Despite its expansionism, however, the 1990 Act is better understood as a case of reform failure. Intended to shift immigrant admissions from family toward high-skilled admissions under a firm numerical cap on overall admissions, the Immigration Act's modest expansion of economic immigration relied on a drastic expansion of overall admissions, rather than a reduction in family-based admissions. The passage of the 1990 Act thus stands in marked contrast to the success of human capital-based immigration reforms in Canada. Whereas Canadian policy makers were able to institutionalize a new immigration paradigm relatively free from external constraints, the reform process in the United States was profoundly shaped by the absence of interest group insulation, which forced policy makers to enlarge, rather than redistribute, the overall supply of available visas. We will now begin this case study with the work of the Select Commission on Immigration and Refugee Policy (SCIRP), which provided the ideational blueprint for immigration reform initiatives throughout the 1980s.

Depoliticizing Immigration: The Agenda-Setting Power of SCIRP

In 1978, Representative Peter Rodino and Senator Edward Kennedy proposed the creation of SCIRP to study the challenge of undocumented immigration and develop long-term recommendations that could serve as the foundation for nonpartisan immigration reform (Fuchs 1980). Fully cognizant of public opposition to policy liberalization, SCIRP was intended "to take xenophobia, race, and even economic conflict out of the debate" (Tichenor 2002, 250). Inspired by Truman's presidential commission that preceded the 1965 Hart–Celler Act, Kennedy envisaged the commission providing "definite information" and "enlightened" proposals that would move policy making beyond populist appeals for "retrograde legislation" (cited in Tichenor 2002, 250). Commission chair Father Theodore Hesburgh similarly conceived the role of the commission as promoting a policy agenda that could be endorsed by Democrats and Republicans alike, rather than as appealing to the public: "As a general rule, the American public ... has been negative toward the admission of immigrants and refugees to the United States. It is the most human thing in the world to fear strangers" (cited in Tichenor 2002, 252).

The commission was composed in equal part of cabinet secretaries, members of the House Judiciary Committee, members of the Senate Judiciary Committee, and nongovernmental experts – a decision that was to prove favorable for the stability of the reform process, as seven of the eight congressional commissioners would remain on the House and Senate Judiciary Committees throughout. The commission was firmly committed to evidence-based, nonpartisan discussion and sought to distance its deliberations from popular emotions. In its final report, *U.S. Immigration Policy and the National Interest* (March 1, 1981), SCIRP sought to frame immigration policy as integral to the national interest, rather than as an act of American generosity. While affirming the three-stream admission of family members – economic (independent) immigrants, and refugees – the commission called for the separation of visa allocation between economic and family immigrants in order to free up visas for independent immigrants. Emphasizing the positive effects of economic immigration, the report called for the liberalized admission of independent immigrants, those with exceptional qualifications, and foreign investors. The commission was unanimous in its support for greater employment-based immigration, with the single exception of investor visas, which were opposed by its chairman, Father Theodore Hesburgh. While the commission's favoring of employment-based immigration did not imply a rejection of the principle of family reunification, commissioners considered narrowing the circle of relatives eligible for sponsorship by abolishing the fifth preference of the brothers and sisters of US citizens. In the end, in a rare instance of partisan voting, the commission decided, by a close vote of 9–7, to retain the preference, with Democratic commissioners voting in favor of retention (Roebuck 1991).

In order to allow for a positive framing of immigration as in the national interest, SCIRP drew a firm line between illegal and legal immigration. Cognizant of mounting public concern about rising undocumented immigration, the commission emphasized the need for more effective immigration control while at the same time affirming the desirability of legal immigration. By drawing contrasting portraits of these two migratory flows, SCIRP facilitated their political decoupling – a move that was to prove instrumental in the passage of immigration reform, which took the form of illegal immigration reform in 1986 and legal immigration reform in 1990. While the commission ended up endorsing a modest expansion in immigration – increasing numerically restricted immigration from 290,000 to 350,000 a year – the voices of expansion skeptics, most importantly Senator Simpson, were clearly heard in the final report: "This is not the time for a large-scale expansion in legal immigration ... because the first order of priority is bringing undocumented/illegal immigration under control, while setting up a rational system for legal immigration" (The Select Commission on Immigration and Refugee Reform March 1, 1981, 37).

Interest Group Pressure and the Failure of Immigration Reform in the 1980s

After the conclusion of the commission's work, its leaders strategically reached out to the media to goad Congress into action. Two legislators with close ties to the commission were particularly well placed to take the lead on immigration reform. Senator Alan Simpson (R-WY), whose service on the commission had ignited a passionate interest in immigration policy, persuaded Judiciary Committee chair Strom Thurmond to place him at the head of the dormant Immigration Subcommittee. In the House, Romano Mazzoli (D-KY), a legislator with ties to Commission chair Father Hesburgh and at his urging, agreed to chair the House Judiciary Immigration Subcommittee (Tichenor 2002). Having developed a close working relationship on the commission, in 1982 Simpson and Mazzoli introduced legislation that entailed both legal and illegal immigration reform. The bill's immigration control provisions echoed many of the commission's proposals for a mix of legalization and employer sanctions. Its legal immigration reform proposals followed the commission's recommendations in liberalizing the admission of skilled workers and proposing a somewhat higher annual cap of 425,000 admissions. At the same time, in a consequential departure from SCIRP, it virtually eliminated visas for brothers and sisters of US citizens.

While the bill was quickly passed by the Senate, it was immediately shut down in the House. A broad coalition of interest groups ranging from business and agricultural growers to religious groups and immigrant rights organizations mobilized against employer sanctions and the restriction on legal admissions. The elimination of the adult sibling preference in particular was strongly opposed by Asian American and Latinx groups.

In the words of one legislator, "the roadblock to getting legislation certainly wasn't the public mood which favored action. It was fierce resistance from an unbelievable variety of groups with clout on the Hill" (cited in Tichenor 2002, 254). Legislators clearly faced a strikingly different interest group environment than during earlier rounds of immigration reform, including the 1965 Act. By the late 1970s the civil rights movement had inspired a historically unprecedented wave of ethnic mobilization, in particular by Mexican American and other Hispanic groups. In the mid-1970s, aided by government contracts and private foundations, no fewer than eight national Latinx organizations set up offices in Washington, DC (Tichenor 2002, 230). Moreover, unlike in the 1960s when Southern Democrats were still firmly restrictionist, immigration politics had become more partisan and politicized, leading to a switch from voice votes to recorded votes (Gimpel and Edwards 1999) – a procedural change that significantly decreased legislators' interest group insulation.

The bill was also opposed by the Reagan administration, whose ideational commitment to large-scale legal immigration and generous temporary foreign worker programs was at odds with the tenor of the bill. Echoing SCIRP's recommendations, the White House lobbied for the separation of legal from illegal immigration reform (Tichenor 2002). This strategic legislative split was in fact the critical lesson to emerge from the failure of immigration reform in 1982. Given the drastic decrease in interest group insulation, it would be impossible to find a legislative compromise encompassing both legal and illegal immigration reform that would be acceptable to a broad coalition of interests. Given heightened public unease with illegal immigration and the commission's pushing for a swift tackling of the issue, reformers decided to deal with illegal immigration first. In 1985 Simpson introduced a bill exclusively focused on the issue that would end up forming the blueprint for the 1986 Immigration Reform and Control Act (IRCA).

In 1988, two years after the passage of IRCA, Senators Kennedy and Simpson co-sponsored omnibus legislation to reform legal immigration. Aside from their shared commitment to immigration reform, the two senators' policy preferences were only partially overlapping. Simpson's commitment to immigration reform was firmly premised on the need to place a strict limit on overall immigration. Representing the state of Wyoming, he was politically unconstrained by immigrant constituencies and clearly favored high-skilled over family immigration. By contrast, Ted Kennedy, who had resumed control of the Immigration

Subcommittee, wanted to expand overall admissions and liberalize the admission of Irish immigrants in particular – a cause that had always been close to his heart. As a bipartisan compromise, the Kennedy–Simpson bill provided for a raised but firm admissions ceiling of 590,000 (exempting only refugees). While the immediate relatives of US citizens would continue to be admitted outside the preference system – free of numerical constraint – the number of nonpreference visas issued in a given year would be subtracted from the preference family visas available in the subsequent year so that as demand for nonpreference visas increased, the number of nonpreference family visas would decrease, hitting the brothers and sisters preference particularly hard (Zolberg 2006). The bill also directly attacked family immigration by lowering the number of visas allocated for the spouses and minor children of permanent residents (the second preference) and by restricting the fifth preference to never-married siblings (thereby excluding not only married siblings but also their spouses and children).

Visas freed up by the reduction in family visas and the raising of the overall ceiling would go to economic immigrants – including investors – whose admission was to be raised from 54,000 to 120,000, a number that exceeded SCIRP's recommendation. Of these visas, 55,000 would be distributed on the basis of a Canadian-style points system that would allocate points for education, skills and work experience, age, English-language proficiency, and, controversially, source country diversity, which would allow the United States, to quote Kennedy, to "open its doors again to those who no longer have immediate family ties in the US" (Zolberg 2006, 377). There is no question that the emphasis on the English language and source country diversity were a thinly veiled strategy to favor the admission of Irish workers, who, as an immigrant group significantly impacted by the 1965 reforms, did not benefit from a family unification-based immigration system. Kennedy's quest for increased Irish admissions did not stop here but also extended to the inclusion of a provision for special visas reserved for Irish nationals. Not surprisingly, non-Irish ethnic lobbies were hostile to the bill's source country diversity provisions, with Latinx and Asian American groups faulting the bill as hostile to nonwhite immigrants (Tichenor 2002). However, given the speed with which the bill moved through the Senate – passing after minimal debate by eighty-eight to four votes (Zolberg 2006) – ethnic groups had little time to mobilize.

Ethnic lobbies found a more hospitable environment in the House, where the bill quickly stalled in committee after most Democrats rejected the bill's pro-Irish bias. As a key Democratic staffer recounted:

for generations we only admitted white, European immigrants, and then, after Asians and Latin Americans finally have an opportunity to get in, there's this proposal to limit their numbers. We simply weren't going to support something so racially biased.

(Cited in Tichenor 2002, 269)

House Democrats were willing to appease Irish American lobbies by proposing a less ethnically conspicuous measure: a visa lottery for nationals of all countries adversely affected by the existing preference system. Latinx, Asian American, and immigrant rights groups, however, joined forces to call for the bill's outright rejection (Tichenor 2002). There was little pushback against these calls, especially as Peter Rodino (D-NJ), chairman of the Judiciary Committee, and Romano Mazzoli (D-KY), chairman of the Immigration Subcommittee and co-sponsor of IRCA, were willing to hold up the bill. Neither Rodino nor Mazzoli were strong supporters of employment-driven immigration, and Mazzoli in particular wanted to hold off with legal immigration reform until the effects of IRCA were better understood (Murphy and Espenshade 1990). Key House legislators had little reason to initiate a complex legislative process that would need to work around vocal interest group opposition. Thus, the Kennedy–Simpson bill died in the House Immigration Subcommittee, freezing any reform movement until after the 1988 midterm elections.

The Immigration Act of 1990: The Limits of Paradigmatic Reform in the Absence of Interest Group Insulation

With the changing of hands of the chairmanships of the House Judiciary Committee and its Immigration Subcommittee in 1989, a window of opportunity for immigration reform opened. After Peter Rodino's retirement, the Judiciary Committee was now led by Jack Brooks (D-TX), who, having showed little interest in immigration reform in the past, delegated policy making to the Immigration Subcommittee under the leadership of Bruce Morrison (D-CT), a supporter of immigration liberalization with close relations to pro-immigration interest groups (Gimpel and Edwards 1999). In response to this more favorable political environment for moving immigration reform through the House, Kennedy and Simpson reintroduced their 1988 bill in the Senate. The omnibus bill called for the capping of annual immigration at 590,000 – a relatively generous but firm cap that would include immediate relatives of US citizens. Senator Simpson was deeply committed to the goal of immigration control and insisted that legal immigration reform would need to be nested within strict numerical controls: "It is darn well time for our government to face the unfortunate but ridiculously cold reality that they are many more people who want to come here than there is room or intent to accommodate" (cited in Murphy and Espenshade 1990, 144). The bill also reflected Simpson's preference for human capital-based over family immigration. While no free market liberal, Simpson agreed with proponents of the human capital paradigm that in order to remain economically competitive the United States needed to shift its immigration skills profile upward:

By placing more emphasis on the skills and qualities that independent immigrants possess, immigration policy will be more closely coordinated with the national interest ... [o]ur legal immigration system is not now serving the national interest as well as it should or could. Today, more than 90 percent – this is a rather startling figure – of all immigrants enter this country without any screening at all of their impact on the US labor market and without any determination of what our labor needs are.

(Cited in Shanks 2001, 211)

In addition to restricting the overall size of family immigration by subsuming all (including nonpreference) family visas under a numerical cap, the bill sought to reign in the sponsorship of extended family members in particular. Like its predecessor, the bill excluded married brothers and sisters from sponsorship under the fifth preference while at the same time reducing the number of visas available under the fifth preference. It also provided for a lowering of visa allotment for the second preference, the spouses and dependent children of noncitizen permanent residents. On the economic side the bill created a new preference category for high-skilled immigration.

Kennedy's fingerprint, on the other hand, was clearly visible in the proposal to increase levels of immigration overall – a concession made by Simpson, who opposed expanding immigration. As far as changes to the composition of immigration was concerned, Kennedy opposed the shift toward economic immigration, arguing that liberalized economic preferences would be an open invitation for employers to hire cheap foreign labor. Having conceded to Simpson on the point of economic immigration, Kennedy in turn insisted on legislating openings for diversity immigration in order to facilitate Irish immigration: "the most important provisions of the bill will open up immigration for countries that suffer unfair discrimination under the current system" (cited in Murphy and Espenshade 1990, 144–5).

Had it not been for Simpson's and Kennedy's shared commitment to bipartisan immigration reform and their close working relationship that developed during their work on the Select Commission, it is unlikely that the two senators would have agreed to co-sponsor an immigration bill, given their divergent substantive preferences. Their ideological differences were amplified by the fact that they represented starkly differing constituencies. As a senator from Wyoming, where immigration rarely featured politically, Simpson was not beholden to pro-immigration constituencies. Kennedy, by contrast, represented a state with powerful ethnic and immigrant advocacy groups and, as a Northern Democrat, held close ties to trade unions.

Weakened Interest Group Insulation in the Senate

The Kennedy–Simpson bill faced its first challenge even before it could make its way out of the Senate Immigration Subcommittee, with recently joined Paul Simon (D-IL) demanding that the sponsorship of brothers and sisters be fully restored. A senator with close ties to Latinx, Asian American, and immigrant rights groups, Simon viewed the preservation of family reunification – including the sponsorship of extended family members – as the heart of US immigration policy. In a first concession to Simon and ethnic groups, Simpson yielded. Consequently the revised bill fully restored the fifth preference by moving some visas from the economic immigration stream and by increasing the overall supply of visas by 10,000 (Murphy and Espenshade 1990).

As the Judiciary Committee's deliberations began, the bill came under sustained attack, much to Simpson's and Kennedy's surprise. After all, less than two years earlier a comparable bill had sailed through the Senate without eliciting much debate. This sudden mobilization of members of the Judiciary Committee was the result of intense interest group lobbying. With the recent changes in House immigration leadership, immigration lobbies had shifted their focus from their favored target, the House Judiciary Committee, to the Senate Judiciary Committee (Murphy and Espenshade 1990). Given its curtailment of family unification, ethnic lobbies were most strongly opposed to the bill. Referencing a recent Government Accountability Office report that projected family immigration to drop to zero by the year 1999 under the Kennedy–Simpson bill (Murphy and Espenshade 1990), ethnic groups made their support for employment-based immigration and Simpson's immigration ceiling contingent on an increase in visas for the second preference and protection of the fifth preference from cuts (Zolberg 2006). Asian American and Hispanic groups further objected to the English-language provisions for skilled workers. Strikingly, there was no mobilization against Kennedy's proposal for diversity visas. Opposition to the bill was spearheaded by Paul Simon on the left and Orrin Hatch (R-UT) on the right. Whereas committee Democrats spoke of the benefits of reuniting transnational families, Republicans extolled the contributions of immigrant workers to the country's global competitiveness. When the committee reported the bill, virtually all of Simpson's restrictions on family unification had been retracted, as had the English-language stipulation for skilled workers (Gimpel and Edwards 1999). One of the few contested provisions that did survive intact was Simpson's cap on immigration.

On the Senate floor, however, the immigration cap quickly became the target of attack. Orrin Hatch and Dennis DeConcini (D-AZ) secured an amendment that set a floor of 216,000 for family preference visas and allowed the ceiling to be pierced by the admission of immediate family members of US citizens. The Hatch–DeConcini amendment in effect rendered Simpson's cap meaningless, prompting the latter to protest:

This removes the last essential element of the bill that passed the Senate in 1988. There is nothing that Senator Kennedy, Senator Simpson, and I have not compromised to get to this point. ... I really do not know the purpose of this amendment other than just tremendous group pressure ... But I can tell you that it strikes at the very heart of this legislation.

(US Congress July 12, 1989, S.7782)

Another significant amendment was introduced by Arlen Specter (R-PA) in response to business concerns about the difficulty of recruiting certain skilled workers. The Specter amendment restored the 30,000 visas that had been subtracted from the economic category as part of the subcommittee compromise, thereby raising the cap from 600,000 to 630,000 – 480,000 for family reunification and 150,000 for skilled immigrants (Murphy and Espenshade 1990).

The difference between the original Kennedy–Simpson bill and the bill that was passed by the full Senate was vast. Whereas two years before a largely equivalent bill co-sponsored by the two senators had passed through the chamber largely unscathed, this time around the legislative process stripped the bill of most of its central provisions, in particular those introduced by Simpson. What had changed, of course, was the mounting interest group pressures faced by senators in 1989. The fingerprints of ethnic lobbies in particular on this bill are impossible to ignore. Speaking before the final vote on the bill, Senate Majority Whip Alan Senator (D-CA) commented:

California is home to more Asians and Hispanics than any other state in the country. No single issue nor piece of legislation has raised their concern as much as this legislation we are voting on today ... The message I have received from these individuals is that they would prefer to see no reform legislation at all rather than see reforms which would include placing a new cap on family sponsored immigration.

(US Congress July 13, 1989, S.7904)

Building a Pro-immigration Interest Coalition: Immigration Reform in the House

Meanwhile, policy makers in the House had started work on their own immigration bill. Firmly committed to immigration liberalization, Immigration Subcommittee chair Bruce Morrison was concerned that the window for policy reform was about to close after Kennedy had confided in House Judiciary chairman Brooks and Morrison that he was not willing to waste any more time on unsuccessful immigration bills and that this was the last chance for reform (Schuck 1992). Recognizing hostile interest group mobilization as the greatest threat to reform, Morrison sought to assemble a pro-reform coalition that would involve all of the major stakeholders: ethnic groups, employers, and organized labor. Rather than focusing on popular fears about immigration – a dynamic that drove illegal immigration reform in 1986 – Morrison wanted to turn immigration reform into a win-win for all affected (and organized) interests. As Tichenor writes, "[a]t a time of budget austerity, legal immigration reform seemed to provide Morrison and his colleagues with a unique form of distributive politics that carried few apparent costs: namely the allocation of visas" (2002, 271). While this coalition-building and log-rolling political strategy was well tried by US legislators, it had never been used for immigration bills because of the strength of congressional restrictionism (Schuck 1992) – recall the centrality of the promise of numerical restriction as a precondition for the passage of the 1965 Act. Central to Morrison's log-rolling strategy was the need to expand immigration, which precluded the imposition of a firm cap. In order to secure buy-in by all, each stakeholder had to be given a piece of the pie – a strategy that critically hinged on increasing the size of the pie.

While Senate reformers had managed to stay clear of certain politically explosive issues, mounting interest group mobilization meant that these issues now would have to be addressed head-on in the House. Among the most volatile issues was that of temporary foreign worker recruitment. In the extensive subcommittee hearings, most of which were held jointly with the Education and Labor Committee, employers insisted on more flexible access to a greater number of temporary work visas, while the AFL-CIO demanded restrictions on the scale of temporary employment (Schuck 1992). In the Senate, Simpson had done little to secure the support of employers for his bill, and it now fell to House Immigration Subcommittee chair Morrison to court business support. Reflecting Morrison's determination to secure both labor and business buy-in, the House bill incorporated key labor demands, including a cap on temporary employment visas and enhanced worker protections – some of which would later be retracted in order to neutralize employer opposition to these provisions. Seeking to win over business, Morrison sought to increase the number of permanent employment visas to 95,000 but in the end had to settle for 65,000, given the unease felt by many House Democrats with employment-based immigration and its associated harm of wage depression (Gimpel and Edwards 1999).

Among the organized interests, ethnic lobbies were in an especially favorable position to influence policy, as the geographical concentration of immigrant communities in key electoral districts provided these groups with leverage in the House. Moreover, Morrison was known to hold close ties to ethnic and immigrant rights groups. Hispanic and Asian American groups had followed the progress of the Senate bill closely and were unhappy with what they considered to be unjustifiable cuts in family immigration. Given the already mounting backlog of family preference visas and its resultant lengthy wait times for family reunification, ethnic groups not only opposed the proposed cuts to family sponsorship but demanded the liberalization of the status quo, which they described as anti-family and as promoting illegal immigration. One prominent lobbyist for the Asian community provocatively called the Senate bill "the Asian and Latino Exclusion Act of 1989" (Jacob 1992, 314).

While Hispanic and Asian American groups were natural allies as the prospective losers from cuts to family immigration, the Irish for some time had sought to secure immigration openings through a liberalized economic stream, emphasizing education and English fluency as criteria for admission. Yet by the time the House Immigration Subcommittee had begun its work, Irish groups had come to consider the economic admissions approach, which the Senate had pursued in 1988 and again in 1989, as too limited a measure. Instead, led by the Irish Immigration Reform Movement (IIRM), Irish interests lobbied for the adoption of a diversity visa program designed to favor their fellow nationals. In the lead-up to the Kennedy–Simpson bill the IIRM had raised hundreds of thousands of dollars and hired an experienced lobbyist, Harris Miller, who had previously worked as an aide to Mazzoli on the Immigration Subcommittee (Jacob 1992). The organization also launched a well-coordinated campaign of letters, telephone calls, and personal visits by dozens of IIRM members to all legislators of the Immigration Subcommittee, recognizing that "[t]his campaign was unique because the issue was personal. It required more than a paid lobbyist. It required face-to-face presentations." (Jacob 1992, 323). The IIRM not only had a powerful ally in Senator Kennedy but also held unusually strong political cards in the House. Morrison himself was of Irish descent and had just launched a campaign for governor in Connecticut, where the Irish formed an important constituency. The Ancient Order of Hibernians of America, an Irish Catholic organization, honored Morrison with an award at their Washington, DC convention, where the IIRM approached Morrison to discuss the possibility of organizing fundraisers for his gubernatorial campaign by Irish American, Polish American, and Italian American groups with an interest in visas for "adversely affected nations" (Jacob 1992, 326). While the IIRM in the end failed to win the support of other ethnic groups – the latter either were indifferent or objected to the idea of bringing nationality back into US immigration law – Hispanic and Asian American lobbies decided not to mount active opposition against the IIRM's campaign for diversity visas, concentrating their efforts on reversing the cuts to family sponsorship instead.

The cause of the IIRM was first taken on by Representative Charles Schumer (D-NY), who had introduced an immigration bill with a provision for 75,000 "diversity" visas for immigrants from "low-admission" regions, with a 7 percent ceiling on any given country. In drafting the bill, Schumer had worked closely with the IIRM's Harris Miller, who subsequently admitted that Schumer's "diversity" proposal was "not quite as neutral as it seems" (Jacob 1992, 318). The pro-Irish bias was clearly evident in the provision – pushed for by the IIRM – to treat Northern Ireland as a separate state, thereby capping Irish diversity immigration at 14 percent rather than 7 percent. In March 1990, Morrison took the subcommittee by surprise by introducing his own immigration bill. Following Schumer, Morrison proposed the allocation of 75,000 visas to a diversity program that, however, was only to operate on a temporary basis. Morrison went beyond Schumer's bill in setting aside a third of diversity visas for undocumented immigrants from "adversely affected" countries – targeting the IIRM's constituency of undocumented immigrants from Ireland who had arrived in the United States too late to benefit from legalization under the IRCA (Jacob 1992). When the subcommittee finished its markup, the immigration bill not only included Morrison's diversity provisions but also made the (nonamnesty) diversity visa program permanent, as proposed by Schumer. The provision moved through the Judiciary Committee unscathed, despite lackluster support from Judiciary Committee chair, Jack Brooks. Brooks' decision to nevertheless move the bill forward was influenced by Senator Kennedy's lobbying efforts, on the one hand, and the Democratic Party's investment in the success of Morrison's gubernatorial campaign, on the other (Jacob 1992).

The diversity visa program was not the only concession made to ethnic groups. Faced with the onslaught of lobbying by Hispanic and Asian American groups, Morrison proposed an increase in visas for both the second and the fifth preference groups – precisely the preferences that Simpson had sought to limit. Representative Howard Berman, a California Democrat, proposed even more radical legislation that would have moved the immediate family members of permanent residents – the second preference – outside the preference system, in effect extending the right of unrestricted admission hitherto enjoyed exclusively by close family members of US citizens to those of permanent residents (Gimpel and Edwards 1999). Berman's proposal, however, died in committee once it was clear Morrison's bill would be advanced through the House.

After the immigration bill had passed the Judiciary Committee, Lamar Smith (R-TX), a conservative member of the subcommittee that led the dissent of eight members of the Judiciary Committee, criticized the bill as accommodating "every special interest group that has made a demand on the US immigration system" (Jacob 1992, 327). There is no question that the bill was the product of Morrison's masterful accommodation of a powerful interest group coalition. Although the business and ethnic lobbies did not formally join forces, there was a tacit agreement that each side would support the other and not oppose their demands (Fitzgerald and Cook-Martín 2014). In order to turn the bill into a win-win situation, both sides knew that they needed to defeat Simpson's push for a firm cap on immigration. Warren Leiden, leader of the American Immigration Lawyers Associations, whose constituents spanned both economic and family immigration, and who served as a bridge between the two groups, put it as follows:

We realize that if each side thought of immigration reform as a zero-sum game in which visas from a group were seen as a loss for the other, there would be an ugly fight and someone would lose. The solution was to work together to make the pie bigger.

(Cited in Tichenor 2002, 269)

This is precisely what Morrison's House bill had done. It is no surprise that after the bill had cleared the Judiciary Committee, Morrison declared:

The business community is getting the things it wants. Labor unions are satisfied. The family-based and diversity immigrant groups are on board. It is a bill that has enough benefits and improvements for everybody.

(Cited in Jacob 1992, 327)

Once the bill was reported to the full House, lobbying shifted into high gear. The IIRM alone visited over two-thirds of all legislators, supported by staffers of the Irish embassy (Jacob 1992, 328). For the most part, lobbies fought to retain the gains already made. Only business was dissatisfied with the committee bill, because of its restrictions on temporary foreign worker visas – an issue that Morrison promised to address in conference. Before the floor debate began, the House decided to limit the ability of representatives to introduce amendments to only those specified on a House Rules Committee list – thereby preempting the need to make major concessions to opponents of the bill. Opposition to the bill was led by two members of the Immigration Subcommittee, Lamar Smith and John Bryant (D-TX), together with Bill McCollum (R-FL). Bryant introduced an amendment to delete the entire bill except for its family reunification provisions. Smith proposed an amendment to lower the number of annual admissions from 800,000 to 630,000, comparable to the Senate bill (Gimpel and Edwards 1999). Having been opposed to the brothers and sisters preference from the outset, Smith argued in favor of a more selective immigration policy that would prioritize immediate family members and skilled workers for admission. The amendments were easily defeated, and the aptly named Family Unity and Employment Opportunity Act of 1990 passed the House in October 1990 by a relatively narrow margin of 231 to 192 (Gimpel and Edwards 1999). While Morrison's bill had remained largely intact as it made its way through the House, its future remained uncertain. Not only did it now face the threat of presidential veto because of its high immigration levels, but it also bore little resemblance to the Senate bill. With Congress due to adjourn soon, immigration reformers were running out of time. Senator Kennedy was justifiably concerned that the tight schedule would allow other legislators, including Simpson, to demand further concessions and frustrate immigration reform once again (Schuck 1992).

Protecting the Spoils in Conference Committee

Charged with reconciling two dissimilar bills, the Conference Committee faced the daunting task of forging a compromise between the expansionist House measure, which set annual admissions at 800,000, and the more moderate Senate bill, which limited admissions to 630,000. The committee comprised members of both chambers, most of whom faced strong incentives to extract concessions on the road to a legislative compromise. This was encapsulated in a statement by Senator Simpson, who soon complained that "[i]n all my years of law and public service, I've never seen so many shifting bottom lines ... This turkey gets more feathers every day" (cited in Tichenor 1994, 353). Simpson clearly posed the biggest risk to the passage of immigration reform, as he held strong objections to many of the House measures and threatened to filibuster it to death (Schuck 1992). Specifically, while Simpson wanted to retain the increase in high-skilled immigration visas, he sought to firmly cap immigration and lower admissions levels by reducing the proportion of family visas and eliminating unskilled worker visas. In contrast, Ted Kennedy, who was cognizant that the next Congress was unlikely to touch immigration legislation in the lead-up to a presidential election, was determined to see the bill succeed at all costs. If Simpson agreed to not block the conference, Kennedy promised to not sign the conference report if it turned out to be unacceptable to Simpson. With this agreement in place, other key players on the committee announced their bottom lines. Morrison reiterated his demands for the favorable treatment of the Irish, Schumer similarly insisted on the new diversity programs, and Berman demanded generous family unification provisions (Schuck 1992).

In order to win over Simpson, Kennedy proposed an increase in legal admissions from 630,000 to 700,000 for the next three years and 675,000 thereafter in exchange for provisions aimed at restricting the rights of immigrants convicted of criminal offenses, stepping up deportations, and curbing undocumented immigration – including a pilot program for a tamper-proof identification card linked to employer sanctions (Tichenor 2002). The latter was a measure that had long been close to Simpson's heart: he had pursued it in the context of the 1986 IRCA but had been forced to concede because a powerful coalition of business and civil rights groups opposed it. Having secured this small victory on immigration control, Simpson grudgingly dropped his opposition to the compromise bill. Even though family-based immigration had survived unscathed, annual ceilings could be pierced whenever the admission of immediate family members of US citizens exceeded 226,000. Moreover, the transitional (reserving 40 percent of its visas for the Irish) and permanent diversity programs were retained. Lastly, even with Kennedy's compromise provision the bill authorized an increase of 40 percent over current admissions.

Thus, after the conclusion of the last closed-door meeting, conferees praised their compromise bill as a triumph for "family unity," "cultural diversity," and "job creation" (Tichenor 2002, 274). The compromise was swiftly passed by the Senate but stalled on the House floor, where the Hispanic Caucus, supported by the Black Caucus, blocked Simpson's tamper-proof identification card. On the final day of the House legislative sessions, a group of prominent legislators (including Morrison and Berman) asked Simpson to save the bill by yielding on the question of the pilot identification card. Representative Barney Frank (D-MA), an openly gay legislator who did not want to see the bill fail after he had secured an end to ideological and sexual preference exclusions in the Conference Committee, promised Simpson that he would lobby Senate liberals to reconsider the pilot program in the next Congress. Simpson quietly conceded (Schuck 1992).

The Executive Arena: From Veto Point to Interest Group Access Point

The making of the 1990 Immigration Act follows a longstanding pattern in US immigration politics that places Congress at the center of policy making (excepting refugee policy, which historically has been closely tied to US foreign policy). Nonetheless, compared to the Hart–Celler Act there was strikingly little presidential involvement in the legislative struggles over immigration in the late 1980s. The White House was slow to articulate a distinct position and did little to shape the policy-making process. In contrast to the 1965 reforms, which were in part driven by the diplomatic costs incurred by a racist policy status quo, there were few diplomatic pressures bearing on the presidency at the time. Unlike policy areas such as immigration control and refugee policy, which directly impinge on the interests of foreign governments, legal immigration reform is less likely to elicit diplomatic interference, provided it does not select by national origin. The main source of diplomatic pressure originated from the Irish government, who pushed for the legalization of its undocumented nationals and the creation of new legal immigration pathways. Yet, unlike the influence exerted by the IIRM over key members of Congress, the Irish government held little diplomatic leverage over the White House. Not only were its demands vulnerable to accusations of ethnic favoritism, but Ireland was too minor a player in the international arena to be of much concern to the United States. Whatever interest the

Bush administration had in immigration reform, it was unlikely to be shaped by diplomatic pressure.

Initially, even though Labor Secretary Elizabeth Dole privately criticized the White House for its failure to articulate a position on immigration reform (Tichenor 2002), the administration remained silent. It was only in late 1990 that the White House spoke out, declaring: "The Administration supports legal immigration reform that would enhance skill-based immigration while facilitating the unification of families. It also supports an increase in immigration levels above those in current law" (Bush September 25, 1990). The White House sided with the Senate bill, with the US attorney general and the secretaries of labor and transportation recommending a presidential veto of the House bill on the basis of its expansive family sponsorship provisions and the small proportion of visas allocated to employment-related immigration (Bush September 25, 1990). After this official statement the administration retreated into passivity and remained on the sidelines as legislators struggled to reach a compromise between the bills.

In early October 1990 – less than a month before the president's signing of the Immigration Act – the *Wall Street Journal* applauded the House bill for its higher ceilings for skilled workers and decried the administration's passivity on the issue of immigration reform. The president's domestic policy advisor cautioned the administration that it was on the wrong side of the issue (Schuck 1992), and the chief White House economist quickly offered public assurances of the administration's support for increased employment-based immigration (Tichenor 2002). Now that the White House had become a player in immigration reform, ethnic lobbies let the White House feel the heat for supporting Simpson's proposal to reduce family-based immigration. To cite an internal White House memorandum:

It requires constant vigilance against the charge that the Administration supports retreating from or is insensitive to this nation's traditional commitment to the institution of the family – and the President's strong pro-family stance. Could raise the ire of the Asian and Hispanic communities. ... The greatest danger may be our identification with those whom the press calls the immigration "restrictionists" or "exclusionists."

(Cited in Tichenor 2002, 273)

Similarly, after a meeting with Asian American lobbyists a White House advisor posed the clearly rhetorical question: "How could any president, let alone President Bush, oppose an immigration package so closely identified with economic growth and family values?" (cited in Tichenor

2002, 273). Thus, at the last minute the president came to publicly endorse increases in both family- and employment-based admissions – a position the White House had initially threatened to veto – demonstrating the influence of interest group lobbying in the absence of countervailing diplomatic or popular pressure.

Getting Away with Immigration Liberalization: Policy Making in the Absence of Popular Mobilization

More than any other major piece of immigration legislation in recent US history, the 1990 Immigration Act constituted a remarkable victory for pro-immigration interest groups. As signed into law by President George H. W. Bush, the immigration reform bore little semblance to its original policy blueprint, the Simpson–Kennedy Senate bill. This initial reform proposal followed in the footsteps of the SCIRP, whose report attested to the growing influence of a human capital immigration paradigm, on the one hand, and a strategic concern with limiting immigration, on the other. However, instead of a proposed modest increase in admissions and the adoption of a points system, intended to shift the selection of immigrants from sponsored family members toward high-skilled workers, the 1990 Immigration Act drastically increased the annual admission of preference immigrants from 290,000 to 675,000, blocked any cuts to family immigration, and modestly expanded employment-based immigration. As a result, a quarter-century after the Act's passage – with its provisions still in place – family immigration continues to dominate US immigration policy, accounting for 64 percent of annual admissions in 2014 (down from 68 percent in 1990). Employment-based immigration, by contrast, makes up only 15 percent of admissions, reflecting a modest increase from 9 percent in 1990 (Chishti et al. October 15, 2015, 10).

The unbridled influence of interest groups as the key driver of immigration liberalization in 1990 critically depended on the popular insulation of immigration policy makers. Since the last major round of legal immigration reform, public support for immigration restrictionism had virtually doubled, increasing from 33 percent in 1965 to 42 percent in 1986 and 65 percent in 1993. At the same time the proportion of Americans favoring current levels of immigration declined from 39 percent to 35 percent in 1986 and 27 percent in 1986 (Gallup n.d.). What accounts for the absence of popular mobilization against immigration expansionism, given the vast gap between public preferences and policy output?

The caution that marked the early stages of the policy-making process in the late 1980s clearly indicates congressional awareness of the political liability of immigration liberalization. With the passage of illegal immigration reform in 1986, however, policy makers could position themselves as responsive to public concerns. Having put in place a policy framework to address the problem of illegal immigration, legislators could now frame the liberalized admission of high-skilled immigrants as conducive to the national interest. Yet even assuming some popular receptivity to an increase in legal and skills-based immigration, policy makers could not rely on public support for drastically expanded immigrant admissions. Thus, policy liberalization depended on minimizing public engagement, preserving a pattern of client politics (Wilson 1980, Freeman 1995) where policy making in congressional committees provided opportunities for interest lobbies, but not the unorganized public, to influence policy. Given the active support of both business and ethnic and civil rights groups for the expansion of immigration, politicizing immigration reform was in neither party's interest. In the absence of partisan incentives for politicization, there was no catalyst for public mobilization against immigration liberalization.

The lack of a public immigration debate in the late 1980s and early 1990s is reflected in the sparse media coverage of the new immigration act. CBS Evening News coverage of the reform was negligible. Even the *New York Times*, one of the most consistent sources of news coverage on immigration, paid little attention to the reform process. While the paper had provided extensive coverage of the 1986 IRCA – reflecting the politicization of illegal immigration in the 1980s – the number of annual news articles on immigration declined in a linear fashion from about 140 in 1986 to just over forty in 1991 (Suro 2009, 8). In a similar vein the *Washington Post* covered the debates leading up to the 1990 Act in just 2,078 words in four routine Capitol Hill stories, and examined the bill's implications only a week after its passage (Suro 2009, 9). More broadly, until the 1990s political elites had more leeway in ignoring a mostly latent public restrictionism, which is reflected in the absence of public opinion polling. Gallup, for instance, only started annual immigration polling in 1999, having conducted no more than three immigration polls in the close to three decades between 1965 and 1993. Looking at the period of immigration reform itself, not a single immigration survey by any polling institute took place between 1986 and 1989 (Fogleman and Kellstedt 2012).

In sum, the politics of immigration reform leading up to the 1990 Immigration Act was marked by high levels of popular and diplomatic insulation, on the one hand, and an acute vulnerability to interest group pressure, on the other. The Act's passage contrasts with the failure

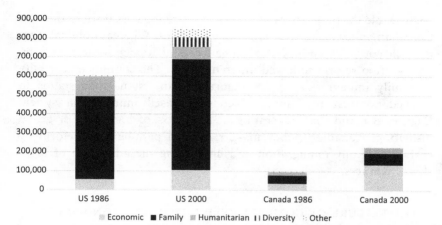

FIGURE 6.1 US and Canadian immigrant admissions, stacked by category, 1986 and 2000.

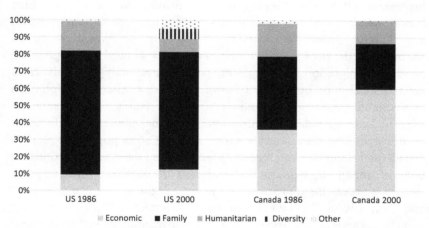

FIGURE 6.2 US and Canadian immigrant admissions, 100 percent stacked, 1986 and 2000.

of a comparable reform effort by Senators Simpson and Kennedy just two years prior, which also took place in a context of a Democratically controlled Congress and a Republican White House. Thus the success of the 1989/90 reform effort can be attributed to the decision by key policy makers to accommodate numerous societal stakeholders – ranging from ethnic groups to employers – by drastically expanding the number of visas. Returning to the Canadian case (Chapter 5), it is striking how comparable the preferences of US policy entrepreneurs were to those of Canadian policy makers in the 1980s and 1990s. Whereas political elites in both countries embraced a human capital immigration paradigm, immigration reform followed different paths. The continued centrality of family immigration in US immigrant admissions thus stands in marked contrast to Canada's economic-based immigration system (Figures 6.1 and 6.2). Operating in a context of high interest group insulation, Canadian policy makers enacted paradigmatic reform by curtailing family immigration and liberalizing the admission of high-skilled workers.

THE FAILURE OF COMPREHENSIVE IMMIGRATION REFORM UNDER THE BUSH AND OBAMA PRESIDENCIES

After the 1990 Act the immigration agenda shifted to the enactment of stricter immigration control, resulting in the passage of the 1996 Illegal Immigration Reform and Immigrant Responsibility Act, which redoubled border enforcement, dramatically widened the grounds for deportability, and limited access to welfare benefits for permanent residents. Throughout the decade, public opinion surveys showed a resurgence of popular immigration restrictionism. Nonetheless, immigrant advocates greeted the election of President George W. Bush in 2000 with optimism as electoral, interest group, and diplomatic pressures now appeared to align in favor of policy liberalization. As former governor of Texas, a border state with the country's second largest Latinx population, Bush's presidential campaign had repeatedly emphasized the economic contributions of immigrant workers and endorsed the legalization of undocumented workers for humanitarian reasons, arguing that "compassion" and "family values" "don't stop at the Rio Grande" (Allen December 24, 2003, 1). Targeting Latinx voters as a key constituency in battleground states and spending millions of campaign dollars on Spanish-language advertising and direct-mail appeals, Bush promised to speed up visa processing for family sponsors and employers and affirmed that "immigration is not a problem to be solved; it is the sign of a successful nation" (Bush 2000, 195–7). Even though Democrats retained their longstanding edge among Latinx voters, Bush won an impressive 34 percent of the Latinx vote. In addition to courting Latinx voters, Bush reached out to the business community (in particular the low-wage, low-skilled sector) as an integral part of his electoral coalition and called for a large-scale temporary foreign worker program.

Bush's commitment to immigration reform gained further momentum when Vincente Fox, a fellow border-state governor, won the Mexican presidential election after running on a platform of being a president to "all Mexicans," including the diaspora in the United States. After winning the White House, Bush considered the strengthening of diplomatic relations with Mexico as his "signature foreign policy legacy" (Rosenblum 2011, 3) and the two presidents met five times during the first nine months of 2001. Together they developed policy blueprints for a temporary foreign worker program and the legalization of undocumented Mexican workers, prompting political observers to forecast "more and more a kind of merged country on the border" (cited in Rosenblum 2011, 3). However, this auspicious reform momentum came to an abrupt halt with the terrorist attacks of September 11, 2001, when the White House decided that it had little choice but to shelve the president's reform agenda (Tichenor 2009). As national security concerns came to dominate US foreign policy, the window for diplomatically driven policy liberalization closed.

The September 11 terrorist attacks propelled forward the securitization of immigration that had already been under way in the 1990s. Now undocumented immigration was widely seen not only as indicative of a broken immigration system but also as a serious threat to national security. More broadly, demands for immigration restrictions were now framed "as key to homeland and cultural protection" (Barry 2005, 29). In the House the conservative and fiercely restrictionist Immigration Reform Caucus, under the leadership of Colorado Republican Tom Tancredo, gathered steam and by 2007 counted over a hundred members – a quarter of all House lawmakers. As a highly ideologically cohesive congressional organization, the Immigration Reform Caucus' obstructionist tactics during the Bush presidency quickly came to serve as "a wake-up call to the political establishment that the business-as-usual approach to immigration policy was no longer viable" (Barry 2005, 29).

Given the political salience of undocumented immigration and the attendant decrease in popular insulation, immigration moderates now no longer had the option – as they'd had in 1990 – of passing a legal-immigration-only bill. Rather, operating in a context of historically low popular insulation, any viable reform endeavor would need to include the challenge of measures for securing the border. Not only had immigration restrictionism come to dominate the political agenda, but the presence of millions of undocumented immigrants was widely regarded as evidence that the 1986 IRCA's two-pronged strategy of immigrant legalization ("amnesty") and border enforcement had failed. Proponents of legalization could no longer convince skeptics that with the right set of accompanying enforcement measures, offering undocumented immigrants a path to legal status would once and for all solve the problem of undocumented immigration.

The Failure of Comprehensive Immigration Reform in 2005–2006: Popular Insulation and the Break-up of the Republican Coalition

In 2004, just days after winning his second term, Bush convened a meeting with a group of pro-immigration Republican centrists in the hope of resurrecting his plans for Comprehensive Immigration Reform. White House political strategist Karl Rove publicly affirmed Bush's commitment to immigration reform, announcing that "[w]e are formulating plans for the legislative agenda for next year. And immigration will be on that agenda" (Sammon November 10, 2004, 1). Despite a Republican-controlled Congress, however, the prospects for Bush's reform proposals were far from bright. Given the heightened politicization of immigration post 9/11 and the attendant influence of Tancredo's anti-immigration coalition within the House, Bush's commitment to immigration liberalization carried the risk of alienating the Republican base. As a Republican strategist commented, "[i]t is highly unusual for an administration to use their political capital that was given by the base against the base" (Sammon November 10, 2004, 1). Similarly, David Frum, a renowned neoconservative and former speechwriter to Bush, wrote in a *National Review* cover article titled "GOP Be Warned" that "no issue, not one, threatens to do more damage to the Republican coalition than immigration. ... There is no issue where the beliefs and interests of the party rank-and-file diverge more radically from the beliefs and interests of the party's leaders" (cited in Barry 2005, 31).

Confirming these predictions, congressional immigration restrictionists fought back immediately. Representative Tancredo accused the president of betraying law-and-order values and declared that "their amnesty plan was dead on arrival" (Sammon November 10, 2004). The same month, House Republicans obstructed the quick passage of an intelligence reform bill by tagging on immigration restriction measures, "signal[ing] to Bush that his immigration initiative would split the party and stall action in his second term" (Tichenor 2009, 15). While Bush's commitment to legalization threatened to alienate both the party's popular base and restrictionist House Republicans, a new guest worker program greatly appealed to the party's business base. Represented by the Essential Worker Immigration Coalition led by the US Chamber of Commerce, this coalition included immigrant-dependent employers in industries covering health care, hospitality, retail, and construction (Tichenor 2009). Thus, with the preferences of business and social conservatives – the party's key constituencies – pulling in opposing directions, "the most notable political dynamic [from the beginning of immigration reform] was the split within the Republican Party" (Leal 2009, 3).

While Bush had affirmed immigration reform as one of his legislative priorities in the 2005 State of the Union address, he did not submit a legislative proposal to Congress. Both chambers subsequently proceeded along two separate tracks. With the Senate Judiciary Committee tied up in Supreme Court appointments, the House moved first. House Republicans wanted a two-step process that would start with a border enforcement bill, followed by guest worker legislation. While all opposed "amnesty" (i.e., legalization) of any kind, Republicans were divided on the question of guest worker recruitment. Nonetheless, as political analyst Stuart Rothenberg commented, "you don't have to speak with many House Republicans to understand that many of them wouldn't care if they ever get to the second bill" (cited in Leal 2009, 3).

Under pressure from Tancredo and his Immigration Reform Caucus, Judiciary Committee chairman Jim Sensenbrenner (R-WI) – himself an immigration restrictionist – drafted the Border Protection, Anti-Terrorism and Illegal Immigration Control Act, informally referred to as the Sensenbrenner Bill. Disregarding Bush's two key proposals – immigrant legalization and a guest worker program – and without holding any hearings, the committee passed a draconian "enforcement-only" bill at breakneck speed. Most controversially, it proposed to make unlawful presence in the United States a criminal felony rather than a civil offense and to punish with up to five years' imprisonment individuals who assisted undocumented immigrants. The Sensenbrenner Bill remained mostly silent on questions of immigrant admissions except for the 1990 Act's Diversity Visa program, which it proposed to abolish, and high-skilled admissions, which it proposed to modestly increase by means of ceiling exemptions.[8]

---

[8] The bill provided for 20,000 highly skilled immigrants to enter exempt from the H-1B visa cap, in addition to foreign nationals already working in STEM (science, technology, engineering, and mathematics) fields on temporary visas. Both groups would be allowed to bring in their immediate family members.

After the Judiciary Committee had voted on the bill, the Rules Committee rejected a motion to allow a bipartisan amendment that permitted undocumented immigrants to apply for new guest worker visas (Wasem February 27, 2013), thereby ensuring that the bill would remain firmly punitive in nature. Sensenbrenner recognized – too late as it turned out – that the bill would provoke fierce opposition within immigrant communities and subsequently proposed a floor amendment to reduce the penalty for unlawful presence from a felony to a misdemeanor (Graham 2010). Democrats joined Republican restrictionists to vote against the proposed amendment, reasoning that Republican extremism would strengthen their own position with Latinx voters at the 2006 midterm elections (Lam 2015). As Minority Leader Nancy Pelosi's spokesperson explained, "[t]he Democrats were not going to do anything to make it easier for Republicans to pass an atrocious bill" (Weisman April 12, 2006, A1). The full House approved the bill with a vote that was largely along partisan lines. The speed with which it was passed was essential for its success, allowing House restrictionists to preempt interest group opposition. As a prominent immigrant advocate commented:

A particularly stunning aspect of this process is that the House Judiciary Committee reviewed and voted on the bill in two days, and the House of Representatives affirmed the bill just one week later, with minimal debate in Congress or the public. The sheer speed and magnitude of the legislation took the immigrant community by surprise, eliminating the ability to craft an effective response strategy. In fact, not even furious lobbying by high powered corporate interests on Capitol Hill could stop the legislation.

(Noorani 2007, 192)

Interest groups and immigrant communities were not the only actors who were taken by surprise. The bill unleashed a flurry of diplomatic activity as eleven Latin American countries, including Mexico, sought to reverse some of its harsh enforcement provisions (Weisman April 12, 2006). At home, as anticipated by Sensenbrenner, the felony provisions took the brunt of interest group outrage. At the same time as the Senate turned its attention to the bill in early 2005, immigrant and church groups, supported by the foreign-language media, mobilized what "in all likelihood ... were the largest civil rights actions in US history [and] the biggest immigrant rights protests the world has ever witnessed" (Zepeda-Millán 2017, 2). By the end of the protest wave up to five million people had marched in nearly 400 demonstrations across the country (Wallace et al. 2014), including 500,000 in both Los Angeles and Dallas, and tens of thousands of Latinx high-school students had boycotted classes in California (Fetzer 2006).

Concerned that immigrant activism would undermine congressional reform efforts and provoke public and congressional backlash, pro-immigration policy makers had warned immigrant rights groups against participating in the protests.[9] While the protests did send a strong message to policy makers that Latinx voters were highly mobilized, they did not meet with widespread popular support. Only 24 percent of Americans held a positive view of those who marched for immigrant rights (compared to 52 percent whose views were unfavorable) (Rasmussen Reports May 1, 2006), although the marches themselves did not appear to have changed attitudes toward immigration (Rasmussen Reports May 3, 2006). As Tichenor's overview of polling data shows, public opinion "was ... far from locked in either a restrictive or expansive direction" (2009, 17). A majority of the public appeared to support a path to legalization – "earned citizenship" – for undocumented immigrants, provided this went hand in hand with tougher border and worksite enforcement. At the same time support for legalization was highly contingent on wording: while 53 percent of Americans favored "earned citizenship," a concept that emphasized conditions attached to legalization (e.g., payment of taxes and fines), only 12 percent supported "amnesty," a term associated with unconditionality (Rasmussen Reports May 1, 2006). Polling data also showed that over two-thirds of Americans wanted to see stricter border enforcement before the passage of further immigration reforms (Rasmussen Reports May 7, 2006). Finally, the public was evenly divided on Bush's approach to immigration reform (with 39 percent in favor and the same percentage against) (Rassmussen Reports May 17, 2006), confirming that Comprehensive Immigration Reform was unlikely to yield electoral gains outside of Latinx and other immigrant communities.

Given the multifaceted nature of Comprehensive Immigration Reform, public opinion could at best be described as ambivalent. Setting aside actual popular attitudes, what matters most for the politics of immigration reform is policy makers' *perceptions* of public opinion and the associated likelihood of electoral mobilization. Institutionalized by means of redistricting and gerrymandering, the highly partisan nature of US primary elections makes the electoral arena particularly risky to navigate for House Republicans who fear primary challenges from the right. As *Roll Call* noted in November 2005, "the most hotly contested races

---

[9] I owe this point to Dan Tichenor.

involving immigration appear to be in primaries in safe Republican districts" (Jacobson November 16, 2005). This vulnerability was clearly heightened by the Iraq War's mounting unpopularity. Moreover, there was a prevailing sense among House Republicans that their reelection was at risk, and that support for Comprehensive Immigration Reform would amount to political suicide. Confronted with acutely low levels of popular insulation, in the end even restrictionist immigration positioning failed to protect House Republicans from electoral loss in 2006 (Leal 2009).

Whereas legislators in the House were largely concerned with how immigration reform would impact their reelection prospects in the 2006 midterm elections, the Senate was more attuned to presidential politics. Judiciary Committee chair Arlen Specter (R-PA), a Republican centrist, drafted his own bill at the same time as Senators Edward Kennedy (D-MA) and presidential hopeful John McCain (R-AZ) drafted a bipartisan bill. Intent on softening his maverick image, McCain embraced bipartisan immigration reform to win over establishment Republicans and appeal to general election moderates and the Latinx population. Both bills proposed relatively liberal legislation in the form of Comprehensive Immigration Reform, which included legalization and guest worker programs and stricter border enforcement, as well as increases in legal immigration.

In addition to facing institutional incentives for greater centrism, the Senate's embrace of bipartisan immigration reform was externally bolstered by the wave of pro-immigrant protests. As the *New York Times* reported, "[l]awmakers central to the immigration debate acknowledged that the televised images of tens of thousands of demonstrators, waving flags and fliers, marching in opposition to tough immigration legislation helped persuade the [Judiciary Committee] to find a bipartisan compromise" (Swarns March 28, 2006, A1). In a similar vein, a congressional staffer involved in the reform process recalls: "I felt like that specific series of rallies really meant something. And I'm sure that lobbying did too but that was a really powerful political statement. And they were watching. The Members knew that was happening" (Lam 2015, 203). Senate reformers certainly made frequent reference to the protesters when rallying support for Comprehensive Immigration Reform. Ted Kennedy, who co-sponsored the legalization measures with John McCain, described the bill's beneficiaries as "our neighbors," adding "[t]hey're churchgoers. They're the shop owners down the street. They're the people we know" (Swarns March 28, 2006). Immigrant advocates followed the legislative process closely, and when the Senate Judiciary Committee was drafting its bills, hundreds of religious leaders and immigrant advocates descended upon Washington, DC, "Wearing handcuffs to signify their impending convictions under H.R. 4437 [the Sensenbrenner Bill], clergymen personally challenged the Senate Judiciary Committee to incarcerate them by passing enforcement-only legislation. .... Immigration-related news blanketed the airwaves as national and local media covered the sudden explosion of energy" (Noorani 2007, 196–7).

The bipartisan reform process was repeatedly put under pressure, particularly by Senate Majority Leader Bill Frist (R-TN), who tried to sideline Comprehensive Immigration Reform, prompting both Democrats and Republicans to complain that Frist put his presidential ambitions before his institutional responsibilities (Babington March 30, 2006). In contrast, Minority Leader Harry Reid (D-NV) sought to achieve as liberal a bill as possible, blocking a vote on Judiciary Committee chairman Specter's bill because he favored the more liberal McCain–Kennedy alternative. Senate debate came to a halt, and the impasse was only broken when McCain announced his support for a new compromise bill written by Chuck Hagel and Mel Martinez, two Republican senators. Even though two-thirds of senators indicated their support, partisan disagreements prevented a vote on the bill, as several Republican senators wanted to delay the introduction of the guest worker and legalization programs until the border was verified to be secure (Wroe 2007).

The Senate debate coincided with the "Day without an Immigrant," a one-day boycott of schools and businesses organized by grassroots immigrant advocates, with hundreds of thousands of protesters marching in Los Angeles and carrying signs reading "today we march, tomorrow we vote." The boycotts threatened to further polarize public debate. President Bush publicly opposed the boycotts, while Senator Martinez appealed to his fellow legislators that "[b]oycotts, walkouts or protests are not going to get this done. This is an issue that isn't going to get fixed on the streets. It's going to take thoughtful action by Congress" (Weisman April 12, 2006).

With Senate in a deadlock, Bush took the unusual step of appealing directly to the American public in his first televised presidential address on a domestic issue. Reaching out to immigration conservatives, his address was largely focused on border enforcement, though he also restated his case for a guest worker system and immigrant legalization. Recognizing widespread concern within the Republican Party that a new legalization program would lead to history repeating itself, Bush went to great lengths to emphasize the strict conditionalities attached to the proposed program, which included a requirement to get in line behind existing applicants for naturalization. This stood in stark contrast to 1986, when the IRCA had fast-tracked these applications (Wroe 2007). The address was followed by meetings of members of the administration with key congressional actors.

Bush's intervention ended up providing new momentum to the stalled Senate debate and, after a series of security amendments (including 370 miles of border fence) that were intended to move the two chambers closer together, the Senate passed the Comprehensive Immigration Reform Act of 2006. Even though the bill was passed by a comfortable margin, a majority of Republican senators ended up voting against it (32–23), while nearly all Democrats voted in favor (38–4). In addition to ramped-up border enforcement, increases in low-skilled and high-skilled economic admissions,[10] and reductions in family backlogs, the Senate's Comprehensive Immigration Reform Act included a temporary guest worker program[11] and legalization provisions that allowed undocumented immigrants who had been in the country for more than five years to apply for citizenship, subject to payment of fines and back taxes.

Meanwhile, House Republicans left no doubt that any chance of compromise between the House and Senate bills was doomed. While some (including Sensenbrenner himself) were willing to consider a guest worker program, Republican members were firmly opposed to immigrant legalization. Despite enjoying a close working relationship with President Bush, House Speaker Dennis Hastert insisted that he would only bring a compromise bill to the floor if it was likely to win the support of at least half of the Republican caucus (Wroe 2007). This "majority of the majority" rule, informally instituted two years prior, provided that only bills that were supported by a majority of Republicans would be voted on. Far from being an isolated instance of partisanship, the rule reflected a more pervasive pattern of highly partisan congressional leadership under Hastert:

The regular order – a mix of rules and norms that allows debate, deliberation, and amendments in committees and on the House floor, that incorporates and does not shut out the minority (even if it still loses most of the time), that takes bills that pass both houses to a conference committee to reconcile differences ... – is a mainstay of a functional legislative process ... But no speaker did more to relegate the regular order to the sidelines than Hastert. ... Under Hastert, amendments

---

[10] High-skilled immigration was expanded by raising the H-1B visa cap from 65,000 to 115,000 and escalating the ceiling by 20 percent each subsequent year until numerical limits were reached.

[11] The H-2C visa or "Blue Card."

from Democrats and Republicans alike were squelched by a strikingly pliant Rules Committee; conferences were rarely held, and if they were, it was late at night and they were closed to input from all except loyal lieutenants. ... And, of course, Hastert presided over the informal "Hastert rule," doing whatever he could to avoid input from Democrats, trying to pass bills with Republicans alone. The House is a very partisan institution, with rules structured to give even tiny majorities enormous leverage. But Hastert took those realities to a new and more tribalized, partisan plane.

(Ornstein June 3, 2015)

By insisting on majority Republican support for a vote on an immigration bill, Hastert foreclosed the possibility that Comprehensive Immigration Reform could have won a House majority if supported by most Democrats and some Republicans. Even more consequentially, Republican leaders stalled on appointing members to the Conference Committee that would have worked on reconciling the two competing bills, thereby effectively killing immigration reform.

Instead of continuing along the legislative path, Hastert announced that the House was to hold twenty-one "immigration hearings" in thirteen states over the summer recess (Wroe 2007). Just days earlier, Brian Bilbray, a Republican candidate running on an enforcement-only immigration platform, had won a seat in a special election in California, confirming Republican fears that any pursuit of immigration reform beyond border enforcement would prove electorally risky in the lead-up to the 2006 midterm elections. Justified as an exercise in public consultation, the hearings were in fact a thinly veiled attack on the Senate bill and the president's immigration agenda. For instance, one session was titled "Whether Attempted Implementation of the Senate Immigration Bill Will Result in an Administrative and National Security Nightmare" (Wroe 2007, 281). If there ever was any doubt about the future of the Senate bill, it was now dispelled. By moving immigration reform into the electoral arena, restrictionist legislators effectively closed the window for Comprehensive Immigration Reform. To quote Representative Tancredo, the "[o]dds were long that any so-called compromise bill would get to the president's desk this year. ... The nail was already in the coffin of the Senate's amnesty plan. These hearings probably lowered it into the grave" (cited in Wroe 2007, 281). After about two dozen field hearings, House Republicans pronounced the Senate bill to be fundamentally unacceptable (Leal 2009).

House Republicans returned from summer recess determined to pass enforcement-only reform. Driven by projections of midterm seat losses and Bush's waning popularity, legislators broke the 2005 Sensenbrenner

Bill into smaller bills, which were assured easy passage through the House. Several measures were supported by the Senate and, just days before the midterm elections, George W. Bush signed the Secure Fence Act of 2006, which authorized the construction of 700 miles of double-fencing along the US–Mexico border. Despite their longstanding opposition to enforcement-only immigration reform, many senators were willing to support these comparatively moderate enforcement measures as a first step toward Comprehensive Immigration Reform. To quote Senator Sam Brownback (R-KS), a centrist Republican who co-sponsored the 2006 Comprehensive Immigration Reform Act: "Many people have told me they will support Comprehensive Immigration Reform if we secure the border first. I hope we can use passage of this bill as a starting point toward long-term, comprehensive immigration reform" (cited in Gaouette September 30, 2006). Thus, with the end of the 109th Congress, the House's Border Protection, Anti-terrorism, and Illegal Immigration Control Act (the Sensenbrenner bill) and the Senate's Comprehensive Immigration Reform Act expired, leaving the Secure Fence Act as its sole legislative achievement.

The Failure of Comprehensive Immigration Reform in 2007: Policy Making in the Crossfire of Popular and Interest Group Pressure

The Republican right turn on immigration could not avert the electoral losses that followed in the wake of widespread public dissatisfaction with the Bush administration's handling of the war in Iraq and Hurricane Katrina. With the 2006 midterm elections, Democrats gained control of both houses of Congress for the first time since 1994, although not by a sufficient margin to garner the sixty votes necessary to invoke cloture (end debate) in the Senate. The Democratic electoral victory invigorated reformers to once more tackle Comprehensive Immigration Reform by assembling a coalition of congressional Democrats, moderate congressional Republicans, and the White House. Bush reaffirmed his support for Comprehensive Immigration Reform in his State of the Union address, and, given that it faced higher procedural hurdles than the more liberal House, the Senate moved first.

Right from the beginning of the reform process it became clear that Democratic congressional gains could not offset the restrictionist shift within the Republican Party. On May 9, Majority Leader Harry Reid introduced the Comprehensive Immigration Act of 2007, which was virtually identical to the previous year's Senate bill that had been supported by a bipartisan core. Nonetheless, Republican senators immediately withdrew their support of the bill. According to *Roll Call*, "all 23 Republicans who voted for last year's immigration bill sent a letter to Majority Leader Reid on Wednesday warning they would not vote for that measure again and calling on the Majority Leader to allow more time to work out a bipartisan deal" (Stanton and Billings May 10, 2007). Faced with either reelection (Lindsey Graham) or the possibility of a presidential run in 2008 (John McCain, Sam Brownback, and Chuck Hagel), key Republican moderates who had been part of the bipartisan core in 2006 had either shifted their immigration positions to the right or were unwilling to take a position altogether. When Mel Martinez also stepped back from the reform process after becoming chairman of the Republican National Committee, the White House decided that immigration reform could only proceed if it could get Senator Jon Kyl, who had led the opposition to the 2006 bill, on board (Butterfield January 29, 2008).

Meanwhile, in the public sphere the immigration debate quickly became dominated by conservative talk radio and cable television hosts, who came out in full force to mobilize against Comprehensive Immigration Reform. Conservative talk radio shows, which had gained unprecedented prominence in the wake of the terrorist attacks of September 2001, had already played a role in mobilizing opposition to Comprehensive Immigration Reform in 2006, with some observers arguing that a majority of House members would have voted in favor of comprehensive reform had it not been for talk-show hosts "poison[ing] the atmosphere" (Currie November 27, 2006). Now, talk radio hosts were at the helm of intense populist mobilization against the Senate bill, with several Republican legislators stating that this was the first time "that they have felt the full brunt of an advocacy machine built around conservative talk radio and cable television programs" (Zeleny June 28, 2007). While the Senate bill received 9 percent of mainstream media time, it took up 19 percent of talk radio show time (Wasserman July 9, 2006). Many legislators reported getting inundated with angry phone calls, emails, and letters from constituents, reflecting a well-organized and vocal opposition (Butterfield January 29, 2008). According to one analysis, calls to congressional offices from restrictionist groups outnumbered calls from supporters by 400 to one (Sandler June 28, 2007).

Operating within a context of severely weakened popular insulation, Senate reformers worked together with the Bush administration to draw up a compromise bill with sufficiently broad appeal to stand a realistic chance of passage. In addition to providing for stricter worksite and border enforcement, the bill introduced by Judiciary Committee chairman Specter as a "grand bargain" included legalization provisions as well as a guest worker program that would allow workers to apply for permanent residence through a points system based on education, job skills, labor market demand, and English proficiency. The bill further legislated a reduction of the family sponsorship backlog and the creation of a broader points system that would shift admissions from family ties to education and work skills. Days later a bipartisan coalition led by Senators Kennedy and Kyl and supported by the White House introduced a substitute amendment that also included a points system. Over the next two weeks the Senate voted on a series of amendments to the substitute amendment, a contentious process that undid the fragile alliance supporting Comprehensive Immigration Reform resulting in Senator Reid withdrawing the legislation (Abramovitz May 27, 2007).

Once again, seeking to revive the legislation, President Bush intervened with public statements and private meetings with key legislators, resulting in the introduction of a new compromise bill: the Secure Borders, Economic Opportunity and Immigration Reform Act of 2007 (also referred to as the Comprehensive Reform Act of 2007) (Freeman et al. 2013). Even though the bill's sole sponsor was Majority Leader Harry Reid, it was the result of the collective effort of the bipartisan "Gang of 12," in particular Senators Kennedy, McCain, Kyl, and Graham, supported by Bush. Responding to Republican concerns, the bill added over four billion in new enforcement funds to a long list of beefed-up border and worksite enforcement provisions. Other provisions were clearly compromises between supporters of Comprehensive Immigration Reform and Republican restrictionists: the bill liberalized access to legalization while at the same time rendering its prospects uncertain by requiring that certain enforcement targets be reached before legalization could begin. It provided for a guest worker program but required that its agricultural component be terminated after five years. The bill's most far-reaching provisions, however, targeted permanent admissions. In addition to abolishing the diversity visa program and increasing the per-country limits for both economic and legal admissions, the bill outlined a skills-based points system and enacted restrictions to family sponsorship.

First championed in the executive arena by Secretary of the US Department of Homeland Security, Michael Chertoff, and in large part modeled after the Canadian and Australian models (Abramovitz May 27, 2007), the idea of a points system had already been floated in Specter's "grand bargain" bill and in the Kennedy–Kyl substitute amendment. By now the workings of the proposed system were clearly specified. Like Canadian policy makers, American reformers sought to instrumentalize the points system in order to restrict the immigration of extended family members. Thus, the bill proposed to eliminate the sponsorship of adult children and siblings and instead allowed for a family ties points boost for points system entries if applicants met a threshold of fifty-five points earned through education, employment, and knowledge of English.[12] If enacted, the bill would reduce family-based immigration from approximately two-thirds to half of all immigration and increase employment-based immigration from one-fifth to two-fifths of total permanent admissions (Migration Policy Institute 2007).

These proposed changes to the US immigration regime were clearly intended to secure the support of Kyl and other Senate Republicans, given longstanding Republican unease with the sponsorship of extended family members and its propensity to generate "chain migration." Kyl himself pushed for immigration reform that would bring in "the best and the brightest." White House officials and Senate reformers justified the proposed points system as a rational response to a changing global economy. As Joel Kaplan, White House deputy chief of staff and point person on immigration, explains:

We have a system today that is very heavily weighted to whether or not you happen to have a family member in the United States. There was a view that, if you really wanted to have an immigration system that was geared to making sure we were competitive in the 21st century, we had to try to rebalance that ... and focus more on our national interests.

(Abramovitz May 27, 2007)

Executive officials further noted that the changes to family sponsorship would make immigrant legalization more politically palatable, as it would prevent those who gained US citizenship from bringing in extended family members (Abramovitz May 27, 2007).

Whereas Republicans pushed for a shift to high-skilled immigration, Senator Kennedy and other Democrats demanded immigration avenues for lower-skilled immigrants, no doubt seeking to compensate for the elimination of extended family-based preferences. The bill's "merit-based evaluation system" reflected the competing preferences of both Republican and Democratic legislators: immigrants in "high-demand"

---

[12] Eight points for adult children of US citizens, six points for adult children of permanent residents, and four points for adult siblings of US citizens and permanent residents.

occupations, such as janitors and landscapers, would get sixteen points compared to twenty points for "specialty" occupations, such as engineers and scientists. Aside from specific occupations, the points system heavily rewarded education (28 points for a graduate degree) and English proficiency (15 points).

As in 1990, ethnic lobbies fiercely opposed the proposed elimination of family preference categories. The Mexican American Legal Defense and Educational Fund, the National Association of Latino Elected and Appointed Officials, the League of United Latin American Citizens, US Catholic Bishops, the Interfaith Immigration Coalition, and the Jewish Council for Public Affairs all criticized the points system for prioritizing skills over family ties and demanded amendments that would reverse the proposed restriction of family immigration. Latinx groups were most strongly opposed to the proposed changes, as a selection system based on education and language would close the door to many immigrants from Mexico and Latin America (see Migration Policy Institute 2007). Many Democratic legislators were receptive to these concerns, with Senators Bob Menendez (D-NJ), Christopher Dodd (D-CT), and Barack Obama (D-IL) all proposing amendments to revise the proposed points system in favor of family reunification. Senator Obama, preparing for his presidential bid and seeking to mobilize Latinx voters, introduced an amendment to terminate the points system after five, instead of fourteen, years. Criticizing the bill as a "radical experiment in social engineering," he argued that it "fails to recognize the fundamental morality of uniting Americans with their family members. It also places a person's job skills over his character and work ethic. How many of our forefathers would have measured up under the point system?" (Abramovitz May 27, 2007). Obama repeatedly emphasized the adverse impacts a points system would have on the Latinx community:

> [The] new points system shifts us too far away from the value we place on family ties and moves us toward a class-based immigration system, where some people are welcome only as guest workers but never as full participants in our democracy. Indeed, the practical effect of the points system is to make it more difficult for Americans and legal permanent residents with family living in Latin America to bring them here. [The points system pushes] workers from Latin America to the back of an endless line with no hope of ever reaching the front.
>
> (Obama, US Senate June 6, 2007, 7155)

On the other side of the political divide was a group of Republican senators – Jon Kyl, John McCain, Lindsey Graham, and Jeff Sessions – who passionately argued that the US should adopt "some of the principles

Canada has: its point system, its merit-based system" (Sessions, US Senate May 7, 2007, S5672). Whereas Democrats argued that family reunification had made the family the "bedrock" and "fabric" of America (Menendez, US Senate May 7, 2007, S6255), Republicans framed family immigration as unconnected to the national interest. As Senator Sessions argued:

> If a person comes, then you can bring your brother and sister. If your brother is married, the wife comes with your brother. If they have three children, those come. If she moves forward to a green card or citizenship, she can also bring in her relatives. Then the wife can bring in her brothers and sisters. So that is how this system works. It is unrelated to skills and the productivity of the person intending to come. It is unrelated, therefore, to the national interests of the United States. It is unconnected to them. It is their interest they are concerned about and not the national interest, which is to make sure the persons who come are honest, hard-working, decent people with skills and capabilities to be successful in America.
>
> (Sessions, US Senate May 22, 2007, S6432)

For the immigration bill's drafters, the points system served as the linchpin for securing a minimum bipartisan consensus among negotiators (Leal 2009). Democratic senators strategized that in conjunction with the border enforcement provisions the points system would allow for sufficient Republican buy-in to ensure the bill's passage, in addition to being endorsed by the business lobby. There was no question that the high-tech business lobby was deeply frustrated with the policy status quo, repeatedly lobbying for more H1-B visas and green cards to be made available to their workforce.[13] While Senate reformers were drafting their bill, Bill Gates of Microsoft led a group of high-tech executives to Capitol Hill and urged senators to authorize more visas for temporary foreign workers and permanent immigrants. In fact, in the spring of 2007 several bills that would have raised the H1-B visa cap had already been considered by Congress.[14] The architects of the Senate bill were thus taken by surprise when high-tech companies scathingly criticized the points system, despite the fact that it would provide new immigration pathways for those with advanced degrees and other relevant job skills. E. John Krumholtz, Director of Federal Affairs at Microsoft, dismissed the bill as "worse than the status quo, and the status quo is a disaster" (Pear June 25, 2007).

---

[13] High-skilled foreign workers typically enter on a temporary H1-B visa and later apply for permanent residence from inside the US.

[14] The Secure Knowledge, Innovation, and Leadership Act of 2007, introduced in both houses of Congress; the High-Tech Worker Relief Act of 2007, introduced in the Senate.

High-tech executives opposed the points system because it would strip employers of the ability to handpick and sponsor individual immigrants. The points system thus became framed as "creating a government-imposed limitation on employer flexibility to respond quickly to their labor market needs" (Pear June 25, 2007). In subsequent weeks, Senate offices were inundated with letters, e-mail messages, phone calls, and personal visits from high-tech executives, all seeking an amendment to the bill. Edward Sweeney, senior vice president of National Semiconductor, commented, "I've spent many hours in Washington talking with senators to get their support on this amendment," and William Watkins, chief executive of Seagate Technology, the world's leading producer of computer disk drives, was reported to have met with five or six senators (Pear June 25, 2007). Seeking to win over business, Senator Kyl and his Democratic colleague Cantwell drafted an amendment that, among other provisions, proposed an H-1B exemption for STEM workers and set aside 20,000 green cards for immigrants of extraordinary ability and other highly skilled immigrants, thereby retaining the preference for such workers that the shift to a points system would eliminate.

Despite the political appeal of simply increasing existing economic preference caps and continuing the longstanding practice of adding more exemptions to visa caps, policy makers refused to give in to the demands of high-tech business. To eliminate the points system would not only run counter to the ambition of policy makers to pass a "comprehensive" bill that would simplify and streamline a messy immigration system, but it also would deprive policy makers of a tool for making significant cuts to family immigration. Moreover, accommodating business preferences would likely strengthen the opposition of social conservatives. As Stephen Yale-Loehr, a prominent immigration law professor and attorney, explains:

High-tech companies are very organized. They have numerous lobby groups. When Bill Gates advocates more H-1B visas and green cards for tech workers, everyone listens. But that supposed influence has not translated into legislative results. . . . High-tech companies have been lobbying unsuccessfully since 2003 for more H-1B visas. It's hard to get anything through Congress these days. In addition, anti-immigrant groups are well organized.

(Cited in Pear June 25, 2007)

The final days leading up to the floor debate were marked not only by intense interest group lobbying but also by heightened popular mobilization. As *Congressional Quarterly* reported, "[h]ours before the demise of the complex and highly contentious bill, a deluge of phone calls from constituents, mostly clamoring for the measures' defeat, tied up the line to several Senate offices (Sandler June 28, 2007). A leading anti-immigrant group, Grassfire.org, claimed that in the week leading up to the vote its members had made 250,000 contacts with Senate offices. Senator Warner (R-VA) commented that "[i]n my 29 years, I've experienced all the events in that time period, but this is clearly the high-water mark" (cited in Zeleny June 28, 2007). Another commentator argues, "[t]he anger of those callers apparently had some resonance in the Senate, because in the end only 46 lawmakers stood behind the compromise measure" (Wasserman July 9, 2006). According to opinion surveys, now only 23 percent of Americans supported the bill whereas 80 percent believed that the bill would fail to reduce illegal immigration. Republican voters were overwhelmingly opposed to the bill and disillusioned with Bush, while Democrats were evenly split (Tichenor 2009, 18). Of course, skepticism about the efficacy of the bill's enforcement provisions was not limited to the public but was openly expressed by legislators. As Republican Senator Charles Grassley, referring to the 1986 IRCA, put it, "I was fooled once, and history has taught me a valuable lesson" (cited in Dinan June 22, 2007).

With Comprehensive Immigration Reform now widely regarded as a third rail, senators who were still on the fence decided to play it safe by voting against it. As Senator Graham explains, "I think it was a situation where they knew we weren't going to make it, and people felt like a 'no' vote was in their best interest" (cited in Sandler June 28, 2007). On June 18, 2007, the Comprehensive Immigration Reform Act of 2007 was brought to the floor under a rarely used parliamentary procedure known as "clay pigeon." Intended to curtail debate on the bill, this tactic protected twenty-two of the twenty-seven amendments that were to be voted on from extended debate. Yet the fragile reform coalition quickly fell apart, and two-thirds of Republicans and one-third of Democrats refused to end the debate. Majority Leader Reid pulled the bill from the Senate floor, thereby ending all efforts for Comprehensive Immigration Reform for the remainder of Bush's presidency. As *Congressional Quarterly* commented, "[a]fter the immigration bill died and the Senate turned out its light for the July Fourth recess, in the quiet you could almost hear the sound of the conservative talk-show hosts slapping one another on the back and clinking their champagne flutes" (Wasserman July 9, 2006).

The Failure of Comprehensive Immigration Reform in 2013: Latinx Electoral Strength Meets Anti-immigration Populism

In May 2008, Democratic presidential candidate Barack Obama announced in a town hall meeting: "I can guarantee that we will have, in the first year, an immigration bill that I strongly support" (cited in Rodriguez November 9, 2012). However, despite winning the White House with the support of 67 percent of Latinx voters, Comprehensive Immigration Reform was relegated to the back burner as Obama's first term came to be defined by the financial crisis and the decision to prioritize health care reform over Comprehensive Immigration Reform. In the meantime, the White House pursued an enforcement-first immigration strategy, reasoning that this would lay the groundwork for bipartisan support for comprehensive reform. As US Secretary of Homeland Security Janet Napolitano acknowledged, the hope was that enforcement-first would prove to Congress that unlike other post-IRCA administrations, President Obama was committed to enforcing immigration laws and, as a result, a grand bargain on immigration would not risk repeating the IRCA's failure to contain undocumented immigration (Skrentny 2011).

Obama's enforcement-first strategy included ramped-up deportations. The increase was such that under the Obama White House, more people were deported compared to any other administration in US history, prompting immigrant rights groups to refer to Obama as "Deporter-in-Chief" (Marshall August 29, 2016). Enforcement-first also focused on intensifying work audits and prosecuting employers of undocumented workers, increasing staffing at the US–Mexico border, and improving cooperation between local and federal law officials in identifying undocumented immigrants with criminal records. Just before the 2010 midterm elections, Congress passed a $600 million enforcement-only border security bill. Signing the bill, Obama reiterated that enforcement-only policy reform was a necessary step toward bipartisan Comprehensive Immigration Reform (Skrentny 2011).

While enforcement-only immigration reform enjoyed a smooth passage through Congress, early efforts by the White House to forge a comprehensive reform coalition met with little success. At a meeting with a bipartisan group of senators, including Republican Senators McCain and Graham, Obama announced that his Secretary for Homeland Security was going to take the lead in crafting the administration's policy blueprint for comprehensive reform. While John McCain withdrew from the reform effort after facing a tough primary challenge by an immigration restrictionist, Lindsey Graham continued to work with Obama's key Democratic ally, Chuck Schumer, to craft a reform plan that they outlined in a *Washington Post* op-ed in March 2010. However, just a month later Graham jumped ship, complaining that Democrats were only interested in securing the Latinx vote. To quote from a publicly circulated letter

Graham wrote to Senators Kerry and Lieberman, "moving forward on immigration – in this hurried, panicked manner – is nothing more than a cynical political ploy" (Skrentny 2011, 283). Thus, in contrast to Bush's efforts at Comprehensive Immigration Reform in 2006 and 2007, now "not a single Republican was willing to support CIR [Comprehensive Immigration Reform] in Obama's first term ... this unprecedented polarization stopped Obama's CIR legislative agenda dead in its tracks" (Skrentny and Lopez 2013, 66)

The White House threw its support behind the DREAM Act (the Development, Relief, and Education for Alien Minors Act), a bill with a bipartisan history dating back to 2001 that provided for the legalization of undocumented minors who fulfilled certain educational or military requirements. Once again, however, the bill floundered. This time it was in the Senate, where Democrats came up five votes short of the sixty needed to advance the bill. In June 2012, nearing the election and under growing pressure from Latinx leaders and Democrats, who warned that Obama's harsh enforcement-first record may cost him critical Latinx votes (Cohen June 16, 2012), the president used his executive powers to enact a policy directive, DACA (Deferred Action for Childhood Arrivals), which provided qualified "Dreamers" with a two-year reprieve from deportation and the opportunity to apply for work authorization. Reactions were swift and polarized: whereas Republicans reacted with anger and accused Obama of overstepping his constitutional powers, Latinx leaders, together with the US Council of Catholic Bishops and some Jewish and Evangelical Christian groups, praised the decision. There was broad agreement, however, that "the president's move was a clear play for a crucial voting bloc in states that will decide whether he gets another term" (Preston and Cushman June 15, 2012).

In the fall of 2011, Obama had declared in an originally off-the-record media interview, that he was

confident about immigration reform in the second term. ... And since this is off the record, I will just be very blunt. Should I win a second term, a big reason I will win a second term is because the Republican nominee and the Republican Party have so alienated the fastest-growing demographic group in the country, the Latino community.

(Rodriguez November 9, 2012)

The 2012 election proved Obama right: now accounting for 10 percent of the electorate, Latinx voters helped the president secure election victories in key battleground states. With the Latinx population voting for Obama over Republican candidate Mitt Romney 71 percent to 27 percent,

Republican strategist Ann Navarro warned that "[i]f we don't do better with Hispanics, we'll be out of the White House forever" (cited in Rodriguez November 9, 2012). Democrats also expanded their control of the Senate, prompting one liberal immigration reformer to venture that "[t]he GOP's lurch to the right on immigration destroyed their chances of re-taking the White House and the Senate" (*America's Voice* November 8, 2012). Fears of the long-term consequences of alienating Latinx voters were echoed by several legislators, in particular by members of the Senate, who were more dependent on assembling broad electoral coalitions than members of the House with its smaller and racially redistricted districts. Thus, Senator Lindsay Graham (R-SC) cautioned, "[Latinx voters are] the fastest-growing demographic in the country and we're losing votes every election cycle, it has to stop. . . . It's one thing to shoot yourself in the foot – just don't reload the gun" (Fathali 2013, 252–3). Likewise, Senator Chuck Schumer (D-NY) noted that "the Republican Party has learned that being . . . anti-immigrant doesn't work for them politically. And they know it" (Fathali 2013, 253). Even though Democrats had not been able to take back the House, some House Republicans shared concerns with Obama's success among Latinx voters, most notably House Speaker John Boehner, who days after the election suggested that Congress needed to pass Comprehensive Immigration Reform (DeSipio and de la Garza 2015).

Invigorated by the Democratic victories and the high Latinx election turnout, a bipartisan group of senators commenced work on a comprehensive immigration bill in earnest. The "Gang of Eight," as they quickly became known, was made up of eight high-profile senators: John McCain, Lindsay Graham, Marco Rubio, and Jeff Flake on the Republican side, and Chuck Schumer, Dick Durbin, Bob Menendez, and Michael Bennet on the Democratic side. In January, the Gang of Eight publicly outlined their immigration plan, which included the major components of Comprehensive Immigration Reform. Speaking to the press, the Gang of Eight expressed optimism that the momentum of the 2012 election would carry over into immigration reform. "The politics on these issues have turned upside down," Chuck Schumer declared. "For the first time ever, there is more political risk in opposing immigration reform than in supporting it" (cited in Whitesides January 29, 2013). John McCain, asked how the 2012 election result would impact Republican support for the reform bill, responded: "a little straight-talk here: Republicans have got to compete – and I say compete – for the Hispanic voter" (*CSPAN* April 18, 2013). In a similar vein, Lindsey Graham argued in an interview with *TIME Magazine*:

We need a bill because our immigration system is so broken. But politically, if the bill fails and Republicans are blamed in the eyes of the public for not being practical it makes it virtually impossible for us to win the White House in 2016. . . . I think most Republicans understand that we've dug a hole and we need to get this immigration issue off the table and behind us. And if we don't, we understand things will be bad.

(Newton-Small June 11, 2013)

Following the Senate plan's public release, President Obama outlined his own vision, which was compatible with the Senate proposal. In response, Brookings scholar Darrell West provided an optimistic appraisal of the prospects of immigration reform:

Last fall, it would have been hard to imagine Republicans and Democrats working together to fix our broken immigration system. . . . But now we have leading Democrats and Republicans who have announced their support of a bipartisan reform package. With the Senate moving toward action, House Republicans indicating we should be open to immigrants, and President Barack Obama making immigration reform a top priority, the country appears close to taking meaningful action on this important issue.

(Preston June 28, 2013)

The bipartisan group, with White House support, successfully shepherded the bill through the Judiciary Committee, where a detailed bill was passed with a strong bipartisan vote of 13–5. The Border Security, Economic Opportunity, and Immigration Modernization Act created a lengthy (thirteen-year) pathway to citizenship. Undocumented immigrants who had entered the US prior to January 2012 could, subject to certain conditions, gain registered provisional immigrant (RPI) status, which would protect its holders from deportation and give them the right to work. After ten years RPIs would be able to become permanent residents and, three years later, US citizens, provided that certain triggers were activated, most importantly a 90 percent apprehension rate of undocumented migrants crossing the southwest border. In addition, existing visa backlogs had to be cleared before any adjustment from RPI to permanent resident could take place – the "back of the line" provision. The bill also proposed accelerated pathways to citizenship for "Dreamers" and agricultural workers. The bill further provided for a guest worker program for agricultural and nonagricultural workers, which would allow visa holders to change employers and provide some of them with access to permanent residence. On the issue of border enforcement, the bill stipulated the use of an exit variation system at ports of entry and the use of a work authorization database by all US employers.

On the regulation of legal immigration, the bill – like its predecessors – proposed the relatively uncontroversial abolition of the Diversity Visa program. More controversially, it once again sought to limit family immigration by abolishing family visas for the siblings of US citizens and limiting the sponsorship of married children of US citizens to children under the age of 31. At the same time the bill took a significant step toward reducing processing backlogs for the spouses and minor children of permanent residents by reclassifying these family members as "immediate relatives," thereby exempting their sponsorship from any numerical caps. The bill liberalized economic immigrant admissions by making the spouses and children of employment-based immigrants exempt from numerical limits, thereby freeing up visas for economic admissions. Like its predecessors, the bill provided for additional cap exemptions for immigrants of "extraordinary ability" and certain STEM workers. On the contested notion of a points system, the bill proposed the creation of new merit-based visas that would provide two distinct pathways to permanent residence. Under "Merit Based Track One," between 120,000 and 250,000 visas would be made available to immigrants scoring high under a points system that rewarded education, US work experience, job skills in high demand, and family ties. Under "Merit Based Track Two," an unlimited number of visas would be made available to clear the existing backlogs of millions of noncitizens waiting under both employment-based and family-based admissions.

Importantly, this time around reformers were able to assemble a broad interest group coalition that included all key economic stakeholders, ranging from high-tech companies to agricultural growers to trade unions. Unlike the 2007 bill, which had lacked buy-in from both Silicon Valley companies and trade unions, the 2013 bill's provisions appealed to all major economic interests. As the Executive Director of Compete America, which represents tech companies, commented, "What will shock a lot of people in the House is the level and intensity of the business community compared to 2007" (Preston June 28, 2013). High-tech companies stood to gain from significant increases in high-skilled visas, while agricultural growers got their guest worker program. Importantly, trade unions supported the bill after a carefully negotiated compromise was agreed upon between the US Chamber of Commerce and the AFL-CIO. The demands of unions were reflected in several guest worker protections – such as the portability of visas – and access for some guest workers to citizenship. The AFL-CIO also embraced the expansiveness of the legalization program, stating in a letter that:

The AFL-CIO is fully committed to achieving a roadmap to citizenship for the 11 million aspiring Americans who live and work in our communities. This is the preeminent civil rights issue of our time and the AFL-CIO will continue to dedicate the full resources of our Federation to ensure that we achieve this vital goal.

(American Federation of Labor and Congress of Industrial Organizations
June 13, 2013)

Not only did unions put their support behind legalization, but tech companies also argued that economic immigration reform had to be part of a more comprehensive reform package that needed to include a path to citizenship for undocumented immigrants (Preston June 28, 2013). While the bill was on the Senate floor the Partnership for a New American Economy, a coalition of major business leaders (including Oracle, Disney, Marriott, and Boeing) and majors of mayor US cities, organized a "virtual march" on Washington by carrying off one of the largest simultaneous "thunderclaps" of Twitter and Facebook posts. The organization also sent a letter signed by twenty-one Tennessee university presidents to the state's senators, Republicans Bob Corker and Lamar Alexander, both of whom voted for the Senate bill (Preston June 28, 2013). The following excerpt from a floor speech by Republican Jeff Sessions, who led the Senate opposition to the bill, critiques the importance of the interest group coalition to the reform process, including the possible influence of lobbying by Mexican diplomats:

Powerful groups met, excluding the interests of the American people. Even foreign countries had a say in drafting our law. Mexico's new ambassador to the US ... has had a number of meetings with the administration where the issue of immigration has come up ... This [reform] bill is far weaker than the 2007 legislation rejected by the American people ... But the people who came illegally get exactly what they wanted immediately. ... The special interests, La Raza, the unions, the corporate world, the big agriculture businesses ... they are the ones that made the agreement in this process.

(Cited in Felicity 2014, 28)

The 2013 Senate reform process thus differed in critical ways from that of 2007. First, the 2013 bill made strategic concessions to major organized interests, allowing reformers to assemble a broad-based interest group coalition. Second, there was a bipartisan core – the Gang of Eight – that was firmly committed to the success of Comprehensive Immigration Reform and kept their course in the face of opposition. In fact, "[m]any experts believe that the bill's successful and relatively smooth journey through the Senate was owed to the Gang of Eight, which after authoring the bill, remained united in its strategy to keep its product intact and fend off 'poison pill' amendments that would have led to the bill's failure" (Chishti and Hipsman 2014). The bipartisan core remained united even when, in April, with the bill still in committee, the Boston Marathon bombings threatened to derail the reform process as some supporters began to waver and the immigration debate stalled. Most prominently, Kentucky Senator Rand Paul, a prominent Republican with presidential ambitions and an early proponent of immigration reform, publicly circulated a letter to the Senate leadership, which tied the fate of the bill to national security imperatives and urged that the reform process be put on hold (Parker April 22, 2013). Yet despite these challenges the bill eventually cleared the committee stage after its members agreed to an amendment by Chuck Grassley (R-IA) to provide immigration officers at US ports of entry with information on the status of student visas (one of the men assisting the bombers had held a student visa).

On the Senate floor numerous amendments were introduced, two of which were widely regarded as critical. Republican Senator Chuck Grassley proposed to add a legalization trigger that would make the adjustment from RPI to permanent resident contingent on the border having been secured for six consecutive months. Fearing that the amendment would result in the indefinite postponement of legalization, Senate Democrats fought to defeat the amendment 53–47. The second major amendment, which was introduced by Republicans Bob Corker and John Hoeven, proposed to authorize an additional $40 billion for 700 miles of border fencing and 20,000 border patrol positions, among other enforcement spending items. After more than a dozen reluctant senators suggested that this amendment would assuage their concerns with the bill, Democrats rallied behind the amendment, which passed 67–27 (Graham 2016). In its final form, the Border Security, Economic Opportunity, and Immigration Modernization Act of 2013 passed with a rare show of bipartisan support for such major legislation, with a 68–32 vote, with all fifty-two Democrats, both Independents, and fourteen Republicans voting in favor.

The immigration interest group coalition left no doubt it was willing to take on restrictionists in the House. "The House has not felt our love yet," announced a representative of the Service Employees International Union, a leading labor group in the campaign for Comprehensive Immigration Reform (Preston June 28, 2013). Business groups similarly pledged to stay the course. Likewise, a Christian Evangelical member of the coalition declared:

We were at the edge of the Jordan River, but after the Senate, we officially got our feet wet. If 11 million immigrants are left in the middle of the water and do not reach the promised land, neither will the Republican Party reach the promised land of the White House.

(Preston June 28, 2013)

Yet the populist pressures bearing on Republican House members were much more powerful than what senators had to contend with. Most importantly, with the founding of the Tea Party movement in 2009 a new and powerful catalyst for immigration restrictionism had emerged. Given their firmly restrictionist position on immigration, Tea Party patriots were heavily invested in defeating comprehensive reform and, in June 2013, pledged a primary challenge to any Republican member of Congress who supported the immigration bill (Graham 2016). The Tea Party's influence was magnified by the fact that partly because of redistricting, most seats controlled by House Republicans had few Latinx constituents. Unlike the national-level Republican Party, which in March 2013 endorsed the principles of Comprehensive Immigration Reform, House Republicans faced few electoral incentives to moderate their positions. As Republican representative Kenny Marchant of Dallas explained, "[the Senate bill] is very unpopular in my district." In fact, legalization would likely end up posing an electoral threat to Republicans. As Marchant argued: "Republican primary voters are pretty vocal with me on this subject . . . if you give the legal right to vote to 10 Hispanics in my district, 7 to 8 of them are going to vote Democratic'" (cited in Graham 2016, 290). Even though, as policy analyst John Graham argues, public opinion polls at the time suggested that the American public might have supported key pillars of Comprehensive Immigration Reform, "[t]hose national polls were largely irrelevant to the calculus of House Republicans who were concerned with the opinions of their own constituents and especially how Republican primary voters might react to immigration reform" (Graham 2016, 290). Moreover, House Republicans had little reason to fear that blocking immigration reform would end up compromising their chances of winning back control of the Senate in midterm elections. Among the nine states with competitive Senate races in 2014, only one (Colorado) had a sizable population of Latinx eligible voters, whereas in the other battleground states the Latinx population accounted for fewer than 5 percent of the electorate (compared to 11 percent nationally) (Graham 2016, 77). Senator Graham summed up the House's electoral considerations when answering a reporter's question about the impact of Comprehensive Immigration Reform on the 2014 midterm elections:

It's more a presidential issue. The House politics aren't affected too much by demographics at the moment. Senate a little more so, the White House dramatically. If you want to be a congressional party, fine, but I'd like to be a part of the party that can also win the White House.

(Newton-Small June 11, 2013)

Even before the passage of the Senate Bill, House Speaker Boehner declared that any reform measure must have the support of the majority of House Republicans in order to be considered by the House. In other words, the Senate bill would not be brought to the House floor. In doing so, the speaker strategically precluded the possibility of the House passing Comprehensive Immigration Reform on the basis of bipartisan support. By some analyses this was a distinct possibility, with forty to fifty House Republicans and 185 to 190 House Democrats willing to support Comprehensive Immigration Reform (Graham 2016, 292). Passing immigration reform with predominantly Democratic support, however, would likely have cost Boehner the speakership and thus was not something he was willing to entertain (DeSipio and de la Garza 2015).

As long as immigration reform included a path to citizenship, majority Republican support for an immigration bill was out of the question. Republican opposition focused on the very principle of "amnesty" (it rewarded law breaking), its electoral repercussions (see Marchant's comment above), and several pragmatic concerns. How could one ever establish that an undocumented immigrant owed no back taxes? When can a border be considered secure? What would be the impact on emergency rooms by the exclusion of RPIs from medical coverage under the Affordable Care Act? In the end it was the question of health care coverage that was the nail in the coffin of early House attempts at bipartisan reform. Of a loosely organized bipartisan group of four Republicans and four Democrats, by September only one Republican remained. Aside from disagreements about health care funding for undocumented immigrants, Republicans' departure was largely driven by anger with Obama's implementation of the Affordable Care Act, which prompted them to conclude that the president could not be trusted with implementing immigration reform (Graham 2016).

In September, Boehner reassured Republican conservatives by stating: "We have no intention of ever going to conference on the Senate bill" (Meckler September 4, 2013). Instead, the House Judiciary and Homeland Security Committees proceeded with five issue-specific immigration bills, which stood a greater chance of winning a Republican majority than a Comprehensive Immigration Reform bill. In January congressional Republicans released a one-page document outlining the party's principles for immigration reform. In addition to prioritizing border security, the document criticized the policy status quo as "emphasiz[ing] family members and pure luck over employment-based immigration" and demanded an employer-focused immigration policy instead.

The document further stated that except for those brought into the country as children, "[t]here will be no special path to citizenship for individuals who broke our nation's immigration laws" (*New York Times* January 30, 2014). Seeking to protect Republican incumbents from Tea Party challenges, Boehner strategically scheduled the floor debate for April 2014, which was after the filing deadline for challengers in congressional races (Graham 2016).

Despite these precautions, a stunning primary defeat rocked the party in June. Eric Cantor, the House Majority Leader from Virginia and second most powerful member of the House, unexpectedly lost the primary to a poorly funded, unknown Tea Party challenger, Dave Brat. Brat had run on an anti-immigration platform and had accused Cantor of supporting "amnesty" for undocumented immigrants. Even though the reasons for Cantor's defeat were complex, "the take-home message from Cantor's defeat among campaign experts was the immigration issue: it is volatile and provokes anger among many highly conservative voters. A bad place to be in politics is on the wrong side of the immigration issue when faced by a Tea Party challenger in a Republican primary" (Graham 2016, 294). Cantor's defeat marked end of any viable immigration reform effort in the 113th Congress.

By the summer of 2014 even those Republicans who genuinely believed that policy liberalization was possible once the border had been secured were unwilling to move ahead with Comprehensive Immigration Reform. Cantor's defeat coincided with the peak of a child refugee crisis triggered by the arrival of over 50,000 unaccompanied minors fleeing gang violence, drug cartels, and poverty in Central America between late 2012 and the summer of 2014. The severity of the crisis undermined claims that Obama's enforcement-first strategy had worked, and the White House's late recognition of the need for action led to broad public disapproval of his handling of the crisis (Baker August 11, 2014). In June, Luis Gutiérrez, who was at the helm of Democratic efforts at bipartisan immigration reform in the House, announced that he was giving up on a bipartisan reform bill (Graham 2016), thereby dispelling any remaining doubt that Comprehensive Immigration Reform was dead for good.

To sum up, under the Bush and Obama presidencies repeated efforts to pass Comprehensive Immigration Reform were all defeated, during times of divided and unified government. Contrasting the failure of Comprehensive Immigration Reform with the successful passage of the 1990 Immigration Act, several findings stand out. First, given the relatively low levels of interest group insulation of US legislators, successful immigration reform requires the support of a broad interest group coalition. The passage of Comprehensive Immigration Reform by the Senate in 2013, which was supported by both business and labor, stands in marked contrast to the failure of CIR in 2007, when the lack of business buy-in was a critical factor in preventing the bill's passage by the Senate. Yet while necessary, since the 2000s, interest group support is no longer sufficient for the liberalization of immigration policy. The growing clout of immigration restrictionists in the Republican Party – first organized by the Congressional Immigration Reform Caucus and, later, the Tea Party, and more broadly supported by anti-immigration activists in think tanks, the conservative media, and social media – has significantly weakened policy makers' popular insulation. Playing a role comparable to that of anti-immigrant parties in Europe, Tea Party Republicans now ensure that Republican legislators must carefully consider the electoral implications of every step toward immigration liberalization. The opposition of House Republicans to immigrant legalization in particular has become the biggest stumbling block to the liberalization of immigration policy. By contrast, the growing electoral strength of immigrant and ethnic voters provided an impetus for the pursuit of comprehensive reform, by presidents of both parties and Democratic legislators. Finally, comparing this case study to Canadian immigration, the primacy of the legislative arena in US immigration policy making stands out. Whereas the Canadian points system was introduced in the form of executive regulation and, to this day, selection criteria and their weights continue to be fine-tuned in the executive arena, attempts by US policy makers to enact such a system failed in part because decision-making was set in the legislative arena, with its multiple access points for opposition interests.

Postscript

The election that propelled Republican Donald J. Trump into the White House marked a caesura in US immigration politics. In one of the most acrimonious and populist presidential campaigns in US history, Trump offered a more detailed agenda on immigration than on any other policy issue. In stark contrast to the conciliatory tone struck by his predecessors, Trump's immigration agenda played to the Republican base, promising that "I will build a great, great wall on our southern border" (Scott June 20, 2015). Likewise, Trump called "for a total and complete shutdown of Muslims entering the United States until our country's representatives can figure out what is going on" (Khan et al. 2019) and pledged to repeal

DACA – the Obama-era program that provides temporary protection from deportation to undocumented immigrants who were brought to the United States as children – on "day one" of his presidency (Bennett and Memoli February 16, 2017). These campaign promises exemplified a departure from the usual politics of presidential positioning. First, by singling out entire groups of nonwhite (in particular Latinx and Muslim) immigrants as prejudicial to the national interest, Trump presented himself as a divider rather than unifier. Second, in playing to popular anti-immigration attitudes, Trump willfully disregarded any diplomatic costs incurred by such positioning. Whereas presidents are typically closely attuned to the diplomatic repercussions of their rhetoric and action, Trump's positions on immigration showed a striking disregard for how they would be received by foreign governments. Third, as was going to become evident early into this presidency, Trump's promises and actions more often than not were those of a president acting independently of both his administration and his party. As a Republican member of Congress recalled the moment he heard about the travel ban: "It was a fiasco. I called the White House and said, 'What's going on?' It took about five minutes to understand that they didn't run it by the Department of Defense, or State, or Homeland Security, or Justice. He just signed the Executive Order and sent out a press release" (cited in Ball and Elliott January 11, 2018)

Contrary to most predictions, once in office Trump moderated neither his immigration rhetoric nor his reform agenda. Instead of yielding to institutional constraints and incentives that have long characterized policy making in the executive arena, Trump's governance style bears greater semblance to congressional restrictionists who pander to white and socially conservative constituencies than to a president representing an entire nation. The list of Trump's executive activism on immigration to date is long. In the area of asylum and refugee policy alone, it includes the indefinite stop of the admission of Syrian refugees and a temporary stop of all refugee admissions (Executive Order 13769), the subsequent reduction of refugee admissions to the lowest level since the passage of the Refugee Act of 1980, an end to the designation of Temporary Protected Status for Haitian, Nicaraguan, and Sudanese nationals, a ban on asylum claims by migrants traveling through Mexico, the suspension of the right of asylum for any migrant crossing the US–Mexico border outside of official ports of entry (at the time of writing, pending in Supreme Court), and the "Remain in Mexico" policy that allows the US government to return asylum seekers to Mexico while their claims are being adjudicated. Other executive actions include the unprecedented entry (or travel) ban on nationals from eight mostly Muslim-majority countries (Presidential Proclamation 9647), a repeal of DACA (still pending in the Supreme Court), a slowing of visa applications and renewals, including the exclusion of poor immigrants from access to green cards, and a vast augmentation of border enforcement powers, including the denial of federal grants to "sanctuary" cities who limit cooperation with federal immigration law enforcement (Executive Order 13768) and a zero-tolerance policy toward unauthorized border crossings that includes the forced separation of children from their parents (also still in front of the courts).

In the legislative arena Trump has embraced the Reforming American Immigration for a Strong Economy (RAISE) Act, which seeks to reduce legal immigration and reorient permanent admissions toward a high-skilled immigration system. The RAISE Act proposes to halve the number of green cards through drastic cuts to family immigration, to impose a ceiling on refugee admissions, to abolish the diversity visa program, and to anchor economic admissions in a points system. Despite unified Republican control of Congress and the White House for Trump's first two years in office, no changes to US immigration legislation have been enacted to date. New congressional appropriations for executive policy changes have been equally slow in coming, with the most contested of appropriations requests being Executive Order 13767, which provided for the construction of a border wall along the US–Mexico border. The resulting battle between the White House and Congress culminated in a thirty-five-day shutdown of the federal government, followed by Trump declaring a national emergency. The issue made its way into the judicial arena, where the Supreme Court overrode the decisions of lower courts and affirmed Trump's decision to divert $2.5 billion in Defense Department anti-drug funding for wall construction.

With a president who is renowned for his dominance of the executive branch and his congressional party, the judicial arena has gained in significance as a potential veto point. The majority of Trump's executive actions on immigration have triggered legal challenges, several of which have wound their way up to the Supreme Court. Almost fifty cases were filed in the federal courts against Executive Order 13769 (the "Muslim ban"), prompting a temporary restraining order and two rounds of revisions that partially changed its target countries and excluded US permanent residents from its reach. In the end the Supreme Court permitted the now labeled Presidential Proclamation 9645 and its accompanying travel

TABLE 6.1 *US case studies summary*

Policy episode	Policy choice	Policy arenas and veto points	Popular insulation	Interest group insulation	Diplomatic insulation
Case study 1					
1952 McCarran–Walter Act	*Failed liberalization*	Executive arena Legislative arena	Intermediate	Intermediate	Intermediate
1965 Immigration and Nationality Act	*Paradigmatic liberalization* Selective restriction	Executive arena Legislative arena	Intermediate	Intermediate	Low
Case study 2					
1988 Kennedy–Simpson bill	*Failed paradigmatic liberalization*	Legislative area	Intermediate	Low	High
1990 Immigration Act	*Partial paradigmatic liberalization*	Legislative arena Executive arena	Intermediate	Low	High
Case study 3					
2005/2006 CIR	*Failed paradigmatic liberalization*	Executive arena Legislative arena	Low	Intermediate	High
2007 CIR	*Failed paradigmatic liberalization*	Executive arena Legislative arena	Low	Low	High
2013 CIR	*Failed paradigmatic liberalization*	Executive arena Legislative arena	Low	Low	High

ban to come into effect, ruling 5–4 along ideological lines. Trump was handed another victory when the Supreme Court signed an order to allow the administration to enforce new rules that exclude migrants traveling through Mexico from access to the US asylum system. While the Supreme Court for now has upheld an injunction by the Northern California District Court against limiting asylum claims to those crossing at official ports of entry, the court so far has not served as a veto point in the way anticipated by pro-immigration interests.

CONCLUSION

The making of economic and family immigration policy in the United States is marked by several patterns that distinguish it from those of other countries examined in this book. First and foremost, the institution of Congress is at the center of the policy-making process. Whereas the politics of immigration is dominated by the executive arena in Canada and the electoral arena in Switzerland, the locus of policy making in the United States has always been the legislative arena (Table 6.1). Even though US presidents have sought to flex their muscles by issuing executive orders, and occasionally vetoes, Congress always has been, and continues to be, the most important institution for the making of immigration policy (at least until the Trump presidency). In the US separation-of-powers system, members of Congress seek to assert control over policy by writing immigration laws that routinely specify the kind of policy minutiae that, in other countries, are determined by executive regulation.

Second, with its two chambers and decentralized committee system Congress offers multiple access points for organized interests. More than any other country examined here, US immigration policy is the product of interest group politics. Because those who stand to gain from immigration face the strongest incentives to mobilize, interest group influence has pushed US immigrant admissions toward openness, rather than closure. With economic and family immigration policy routinely legislated in the form of vast omnibus bills, interest groups have formed strange bedfellow coalitions that have been instrumental in the passage of liberalizing policy reform. Because of their breadth, these interest group coalitions have – at least until recently – appealed to legislators from both parties, resulting in congressional bipartisan reform coalitions made up of economic and social liberals.

This pattern of interest group politics and bipartisan reform coalitions came under threat in the 1990s, however, when the rise of the populist

Congressional Immigration Reform Caucus and the Tea Party allowed immigration restrictionism to strengthen its hold on the Republican Party. As the balance between social conservatives and economic liberals within the Republican Party tilted toward the former, congressional Republicans moved to the right, precipitating growing partisan polarization in Congress. Analogous to the rise of far-right parties in Europe, the strengthening of the anti-immigration wing within the Republican Party has weakened policy makers' popular insulation. Given the short electoral horizons of members of the House in particular, the need to secure popular support for reelection at a time of highly politicized immigration has made the embrace of policy liberalization too risky for many. As the repeated failure of Comprehensive Immigration Reform in the 2000s demonstrates, policy liberalization now requires more than the presence of strong pro-reform interest group coalitions. With legislators operating in a context of weak interest group *and* weak popular insulation, policy gridlock has become the rule. Whereas the institutional fragmentation of Congress has always made paradigmatic immigration reform a tall order, with immigration squarely in the electoral arena even incremental reform of legal immigration now seems to be out of reach. The future of US immigration reform will likely be closely tied up with the fate of the Republican Party. With the election of Donald Trump, the White House, for the first time in recent history, is held by a populist and openly restrictionist president. Given the symbiotic relationship between Trump and congressional Republicans, the Republican Party's ideological direction (and future immigration positioning) will likely be determined by whether or not Trump wins a second term and, by extension, how his party will come to interpret his legacy.

7

Conclusion

This chapter begins by revisiting the book's core theoretical argument and its most significant empirical findings. It then explores two extensions of the argument beyond the cases examined in Chapters 3 to 6. First, the chapter applies the insulation framework to policy areas other than economic and family admissions: asylum policy, refugee policy, migration control, immigrant integration, and citizenship policy. Second, the analysis moves beyond the national level of policy making and explores the insulation framework's transferability to contexts of supranational (the case of the European Union) and subnational policy making. The chapter concludes with some thoughts on the future politics of immigration policy making.

POLITICAL INSULATION AND THE MAKING
OF IMMIGRATION POLICY

This book has been motivated by two basic questions. First, grappling with the puzzle of cross-national variation in immigration policy, we asked: why do states that confront comparable immigration challenges so often adopt different policy solutions? I have argued that the capacity of policy makers to turn their immigration preferences into policy is fundamentally shaped by three distinct types of political insulation. Whereas popular insulation will shield policy makers from public pressure for policy restrictionism, interest group insulation and diplomatic insulation from sending states are necessary if policy makers are to enjoy reprieves from the demands of domestic lobbies and foreign governments for the liberalization of immigration policy. Importantly, the relative strength of popular, interest group, and diplomatic insulation varies across institutional arenas. As a result, the locus of policy making matters greatly for the outcome of policy reform. Immigration policy choices thus vary across countries and, in contexts where actors can strategically manipulate the institutional locus of policy making, over time.

Whereas the first question driving this analysis focused on the *direction* of policy change, the second question grapples with its *scope*. Why does immigration policy change radically at certain points in time while remaining stable at others? Under what conditions is paradigmatic immigration reform – reform that alters the overarching goals of policy – possible? I have argued that paradigmatic reform is preceded by a loss of congruence between the prevalent immigration paradigm and its environment. Once the loss of congruence has eroded a paradigm's legitimacy, a process of competition over alternative paradigms is set in motion. Because of the need for broad-based legitimation, however, a new paradigm can only win out if its legitimacy is affirmed in the context of public debate. This process is by necessity contentious and, as a result, its success hinges on the absence of institutional veto points that could be exploited by reform opponents.

Comparing the politics of immigration policy making across the four countries of Switzerland, Germany, Canada, and the United States, this book has uncovered distinct policy-making logics. First, the case of Switzerland stands out due to the striking lack of insulation afforded to its policy makers. Given Swiss institutions of direct democracy – the ever present referendum threat – neither executives nor legislators enjoy meaningful insulation from popular immigration restrictionism. At the same time, legislators' close affiliation with interest groups erases any meaningful interest group insulation. Finally, the country's small size and economic dependence on access to the European market makes for perpetually weak diplomatic insulation. As a result, the making of Swiss immigration policy is best conceived of as a tightrope walk by policy makers seeking to accommodate simultaneous and contradictory pressures.

Immigration politics in Germany, our second case, has been shaped by distinct changes in its policy-making context over time. Whereas in the postwar decades the locus of policy making was firmly in the executive arena leaving policy makers to grapple with the country's weak diplomatic insulation – more recent reform initiatives have exposed the growing importance of the legislative arena and a rapid decrease in popular insulation. Perhaps most significantly, the case of Germany illustrates the challenge of paradigmatic policy liberalization in contexts where a long-standing paradigm opposes, rather than embraces, immigration. Despite the discreditation of the country's non-immigration paradigm several decades ago, the adoption of a new paradigm has proceeded in a piecemeal manner and is still not fully concluded today, as reform opponents have availed themselves of veto points to block paradigmatic reform.

The book's chapter on Canadian immigration politics offers a particularly striking contrast to the Swiss case. Whereas Swiss policy makers enjoy neither popular, interest group, nor diplomatic insulation, their Canadian counterparts pursue their policy goals in a context marked by exceptionally strong insulation. Most significantly, more than any other politicians examined in this book Canadian policy makers make immigration policy shielded from popular restrictionism. In a related finding, and once again in marked contrast to the other cases, Canada's politics of immigration is defined by the centrality of the executive arena as the locus of policy making. While this is a pattern shared with other Westminster systems, Canada is unique in legislating immigration policy in the form of framework legislation, which delegates far-reaching policy decisions to the regulatory process. Finally, because of policy makers' strong political insulation, Canadian immigration politics distinguishes itself by the frequency of enacted paradigmatic reform.

Whereas the politics of immigration is dominated by the electoral arena in Switzerland and the executive arena in Canada, the locus of US policy making is the legislative arena. In contrast to Canada, where legislators routinely leave policy decisions to the regulatory process, the US Congress exercises tight control by writing extraordinarily detailed immigration bills. Given the legislative arena's multiple access points, policy makers enjoy little interest group insulation. Thus, more so than in any other country examined in this book, US immigration policy making has been the product of interest group politics. Until recently the breadth of these interest group coalitions have facilitated the cobbling together of bipartisan compromise bills. With the rise of immigration restrictionism within the Republican Party, however, interest group politics has given way to partisan polarization, thereby weakening policy makers' popular insulation. Thus, much like their Swiss counterparts, US legislators now operate in a context of simultaneously weak interest group and popular insulation. As a result, immigration reform has shifted from taking the form of compromise bills to being stymied by policy gridlock.

BEYOND FAMILY AND ECONOMIC IMMIGRATION POLICY

Having examined the politics of family and economic immigration policy making throughout this book, we now consider whether its insulation framework can travel beyond these particular areas of immigration policy. This section examines the areas of asylum, refugee, migration control, and integration and citizenship policy. For each policy field we compare the expected dynamics of popular, interest group, and diplomatic pressure to those observed in the politics of family and economic immigration. I conclude that the insulation framework allows for the comparative study of immigration and integration policy making more broadly.

The Politics of Asylum Policy

As signatories to the 1951 Refugee Convention and its 1967 Protocol, liberal democracies have in place policies that regulate access to protection for non-nationals filing for asylum at their borders and in their territory. Originally designed to cope with the large-scale population displacement in the aftermath of World War II, the golden age of protection-driven asylum policy was short-lived, beginning with the signing of the Refugee Convention in 1951 and petering out by late 1970s. During the Cold War, liberal democracies willingly opened their arms to the relatively few asylum seekers who managed to escape from behind the Iron Curtain, heralding the arrival of Eastern Bloc refugees as a sign of the superiority of the capitalist West. With the end of the Cold War and the escalation of refugee-producing events in the Global South, however, asylum applications from non-Western regions rose rapidly, while the foreign policy benefits of granting asylum vanished. In response, liberal states adopted a defensive stance and implemented a multitude of control measures designed to deter and redirect humanitarian flows away from their borders. This new and "mean-spirited" (Dauvergne 2016) politics of asylum, which began in the 1980s and gathered full steam in the 1990s, is now firmly institutionalized and bound to continue for the foreseeable future.

Compared to the politics of economic and family immigration policy, asylum policy distinguishes itself by the intensity of restrictionist pressures bearing on the policy process. Unlike economic immigration, and much more so than is the case for family admissions, asylum migration is "unwanted" (Joppke 1998b). Because contemporary asylum flows are "endured" rather than actively solicited, they are broadly viewed as a fundamental challenge to states' ability to manage and control immigration. Striking at the heart of states' capacity for territorial closure, asylum migration thus triggers particularly intense public restrictionism. During times of heightened displacement, asylum migration takes on highly visible forms that are vividly captured by the media, broadcasting footage of migrants arriving on jerry-rigged boats or crossing land borders in caravans and on trains. These images are easily exploited by anti-immigrant actors who frame asylum immigration as a loss of territorial control. As a result, to a greater degree than is the case with economic and family immigration, mobilized public opinion on asylum seekers is restrictionist, and more intensely so.

These restrictionist popular pressures are unlikely to be offset by liberalizing interest group pressure. While those who stand to reap the concentrated benefits of liberalized admissions – collective actors ranging from co-ethnics, refugee advocacy groups, and faith-based organizations – face strong incentives to mobilize, pro-asylum lobbies hold much weaker political clout than the interest groups that demand the expansion of economic and family admissions. Most importantly, as the most powerful of interest group lobbies, employers are typically silent on questions of asylum policy. Similarly, in contrast to family admissions, where the benefits of policy liberalization accrue to many ethnic groups, asylum reform is rarely supported by broad-based ethnic coalitions because asylum flows tend to be dominated by a few source countries. While this book's theoretical framework predicts that interest group pressure will point toward the liberalization of asylum policy, we would expect this pressure to be weaker, and hence less effective, than interest group pressure in areas of economic and family immigration.

Turning to diplomatic pressure, yet another pattern of restrictionism emerges. As I have argued in Chapter 2, in contrast to sending-state governments, fellow receiving states in the region will exert diplomatic pressure for policy restrictionism. Neighboring states will consider liberal asylum policies to be a political liability to the extent that these policies are perceived as "magnets" for asylum flows that might spill over into the entire region. Consider, for instance, the Canadian government's demand that the United States restrict the issuing of visitor visas to Nigerian nationals after the number of asylum seekers with Nigerian passports who crossed into Canada from the US suddenly increased in 2018 (*iPolitics* April 30, 2018). In a similar vein, after German Chancellor

Angela Merkel opened the door to Syrian refugees in 2015, she quickly came under fire from neighboring governments who argued that her open border policy was fueling asylum migration into Europe.

When it comes to the making of asylum policy, then, policy makers are confronted with strong popular and diplomatic pressures for closure, pressures which are only weakly counterbalanced by interest group demands for greater openness. In other words, to a much greater extent than is the case in the areas of family and economic immigration, asylum policy making takes place in a context of simultaneously weak popular and diplomatic insulation, paired with relatively strong interest group insulation. As a result, it generates a political dynamic that pushes asylum policy toward ever greater closure and turns humanitarian flows into political liabilities, erecting high hurdles to policy liberalization.

The Politics of Refugee Policy

Refugee policy takes the form of humanitarian admissions programs that facilitate the resettlement of refugees from overseas. While refugee and asylum policy both provide protection to those fleeing persecution and harm, they represent distinct policy areas with contrasting political dynamics. Whereas asylum policy regulates the processing of "spontaneous arrivals" who have made their own way into receiving regions (many with the help of smugglers), refugee policy is premised on selecting and screening refugees prior to admission. Unlike asylum policy, refugee policy allows for both "qualitative" and quantitative control of humanitarian admissions. Thus, whereas asylum policy fundamentally constrains state sovereignty, refugee policy affirms states' capacity to manage and control humanitarian immigration. In fact, precisely because refugee resettlement is a discretionary act, only some states have in place refugee policies. And whereas the ability of states to use asylum policy for ends other than humanitarian protection has steadily diminished since the end of the Cold War, this has not been the case for refugee policy, which, by targeting specific populations, oftentimes remains an integral aspect of foreign policy. For instance, as the global leader in refugee resettlement (at least until the Trump presidency), the United States has long used refugee policy to support stability in conflict regions, foster cooperation with military allies, and enhance the country's reputational standing abroad.

Because refugee policy so often takes the form of foreign policy, it is usually crafted in the executive arena. This is even the case for the United States, where the legislative arena is otherwise central to the making of immigration policy. As legal scholar Stephen Legomsky has noted, with the Refugee Act of 1980, "Congress virtually wrote the President a blank check to decide how many overseas refugees to admit and which ones," thus presenting the "one gaping exception" to congressional dominance over immigration policy making (1995, 676). Not only is the making of refugee policy anchored in the most politically insulated of arenas, but because the number of resettled refugees tends to be small and is firmly subject to state control, refugee resettlement rarely elicits popular backlash. As a result, the relative absence of popular restrictionism provides openings for domestic pro-refugee groups and foreign governments to lobby for liberalized refugee admissions. In sum, despite being central pillars of the international refugee regime, asylum policy and refugee policy exhibit strikingly different political dynamics, both of which can be accounted for by this book's insulation framework.

The Politics of Migration Control

Migration control policy describes the vast array of measures devised to prevent entry and ensure the departure of foreign nationals without legal immigration status. This includes "remote" control measures (Zolberg 2003) such as visas and carrier sanctions, border controls such as port-of-entry inspections and border patrols, and interior controls such as work-site enforcement, detention, and deportation. As I argued in Chapter 2, with the growing securitization of migration, states' capacity for migration control is now seen as critical for states' legitimation as security providers. In other words, unauthorized immigration is broadly understood as inimical to state sovereignty. As a result, and echoing the dynamics of asylum politics, the politics of migration control stands out for the ease with which popular pressure for territorial closure can be mobilized. As I have shown in the context of deportation (Ellermann 2009), "demonizing" frames of undocumented immigrants easily resonate with the public and provide proponents of stricter migration controls with a comparative advantage when mobilizing latent anti-immigration sentiment. Unless they are firmly insulated from popular pressures, few policy makers can afford to be seen as "soft" on questions of law and order.

This is not to argue that the public never differentiates between different categories of undocumented immigrants. In fact, policies that seek to reduce illegal immigration by creating pathways for legalization can garner significant public support if they succeed in framing undocumented immigrants as "innocent" (the case of the "Dreamers" who were brought to the United States as children) or "deserving" (long-term undocumented residents with solid employment records and local family and community ties). Yet, as we saw in Chapter 6, even in this "most favorable" scenario, immigrant legalization remains politically risky. Wright et al.'s (2016) study of the role of categorical judgment in immigration attitudes offers a sobering corrective to assumptions about a broadly malleable public opinion in this regard. The authors find that those who categorically support the principle of law and order – over a quarter of respondents – are unwilling to make distinctions between undocumented immigrants based on individual attributes and circumstance. Moreover, while the legalization of long-established community members can garner significant public backing, support for tougher migration control is bound to increase in cases where migrants have no discernible ties to their country of destination or where the human costs of denying entry or membership are rendered invisible by distance (e.g., remote control) or mode of implementation (e.g., deportation via charter flights) (Ellermann 2006).

Given the strength of popular restrictionism, advocates for the liberalization of migration control are in an unviable position. Interest group lobbying in favor of more permeable borders or a more permissive approach to migration enforcement will only be successful during times when illegal immigration is not politicized. Until the heightened politicization of undocumented immigration in the 1990s, for instance, US employers in labor-intensive industries such as agriculture or meat-packing were routinely able to negotiate exemptions from worksite enforcement. Given today's pervasiveness of immigration populism, however, we have little reason to assume that popular pressure for tougher migration controls is about to abate.

Like domestic organized interests, governments of immigrant-sending states support the liberalization of migration control policies, either because of material interests – such as remittances – or to avert the reputational damage of seeing their diasporas targeted by policy restrictionism. As we have seen in this book's empirical chapters, diplomatic pressure for policy liberalization can have a significant impact on the making of immigration policy, but only when policy makers are well insulated from opposing popular pressures, a condition that is unlikely to be met in this policy area. Thus, we expect the politics of migration control to follow a dynamic comparable to that of asylum politics: pervasive popular pressure for restrictionism that will render any liberalizing policy reform a political liability.

The Politics of Integration and Citizenship

The book's insulation framework was developed with immigration policy in mind. Regulating the entry of non-nationals, however, is not the only challenge facing the makers of immigration policy. As sustained immigration transforms nation-states into countries of immigration, policy makers turn their attention to questions of integration. Until recently, migration scholars approached integration policies as a reflection of nationally distinct models of integration, which evolved from unique national histories, conceptions of national identity, and understandings of the role of the state. Thus, scholars of Europe posited a French republican model of civic assimilation (Favell 1998), a German model of ethnocultural differentiation (Brubaker 1992), a British race relations model (Favell 1998), and a Dutch multicultural model (Koopmans 2007). Similarly, in North America Bloemraad contrasted Canada's interventionist multiculturalism with a US laissez-faire approach to immigrant integration that emphasizes immigrant autonomy (Bloemraad 2002). These models were understood to be relatively immutable paradigms or "philosophies" (Favell 1998) rather than sets of policies shaped by political contestation. Since the turn of the millennium, however, the rise of civic integration in Europe (Goodman 2014) and the associated "multicultural backlash" (Vertovec and Wessendorf 2010) have increasingly called into question the continued viability of national models. With the growing popularity of civic integration many European governments adopted such policies, including countries that, until the 2000s, had no official integration policy in place. As the study of integration shifted from identifying national models to examining policies of integration, integration scholars cast doubt on the internal validity of national integration models. They did so by examining changes in integration policy over time that could not be contained under a single integration model (Bertossi 2011), and by identifying cross-national policy convergence between seemingly incompatible integration regimes (Banting 2014). To what extent, then, is this book's insulation framework transferrable to the comparative study of integration policy?

While less is known about popular attitudes on immigrant integration than on immigration, existing scholarship points to a strong public preference for cultural assimilation over multiculturalism (Zick et al. 2001, Breugelmans and Van De Vijver 2004, Arends-Tóth and Vijver 2003). Across European countries, public opinion associates multicultural policy with ethnic segregation and, hence, threats to social cohesion. While the public recognizes integration to be a complex and multidimensional process, in a recent study of British and Dutch popular attitudes, Sobolewska et al. (2017) find a strong preference for cultural assimilation, expressed as the expectation that immigrants speak the host country's language in the home and support women's employment. Research on American public opinion likewise confirms strong public support for linguistic assimilation (Citrin and Sides 2008). Thus, while more research is needed to fully understand public views on integration – including the full range of attitudinal dimensions pertaining to integration – existing studies suggest a strong public preference for assimilation. In other words, we would expect popular "assimilationism" to operate in a manner comparable to that of immigration restrictionism.

This political logic is borne out by Marc Howard's comparative study of citizenship reform (2006), which finds that policy liberalization – typically the lowering of residency requirements or, more controversially, the acceptance of dual nationality – is only feasible in the absence of populist far-right parties that can mobilize public opposition. Perhaps most famously, when German policy makers sought to liberalize the country's notoriously closed citizenship law by introducing conditional birthright citizenship, lowering residence requirements, and accepting dual nationality, reform opponents mobilized public opposition by means of a countrywide petition drive that forced reformers to abandon the proposed acceptance of dual nationality. By framing dual nationality as a toleration of divided loyalties and, hence, a sanctioning of sociocultural and political dissimilation, opponents skillfully exploited popular assimilationism to defeat reform.

As in the case of family immigration, our framework predicts interest group mobilization in favor of a liberalized integration policy. Thus, ethnic groups and immigrant advocates will join forces to demand greater immigrant rights and fewer hurdles to immigrant inclusion. In a similar vein, sending-state governments will advocate on behalf of their nationals abroad, seeking to ensure favorable legal treatment, including the possibility of dual nationality. As a result, just as in the case of family and economic immigration the makers of integration and citizenship policy will be exposed to the cross-cutting pressures of popular restrictionism, on the one hand, and interest group and diplomatic pressures for liberalization, on the other.

BEYOND NATIONAL-LEVEL POLICY MAKING

The comparative politics of immigration examined in this book has focused exclusively on national-level policy making, leaving open the

question of whether its framework can travel to other levels of governance. Can the insulation framework help us make sense of policy making
at the supranational level – the case of the European Union – or, alternatively, at subnational levels of government? While an in-depth analysis of
these questions is beyond the scope of this chapter, a cursory exploration
of examples of supranational and subnational policy making suggests
that the framework can in fact shed light on the drivers of immigration
policy beyond the national level.

Shifting Policy Up: Supranational Policy Making in the European Union

Over the past two decades the European Union has become a policy
maker in its own right when it comes to the regulation of movement
within its territory and across its external borders. Its policy-making
powers are now far reaching in the areas of European Union citizenship –
including its crown jewel, freedom of movement and residence for EU
citizens – and protection of its external borders. Beyond this, supranational policy development has been largely confined to the field of
asylum, after the abolition of internal border controls allowed asylum
seekers to move freely across borders. Most notably, the EU to date has
found little common ground on matters of legal immigration, with the
result that little policy development has taken place in areas of family
immigration, economic admissions, and immigrant integration.
Complicating our analysis is the fact that much more so than is the case
with the study of national-level policy making, the institutional context of
policy making in the European Union is a work-in-progress, with the
relative significance of its policy-making arenas having undergone significant change over the past three decades. We begin this section with a brief
history of the institutional configuration of EU immigration policy
making. The chapter then identifies the political dynamics that have
driven EU policy making on matters of immigration and asylum.

The Constitutional Evolution of EU Asylum and Immigration Policy Making

In the 1980s immigration appeared on the agenda of intergovernmental
groups of justice and interior officials working in the fields of anti-
terrorism and drug enforcement. With the signing of the Schengen
Agreement in 1985, the Ad Hoc Immigration Group was created as an
intergovernmental forum for security-focused cooperation. The following
decade saw increased intergovernmental cooperation on questions of

migration control and asylum. Two key policy milestones – the 1985 Schengen Agreement, which provided for the abolition of internal borders, and the 1990 Dublin Convention, which determined the member state responsible for the adjudication of asylum applications – were first adopted outside the EU legal framework on a strictly intergovernmental basis and, given unanimity rules, saw long delays in implementation (ten years for Schengen, seven years for Dublin). With the signing of the Treaty of Maastricht in 1993, cooperation on migration and asylum became integrated into the institutional framework of the European Union, though on a strictly intergovernmental (rather than European Community) basis. Maastricht created an intergovernmental Justice and Home Affairs pillar and dedicated one of its groups exclusively to matters of asylum, visas, and migration. Because member states continued to object to supranational decision-making in this politically sensitive area, intra-EU cooperation remained limited to intergovernmental decision-making. With immigration and asylum not yet integrated in the Community legal order, within the Council of Ministers, the Justice and Home Affairs Council – composed of the member states' immigration executives – established itself as the central EU actor in this policy field. The intergovernmental policy-making framework assured member state governments of tight control over policy development and denied the European Parliament and the European Commission any meaningful policy-making powers. Likewise, the European Court of Justice did not hold jurisdiction over questions of asylum and migration.

In the 2000s, this policy-making logic shifted in response to changes in the European Union's institutional architecture. With the signing of the Treaty of Amsterdam, both legislative institutions – the Council of Ministers and the European Parliament – were empowered to adopt legislation on migration and asylum. At the same time, the European Commission – the EU's executive – was given the sole right of legislative initiative. In order to ease the transition and set a temporary brake on the Commission's new legislative powers, during a five-year transitional period legislative initiative taking was to be shared between the Commission and the Council. At the end of the transition period, the Commission was given the sole right of legislative initiative, and the Council's decision-making rules changed from unanimity to qualified majority. Furthermore, with the Treaty of Amsterdam, the European Court of Justice was granted the power to rule on migration and asylum cases brought before member state courts that have no judicial remedy under national law. In sum, by increasing the powers of the Commission, the Parliament, and the Court of Justice, the Treaty of Amsterdam moved EU-level migration and asylum policy making from a strictly intergovernmental basis – dominated by the Council of Ministers – toward communitarization and judicialization. All four institutions now constitute potential veto points in the making of immigration and asylum policy. In 2007 this dynamic was reinforced when the Treaty of Lisbon further strengthened the role of the Parliament and Court of Justice.

The Politics of EU Migration and Asylum Policy

Prior to the constitutional reforms of the Treaty of Amsterdam, the logic of EU-level policy making on migration and asylum followed a strictly intergovernmental logic. Firmly in control of policy development, the Council of Ministers gave expression to the interests of the member states to strengthen the Union's external borders and exert greater control over asylum migration. Thus, Virginie Guiraudon's (2000b) seminal study of pre-Amsterdam migration policy making shows how, in the early 1980s, national immigration officials used intergovernmental venues to circumvent domestic obstacles to tighter migration control. During this time, domestic court rulings, integration-focused ministries, and, to a lesser extent, pro-immigrant lobbies constrained the decision-making autonomy of interior and justice officials. By shifting policy to intergovernmental spaces that had opened up with the negotiation of the Schengen Agreement, immigration officials strategically moved policy making into an arena more amenable to the pursuit of restrictionist policy preferences. In this new intergovernmental space, immigration officials exerted tight control over the policy agenda and enjoyed extraordinarily strong interest group insulation. Not only did the Justice and Home Affairs Council's meetings take place behind closed doors, but domestic interest group lobbies had hitherto organized only at the national level and were thus deprived of previous access points to the policy-making process. As a result, throughout the 1990s immigration officials were able to shift migration control and asylum policy toward greater restrictionism, unencumbered by the constraints of judicial review and shielded from more immigrant-friendly collective actors, at both the European and the national level.

With the treaty changes of the 2000s, however, the political logic of European migration governance shifted in important ways, as the number of veto points increased and the Council came to share power with institutions governed by supranational logics. Whereas decision-making by the Council continued to follow a lowest common denominator logic that favored immigration restrictionism (Cerna 2014b, Guiraudon 2000b, Huysmans 2006), decision-making in the supranational institutions of the Commission, the Parliament, and the Court of Justice favored more liberal positions on asylum and immigration. The Commission's and Court's positioning in particular have been consistently found to be "refugee-friendly" (Kaunert and Léonard 2012), "rights-oriented," (Thielemann and El-Enany 2010), and taking on the role of "protectors of family migration rights" (Block and Bonjour 2013, 223). The sole substantive exception to this logic is in the area of visa and border policies, where the Commission has shown itself as an "ally [to the Council of Ministers] in tougher border control and immigration enforcement" (Lahav and Luedtke 2013, 111). The Court of Justice has played an especially influential role in constraining the Council in areas of family unification and expulsion (Acosta Arcarazo and Geddes 2013, Bonjour and Vink 2013).

By contrast, the immigration positioning of the European Parliament has undergone a shift from playing the role of "pro-migrant actor" when policy making was still dominated by the Council, to adopting "more consensual behavior vis-à-vis the Council" after it was granted full legislative powers (Trauner and Ripoll Servent 2016, 1429). Since then, Parliament's positioning has fluctuated with the ability of parliamentary groups to form coalitions. Thus, whereas a left-liberal parliamentary coalition supported the European Commission's proposals for more harmonized and liberal asylum policies, after the conservatives' victory in 2009 the Council of Ministers was able to co-opt the liberal parties to join its restrictionist coalition with parliamentary conservatives (Trauner and Ripoll Servent 2016). We now offer a brief appraisal of the insulation logics of these policy-making institutions in order to gauge whether the insulation framework can help us make sense of these patterns.

THE EUROPEAN COMMISSION AND THE EUROPEAN COURT OF JUSTICE As the European Union's executive, the Commission holds greater power than national-level executives. Not only does it have the oversight and implementation responsibilities associated with executives elsewhere, but its monopoly over the initiation of legislation closely resembles that of federal legislatures and unitary executives (Schmidt 2012). As an unelected bureaucracy whose commissioners are appointed by the Council of Ministers and approved by the European Parliament, the Commission is directly accountable neither to the European public nor to the member state publics and hence enjoys exceptionally strong popular insulation. In the face of mounting concerns about the European Union's "democratic deficit," the Commission has sought to compensate for its lack of electoral legitimacy through consultation with organized interests and civil society. Because the Commission considers civil society a critical ally in establishing its legitimacy (Pollack 1997), it has become the most important access point for interest groups in Brussels (Eising 2007).

This combination of strong popular insulation and weak interest group insulation, it follows, allows the Commission to pursue its supranational policy agenda of expansive immigration and immigrant rights. Further, in the European Union's external relations the Commission bears primary responsibility for trade negotiations and development policy. Diplomatic pressures from third countries who seek immigration concessions in exchange for greater trade openness or stricter immigration controls are likely to push Commission proposals toward greater openness (with the exception of external border controls). The Commission's progressive policy agenda has been largely supported by the rulings of the European Court of Justice as another constitutionally powerful player within the European Union. The Court of Justice enjoys greater independence than national-level courts in Europe (Schmidt 2012). And while judicial rulings do not exist in a political vacuum, as an unelected body with a mandate of interpreting EU law, the Court clearly enjoys a high degree of political insulation. Perhaps most importantly, both the Court and the Commission make decisions in an institutional context of high popular insulation, prompting assessments of their immigration expansionism as rooted in "the relative 'insulation' of technocrats and judges from the harsher glare of electoral politics" (Geddes 2000, 633).

THE EUROPEAN PARLIAMENT Despite the constitutional changes of the 2000s, which gave the European Parliament the power to adopt and amend legislation, it lacks some of the basic competencies associated with national parliaments, most importantly the power to initiate legislation. Not only is the European Parliament constitutionally weaker than its member state counterparts, but the absence of a regional electoral system has impeded the development of Europe-wide party identities. Instead, legislators are elected on the basis of national electoral rules and tend to campaign on domestic issue platforms. European Parliament elections are marked by low (and declining) turnout, flying below the radar of most voters who pay little attention to the substance of European Union politics. Given the distance between EU parliamentarians and member state electorates, legislators' popular insulation is likely greater than is the case for members of national parliaments (though lower than for the Commission and Court). Moreover, as the Parliament's constitutional powers have grown it has become a locus of interest group lobbying in its own right, second only to the Commission. Thus, even in the absence of diplomatic pressure for policy liberalization (as the Parliament plays no role in EU external relations), interest group lobbying will support progressive positioning on immigration.

THE COUNCIL OF MINISTERS The Council of Ministers (the Council of the European Union), a diplomatic body composed of ministers of the member states, is designed to represent the interests of the member states and to facilitate joint decision-making. The Council of Ministers and the European Parliament are co-legislators. Whereas the European Parliament has direct but weak representation, the Council has indirect but strong representation (Schmidt 2012). Ministers attend Council meetings based on their portfolio, with the Justice and Home Affairs Council deciding on migration-related legislation on the basis of qualified majority voting. While much has been made of the Council's move from unanimity to qualified majority voting in 2005, its decision-making style remains premised on consensus seeking rather than formal voting (Lewis 2012). Thus, despite a highly ordered system of voting rules that sets minimum blocking thresholds and policy-specific vetoes, there are also strong norms "which aim toward mutual accommodating for domestic difficulties based on group standards for legitimating such accommodation" (Lewis 2012, 3).

This collective preference for consensus-based decision-making is borne out by the Council's voting record, where the vast majority of legislation subject to qualified majority voting is adopted without the need for a formal vote because of the absence of dissension (Lewis 2012). Council decision-making has long been cloaked in secrecy, with its deliberations taking the form of *in camera* negotiations. While the Council has recently introduced some "transparency-enhancing" measures, it "continues to operate in mostly closed settings with a relatively high degree of insulation for national negotiators" (Lewis 2012, 6). Many accounts of the Council's work have attributed its consensus-finding abilities to this insulation. David Stavasage argues that the Council's lack of transparency has removed incentives for negotiators to pander to public opinion and to engage in posturing by adopting uncompromising positions (Stasavage 2004). The Council itself provided a formal defense of its negotiating procedures in a court case launched by *The Guardian*:

> The Council normally works through a process of negotiation and compromise, in the course of which its members freely express their national preoccupations and positions. If agreement is to be reached, they will frequently be called upon to move from those positions, perhaps to the extent of abandoning their national instructions on a particular point or points. This process, *vital to the adoption of Community legislation*, would be compromised if delegations were constantly mindful of the fact that the positions they were taking, as recorded in Council minutes, could at any time be made public through the granting of access to these documents, independently of a positive Council decision.
>
> (Council of the European Union July 13, 1994, emphasis in original)

To a much greater extent than is the case for the Commission and Parliament, the Council of Ministers is a highly insulated policy-making body and enjoys unparalleled interest group insulation. Despite the Council's undisputed locus of power, the lack of direct interest group lobbying directed at the Council has been described as an "EU lobbying anomaly" (Coen 2007, 341). Most lobbying appears to take place indirectly, with domestic interests turning to domestic government ministries who send delegations to the Council working groups (Bouwen 2004). Assessing the Council's popular insulation is less straightforward, however. On the one hand, Council members serve as the representatives of member state interests, and hence will be held accountable by domestic audiences. On the other hand, the Council's closed-door decision-making style offers significant insulation. Equally important is the fact that, in the area of justice and home affairs, the positions of Council members are much closer to public opinion than is true for just about any other policy-making body. Thus, as Bonjour and colleagues have argued, member state positions in the Council "might be more restrictive at the EU than at the national level due to the central control role played by Justice and Home Affairs officials who are used to framing issues of immigration in terms of security rather than in terms of human rights" (Bonjour et al. 2018, 414). Some observers have attributed the Council's immigration restrictionism to concerns about domestic backlash. To cite a spokesman for the NGO Caritas:

[T]here is not much hope that (the proposals) will go anywhere as long as this is a matter for the council of ministers to decide ... they are motivated by public opinion and re-election concerns ... but without a clear European immigration policy we won't be able to fight xenophobia.

(Cited in Schilde 2017, 204)

There is substantial evidence to suggest that members of the Council seek to upload domestic restrictionist policies in order to legitimate domestic immigration restrictionism, or pursue supranational policy making in order to force domestic policy adjustments toward greater restrictionism. For instance, several analyses of the European Union's Family Reunification Directive of 2003 posit that the Council's positioning was motivated by the need to legitimize domestic restrictive policies (Goodman 2011, Groenendijk 2011, Luedtke 2011). Adam Luedtke convincingly shows that member states' support for both the Family Reunification Directive and the Long Term Residents' Directive "stemmed from a desire to scale down generous domestic legislation that could not be scaled down domestically, due to institutional constraints at the national level" (2011, 15). For instance, France and Belgium, both key supporters of the Family Reunification Directive, favored supranational policy harmonization as this would require both governments to scale back immigrant rights. One Belgian ex-civil servant interviewed by Luedtke asserted that Belgium supported the directive because it was expected to take the wind out of the sails of the far-right Vlaams Belang party. Tellingly, the French government, another supporter of the directive, subsequently relied on it to pursue domestic reforms that mandated DNA testing for family immigrants. Likewise, Spain implemented the directive's provision for integration tests for minors in order to block the entry of immigrant youths (Luedtke 2011). Thus, a Commission proposal that was designed to guarantee family migrants a minimum set of rights in the end came to mark a restrictive turn in family admissions.

Conversely, the Council has blocked legislative action in areas where liberalizing policy harmonization would not have been supported by domestic electorates. Despite the European Commission's commitment to an EU-wide framework for legal immigration, the Council has repeatedly vetoed proposals in this area, including temporary visas for agricultural workers and the creation of an EU-wide "green card" system to regulate labor migration. The only Commission proposal that saw the light of day was the Blue Card Directive for highly skilled workers. Because member states' positions on the Blue Card varied so widely, however, the final directive was a much watered down version of the

Commission's proposal, amounting to little more than an "advertising tool" (Cerna 2014b).

Some scholars have argued that constitutional changes that have led to the communitarization of the formerly intergovernmental area of justice and home affairs has shifted policy toward liberalization (Bonjour and Vink 2013, Zaun 2016, Kaunert and Léonard 2012). While asylum rules underwent some modest liberalization, Ripoll Servent and Trauner (2014) have shown that the final legislation was much closer to the restrictionist position held by the Council and the center-right parliamentary parties, compared to the Commission's and center-left parliamentary groups' preferences. Lastly, Bonjour and Vink (2013) make a compelling argument about the Family Reunification Directive's unintended consequences. The Netherlands' strategic support of the directive rested on the assumption that fellow member states would emulate Dutch practices, thereby enhancing their legitimacy. In the end, however, the directive had a constraining effect on Dutch policy makers, for two distinct reasons. First, the Court of Justice ruled that the directive granted third-country nationals a subjective right to family unification. Second, as the preferences of Dutch policy makers moved toward ever greater restrictionism, the directive's legally binding nature prevented any subsequent legislative pursuit of these preferences.

As policy makers come to realize the unintended consequences of restrictionist EU policy initiatives, the Council is likely to use its veto power to block supranational policy making. Already, the Council's restrictionism has served as a powerful brake on policy harmonization on legal immigration and on policy liberalization in the area of asylum. The restrictionist policy core that predates communitarization has largely remained intact, constraining more liberal-minded actors, whereas the Council has exercised its veto power on virtually all initiatives that have sought to open up immigration. Trauner and Ripoll Servent describe the status quo as one of "policy stability" (2016) – in other words, policy gridlock. Moreover, the Council of Minister's role in the Union's nascent Common Security and Defense Policy is unlikely to force a lessening of this restrictionism. Not only does the national level remain the preeminent locus of decision-making in this area, but because of unanimity rules there are few opportunity points for the exercise of diplomatic pressure.

Shifting Policy Down: Subnational Policy Making

Over the past two decades subnational governments have emerged in many jurisdictions as distinct actors in the making of immigration and integration policy. In Canada and Australia, for instance, some powers over the selection of economic immigrants has been devolved to the provinces, territories, and states, alongside Quebec's much greater autonomy in immigrant admissions. In the United States, states and municipalities now play a significant role in enforcing immigration law. In Europe, Switzerland, Germany, Belgium, and Britain have all witnessed policy-making activity at subnational levels of government on matters of immigrant integration. Given the diversity of constitutional arrangements and patterns of policy devolution, examining the politics of subnational policy making would require a book in its own right. This discussion will therefore be limited to exploring some of the dynamics driving select examples of subnational policy making.

Provincial Nominee Programs in Canada and Subnational Immigration Enforcement in the US

The reasons why subnational governments have engaged in immigration policy making are diverse, and range from meeting regional labor market needs to compensating for federal government failure to enforce immigration law. In Canada the post-Confederation era of uncontested federal immigration policy dominance outside of Quebec came to an end in the 1990s, when subnational governments across the country began to develop PNPs, which allow for the direct selection of potential permanent residents on the basis of employment in the province. As Mireille Paquet (2015) has shown, bureaucrats in the provincial and territorial executive arenas were instrumental in developing PNPs between 1990 and 2010. Mirroring federal policy-making trends, this case of bureaucratic policy entrepreneurship operated in the absence of significant political and societal pressures. Instead it was driven by the view that immigration constituted an important economic and demographic resource and would be in the province's or territory's best interests. The initiation of these programs took place in a context of political insulation, what Paquet describes as "client politics, without clients" (2015, 1831).

Yet, as Paquet concedes, "the absence of client groups at the outset of provincial immigration activism in Canada may only be contingent on the novelty of this level of government's involvement in this policy domain" (2015, 1831). Because the PNP is employment based, employers "act as de facto principals for provincial nominees, selecting workers for nomination directly" (Baxter 2010, 25). With the rapid expansion of these programs, the role of employers in facilitating both skilled and low-skilled immigration has gained in significance. Given the lesser distance between policy makers and societal actors at subnational levels, we would expect both interest group and popular insulation to be lower than at the national level. In the case of the PNPs, whose economic rationale is unlikely to trigger much popular backlash in Canada, employers are likely to have a significant policy-making impact. To return to Triadafilopoulos' work (see Chapter 5), "employers typically set the terms for their provincial government" (Triadafilopoulos 2013b, 14), a point also made by Baglay and Nakache (2014). In the absence of countervailing public pressures, employer lobbies are likely to act as a key driver in immigration expansionism at the provincial level.

In contrast to the Canadian pattern of pro-immigration policy entrepreneurship by provincial bureaucrats, studies of US state- and local-level policy making have focused on restrictionist policy activism on matters of immigration enforcement. Ramakrishnan and Gulasekaram account for the proliferation of restrictionist state and municipal laws as "largely the product of political partisanship, with Republican-heavy areas especially ripe for political action" (2012, 1434). Given the importance of partisanship as a predictor of the emergence and direction of state-level immigration activism (Ramakrishnan and Wong 2011, Provine and Chavez 2009), primary candidates in Republican-heavy districts have used the issue of undocumented immigration to mobilize restrictionist party activists. In particular, jurisdictions with large Republican legislative majorities and Republican governors have been the favored target of restrictionist policy activism. Ramakrishnan and Gulasekaram show how issue entrepreneurs, including elected officials and societal actors, have simultaneously targeted federal and state-level policy arenas to force a crackdown on undocumented immigrants.

Ramakrishnan and Gulasekaram's analysis identifies anti-immigrant organizations as among the most effective of issue entrepreneurs, in particular the Federation for American Immigration Reform (FAIR) and NumbersUSA. Both organizations have mounted intense and sustained activism in the area of immigration enforcement, focused on defeating moderate federal legislation and promoting immigration restrictionism at the subnational level. These organizations have provided legal and political expertise, financial resources, and personnel to subnational legislative campaigns. Most importantly, the constitutional provision of referendums and popular initiatives at the state level drastically reduces the popular insulation of state-level elected officials. Anti-immigrant organizations thus strategically employ resources to, first, mobilize the public to support anti-immigration initiatives in the electoral arena, such as

California's Proposition 187 ("Save our State," 1996) and Arizona's Proposition 200 ("Protect Arizona Now," 2004). Second, these organizations – most importantly, FAIR's legal affiliate, the Immigration Reform Law Institute – use their legal expertise and financial resources to move policy into the judicial arena, either by filing lawsuits to ensure these measures' broadest possible application, or by offering legal counsel to challenge pro-immigration state and local laws in Democratic jurisdictions, such as San Francisco's issuance of municipal identification cards (Ramakrishnan and Gulasekaram 2012).

Despite their vast differences, this cursory examination of Canadian PNPs and US subnational immigration restrictionism shows striking parallels to federal logics of immigration policy making in each country. In each case, lower levels of political insulation at subnational levels of policy making have amplified patterns identified in Chapters 5 and 6. In Canada, PNPs follow the logic of executive-driven policy reform at the federal level, marked by a preference for economic immigration that is supported by employer interests and is marked by low levels of political contestation. It is no coincidence that the only Canadian province in which immigration-skeptic policies have emerged is Quebec, Canada's province with longstanding separatist ambitions. In the United States, in contrast, subnational-level immigration politics mirrors federal-level politics in being driven by partisan polarization. Whereas some municipalities and states have pursued liberalizing policy reforms, others have passed punitive enforcement measures. In either case, policy makers are operating in highly politicized environments, marked by weak popular and interest group insulation. The only type of insulation reliably enjoyed by subnational policy makers is that of diplomatic insulation, as foreign governments continue to direct their demands at national-level policy makers.

THE FUTURE POLITICS OF IMMIGRATION POLICY

This book has traced the development of immigration policy making over the course of seven decades. With the partial exception of Canada, immigration politics across liberal democracies has become more politicized and partisan over time. The growing populism that has emerged over the past decade or two only serves to amplify and accelerate political dynamics that have emerged since the end of the postwar period. There is little reason to believe that this trend will abate any time soon. Policy makers committed to the liberalization of immigration policy will continue to find their room for maneuver constrained by weakened popular insulation, especially in areas of family and humanitarian immigration. At the national and supranational levels, pursuing high-skilled immigration policies will likely remain the politically most viable course of action. The best prospects for progressive immigration agendas more broadly, however, will likely be found in left-leaning subnational jurisdictions, such as "cosmopolitan" urban centers (Maxwell 2019). Given the uneven geographic distribution of "cosmopolitan" and "nationalist" publics, we will likely see increasing state- and local-level variation in policy responses to immigration. Whereas in some locales we will observe the development of creative and inclusive approaches to "superdiversity" (Vertovec 2007), others will come to serve as "laboratories of bigotry" (Wishnie 2001) instead.

It is only with a long-term time horizon that we can expect to observe more fundamental changes to the politics of immigration. Fifty years from now, projected demographic changes will have profoundly diversified our societies, with important ramifications for the popular insulation of policy makers. Once ethnic minorities account for a majority of the electorate, policy makers across jurisdictions will face incentives to appeal to immigrant and ethnic minority voters. While growing ethnic minority electoral clout is unlikely to translate into an across-the-board liberalization of immigration policy, future policy makers will have to balance immigration restrictionism with the political imperative of selective policy liberalization.

References

Aaron, Henry. 2010. *Politics and the Professors: The Great Society in Perspective.* Washington, DC: Brookings Institution Press.

Abou-Chadi, Tarik. 2016. "Political and Institutional Determinants of Immigration Policies." *Journal of Ethnic and Migration Studies* 42 (13): 2087–110.

Abramovitz, Michael. May 27, 2007. "Immigration Bill's Point System Worries Some Groups." *Washington Post.*

Ackermann, Maya, and Markus Freitag. 2015. "What Actually Matters? Understanding Attitudes toward Immigration in Switzerland." *Swiss Political Science Review* 21 (1): 36–47.

Acosta Arcarazo, Diego, and Andrew Geddes. 2013. "The Development, Application and Implications of an EU Rule of Law in the Area of Migration Policy." *Journal of Common Market Studies* 51 (2): 179–93.

Adams, Michael. 2007. *Unlikely Utopia: The Surprising Triumph of Canadian Pluralism.* Toronto: Viking Canada.

Afonso, Alexandre. 2007. "Policy Change and the Politics of Expertise: Economic Ideas and Immigration Control Reforms in Switzerland." *Swiss Political Science Review* 13 (1): 1–38.

———. 2013. "Whose Interests Do Radical Right Parties Really Represent? The Migration Policy Agenda of the Swiss People's Party between Nativism and Neoliberalism." In *The Discourses and Politics of Migration in Europe,* edited by Umut Korkut, Gregg Bucken-Knapp, Aidan McGarry, Jonas Hinnfors, and Helen Drake, 17–35. New York: Palgrave Macmillan.

Aksoy, Deniz. 2012. "The Flag or the Pocketbook: To What Are Immigrants a Threat." *International Migration* 50 (6): 28–41.

Albertazzi, Daniele, and Duncan McDonnell. 2015. *Populists in Power.* Abingdon: Routledge.

Allen, Mike. December 24, 2003. "Immigration Reform on Bush Agenda." *Washington Post.*

America's Voice. November 8, 2012. "New Poll: How Texas Latino and New Citizen Voters Influenced the 2012 Elections." https://americasvoice.org/press_releases/new-poll-how-texas-latino-and-new-citizen-voters-influenced-the-2012-elections/, accessed August 26, 2019.

American Federation of Labor and Congress of Industrial Organizations. June 13, 2013. "Letter to Senators." http://images.politico.com/global/2013/06/17/trumka_s_744_letter_june_17_2013.html, accessed August 27, 2019.

Amtliches Bulletin Nationalrat. May 6, 2004. "Bundesgesetz über die Ausländerinnen und Ausländer."

Angenendt, Steffen. 2002. "Einwanderungspolitik und Einwanderungsgesetzgebung in Deutschland 2000–2001." In *Migrationsreport 2002: Fakten – Analysen – Perspektiven,* edited by Klaus J. Bade and Rainer Münz, 31–60. Frankfurt: Campus.

Angus Reid Global. May 30, 2014. "Temporary Foreign Worker Program: Fine for Older Canadians, Bigger Problem for Young and Unemployed."

Arbenz, Peter. 1995. *Bericht über eine Schweizerische Migrationspolitik.* Bern: Eidgenössisches Justiz- und Polizeidepartement.

Arends-Tóth, Judit, and Fons J. R. Van De Vijver. 2003. "Multiculturalism and Acculturation: Views of Dutch and Turkish-Dutch." *European Journal of Social Psychology* 33 (2): 249–66.

Aubert, Jean-Francois. 1978. "Switzerland." In *Referendums: A Comparative Study of Practice and Theory,* edited by David Butler and Austin Ranney, 39–66. Washington, DC: American Enterprise Institute for Public Policy Research.

Austen-Smith, David, and John R. Wright. 1994. "Counteractive Lobbying." *American Journal of Political Science* 38 (1): 25–44.

Auswärtiges Amt. March 20, 1972. *Memorandum by Referat V6 to Referat IA4 (V6 -80.55): Aussenpolitische Auswirkungen der Beschäftigung ausländischer Arbeitnehmer in der BRD.* Vol. B85, 1031. Berlin: Politisches Archiv des Auswärtigen Amtes.

Babington, Charles. March 30, 2006. "Senate GOP Fears Frist's Ambitions Split Party." *Washington Post.*

Bade, Klaus, J. 1982. "'Kulturkampf' auf dem Arbeitsmarkt: Bismarcks 'Polenpolitik' 1885–1890." In *Innenpolitische Probleme des Bismarck-Reiches,* edited by Olaf Pflanze, 121–42. Munich: R. Oldenbourg.

——— 2014. Kulturrassismus und Willkommens-kultur, Heinrich Böll Stiftung. http://kjbade.de/wp-content/uploads/2014/12/2014-12-12_Potsdam-Kurzfassung.pdf.

Baglay, Sasha, and Delphine Nakache, eds. 2014. *Immigration Regulation in Federal States: Challenges and Responses in Comparative Perspective.* New York and London: Springer Dordrecht Heidelberg.

Baker, Ross K. August 11, 2014. "Liberal Democrats in a Funk over Obama Inaction." USA Today.

Bale, Tim. 2003. "Cinderella and Her Ugly Sisters: The Mainstream and Extreme Right in Europe's Bipolarising Party Systems." *West European Politics* 26 (3): 67–90.

——— 2013. "More and More Restrictive – But Not Always Populist: Explaining Variation in the British Conservative Party's Stance on Immigration and Asylum." *Journal of Contemporary European Studies* 21 (1): 25–37.

Bale, Tim, Christoffer Green-Pedersen, André Krouwel, Kurt Richard Luther, and Nick Sitter. 2010. "If You Can't Beat Them, Join Them? Explaining Social Democratic Responses to the Challenge from the Populist Radical Right in Western Europe." *Political Studies* 58 (3): 410–26.

Bale, Tim, and Rebecca Partos. 2014. "Why Mainstream Parties Change Policy on Migration: A UK Case Study – The Conservative Party, Immigration, and Asylum, 1960–2010." *Comparative European Politics* 12 (6): 603–19.

Ball, Molly, and Philip Elliott. January 11, 2018. "Inside the GOP's Rocky Relationship with Donald Trump." Time. https://time.com/5098403/inside-the-gops-rocky-relationship-with-donald-trump/, accessed September 12, 2019.

Banting, Keith. 2014. "Transatlantic Convergence? The Archeology of Immigrant Integration in Canada and Europe." *International Journal* 69 (1): 66–84.

Barry, Tom. 2005. "Anti-Immigrant Backlash on the 'Home Front'." *NACLA Report on the Americas* 38 (6): 28–32.

Baumgartner, Frank R., and Bryan D. Jones. 1993. *Agenda and Instability in American Politics*. Chicago: Chicago University Press.

Baxter, Jamie. 2010. *Precarious Pathways: Evaluating the Provincial Nominee Programs in Canada*. Toronto: Law Commission of Ontario.

Beauftragte der Bundesregierung für Ausländerfragen. 1999. *Migrationsbericht 1999: Zu- und Abwanderung nach und aus Deutschland*. Bonn: Beauftragte der Bundesregierung für Ausländerfragen.

Beck, Marieluise. 2001. "Ihr Inderlein Kommet." *Blätter für deutsche und internationale Politik* 46 (1): 7–9.

Bennett, Andrew, and Jeffrey T. Checkel, eds. 2014. *Process Tracing: From Metaphor to Analytic Tool*. Cambridge: Cambridge University Press.

Bennett, Brian, and Michael A. Memoli. February 16, 2017. "The White House Has Found Ways to End Protection for 'Dreamers' While Shielding Trump from Blowback." *Los Angeles Times*.

Bennett, Marion T. 1966. "The Immigration and Nationality (McCarran-Walter) Act of 1952, as Amended to 1965." *The Annals of the American Academy of Political and Social Science* 367 (1): 127–36.

Bertossi, Christophe. 2011. "National Models of Integration in Europe: A Comparative and Critical Analysis." *American Behavioral Scientist* 55 (12): 1561–80.

Bethlehem, Siegfried. 1982. *Heimatvertreibung, DDR-Flucht, Gastarbeiterzuwanderung: Wanderungsströme und Wanderungspolitik in der Bundesrepublik Deutschland*. Stuttgart: Klett-Cotta.

Bigo, Didier. 2002. "Security and Immigration: Toward a Critique of the Governmentality of Unease." *Alternatives* 27: 63–92.

Bildzeitung. March 31, 1966. "Gastarbeiter fleissiger als deutsche Arbeiter?"

Binderkrantz, Anne Skorkjæ, Peter Munk Christiansen, and Helene Helboe Pedersen. 2015. "Interest Group Access to the Bureaucracy, Parliament and the Media." *Governance* 28 (1): 95–112.

Black, Jerome H., and Bruce M. Hicks. 2008. "Electoral Politics and Immigration in Canada: How Does Immigration Matter?" *International Migration & Integration* 9 (3): 241–67.

Block, Laura, and Saskia Bonjour. 2013. "Fortress Europe or Europe of Rights? The Europeanisation of Family Migration Policies in France, Germany and the Netherlands." *European Journal of Migration & Law* 15 (2): 203–24.

Bloemraad, Irene. 2002. "The North American Naturalization Gap: An Institutional Approach to Citizenship Acquisition in the United States and Canada." *International Migration Review* 36 (1): 193–228.

  2006. *Becoming a Citizen: Incorporating Immigrants and Refugees in the United States and Canada.* Berkeley: University of California Press.

  2012. *Understanding "Canadian Exceptionalism" in Immigration and Pluralism Policy.* Washington, DC: Migration Policy Institute.

Blumenthal, Sidney. 1982. *The Permanent Campaign.* New York: Touchstone Books.

Bohaker, Heidi, and Franca Iacovetta. 2009. "Making Aboriginal People 'Immigrants Too': A Comparison of Citizenship Programs for Newcomers and Indigenous Peoples in Postwar Canada, 1940s–1960s." *Canadian Historical Review* 90 (3): 427–62.

Bon Tempo, Carl J. 2008. *Americans at the Gate: The United States and Refugees During the Cold War.* Princeton: Princeton University Press.

Bonjour, Saskia. 2011. "The Power and Morals of Policy Makers: Reassessing the Control Gap Debate." *International Migration Review* 45 (1): 89–122.

  2016. "Speaking of Rights: The Influence of Law and Courts on the Making of Family Migration Policies in Germany." *Law & Policy* 38 (4): 328–48.

Bonjour, Saskia, Ariadna Ripoll Servent, and Eiko Thielemann. 2018. "Beyond Venue Shopping and Liberal Constraint: A New Research Agenda for EU Migration Policies and Politics." *Journal of European Public Policy* 25 (3): 409–21.

Bonjour, Saskia, and Maarten Vink. 2013. "When Europeanization Backfires: The Normalization of European Migration Politics." *Acta Politica* 48 (4): 389–407.

Bornschier, Simon. 2010. *Cleavage Politics and the Populist Right: The New Cultural Conflict in Western Europe* Philadelphia: Temple University Press.

Boscardin, Lucio. 1962. *Die italienische Einwanderung in die Schweiz mit besonderer Berücksichtigung der Jahre 1946–1959.* Zürich: Polygraphischer Verlag.

Boswell, Christina. 2003. "The 'External Dimension' of EU Immigration and Asylum Policy." *International Affairs* 79 (3): 619–38.

  2007. "Theorizing Migration Policy: Is There a Third Way?" *International Migration Review* 41 (1): 75–100.

Boswell, Christina, and Dan Hough. 2008. "Politicizing Migration: Opportunity or Liability for the Centre-Right in Germany." *Journal of European Public Policy* 15 (3): 331–48.

Boucher, Anna. 2013. "Bureaucratic Control and Policy Change: A Comparative Venue Shopping Approach to Skilled Immigration Policies in Australia and Canada." *Journal of Comparative Policy Analysis: Research and Practice* 15 (4): 349–67.

  2016. *Gender, Migration and the Global Race for Talent.* Manchester: Manchester University Press.

Boucher, Anna, and Justin Gest. 2017. *Crossroads of Immigration: A Global Approach to National Differences.* New York: Cambridge University Press.

Bourbeau, Philippe. 2011. *The Securitisation of Migration: A Study of Movement and Order.* London: Routledge.

Bouwen, Pieter. 2004. "Exchanging Access Goods for Access: A Comparative Study of Business Lobbying in the European Union Institutions." *European Journal of Political Research* 43 (3): 337–69.

Breugelmans, Seger M., and Fons J. R. Van De Vijver. 2004. "Antecedents and Components of Majority Attitudes toward Multiculturalism in the Netherlands." *Applied Psychology* 53 (3): 400–22.

Brubaker, Rogers. 1992. *Citizenship and Nationhood in France and Germany.* Cambridge, MA: Harvard University Press.

Bucken-Knapp, Gregg. 2009. *Defending the Swedish Model: Social Democrats, Trade Unions, and Labor Migration Policy Reform.* Plymouth: Lexington Books.

Bulmer, Simon. 2011. "Shop Till You Drop? The German Executive as Venue-shopper in Justice and Home Affairs." In *The Europeanization of Control: Venues and Outcomes of EU Justice and Home Affairs Cooperation,* edited by Petra Bendel, Andreas Ette, and Roderick Parkes, 41–76. Berlin: LIT Verlag.

Bundesamt für Industrie Gewerbe und Arbeit. March 31, 1953. *Vorsorgliche Massnahmen gegen die Überfremdung des Arbeitsmarktes:* Schweizerisches Bundesarchiv, E2001E 1970_217, Bd. 205. Memorandum.

1964. *Das Problem der ausländichen Arbeitskräfte: Bericht der Studienkommission für das Problem der ausländischen Arbeitskräfte.* Bern: BIGA.

Bundesamt für Industrie Gewerbe und Arbeit, and Bundesamt für Ausländerfragen. 1991. *Bericht über Konzeption und Prioritäten der schweizerischen Ausländerpolitik der neunziger Jahre.* Bern: BIGA.

Bundesamt für Migration und Flüchtlinge. 2010. *Migrationsbericht 2010.* Berlin: Bundesamt für Migration und Flüchtlinge.

2013. *Migrationsbericht 2012.* Nürnberg: Bundesamt für Migration und Flüchtlinge.

2015. *Migrationsbericht 2014.* Nürnberg: Bundesamt für Migration und Flüchtlinge.

2016. *Migrationsbericht 2015.* Nürnberg: Bundesamt für Migration und Flüchtlinge.

Bundesrat. 2002. Botschaft zum Bundesgesetz über die Ausländerinnen und Ausländer vom 8. März 2002.

Buomberger, Thomas. 2004. *Kampf gegen unerwünschte Fremde: Von James Schwarzenbach bis Christoph Blocher.* Zurich: Orell Füssli.

Burdett, Loomis A. 2009. "Connecting Interest Groups to the Presidency." In *The Oxford Handbook of the American Presidency,* edited by George C. Edwards III and William G. Howell. Oxford: Oxford University Press.

Burgdorff, Stefan. June 12, 2000. "Wettbewerb um die Köpfe." *Der Spiegel* 24: 43.

Busch, Andreas. 2007. "Von der Reformpolitik zur Restriktionspolitik? Die Innen- und Rechtspolitik der zweiten Regierung Schröder." In *Ende des rot-grünen Projektes: Eine Bilanz der Regierung Schröder 2002–2005*, edited by Christoph Egle and Reimut Zohlnhöfter, 408–30. Wiesbaden: Verlag für Sozialwissenschaften.

Bush, George H. W. September 25, 1990. "Statement of Administration Policy: H.R. 4300 – Family Unity and Employment Opportunity Immigration Act of 1990." *The American Presidency Project*, www.presidency.ucsb.edu/node/328943, accessed September 25, 2020.

Bush, George W. 2000. *Renewing America's Purpose: The Policy Addresses of George W. Bush, 1999–2000*. Washington, DC: Republican National Committee.

Butterfield, Jeanne. January 29, 2008. "Senate Bill 1639 and Other Federal Efforts at Reform: What Went Wrong? Keynote Presentation at Loyola Public Interest Law Reporter Symposium." *Public Interest Law Reporter* 13 (3): 213–27.

Byrd, Jodi. 2011. *The Transit of Empire: Indigenous Critiques of Colonialism*. Minneapolis: University of Minnesota Press.

Cairns, Alan C. 1994. "An Election to Be Remembered: Canada 1993." *Canadian Public Policy* 20 (3): 219–34.

Calavita, Kitty. 1992. *Inside the State: The Bracero Program, Immigration, and the I.N.S.* New York: Routledge.

Caldeira, Gregory A., and John R. Wright. 1988. "Organized Interests and Agenda Setting in the U.S. Supreme Court." *American Political Science Review* 82 (4): 1109–27.

Campi, Alicia J. 2004. "The McCarran–Walter Act: A Contradictory Legacy on Race, Quotas, and Ideology." Policy Brief.

Canada Department of Manpower and Immigration. October 1966. *White Paper on Immigration*. Ottawa: Canada Department of Manpower and Immigration.

Canada News Wire. March 22, 2002. "Government Must Adopt Committee's Recommendations to Keep Skilled Workers Coming to Canada."

Card, David, Christian Dustmann, and Ian Preston. 2012. "Immigration, Wages, and Compositional Amenities." *Journal of the European Economic Association* 10 (1): 78–119.

Carty, R. Kenneth. 2015. *Big Tent Politics: The Liberal Party's Long Mastery of Canada's Public Life*. Vancouver: UBC Press.

Carvalho, João, and Didier Ruedin. 2019. "The Positions Mainstream Left Parties Adopt on Immigration: A Cross-cutting Cleavage?" *Party Politics*. http://doi:10.1177/1354068818780533.

Castles, Stephen. 2006. "Guestworkers in Europe: A Resurrection?" *International Migration Review* 40 (4): 741–66.

Castles, Stephen, Hein de Haas, and Mark J. Miller, eds. 2014. *The Age of Migration: International Population Movements in the Modern World*. 5th ed. New York: Guilford.

Castonguay, Alec. February 2, 2013. "The inside Story of Jason Kenney's Campaign to Win over Ethnic Votes: The Secret to the Success of Canada's Immigration Minister." *Maclean's*.

Caviedes, Alexander A. 2010. *Prying Open Fortress Europe: The Turn to Sectoral Labor Migration*. Lanham, MD: Lexington Books.

CBC. October 31, 1972. "Pierre Trudeau Experiences Popularity Backlash after 1972 Election." *CBC Television News Special*. www.cbc.ca/archives/entry/trudeau-backlash-after-1972-election, accessed January 6, 2016.

CBC News. May 10, 2013. "Don't Bring Parents Here for Welfare, Kenney Says." www.cbc.ca/news/politics/don-t-bring-parents-here-for-welfare-kenney-says-1.1351002, accessed September 25, 2020.

September 25, 2015. "Justin Trudeau Promises to Make Family Reunification Easier for Immigration." www.cbc.ca/news/politics/canada-election-2015-trudeau-immigration-reform-1.3243302, accessed September 25, 2020.

Cerna, Lucie. 2013. "Understanding the Diversity of EU Migration Policy in Practice: The Implementation of the Blue Card Initiative." *Policy Studies* 34 (2): 180–200.

2014a. "Attracting High-Skilled Immigration: Policies in Comparative Perspective." *International Migration* 52 (3): 69–84.

2014b. "The EU Blue Card: Preferences, Policies, and Negotiations between Member States." *Migration Studies* 2 (1): 73–96.

2016. "The Crisis as an Opportunity for Change? High-Skilled Immigration Policies across Europe." *Journal of Ethnic and Migration Studies* 42 (10): 1610–30.

Cerny, Philip G. 1997. "Paradoxes of the Competition State: The Dynamics of Political Globalization." *Government and Opposition* 32 (2): 251–74.

Cerutti, Mauro. 2005. "La Politique Migratoire de la Suisse, 1945–1970." In *Histoire de la Politique de Migration, d'Asile et d'Integration en Suisse Depuis 1948*, edited by Hans Mahnig, 89–134. Zürich: Seismo.

Chen, Xiaobei, and Sherry Xiaohan Thorpe. 2015. "Temporary Families? The Parent and Grandparent Sponsorship Program and the Neoliberal Regime of Immigration Governance in Canada." *Migration, Mobility & Displacement* 1 (1): 81–98.

Chin, Gabriel J. 1996. "The Civil Rights Revolution Comes to Immigration Law: A New Look at the Immigration and Nationality Act of 1965." *North Carolina Law Review* 75 (1): 273–346.

Chin, Rita. 2007. *The Guest Worker Question in Postwar Germany*. New York: Cambridge University Press.

Chiose, Simona. March 31, 2016. "Express Entry Program Skewed Too Heavily toward In-demand Jobs: Critics." *The Globe and Mail*.

Chishti, Muzaffar, and Faye Hipsman. 2014. *U.S. Immigration Reform Didn't Happen in 2013; Will 2014 Be the Year?* Washington, DC: Migration Policy Institute.

Chishti, Muzaffar, Faye Hipsman, and Isabel Ball. October 15, 2015. "Fifty Years On, the 1965 Immigration and Nationality Act Continues to Reshape the United States." *Migration Information Source*, www.migrationpolicy.org/article/fifty-years-1965-immigration-and-nationality-act-continues-reshape-united-states, accessed December 10, 2018.

Chuenyan Lai, David. 1988. *Chinatowns: Towns within Cities in Canada*. Vancouver: UBC Press.

Church, Clive C. 2004. "Swiss Euroscepticism: Local Variations on Wider Themes." In *Euroscepticism: Party Politics, National Identity and European Integration*, edited by Robert Harmsen and Menno Spiering, 269–90. Amsterdam: Editions Rodopi.

Citizenship and Immigration Canada. 2001. "Bill C 11 Immigration and Refugee Protection Act: Explanation of Proposed Regulations. Prepared for Members of the House of Commons Standing Committee on Citizenship and Immigration."

2003. *Facts and Figures 2003*. Ottawa: Citizenship and Immigration Canada.

2005. *Annual Report to Parliament on Immigration 2005*. Ottawa: Citizenship and Immigration Canada.

March 6, 2013. "Super Visa Is Super Popular: Over 15,000 Parent and Grandparent Super Visas Issued."

May 18, 2013. "Regulations Amending the Immigration and Refugee Protection Regulations: Regulatory Impact Analysis Statement." *Canada Gazette* 147 (20).

Citrin, Jack, Donald P. Green, Christopher Muste, and Cara Wong. 1997. "Public Opinion toward Immigration Reform: The Role of Economic Motivations." *Journal of Politics* 59 (3): 858–81.

Citrin, Jack, and John Sides. 2008. "Immigration and the Imagined Community in Europe and the United States." *Political Studies* 56 (1): 33–56.

Citrin, Jack, Richard Johnston, and Matthew Wright. 2012. "Do Patriotism and Multiculturalism Collide: Competing Perspectives from Canada and the U.S." *Canadian Journal of Political Science* 45 (3): 531–52.

Cochrane, Christopher. 2011. "The Asymmetrical Structure of Left/Right Disagreement: Left-Wing Coherence and Right-Wing Fragmentation in Comparative Party Policy." *Party Politics* 19 (1): 104–21.

Coen, David. 2007. "Empirical and Theoretical Studies in EU Lobbying." *Journal of European Public Policy* 14 (3): 333–45.

Coffé, Hilda. 2008. "Social Democratic Parties as Buffers against the Extreme Right: The Case of Belgium." *Contemporary Politics* 14 (2): 179–95.

Cohen, Tom. June 16, 2012. "Obama Administration to Stop Deporting Some Young Illegal Immigrants." *CNN Politics*. www.cnn.com/2012/06/15/politics/immigration/index.html, accessed August 27, 2019.

Collins, Paul M. Jr. 2007. "Lobbyists before the U.S. Supreme Court: Investigating the Influence of Amicus Curiae Briefs." *Political Research Quarterly* 60 (1): 55–70.

Commission d'Experts en Migration. 1997. Une nouvelle conception de la politique en matiere de migration: rapport de la commission d'experts en migration. Berne: Office fédéral des réfugiés.

Cooper, Duncan. 2010. *Immigration and German Identity in the Federal Republic of Germany from 1945 to 2006*. Berlin: LIT Verlag.

Cornelius, W. A., Philip L. Martin, and James F. Hollifield. 1994. "Introduction: The Ambivalent Quest for Immigration Control." In *Controlling Immigration: A Global Perspective*, edited by W. A. Cornelius, Philip L. Martin, and James F. Hollifield 3–41. Stanford: Stanford University Press.

Council of the European Union. July 13, 1994. *Statement of Defence of the Council of the European Union in Case T-194094*. Brussels: Council of the European Union.

Cragg, C. Andrew. 2011. *Neoliberalising Immigration in Canada: The Pilot Project for Occupations Requiring Lower-Levels of Formal Training and the Expansion of Canada's Temporary Foreign Worker Program.* Peterborough, ON: Frost Centre for Canadian Studies and Indigenous Studies, Trent University.

CSPAN. April 18, 2013. "Senators on Bipartisan Immigration Legislation." www .c-span.org/video/?312156-1/gang-eight-senators-unveils-bipartisan-immi gration-bill, accessed September 20, 2017 (McCain's response at 46:56).

Currie, Duncan. November 27, 2006. "Republican Border Wars: A House Caucus Divided against Itself." *The Weekly Standard.*

Cyrus, Norbert and Ewa Helias. 1993. "Es ist möglich,die Baukosten zu senken: Zur Problematik der Werkvertragsvereinbarungen mit osteuropäischen Staaten seit 1991." Research Paper. Berliner Institut für Vergleichende Sozialforschung.

D'Amato, Gianni. 2001. *Vom Ausländer zum Bürger: Der Streit um die politische Integration von Einwanderern in Deutschland, Frankreich und der Schweiz.* Münster: LITT.

Dauvergne, Catherine. 2003. "Evaluating Canada's New Immigration and Refugee Protection Act in its Global Context." *Alberta Law Review* 41 (3): 726–44.

2016. *The New Politics of Immigration and the End of Settler Societies.* Cambridge: Cambridge University Press.

De Lange, Sarah L., Wouter van der Brug, and Meindert Fennema. 2014. "The Immigration and Integration Debate in the Netherlands: Discursive and Programmatic Reactions to the Rise of Anti-Immigration Parties." *Journal of Ethnic and Migration Studies* 40 (1): 119–36.

Deffner, Ingo. 2005. *Die Reaktionen der Parteien und der Öffentlichkeit auf die Wahlerfolge der NDP in der zweiten Hälfte der 60er Jahre.* Norderstedt: Grin Verlag.

Der Blick. February 10, 2007. "Jeden Monate 2000 Deutsche mehr."

DeSipio, Louis, and Rodolfo O. de la Garza. 2015. *U.S. Immigration in the Twenty-First Century: Making Americans, Remaking America.* Boulder: Westview Press.

Deutsche Bundesregierung. 2000. "Deutschland schreibt sich mit .de: 'Green Card' für IT-Spezialisten" [Germany is spelled with .de: "Green Card" for IT specialists]. Berlin.

Deutscher Bundestag. February 17, 1955. Stenographischer Bericht, 66. Sitzung.

February 21, 1973. Anlage zum Protokoll der 3. Sitzung des Innenausschusses. Berlin: Politisches Archiv des Auswärtigen Amtes. B85, 1031.

December 9, 1981. Antrag von SPD/FDP "Ausländerpolitik."

January 21, 1982. Antrag der Fraktion der CDU/CSU "Ausländerpolitik."

February 4, 1982. Stenographischer Bericht, 83. Sitzung.

May 5, 1982. Antwort der Bundesregierung auf die Grosse Anfrage der SPD and FDP.

January 20, 1994. "Stenographischer Bericht, 205. Sitzung." Vol. PlPr12/205.

January 26, 2000. "Stenographischer Bericht." Plenarprotokoll 14/83.

Die tageszeitung. January 29, 2010. "Hetze in der Schweiz: 'Kein Hochdeutsch mit den Deutschen'."

Die Woche. November 26, 1998. "Da kommt mir gleich die Galle hoch!"

Die Zeit. December 23, 2002. "Streit um die Zuwanderung."

Dinan, Stephen. June 22, 2007. "Grassley Admits Amnesty Mistake." *Washington Times.*

Divine, Robert A. 1957. *American Immigration Policy, 1924–1952.* New Haven: Yale University Press.

Donzé, René, and Stefan Bühler. September 18, 2016. "Forschungszusammenarbeit mit der EU ist eingebrochen." *Neue Zürcher Zeitung.* www.nzz.ch/nzzas/nzz-am-sonntag/horizon-2020-forschungszusam menarbeit-mit-der-eu-ist-eingebrochen-ld.117359, accessed June 9, 2017.

Duncan, Fraser, and Steven van Hecke. 2008. "Immigration and the Transnational Centre-Right: A Common Programmatic Response?" *Journal of European Public Policy* 15 (3): 432–52.

Dungan, Peter, Tony Fang, and Morley Gunderson. 2012. "Macroeconomic Impacts of Canadian Immigration: Results from a Macro-Model." *IZA Discussion Paper Series* No. 6743.

Dyson, Jane. 1994. *The Reform Party of Canada: Immigration Policy and Leadership-Member Relations.* MA thesis in political science. Vancouver: Simon Fraser University.

Eichenberger, Pierre, and André Mach. 2011. "Organized Capital and Coordinated Market Economy: Swiss Business Interest Associations between Socio-economic Regulation and Political Influence." In *Switzerland in Europe: Continuity and Change in the Swiss Political Economy*, edited by Christine Trampusch and André Mach. Hoboken: Taylor and Francis.

Eidgenössische Kommission gegen Rassismus. 1996. Stellungsnahme der Eidgenössischen Kommission gegen Rassismus zum Drei-Kreise-Modell des Bundesrats über die schweizerische Ausländerpolitik Bern: Eidgenössische Kommission gegen Rassismus.

Eidgenössischer Bundesrat (March 26, 1924). Bundesblatt Nr. 13.

1991. "Bericht des Bundesrates zur Ausländer- und Flüchtlingspolitik vom 15. Mai 1991." *Bundesblatt* 3 (27): 291–323.

1992. Bericht über den Beitritt der Schweiz zum Internationalen Übereinkommen von 1965 zur Beseitigung von jeder Form von Rassendiskriminierung und über die entsprechende Strafrechtsrevision. Bern.

Eidgenössische Fremdenpolizei. December 28, 1950. "Letter to Dr. Heinrich Rothmund, E3/202, Saisonarbeiter Im Baugewerbe. Widerruf Von Aufenthaltsbewilligungen." Schweizerisches Bundesarchiv, E2001E 1967_113 Bd.368.

Eidgenössisches Justiz- und Polizeidepartement. December 12, 1956. Memorandum. Kreisschreiben an die Polizeidirektionen der Kantone. Schweizerisches Bundesarchiv. E2001 E1970_217 Bd 205.

2001. Neues Ausländergesetz: Ergebnis der Vernehmlassung (Zusammenfassung).

Eising, Rainer. 2007. "Institutional Context, Organizational Resources and Strategic Choices: Explaining Interest Group Access in the European Union." *European Union Politics* 8 (3): 329–62.

Ellermann, Antje. 2006. "Street-Level Democracy? How Immigration Bureaucrats Manage Public Opposition." *West European Politics* 29 (2): 287–303.

2008. "The Limits of Unilateral Migration Control: Deportation and Interstate Cooperation." *Government and Opposition* 43 (2): 168–89.

2009. *States against Migrants: Deportation in Germany and the United States*. New York: Cambridge University Press.

2013. "When Can Liberal States Avoid Unwanted Immigration? Self-limited Sovereignty and Guest Worker Recruitment in Switzerland and Germany." *World Politics* 65 (3): 491–538.

2015. "Do Policy Legacies Matter? Past and Present Guest Worker Recruitment in Germany." *Journal of Ethnic and Migration Studies* 41 (8): 1235–53.

2019. "Human-Capital Citizenship and the Changing Logic of Immigrant Admissions." *Journal of Ethnic and Migration Studies*: 1–18. http://doi:10.1080/1369183X.2018.1561062.

Elrick, Jennifer, and Elke Winter. 2018. "Managing the National Status Group: Immigration Policy in Germany." *International Migration* 56 (4): 19–32.

Employment and Immigration Canada. 1990. *Report on the Consultations on Immigration for 1991–95*. Ottawa: Employment and Immigration Canada.

1992. *Managing Immigration: A Framework for the 1990s*. Ottawa: Employment and Immigration Canada.

Esses, Victoria, Lynne Jackson, and Tamara Armstrong. 1998. "Intergroup Competition and Attitudes toward Immigrants and Immigration: An Instrumental Model of Group Conflict." *Journal of Social Issues* 54 (4): 699–724.

Ette, Andreas. 2003. *Germany's Immigration Policy, 2000–2002: Understanding Policy Change with a Political Process Approach Working Paper, Centre on Migration, Citizenship, and Development*. Bremen: COMCAD.

Eule, Tobias G. 2014. *Inside Immigration Law : Migration Management and Policy Application in Germany*. Abingdon: Routledge.

Evangelischer Pressedienst. February 20, 1973. "Proteste gegen die 'Rotation' von Gastarbeitern."

Fathali, Heather. 2013. "The American DREAM: DACA, DREAMers, and Comprehensive Immigration Reform." *Seattle University Law Review* 37 (221): 221–54.

Faist, Thomas. 2003. "Protecting Domestic vs. Foreign Workers: The German Experience during the 1990s." Center on Migration, Citizenship and Development Working Paper Series 1.

Faist, Thomas, Klaus Sieveking, Uwe Reim, and Stefan Sandbrink. 1999. *Ausland im Inland: Die Beschäftigung von Werkvertragsarbeitnehmern in der Bundesrepublik Deutschland*. Baden-Baden: Nomos.

Fassmann, Heinz, and Rainer Münz. 1994. "European East–West Migration, 1945–1992." *The International Migration Review* 28 (3): 520–38.

Favell, Adrian. 1998. *Philosophies of Integration: Immigration and the Idea of Citizenship in France and Britain*. Basingstoke: Macmillan Press.

Felicity, Tan. 2014. "Immigration Policy Narratives and the Politics of Identity: Causal Issue Frames in the Discursive Construction of America's Social Borders." London School of Economics and Political Science.

Fetzer, Joel S. 2000. *Public Attitudes toward Immigration in the United States, France, and Germany*. New York: Cambridge University Press.

2006. "Why Did House Members Vote for H.R. 4437?" *International Migration Review* 40 (3): 698–706.

Fischer, Alex. 2002. "Wirtschaftsbranche, Gewerkschaftsstärke und Interessengegensätze der Arbeitgeber: Der Fall der flankierenden Massnahmen zur Personenfreizügigkeit." *Schweizerische Zeitschrift für Politikwissenschaft* 8 (3): 85–100.

2003a. "Die Schweizer Gewerkschaften und die Europäisierung helvetischer Politik." *Österreichische Zeitschrift für Politikwissenschaft* 32 (3): 303–20.

2003b. "Vetospieler und die Durchsetzbarkeit von Side-Payments: Der schweizerische innenpolitische Entscheidungsprozess um flankierende Massnahmen zur Personenfreizügigkeit mit der Europäischen Union." *Swiss Political Science Review* 9 (2): 27–58.

Fischer, Alex, Sarah Nicolet, and Pascal Sciarini. 2002. "Europeanisation of a Non-EU Country: The Case of Swiss Immigration Policy." *West European Politics* 25 (4): 143–70.

Fitzgerald, David Scott, and David Cook-Martín. 2014. *Culling the Masses: The Democratic Origins of Racist Immigration Policy in the Americas.* Cambridge, MA: Harvard University Press.

Fogleman, Carlie, and Paul M. Kellstedt. 2012. Unpublished paper, University of Oxford.

Ford, Robert. 2011. "Acceptable and Unacceptable Immigrants: How Opposition to Immigration in Britain Is Affected by Migrants' Region of Origin." *Journal of Ethnic and Migration Studies* 37: 1017–37.

Frankfurter Rundschau. December 20, 1954. "Storch: Kein Facharbeitermangel. Ausländische Arbeitskräfte Sollen Nicht vor 1957 Kommen."

February 27, 1961. "Mit Kind und Kegel ins Ruhrgebiet: Ausländische Bergleute holen nach einjähriger Trennung ihre Familien nach."

December 29, 1966. "Gewerkschaft nimmt Gastarbeiter in Schutz."

Freeman, Gary P. 1994. "Can Liberal States Control Unwanted Migration?" *The Annals of The American Academy of Political and Social Science* 534: 17–30.

1995. "Modes of Immigration Politics in Liberal Democratic States." *International Migration Review* 29 (4): 881–913.

2005. "Political Science and Comparative Immigration Politics." In *Reflections on Migration Research*, edited by Michael Bommes and Ewa Morawska, 111–28. Aldershot: Ashgate.

Freeman, Gary, David L. Leal, and Jake Onyett. 2013. "Pointless: On the Failure to Adopt an Immigration Points System in the United States." In *Wanted and Welcome? Policies for Highly Skilled Immigrants in Comparative Perspective*, edited by Triadafilos Triadafilopoulos, 123–43. New York: Springer.

Freeman, Linda. 1997. *The Ambigious Champion: Canada and South Africa in the Trudeau and Mulroney Years.* Toronto: University of Toronto Press.

Frenette, Marc, and René Morissette. 2003. "Will They Ever Converge? Earnings of Immigrant and Canadian-Born Workers over the Last Two Decades." *Analytical Studies Branch Research Paper Series, Statistics Canada*: Catalogue Number 11F0019MIE No. 215.

Fuchs, Lawrence H. 1980. "The Select Commission on Immigration and Refugee Policy: Development of a Fundamental Legislative Policy." *Willamette Law Review* 17: 141–50.

Fudge, Judy, and Fiona MacPhail. 2009. "The Temporary Foreign Worker Program in Canada: Low-Skilled Workers as an Extreme Form of Flexible Labour." *Comparative Labor Law and Policy Journal* 31: 101–39.

Gabaccia, Donna R. 2010. "Nations of Immigrants: Do Words Matter?" *The Pluralist* 5 (3): 5–31.

Gallup. n.d. *Immigration*. https://news.gallup.com/poll/1660/immigration.aspx, accessed September 25, 2020.

Gaouette, Nicole. September 30, 2006. "Border Barrier Approved." *Los Angeles Times*.

Geddes, Andrew. 2000. "Lobbying for Migrant Inclusion in the European Union: New Opportunities for Transnational Advocacy?" *Journal of European Public Policy* 7 (4): 632–49.

Gillon, Steven M. 2000. *That's Not What We Meant to Do: Reform and Its Unintended Consequences in 20th Century America*. New York: W.W. Norton.

February 2, 2018. "Neither Congress Nor the White House Had Carefully Analyzed the Potential Impact of the Family Preference System." *History Reads*. www.history.com/news/1965-immigration-policy-lyndon-johnson, accessed April 2, 2018.

Gimpel, James G., and James R. Edwards. 1999. *The Congressional Politics of Immigration Reform*. Boston, MA: Allyn and Bacon.

Givens, Terri, and Adam Luedtke. 2005. "European Immigration Policies in Comparative Perspective: Issue Salience, Partisanship and Immigrant Rights." *Comparative European Politics* 3 (1): 1–22.

Gmür, Heidi, and Simon Gemperli. April 16, 2016. "Die Umsetzung der Zuwanderungsinitiative verzögert sich: Eine Referendumsabstimmung kann frühestens im Mai 2017 stattfinden." *Neue Zürcher Zeitung*.

Goodman, Sara Wallace. 2011. "Controlling Immigration through Language and Country Knowledge Requirements." *West European Politics* 34 (2): 235–55.

2014. *Immigration and Membership Politics in Western Europe*. Cambridge: Cambridge University Press.

Graham, John. 2010. *Bush on the Home Front: Domestic Policy Triumphs and Setbacks*. Bloomington: Indiana University Press.

2016. *Obama on the Home Front: Domestic Policy Triumphs and Setbacks* Bloomington: Indiana University Press.

Graham, Jr., Otis. L. 2005. "A Vast Social Experiment: The Immigration Act of 1965." *NPG Forum* 106: 1–8.

Green-Pedersen, Christoffer, and Jesper Krogstrup. 2008. "Immigration as a Political Issue in Denmark and Sweden." *European Journal of Political Research* 47 (5): 610–34.

Green, Alan G., and David A. Green. 1999. "The Economic Goals of Canada's Immigration Policy: Past and Present." *Canadian Public Policy* 25: 425–51.

Green, David A., and Christopher Worswick. 2012. "Immigrant Earnings Profiles in the Presence of Human Capital Investment: Measuring Cohort and Macro Effects." *Labor Economics* 19 (2): 241–59.

Green, Simon. 2004. *The Politics of Exclusion: Institutions and Immigration Policy in Contemporary Germany*. Manchester: Manchester University Press.

Greenhill, Kelly M. 2011. *Weapons of Mass Migration: Forced Displacement, Coercion, and Foreign Policy*. Ithaca, NY: Cornell University Press.

Greifenstein, Ralph. 2001. *Die Green Card: Ambitionen, Fakten und Zukunftsaussichten des deutschen Modellversuchs*. Bonn: Friedrich-Ebert-Stiftung.

Groenendijk, Kees. 2011. "Pre-Departure Integration Strategies in the European Union: Integration or Immigration Policy?" *European Journal of Migration and Law* 13 (1): 1–30.

Gudbrandsen, Føy. 2010. "Partisan Influence on Immigration: The Case of Norway." *Scandinavian Political Studies* 33 (3): 248–70.

Guiraudon, Virginie. 2000a. "European Courts and Foreigners' Rights: A Comparative Study of Norms Diffusion." *International Migration Review* 34 (4): 1088–125.

2000b. "European Integration and Migration Policy: Vertical Policy-Making as Venue Shopping." *Journal of Common Market Studies* 38 (2): 251–71.

Guiraudon, Virginie, and Gallya Lahav. 2000. "A Reappraisal of the State Sovereignty Debate: The Case of Migration Control." *Comparative Political Studies* 33 (2): 163–95.

Hainmueller, Jens, and Daniel J. Hopkins. 2012. "The Hidden American Immigration Consensus: A Conjoint Analysis of Attitudes toward Immigrants." SSRN Working Paper 2106116.

2014. "Public Attitudes toward Immigration." *Annual Review of Political Science* 17 (1): 225–49.

Hainmueller, Jens, and Dominik Hangartner. 2013. "Who Gets a Swiss Passport? A Natural Experiment in Immigrant Discrimination." *American Political Science Review* 107 (1): 159–87.

Hainmueller, Jens, and Michael J. Hiscox. 2010. "Attitudes toward Highly Skilled and Low-Skilled Immigration: Evidence from a Survey Experiment." *American Political Science Review* 104 (1): 61–84.

Hall, Peter A. 1993. "Policy Paradigms, Social Learning, and the State: The Case of Economic Policymaking in Britain." *Comparative Politics* 25 (3): 275–96.

Hall, Peter A., and Rosemary C. R. Taylor. 1996. "Political Science and the Three New Institutionalisms." *Political Studies* 44 (5): 936–57.

Hampshire, James. 2013. *The Politics of Immigration: Contradictions of the Liberal State*. Cambridge: Polity.

Harell, Allison. 2009. "Minority-Majority Relations in Canada: The Rights Regime and the Adoption of Multicultural Values." Annual Meeting of the Canadian Political Science Association, Ottawa.

Harell, Allison, Stewart Suroka, Shanto Iyengar, and Nicholas Valentino. 2012. "The Impact of Economic and Cultural Cues on Support for Immigration in Canada and the United States." *Canadian Journal of Political Science* 45 (3): 499–530.

Hawkins, Freda. 1977. "Canadian Immigration: Present Policies, Future Options." *The Round Table: The Commonwealth of International Affairs* 265: 50–63.

1988. *Canada and Immigration: Public Policy and Public Concern.* 2nd ed. Montreal: McGill-Queen's University Press.

1991. *Critical Years in Immigration: Canada and Australia Compared.* 2nd ed. Kingston, ON: McGill-Queen's University Press.

Heclo, Hugh. 1974. *Modern Social Politics in Britain and Sweden: From Relief to Income Maintenance.* Princeton, NJ: Princeton University Press.

Helbling, Marc. 2011. "Why Swiss-Germans Dislike Germans." *European Societies* 13 (1): 5–27.

Helbling, Marc, and David Leblang. 2019. "Controlling Immigration? How Regulations Affect Migration Flows." *European Journal of Political Research* 58 (1): 248–69.

Hell, Matthias. 2005. *Einwanderungsland Deutschland? Die Zuwanderungsdiskussion 1998–2002.* Wiesbaden: VS Verlag für Sozialwissenschaften.

Herbert, Ulrich. 1991. *A History of Foreign Labor in Germany, 1880–1980: Seasonal Workers/Forced Laborers/Guest Workers.* Ann Arbor: University of Michigan Press.

2001. *Geschichte der Ausländerpolitik in Deutschland: Saisonarbeiter, Zwangsarbeiter, Gastarbeiter, Flüchtlinge.* München: C.H. Beck.

Hiebert, Daniel. 2006. "Winning, Losing, and Still Playing the Game: The Political Economy of Immigration in Canada." *Tijdschrift voor Economische en Sociale Geografie* 97 (1): 38–48.

Higham, John. 1955. *Strangers in the Land: Patterns of American Nativism, 1860–1925.* Rutgers: Rutgers University Press.

Hinnfors, Jonas, Andreas Spehar, and Gregg Bucken-Knapp. 2012. "The Missing Factor: Why Social Democracy Can Lead to Restrictive Immigration Policy." *Journal of European Public Policy* 19 (4): 585–603.

Hix, Simon, and Abdul Noury. 2007. "Politics, Not Economic Interests: Determinants of Migration Policies in the European Union." *International Migration Review* 41 (1): 182–205.

Hollifield, James F. 1992. *Immigrants, Markets, and States.* Cambridge, MA: Harvard University Press.

Hollifield, James F., Philip L. Martin, and Pia M. Orrenius, eds. 2014. *Controlling Immigration: A Global Perspective.* 3rd ed. Stanford: Stanford University Press.

Holyoke, Thomas T. 2004. "By Invitation Only: Interest Group Access to the Oval Office." *The American Review of Politics* 25 (Fall): 221–40.

Howard, Marc M. 2006. "Comparative Citizenship: An Agenda for Cross-National Research." *Perspectives on Politics* 4 (3): 443–55.

Howlett, Michael, and Benjamin Cashore. 2009. "The Dependent Variable Problem in the Study of Policy Change: Understanding Policy Change as a Methodological Problem." *Journal of Comparative Policy Analysis: Research and Practice* 11 (1): 33–46.

Hunn, Karin. 2005. *Nächstes Jahr kehren wir zurück ... Die Geschichte der türkischen "Gastarbeiter" in der Bundesrepublik.* Göttingen: Wallstein.

Hutchinson, Edward P. 1981. *Legislative History of American Immigration Policy, 1798–1965.* Philadelphia: University of Philadelphia Press.

Huysmans, Jef. 1998. "Security! What Do You Mean? From Concept to Thick Signifier." *European Journal of International Relations* 4 (2): 226–55.

2000. "The European Union and the Securitization of Migration." *Journal of Common Market Studies* 38 (5): 751–77.

2006. The Politics of Insecurity: Fear, Migration and Asylum in the EU. London: Routledge.

IDEA. 2014. *Funding of Political Parties and Election Campaigns: A Handbook on Political Finance.* Stockholm: International Institute for Democracy and Electoral Assistance.

Imhof, Kurt. November 6, 2008. *Die Schweiz wird Deutsch! In " … und es kommen Frauen," Symposium vom 6. November 2008 in Zürich.* Stadt Zürich: Fachstelle für Gleichstellung.

Immergut, Ellen M. 1990. "Institutions, Veto Points, and Policy Results: A Comparative Analysis of Health Care." *Journal of Public Policy* 10 (4): 391–416.

1992. *Health Politics: Interests and Institutions in Western Europe, Cambridge Series in Comparative Politics.* Cambridge: Cambridge University Press.

Immigration, Refugees and Citizenship Canada. January 11, 2019. "New and Improved Intake Process for Sponsorship of Parents and Grandparents to Launch on January 28, 2019." *News Release.*

iPolitics. April 30, 2018. "Feds Working with Washington to Stop Nigerians Using U.S. Visas as Ticket to Canada."

Iyengar, Shanto, Simon Jackman, Solomon Messing, Nicholas Valentino, Toril Aalberg, Raymond Duch, Kyu S. Hahn, Stewart Soroka, Allison Harell, and Tetsuro Kobayashi. 2013. "Do Attitudes about Immigration Predict Willingness to Admit Individual Immigrants?: A Cross-National Test of the Person-Positivity Bias." *Public Opinion Quarterly* 77 (3): 641–65.

Jacob, Walter. 1992. "Diversity Visas: Muddled Thinking and Pork Barrell Politics." *Georgetown Immigration Law Journal* 6 (2): 297–343.

Jacobs, Alan M. 2009. "How Do Ideas Matter? Mental Models and Attention in German Pension Politics." *Comparative Political Studies* 42 (2): 252–79.

Jacobson, David. 1996. *Rights across Borders: Immigration and the Decline of Citizenship.* Boston, MA: Johns Hopkins University Press.

Jacobson, Gary C. 2012. *The Politics of Congressional Elections.* 8th ed. New York: Pearson.

Jacobson, Louis. November 16, 2005. "Immigration Is Poised to Become a Hot Topic for 2006 Races." *Roll Call.*

Jetten, Jolanda, Russell Spears, and Antony S. R. Manstead. 1998. "Defining Dimensions of Distinctiveness: Group Variability Makes a Difference to Differentiation." *Journal of Personality and Social Psychology* 74 (6): 1481–92.

Jochem, Sven. 2003. "Veto Players or Veto Points? The Politics of Welfare State Reforms in Europe." Presented at the Annual Meeting of the American Political Science Association, Philadelphia, August 28–31, 2003.

Johannesson, Livia. 2018. "Exploring the 'Liberal Paradox' from the Inside: Evidence from the Swedish Migration Courts." *International Migration Review* 52 (4): 1162–85.

Johnson, Lyndon Baines. January 8, 1964. "First State of the Union Address." *American Rhetoric Online Speech Bank*. www.americanrhetoric.com/speeches/lbj1964stateoftheunion.htm, accessed September 26, 2020.

October 3, 1965. "Remarks at the Signing of the Immigration Bill, Liberty Island, New York." *American Presidency Project*. www.presidency.ucsb.edu/ws/index.php?pid=27292, accessed September 26, 2020.

Joppke, Christian. 1998a. *Challenge to the Nation-State: Immigration in Western Europe and the United States*. New York: Oxford University Press.

1998b. "Why Liberal States Accept Unwanted Immigration." *World Politics* 50 (2): 266–93.

1999. *Immigration and the Nation-State: The United States, Germany, and Great Britain*. Oxford: Oxford University Press.

2001. "The Legal-Domestic Sources of Immigrant Rights: The United States, Germany, and the European Union." *Comparative Political Studies* 34 (4): 339–66.

Jurgens, Jeffrey. 2010. "The Legacies of Labor Recruitment: The Guest Worker and Green Card Programs in the Federal Republic of Germany." *Policy and Society* 29: 345–55.

Kalla, Joshua L., and David E. Broockman. 2016. "Campaign Contributions Facilitate Access to Congressional Officials: A Randomized Field Experiment." *American Journal of Political Science* 60 (3): 545–58.

Kaltefleiter, Werner. 1970. "The Impact of the Election of 1969 and the Formation of the New Government on the German Party System." *Comparative Politics* 2 (4): 593–60.

Katzenstein, Peter J. 1987a. Corporatism and Change: Austria, Switzerland, and the Politics of Industry. Ithaca, NY: Cornell University Press

1987b. *Policy and Politics in West Germany: The Growth of a Semisovereign State*. Philadelphia: Temple University Press.

Kaunert, Christian, and Sarah Léonard. 2012. "The Development of the EU Asylum Policy: Venue-Shopping in Perspective." *Journal of European Public Policy* 19 (9): 1396–413.

Kearns Goodwin, Doris. 1991. *Lyndon Johnson and the American Dream*. 8th ed. New York: St. Martin's Griffin.

Kelley, Ninette, and Michael Trebilcock. 1998. *The Making of the Mosaic: A History of Canadian Immigration Policy*. Toronto: University of Toronto Press.

Kelsen, Hans. 1928. "La Garantie Jurisdictionell de la Constitution." *Revue de Droit Public* 44: 197–257.

Kennedy, Edward M. 1966. "The Immigration Act of 1965." *The Annals of the American Academy of Political and Social Science* 367 (1): 137–49.

Kennedy, John F. 1964. *A Nation of Immigrants*. New York City: Harper Collins.

Kent, Tom. 1988. *A Public Purpose: An Experience of Liberal Opposition and Canadian Government*. Kingston and Montreal: McGill-Queen's University Press.

Kessler, Alan, and Gary Freeman. 2005. "Public Opinion in the EU on Immigration from Outside the Community." *Journal of Common Market Studies* 43 (4): 825–50.

Keung, Nicholas. April 25, 2008. "Support for Foreign Worker Program Waning." *Toronto Star*, A23.

Khan, Mohsin Hassan Khan, Hamedi Mohd Adnan Adnan, Surinderpal Kaur, Rashid Ali Khuhro Khuhro, Rohail Asghar, and Sahira Jabeen. 2019. "Muslims' Representation in Donald Trump's Anti-Muslim-Islam Statement: A Critical Discourse Analysis." *Religions* 10 (2). http://doi:www.mdpi.com/2077-1444/10/2/115.

Knopf, Jeffrey W. 1993. "Beyond Two-Level Games: Domestic-International Interaction in the Intermediate-Range Nuclear Forces Negotiations." *International Organization* 47 (4): 599–628.

Knortz, Heike. 2008. *Diplomatische Tauschgeschäfte: Gastarbeiter in der Westdeutschen Diplomatie und Beschäftigungspolitik 1953–1973.* Köln: Böhlau.

Knowles, Valerie. 2007. *Strangers at Our Gates: Canadia Immigration and Immigration Policy, 1540–2006.* Toronto, ON: Dundurn Press.

Kolb, Holger. 2003a. "Die 'gap-Hypothese' in der Migrationsforschung und das Analysepotential der Politikwissenschaft: eine Diskussion am Beispiel der deutschen 'Green Card'." In *Die deutsche "Green Card": Migration von Hochqualifizierten in theoretischer und empirischer Perspektive*, edited by Uwe Hunger and Holger Kolb, 13–38. Osnabrück: IMIS.

— 2003b. "Ein Jahr "Green Card" in Deutschland." In *Migration im Wettbewerbsstaat*, edited by Uwe Hunger and Bernhard Santel, 153–68. Opladen: Leske & Budrich.

trun Kolb, Holger, and Uwe Hunger. 2003. "Von Staatlicher Ausländerbeschäftigungspolitik Zu Internationalen Personalwertschöpfungsketten." *WSI Mitteilungen* 4: 251–6.

Koopmans, Ruud. 2007. "Good Intentions Sometimes Make Bad Policy: A Comparison of Dutch and German Integration Policies." In *Migration, Multiculturalism, and Civil Society*, edited by Friedrich-Ebert-Stiftung, 163–8. Berlin: Friedrich-Ebert-Stiftung.

Köppe, Olaf 2002. MigrantInnen zwischen sozialem Rechtsstaat und nationalem Wettbewerbsstaat. Unpublished dissertation, Gerhard-Mercator–Universität-Duisburg.

Koven, Steven G., and Frank Götzke. 2010. *American Immigration Policy: Confronting the Nation's Challenges.* New York: Springer.

Krause, Christina 2004. *Neue Zuwanderungspolitik? Entwicklungen in der 14. Legislaturperiode in Deutschland.* Kiel: Christian-Albrechts-Universität. Dissertation.

Krehbiel, Keith. 1996. "Institutional and Partisan Source of Gridlock: A Theory of Divided and Unified Government." *Journal of Theoretical Politics* 8: 7–40.

Kriesi, Hanspeter. 1982. "The Structure of the Swiss Political System." In *Patterns of Corporatist Policymaking*, edited by Gerhard Lehmbruch and Philippe C. Schmitter. London: Sage.

— 2001. "The Federal Parliament: The Limits of Institutional Reform." *West European Politics* 24 (2): 59–76.

Kriesi, Hanspeter, Romain Lachat, Martin Dolezal, and Timotheos Frey. 2008. *West European Politics in the Age of Globalization.* Cambridge: Cambridge University Press.

Kruse, Imke, Henry Edward Orren, and Steffen Angenendt. 2003. "The Failure of Immigration Reform in Germany." *German Politics* 12 (3): 129–45.

Kuhn, Thomas S. 1970. *The Structure of Scientific Revolutions*. 2nd ed. Chicago: University of Chicago Press.

Kustec, Stan. 2006. "Family versus Individual Immigration: A New Analytical Perspective." Canadian Issues Spring: 17–20.

2012. *The Role of Migrant Labour Supply in the Canadian Labour Market*. CIC Research and Evaluation. Ottawa: Citizenship and Immigration Canada.

Kymlicka, Will. 2003. "Canadian Multiculturalism in Historical and Comparative Perspective: Is Canada Unique?" *Constitutional Forum* 13 (1): 1–8.

Lachat, Romain, Georg Lutz, and Isabelle Stadelmann-Steffen. 2014. "The 2011 Swiss Elections: Introduction." *Swiss Political Science Review* 20 (4): 515–19.

Lahav, Gallya. 2004. *Immigration and Politics in the New Europe: Reinventing Borders*. Cambridge: Cambridge University Press.

Lahav, Gallya, and Adam Luedtke. 2013. "Immigration Policy." In *The Europeanization of European Politics*, edited by Charlotte Bretherton and Michael Mannin, 109–22. Houndmills: Palgrave Macmillan.

Lam, Livia. 2015. *A Case of Racialization and Immigration Policy: Conceptualizing Interest Group Theory*. Unpublished dissertation, The New School.

Larres, Klaus, and Panikos Panayi. 2014. *The Federal Republic of Germany since 1949: Politics, Society and Economy before and after Unification*. Abingdon: Routledge.

Lauren, Paul Gordon. 1996. *Power and Prejudice: The Politics and Diplomacy of Racial Discrimination*. Boulder, CO: Westview Press.

LaViolette, Nicole. 2004. "Coming out to Canada: The Immigration of Same-Sex Couples under the Immigration and Refugee Protection Act." *McGill Law Journal* 49: 969.

Leal, David L. 2009. "Stalemate: U.S. Immigration Reform Efforts, 2005 to 2007." *People & Place* 17 (3): 1–17.

Lee, Catherine. 2015. "Family Reunification and the Limits of Immigration Reform: Impact and Legacy of the 1965 Immigration Act." *Sociological Forum* 30 (1): 528–48.

Lee, Yueh-Tink, and Victor Ottati. 2002. "Attitudes toward U.S. Immigration Policy: The Roles of In-Group Out-Group Bias, Economic Concern and Obedience to Law." *Journal of Social Psychology* 142 (5): 617–34.

Legislative Review Advisory Group. 1997. *Not Just Numbers: A Canadian Framework for Future Immigration*. Ottawa: Minister of Public Works and Government Services Canada.

Legomsky, Stephen H. 1995. "The Making of United States Refugee Policy: Separation of Powers in the Post-Cold War Era." *Washington Law Review* 70 (3): 675–714.

Lewis, Jeffrey. 2012. "Council of Ministers and European Council." In *The Oxford Handbook of the European Union*, edited by Erik Jones, Anand Menon and Stephen Weatherill. Oxford: Oxford University Press.

Light, Paul. 1999. *The President's Agenda*. Baltimore: Johns Hopkins University Press.

Lindblom, Charles. 1977. *Politics and Markets: The World's Political Economic Systems*. New York: Basic Books.

Linder, Wolf. 2005. *Schweizerische Demokratie: Institutionen, Prozesse, Perspektiven*. 2nd ed. Bern: Haupt.

——. 2009. "Das Politische System der Schweiz." In *Die Politischen Systeme Westeuropas*, edited by Wolfgang Ismayr, 567–605. Wiesbaden: VS Verlag für Sozialwisschenschaften.

——. 2010. *Swiss Democracy: Possible Solutions to Conflict in Multicultural Societies*. 3rd ed. New York: Palgrave Macmillan.

——. 2011. "Europe and Switzerland: Europeanization without EU Membership." In *Switzerland in Europe: Continuity and Change in the Swiss Political Economy*, edited by Christine Trampusch and André March. Oxford: Routledge.

Lucassen, Leo. 2001. "A Many-Headed Monster: The Evolution of the Passport System in the Netherlands and Germany in the Long Nineteenth Century." In *Documenting Individual Identity: The Development of State Practices in the Modern World*, edited by Jane Caplan and John Torpey, 235–55. Princeton: Princeton University Press.

Luedtke, Adam. 2011. "Uncovering European Union Immigration Legislation: Policy Dynamics and Outcomes." *International Migration* 49 (2): 1–27.

Magaña, Lisa. 2003. *Straddling the Border: Immigration Policy and the INS*. Austin, TX: University of Texas Press.

Mahnig, Hans. 2005. "La politique migratoire du milieu des années 1980 jusqu'à 1998." In *Histoire de la politique de migration, d'asile at d'integration en Suisse depuis 1948*, edited by Hans Mahnig, 160–88. Zürich: Seismo.

Mahnig, Hans, and Andreas Wimmer. 2003. "Integration without Immigrant Policy: The Case of Switzerland." In *The Integration of Immigrants in European Societies: National Differences and Trends of Convergence*, edited by Friedrich Heckmann and Dominique Schnapper, 135–60. Stuttgart: Lucius & Lucius.

Mahnig, Hans, and Etienne Piguet. 2004. "Die Immigrationspolitik der Schweiz von 1948–1998." In *Migration und die Schweiz*, edited by Hans-Rudolf Wicker, Rosita Fibbi, and Werner Haug, 63–103. Zürich: Seismo.

Mahony, James. 2000. "Path Dependence in Historical Sociology." *Theory and Society* 29 (4): 507–48.

Manning, Bayless. 1977. "The Congress, the Executive and Intermestic Affairs : Three Proposals." *Foreign Affairs* 55: 306–24.

Marinari, Maddalena. 2014. "'Americans Must Show Justice in Immigration Policies Too': The Passage of the 1965 Immigration Act." *Journal of Policy History* 26 (2): 219–45.

——. 2016. "Divided and Conquered: Immigration Reform Advocates and the Passage of the 1952 Immigration and Nationality Act." *Journal of American Ethnic History* 35 (3): 9–40.

Marshall, Serena. August 29, 2016. "Obama Has Deported More People Than Any Other President." *abcNews*.

Marthaler, Sally. 2008. "Nicolas Sarkozy and the Politics of French Immigration Policy." *Journal of European Public Policy* 15 (3): 382–97.

Marwah, Inder, Triadafilos Triadafilopoulos, and Stephen White. 2013. "Immigration, Citizenship and Canada's New Conservative Party." In *Canadian Conservatism in Comparative Context*, edited by James Farney and David Rayside, 95–119. Toronto, ON: University of Toronto Press.

Mas, Susana. January 8, 2016. "Canada Will Take 10,000 Parent, Grandparent Sponsorship Applications This Year." *CBC*. www.cbc.ca/news/politics/canada-will-take-in-10–000-parent-grandparent-sponsorship-applications-this-year-1.3396179, accessed September 26, 2020.

Maurer, Peter. February 7, 2016. "Umsetzung der Zuwanderungs-Initiative – Was Bisher Geschah." *SRF Schweizer Radio und Fernsehen*, www.srf.ch/news/schweiz/umsetzung-der-zuwanderung-initiative-was-bisher-geschah, accessed September 26, 2020.

Maxwell, Rahsaan. 2019. "Cosmopolitan Immigration Attitudes in Large European Cities: Contextual or Compositional Effects?" *American Political Science Review* 113 (2): 456–74.

May, Peter J. 1992. "Policy Learning and Failure." *Journal of Public Policy* 12 (4): 331–54.

Mazzoleni, Oscar. 2013. "The Swiss People's Party and the Foreign and Security Policy since the 1990s." In *Europe for the Europeans: The Foreign and Security Policy of the Populist Radical Right*, edited by Christina Schori Liang, 223–38. Farnham: Ashgate.

McLaren, Lauren, and Mark Johnson. 2007. "Group Conflict and Symbols: Explaining Anti-immigration Hostility in Britain." *Political Studies* 55 (4): 709–32.

Meckler, Laura. September 4, 2013. "House GOP Puts Immigration Reform on the Backburner." *Wall Street Journal*.

Meguid, Bonnie. 2008. *Party Competition between Unequals: Strategies and Electoral Fortunes in Western Europe*. Cambridge: Cambridge University Press.

Meier-Braun, Karl-Heinz. 1988. *Integration und Rückkehr?* München: Grünewald.

2002. *Deutschland, Einwanderungsland*. Frankfurt am Main: Suhrkamp.

Menz, Georg. 2008. *The Political Economy of Managed Migration: Nonstate Actors, Europeanization, and the Politics of Designing Migration Policies*. Oxford: Oxford University Press.

Messina, Anthony M. 2007. *The Logics and Politics of Post-WWII Migration to Western Europe*. New York: Cambridge University Press.

Meuleman, Bart, Eldad Davidov, and Jaak Billiet. 2009. "Changing Attitudes toward Immigration in Europe, 2002–2007: A Dynamic Group Conflict Theory Approach." *Social Science Research* 38 (2): 352–65.

Meyer, Anneke. June 20, 2016. "Zugang zu EU-Forschungsprogramm auf der Kippe." *Deutschlandfunk*. Zugang zu EU-Forschungsprogramm auf der Kippe.

Migration Policy Institute. 2007. "How Changes to Family Immigration Could Affect Source Countries' Sending Patterns." *Migration Facts* 18: 1–12.

Milic, Thomas. 2015. "'For They Knew What They Did': What Swiss Voters Did (Not) Know about the Mass Immigration Initiative." *Swiss Political Science Review* 21 (1): 48–62.

Milkis, Sidney. 1993. *The Presidents and the Parties.* New York: Oxford University Press.

Minister of Manpower and Immigration. 1974. "Canadian Immigration and Population Study." Immigration Policy Perspectives 1. Ottawa: Canada Department of Manpower and Immigration.

Moe, Terry M., and Scott Wilson. 1994. "Presidents and the Politics of Structure." *Law and Contemporary Problems* 57 (2): 1–44.

Montreal Gazette. October 6, 1993. "Not Much Light Shed."

Murphy, Joseph P., and Thomas J. Espenshade. 1990. "Immigration's Prism: Historical Continuities in the Kennedy–Simpson Legal Immigration Reform Bill." *Population and Environment* 12 (2): 139.

Neue Rhein-Ruhr-Zeitung. December 15, 1966. "Figgen: Verträge der Gastarbeiter überprüfen."

Neue Zürcher Zeitung. November 13, 1946. "Ausländische Arbeitskräfte und Überfremdung."

December 22, 1955. "Italienische Arbeiter für Westdeutschland."

November 21, 1960. "Der Aufenthalt Ausländischer Arbeitskräfte."

May 7, 2004. "Sturmlauf für billige Land- und Bauarbeiter."

February 2018, 2015. "Masseineinwanderungsinitiative: Bundesrat und SVP vollziehen Kehrtwende."

May 4, 2016. "Bilaterale vor Zuwanderungsinitiative."

May 23, 2016. "Mehr Rückhalt für bilaterale Verträge."

June 11, 2016. "EU-Kommissarin dämpft Hoffnungen; Inländervorrang 'nicht möglich'."

December 5, 2016. "Nationalrat beschliesst 'Inländervorrang mittelscharf'."

March 2, 2017. "Referendum dürfte scheitern."

April 27, 2017. "Rasa-Initiative ohne Gegenentwurf: Der Bundesrat vollzieht eine Kehrtwende."

New York Times. January 12, 1964. "Judge Smith Moves with Deliberate Drag: The Powerful Chairman of the House Rules Committee Is in No Hurry to Push Civil Rights."

January 30, 2014. "Text of Republicans' Principles on Immigration."

Newton-Small, Jay. June 11, 2013. "Immigration Reform Q&A with Senator Lindsey Graham." *TIME Magazine.* http://swampland.time.com/2013/06/11/immigration-reform-qa-with-senator-lindsey-graham/, accessed August 26, 2019.

Niederberger, Josef Martin. 1982. "Die politisch-administrative Regelung von Einwanderung und Aufenthalt von Ausländern in der Schweiz : Strukturen, Prozesse, Wirkungen." In *Ausländer in der Bundesrepublik Deutschland und in der Schweiz: Segregation und Integration,* edited by Hans-Joachim Hoffmann-Nowotny and Karl-Otto Hondrich, 11–123. Frankfurt am Main: Campus Verlag.

Niehr, Thomas. 2004. *Der Streit um Migration in der Bundesrepublik Deutschland, der Schweiz und Österreich: Eine vergleichende diskursgeschichtliche Untersuchung.* Heidelberg: Winter.

Noorani, Ali. 2007. "Race, Class, and the Emergence of an Immigrant Rights Movement." *The Fletcher Forum of World Affairs* 31 (1): 185–202.

Nord, Douglas C. 1980. "MPs and Senators as Middlemen: The Special Joint Committee on Immigration Policy." In *Parliament, Policy and Representation*, edited by Harold D. Clarke, Colin Campbell, F. Q. Quo, and Arthur Goddard, 181–92. Toronto: Methuen.

Nuspliger, Niklaus. February 17, 2014. "Barroso markiert Härte." *Neue Zürcher Zeitung*.

O'Connell, Michael. 2011. "How Do High-Skilled Natives View High-Skilled Immigrants: Trade Theory Predictions." *European Journal of Political Economy* 27 (2): 230–40.

Oltmer, Jochen. 2005. *Migration and Politik in der Weimarer Republik*. Göttingen: Vandenhoeck & Ruprecht.

Omidvar, Ratna. May 20, 2013. "Temporary Immigrants Mean Temporary Loyalties." *Globe and Mail*

2016. "The Harper Influence on Immigration." In *The Harper Factor: Assessing a Prime Minister's Policy Legacy*, edited by Jennifer Ditchburn and Graham Fox, 179–95. Montreal: McGill-Queen's University Press.

Ornstein, Norm. June 3, 2015. "This Isn't Dennis Hastert's First Scandal." *The Atlantic*.

Pagenstecher, Cord. 1993. *Rotationsprinzip und Rückkehrorientierung im Einwanderungsprozess: Gastarbeit in der Bundesrepublik Deutschland*. MA thesis, Freie Universität Berlin.

Palan, Ronen, Jason Abbot, and Phil Deans. 1996. London: Pinter.

Palmer, Douglas L. 1996. "Determinants of Canadian Attitudes toward Immigration: More Than Just Racism?" *Canadian Journal of Behavioural Science* 28 (3): 180–92.

Papadopoulos, Yannis. 2013. "How Does Direct Democracy Matter? The Impact of Referendum Votes on Politics and Policy-Making." In *The Swiss Labyrinth: Institutions, Outcomes and Redesign*, edited by Jan-Erik Lane, 25–58. New York: Routledge.

Paperny, Anna Mehler. April 5, 2012. "Jason Kenney Wants to 'Stop the Madness' in Immigration System." *Globe and Mail*.

Paquet, Mireille. 2015. "Bureaucrats as Immigration Policy-Makers: The Case of Subnational Immigration Activism in Canada, 1990–2010." *Journal of Ethnic and Migration Studies* 41 (11): 1815–35.

2016. *La Fédéralisation de l'Immigration au Canada*. Montréal: Les Presses de l'Université de Montréal.

Parai, Louis. 1975. "Canada's Immigration Policy: 1962–1974." *International Migration Review* 9 (4): 449–77.

Parker, Ashley. April 22, 2013. "Heated Questions and Divisions Emerge at Immigration Bill Hearing." *New York Times*.

Parliament of Canada. 1955. *House of Commons Debates* 2.

April 15, 1959. *House of Commons Debates* 3.

January 19, 1962. "The Minister of Citizenship and Immigration, the Hon. Ellen Fairclough, Tables New Immigration Regulations." *House of Commons Debates* 1.

February 27, 1962. "Debate over New Immigration Regulations." *House of Commons Debates* 2: 1326–36.

February 3, 1975. "Tabling of Green Paper of Immigration Policy." *House of Commons Debates*.

March 24, 1987. "Government Orders." *House of Commons Debates*.

May 1, 2000a. "2nd Reading Bill C-31." *House of Commons Debates*, 132.

May 1, 2000b. *House of Commons Debates* 87.

February 26, 2001. "2nd Reading Bill C-11." *House of Commons Debates* 21.

February 27, 2001. "2nd Reading Bill C-11 (Continued)." *House of Commons Debates* 22.

June 13, 2001. "Third Reading Bill C-11." *House of Commons Debates* 78.

Pear, Robert. June 25, 2007. "High-Tech Titans Strike Out on Immigration Bill." *New York Times*.

Perlmutter, Ted. 1996. "Bringing Parties Back in: Comments on 'Modes of Immigration Politics in Liberal Democratic Societies'." *International Migration Review* 30 (1): 375–88.

Pierson, Paul. 1993. "When Effect Becomes Cause: Policy Feedback and Political Change." *World Politics* 45 (4): 595–628.

Piguet, Etienne. 2006a. "Economy Versus the People? Swiss Immigration Policy between Economic Demand, Xenophobia, and International Constraint." In *Dialogues on Migration Policy*, edited by Marco G. Giugni and Florence Passy, 67–89. Lanham: Lexington Books.

2006b. *Einwanderungsland Schweiz: Fünf Jahrzehnte Halb Geöffnete Grenzen*. Bern: Haupt.

Pollack, Mark A. 1997. "Delegation, Agency, and Agenda Setting in the European Community." *International Organization* 51 (1): 99–134.

Powell, Eleanor Neff, and Justin Grimmer. 2016. "Money in Exile: Campaign Contributions and Committee Access." *The Journal of Politics* 78 (4): 974–88.

Preston, Julia. June 28, 2013. "Varied Alliance to Press House on Immigration Bill." *The New York Times*.

Preston, Julia, and John H. Cushman. June 15, 2012. "Obama to Permit Young Migrants to Remain in U.S." *New York Times*.

Provine, Doris Marie, and Jorge M. Chavez. 2009. "Race and the Response of State Legislatures to Unauthorized Immigrants." *Annals of the American Academy of Political and Social Science* 623 (1): 78–92.

Ramakrishnan, S. Karthick, and Pratheepan Gulasekaram. 2012. "The Importance of the Political in Immigration Federalism." *Arizona State Law Journal* 44 (4): 1431–88.

Ramakrishnan, S. Karthick, and Tom Wong. 2011. "Partisanship, Not Spanish: Explaining Municipal Ordinances Affecting Undocumented Immigrants." In *Taking Local Control: Immigration Policy Activism in U.S. Cities and States*, edited by Monica Varsanyi, 73–96. Stanford: Stanford University Press.

Ramsay, Laura. April 15, 2002. "Proposals Will Prevent Desirable Immigrants, Group Fears." *Globe and Mail*.

Rasmussen Reports. May 1, 2006. "24% Have Favorable Opinion of Protestors."

May 3, 2006. "Immigration Rallies Fail to Move Public Opinion."

May 7, 2006. "Politicians Missed Key Point on Immigration Debate."

Rassmussen Reports. May 17, 2006. "39% Agree with President on Immigration."

Reimers, David. 1983. "An Unintended Reform." *Journal of American Ethnic History* 3 (1): 9–28.

1999. *Unwelcome Strangers: American Identity and the Turn against Immigration.* New York: Columbia University Press.

Reisslandt, Carolin. 2002. "Rot-grüne Migrationspolitik und die Zuwanderungsdebatte: Vom 'Paradigmenwechsel' zum Wahlkampfthema?" In *"Deutschland auf den Weg gebracht:" Rot-grüne Wirschafts- und Sozialpolitik zwischen Anspruch und Wirklichkeit,* edited by Kai Eiker-Wolf, Holger Kindler, and Ingo Schäfer, 213–51. Marburg: Metropolis.

Reitz, Jeffrey G. 2011. "Pro-immigration Canada: Social and Economic Roots of Popular Views." *IRPP Study* 20: 1–32.

2014. "Canada: New Initiatives and Approaches to Immigration and Nation Building." In *Controlling Immigration: A Global Perspective,* edited by James F. Hollifield, Philip L. Martin, and Pia M. Orrenius, 88–116. Stanford: Stanford University Press.

Renner, Günther. 1992. *Ausländerrecht: Ausländergesetz und Asylverfahrensgesetz mit materiellem Asylrecht sowie arbeits- und sozialrechtliche Vorschriften.* 5th ed. München: C.H. Beck.

Rheault, Ludovic. 2013. "Corporate Lobbying and Immigration Policies in Canada." *Canadian Journal of Political Science* 46 (3): 791–22.

Rhein-Zeitung. December 14, 1954. "Kommen italienische Arbeiter? Die Verhandlungen haben Begonnen – Eine Million Arbeitslose in der Bundesrepublik."

Riaño, Yvonne, and Doris Wastl-Walter. 2006. "Immigration Policies, State Discourses on Foreigners and the Politics of Identity in Switzerland." *Environment and Planning A* 38 (9): 1693–713.

Ripoll Servent, Ariadna, and Florian Trauner. 2014. "Do Supranational EU Institutions Make a Difference? EU Asylum Law Before and After 'Communitarization'." *Journal of European Public Policy* 21 (8): 1142–62.

Rodriguez, Cindy Y. November 9, 2012. "Latino Vote Key to Obama's Re-election." *CNN Politics.* www.cnn.com/2012/11/09/politics/latino-vote-key-election/index.html, accessed August 26, 2019.

Roebuck, Jr., William V. 1991. "The Move to Employment-Based Immigration in the Immigration Act of 1990: Towards a New Definition of Immigrant." *North Carolina International Law and Commercial Regulation* 16 (3): 523.

Rosenblum, Marc R. 2004. "Beyond the Policy of No-Policy: Emigration from Mexico and Central America." *Latin American Politics and Society* 4 (1): 91–125.

2011. *US Immigration Policy Since 9/11: Understanding the Stalemate over Comprehensive Immigration Reform.* Washington, DC: Migration Policy Institute.

Rudolph, Hedwig. 1996. "The New Gastarbeiter System in Germany." *Journal of Ethnic and Migration Studies* 22 (2): 287–300.

Rustenbach, Elisa. 2010. "Sources of Negative Attitudes toward Immigrants in Europe: A Multi-level Analysis." *International Migration Review* 44 (1): 53–77.

Sammon, Bill. November 10, 2004. "Bush Revives Bid to Legalize Illegal Aliens." *Washington Times*.

Sandler, Michael. June 28, 2007. "Immigration Overhaul Founders." *Congressional Quarterly*.

Sassen, Saskia. 1998. "The *de facto* Transnationalizing of Immigration Policy." In *Challenge to the Nation-State: Immigration in Western Europe and the United States*, edited by Christian Joppke, 49–85. New York: Oxford University Press.

Satzewich, Vic. 2015. *Points of Entry: How Canada's Immigration Officers Decide Who Gets In*. Vancouver: UBC Press.

Savoie, Donald J. 1994. *Thatcher, Reagan, and Mulroney: In Search of a New Bureaucracy*. Pittsburgh: University of Pittsburgh Press.

Schain, Martin A. 2008. *The Politics of Immigration in France, Britain, and the United States: A Comparative Study*. 2nd ed. New York: Palgrave Macmillan.

Scharpf, Fritz W. 2000. "Institutions in Comparative Policy Research." MPIFG Working Paper 00 (3).

Schattschneider, Elmer E. 1975. *The Semi-sovereign People: A Realist View of Democracy in America*. Hindsdale, IL: Dryden Press.

Schilde, Kaija. 2017. *The Political Economy of European Security*. Cambridge: Cambridge University Press.

Schmalz-Jacobsen, Cornelia. 2001. "Der neue politische Diskurs: Ein zaghafter Beginn." In *Deutschland – ein Einwanderungsland? Rückblick, Bilanz, und neue Fragen*, edited by Edda Curle and Tanja Wunderlich, 41–4. Stuttgart: Lucius und Lucius.

Schmid-Drüner, Marion. 2006. "Germany's Immigration Law: A Paradigm Shift?" *European Journal of Migration and Law* 8: 191–214.

Schmidt, Vivien A. 2008. "Discursive Institutionalism: The Explanatory Power of Ideas and Discourse." *Annual Review of Political Science* 11: 303–26.

2012. "Democracy and Legitimacy in the European Union." In *The Oxford Handbook of the European Union*, edited by Erik Jones, Anand Menon and Stephen Weatherill. Oxford: Oxford University Press.

Schmitter Heisler, Barbara. 2000. "Trapped in the Consociational Cage: Trade Unions and Immigration in Switzerland." In *Trade Unions, Immigration and Immigrants in Europe, 1960–1993*, edited by Rinus Penninx and Judith Roosbald, 21–38. New York: Berghahn.

Schönwälder, Karen. 2001. *Einwanderung und Ethnische Pluralität: Politische Entscheidungen in Grossbritannien und der Bundesrepublik von den 1950er bis zu den 1970er Jahren*. Berlin: Klartext.

2004. "Why Germany's Guestworkers Were Largely Europeans: The Selective Principles of Postwar Labour Recruitment Policy." *Ethnic and Racial Studies* 27 (2): 248–65.

2006. "The Difficult Task of Managing Migration: The 1973 Recruitment Stop." In *German History from the Margins*, 252–67. Bloomington: Indiana University Press.

Schuck, Peter H. 1992. "The Politics of Rapid Legal Change: Immigration Policy in the 1980s." *Studies in American Political Development* 6 (1): 37–92.

Schweizer Bundesversammlung. June 10, 1991. "Amtliches Bulletin der Bundesversammlung Nationalrat: Bericht des Bundesrates zur Ausländer- und Flüchtlingspolitik." 91.036.

May 6, 2004. "Amtliches Bulletin Nationalrat." AB 2004 N 711/BO 2004 N 711.

March 16, 2005. "Amtliches Bulletin Ständerat."

Schweizer Bundesversammlung. September 28, 2015. "Amtliches Stenographisches Bulletin der Schweizer Bundesversammlung Nationalrat."

Schweizerische Arbeitgeber-Zeitung. June 20, 1947. "Fremdarbeiter in der Schweiz."

Schweizerische Eidgenossenschaft. February 11, 2015. "Steuerung der Zuwanderung: Bundesrat verabschiedet Gesetzesentwurf und Verhandlungsmandat."

Schweizerischer Metall- und Uhrenarbeiterverband. June 6, 1946. Internal Memorandum. Schweizerisches Sozialarchiv, SMUV 05D-0004, Zirkular.

1955. Bericht über das Fremdarbeiterproblem in der Maschinen- und Metallindustrie. Schweizerisches Sozialarchiv, SMUV 05D-0015, 1947–1963.

1962. SMUV Vortagswoche Oktober 1961. Zurich: Schweizerisches Sozialarchiv.

Scott, Eugene. June 20, 2015. "Trump on the Stump: A Closer Look at The Donald's Proposed Policies." *CNN*. www.cnn.com/2015/06/20/politics/trump-announcement-speech/index.html?fbclid=IwAR2f4-GKDxjozT6ZmIMotVQzoBkgwUiqfq4LY8500dvnH376H7xDYZ67lzY, accessed, September 10, 2019.

Segovia, Francine, and Renata Defever. 2010. "The Polls-Trends: American Public Opinion on Immigrants and Immigration Policy." *Public Opinion Quarterly* 74 (2): 375–94.

Sevastopulo, Demetri, and Simon Doyle. June 21, 2015. "Immigrants Join the Canadian 'Express'." *Forbes*.

Shachar, Ayelet. 2016. "Selecting by Merit: The Brave New World of Stratified Mobility." In *Migration in Political Theory: The Ethics of Movement and Membership*, edited by Sarah Fine and Lea Ypi, 175–204. Oxford: Oxford University Press.

Shanks, Cheryl Lynne. 2001. *Immigration and the Politics of American Sovereignty: 1890–1990*. Michigan: Michigan University Press.

Sheldon, Georg. 2003. "Die Auswirkung der Ausländerbeschäftigung auf die Löhne und das Wirtschaftswachstum in der Schweiz." In *Migration und die Schweiz*, edited by Hans-Rudolf Wicker, Rosita Fibbi, and Werner Haug, 335–70. Zürich: Seismo.

Simmons, Alan B. 2010. *Immigration and Canada: Global and Transnational Perspectives*. Toronto: Canadian Scholars' Press.

Simmons, Alan B., and Kieran Keohane. 1992. "Canadian Immigration Policy: State Strategies and the Quest for Legitimacy." *The Canadian Review of Sociology and Anthropology* 29 (4): 421–52.

Simon, Rita, and James Lynch. 1999. "A Comparative Assessment of Public Opinion toward Immigrants and Immigration Policies." *International Migration Review* 33 (2): 455–67.

Simon, Rita, and Susan Alexander. 1993. *The Ambivalent Welcome: Print Media, Public Opinion and Immigration.* Westport, CT: Praeger.

Skenderovic, Damir, and Gianni D'Amato. 2008. *Mit dem Fremden politisieren: Rechtspopulismums und Migrationspolitik in der Schweiz seit den 1960er Jahren.* Zürich: Chronos.

Skocpol, Theda, and Margaret Weir. 1985. "State Structures and the Possibilities for Keynesian Responses to the Great Depression." In *Bringing the State Back In*, edited by Peter B. B. Evans, Dietrich Rueschemeyer, and Theda Skocpol, 107–63. Cambridge: Cambridge University Press.

Skrentny, John. 2011. "Obama's Immigration Reform: A Tough Sell for a Grand Bargain." In *Reaching for a New Deal: Ambitious Governance, Economic Meltdown, and Polarized Politics in Obama's First Two Years*, edited by Theda Skocpol and Larry Jacobs, 273–320. New York: Russell Sage Foundation.

Skrentny, John, and Jane Lopez. 2013. "Obama's Immigration Reform: The Triumph of Executive Action." *Indiana Journal of Law and Social Equality* 2 (1): 62–79.

Sniderman, Paul M., Louk Haagendorn, and Markus Prior. 2004. "Predisposing Factors and Situational Triggers: Exclusionary Reactions to Immigrant Minorities." *American Political Science Review* 98 (1): 35–49.

Soberman, Liane. 1999. "Immigration and the Canadian Federal Election of 1993: The Press as a Political Educator." In *Ethnicity, Politics, and Public Policy: Case Studies in Canadian Diversity*, edited by Harold Troper and Morton Weinfeld, 253–82. Toronto: Toronto University Press.

Sobolewska, Maria, Silvia Galandini, and Laurence Lessard-Phillips. 2017. "The Public View of Immigrant Integration: Multidimensional and Consensual. Evidence from Survey Experiments in the UK and the Netherlands." *Journal of Ethnic and Migration Studies* 43 (1): 58–79.

Soysal, Yasemin Nuhoglu. 1994. *Limits of Citizenship: Migrants and Postnational Membership in Europe.* Chicago: University of Chicago.

Standing Committee on Citizenship and Immigration. 2002. *Building a Nation: The Regulations under the Immigration and Refugee Protection Act.* Ottawa: Public Works and Government Services Canada.

Stanton, John, and Erin P. Billings. May 10, 2007. "Reid Set to Move Border Bill." *Roll Call.*

Stasavage, David. 2004. "Open-Door or Closed-Door? Transparency in Domestic and International Bargaining." *International Organization* 58 (4): 667–703.

Statistics Canada. 2015. "Same-Sex Couples Across Canada." www12.statcan.gc.ca/census-recensement/index-eng.cfm, accessed February 6, 2017.

Steinmo, Sven, Kathleen Thelen, and Frank Longstreth, eds. 1992. *Structuring Politics: Historical Institutionalism in Comparative Analysis.* New York: Cambridge University Press.

Stone, Alec. 1990. "The Birth and Development of Abstract Review: Constitutional Courts and Policymaking in Western Europe." *Policy Studies Journal* 19 (1): 81–95.

Strahm, Rudolf H. October 1, 1992. "Mein kritisches Ja zum kleineren Übel." *Weltwoche*.

Stratmann-Mertens, Eckhard. July 6, 2019. "Fachkräfteeinwanderungsgesetz: Im Fetischdreieck Wohlstand – Wachstum – Einwanderung." *GlobKult Magazin*. www.globkult.de/politik/deutschland/1775-fachkraefteeinwander ungsgesetz-im-fetischdreieck-wohlstand-%E2%80%93-wachstum-einwan derung, accessed September 6, 2019.

Straubhaar, Thomas. 1989. "Grundzüge einer schweizerischen Migrationspolitik der 90er Jahre." *Wirtschaftspolitische Mitteilungen* 45 (9/10): 1–46.

Stuttgarter Zeitung. January 22, 1973. "Sesshaftwerden von Gastarbeitern unerwünscht."

Stüwe, Klaus. 2001. "Das Bundesverfassungsgericht als verlängerter Arm der Opposition? Eine Bilanz seit 1951." *Aus Politik und Zeitgeschichte* 37–8: 34–44.

Süddeutsche Zeitung. December 21, 1954. "Fremdarbeiter nur im Bedarfsfall." November 15, 1966. "Langer Kündigungsschutz nur für wenige Gastarbeiter." February 23, 2000. "75,000 Fachkräfte fehlen."

Suro, Roberto. 2009. *Promoting Stalemate: The Media and U.S. Policy on Migration* Washington, DC: Migration Policy Institute.

Suyama, Nobuaki. 1994. "State Autonomy and Canadian Immigration Policy." *The Journal of American and Canadian Studies* 12: 89–105.

Swarns, Rachel L. March 28, 2006. "Bill to Broaden Immigration Law Gains in Senate." *New York Times*.

Tages Anzeiger. June 24, 1991. "Die EWR stellt die Ausländerpolitik auf den Kopf." December 13, 2016. "Der Inländervorrang ist fertig kreiert." November 27, 2018. "Eine Partei im Selbstzweifel."

Tagesspiegel. November 15, 1998. "Der Rechtsextremismus is die grösste Gefahr."

Task Force on Program Review. 1986. *Citizenship, Labour, and Immigration*. Ottawa: Minister of Supply and Services.

Taunert, Florian, and Jocelyn Turton. 2017. "'Welcome Culture': The Emergence and Transformation of a Public Debate on Migration." *Austrian Journal of Political Science* 46 (1): 33–42.

The American Presidency Project. July 11, 1960. *1960 Democratic Party Platform, Political Party Platforms: Parties Receiving Electoral Votes: 1840–2016*.

The Federal Council. February 11, 2015. "Controlling Immigration: Federal Council Approves Draft Legislation and Negotiating Mandate." *Press Release of the Federal Council*. www.admin.ch/gov/en/start/documentation/ media-releases/media-releases-federal-council.msg-id-56194.html, accessed September 26, 2020.

The German Marshall Fund of the United States. September 10, 2014. *Transatlantic Trends: Mobility, Migration, and Integration*. Washington, DC: The German Marshall Fund of the United States.

The Select Commission on Immigration and Refugee Reform. March 1, 1981. *U.S. Immigration Policy and the National Interest: The Final Report and Recommendations of the Select Commission on Immigration and Refugee Policy with Supplemental Views by Commissioners.* Washington, DC: The Select Commission on Immigration and Refugee Reform.

Thielemann, Eiko, and Nadine El-Enany. 2010. "Refugee Protection as a Collective Action Problem: Is the EU Shirking Its Responsibilities?" *European Security* 19 (2): 209–29.

Tichenor, Daniel J. 1994. "The Politics of Immigration Reform in the United States, 1981–1990." *Polity* 26 (3): 333–62.

2002. *Dividing Lines: The Politics of Immigration Control in America.* Princeton, NJ: Princeton University Press.

2009. "Navigating an American Minefield: The Politics of Illegal Immigration." *The Forum* 7 (3): 1–21.

Tietze, Klaudia. 2008. *Einwanderung und die Deutschen Parteien: Akzeptanz und Abwehr von Migranten im Widerstreit in der Programmatik von SPD, FDP, den Grünen und CDU/CSU.* Berlin: LIT Verlag.

Timmermans, Arco. 2001. "Arenas as Institutional Sites for Policymaking: Patterns and Effects in Comparative Perspective." *Journal of Comparative Policy Analysis: Research and Practice* 3 (3): 311–37.

Torpey, John. 2000. *The Invention of the Passport: Surveillance, Citizenship and the State.* Cambridge: Cambridge University Press.

Transparency International. 2015. *Lobbying in Europe: Hidden Influence, Privileged Access.* Berlin: Transparency International.

Transparency International Schweiz. 2019. *Lobbying in der Schweiz: Verdeckter Einfluss, heikle Verflechtungen, privilegierter Zugang.* Bern: Transparency International Schweiz.

Trauner, Florian, and Ariadna Ripoll Servent. 2016. "The Communitarization of the Area of Freedom, Security and Justice: Why Institutional Change Does Not Translate into Policy Change." *JCMS: Journal of Common Market Studies* 54 (6): 1417–32.

Triadafilopoulos, Triadafilos. 2010. "Global Norms Domestic Institutions and the Transformation of Immigration Policy in Canada and the United States." *Review of International Studies* 36 (1): 169–93.

2012. *Becoming Multicultural: Immigration and the Politics of Membership in Canada and Germany.* Vancouver: UBC.

2013a. "Dismantling White Canada: Race, Rights, and the Origins of the Points System." In *Wanted and Welcome: Immigrants and Minorities*, edited by Triadafilos Triadafilopoulos, 15–37. New York: Springer.

2013b. "Institutions and the Politics of Power and Persuasion: Canadian Immigration Policy under the Conservative Party, 2006–2012." Meeting of the American Political Science Association, Chicago.

Triadafilopoulos, Triadafilos, and Karen Schönwälder. 2006. "How the Federal Republic Became an Immigration Country: Norms, Politics, and the Failure of West Germany's Guestworker System." *German Politics and Society* 24 (3): 1–19.

Truman, Harry S. June 25, 1952. *Veto of Bill to Revise the Laws Relating to Immigration, Naturalization, and Nationality*, edited by Public Papers Harry S. Truman 1945–1953. Independence, MO: Harry S. Truman Presidential Library & Museum.

Tsebelis, George. 2002. *Veto Players: How Political Institutions Work*. Princeton, NJ: Princeton University Press.

Unabhängige Kommission "Zuwanderung." 2001. *Zuwanderung gestalten, Integration fördern. Bericht der Unabhängigen Kommission "Zuwanderung."* Berlin: Bundesministerium des Innern.

US Congress. July 12, 1989. *Congressional Record* 135 (92).

July 13, 1989. *Congressional Record* 135 (93).

US President's Commission on Immigration and Naturalization. 1953. *Whom Shall We Welcome? Report of the President's Commission on Immigration and Naturalization*. Washington, DC: US Government Printing Office

US Senate. June 6, 2007. "Proceedings and Debates of the 110th Congress, First Session." *Congressional Record* 153 (90).

May 7, 2007. "Proceedings and Debates of the 110th Congress, First Session." *Congressional Record* 153 (74).

May 22, 2007. "Proceedings and Debates of the 110th Congress, First Session." *Congressional Record* 153 (74).

Van der Brug, Wouter, and Joost van Spanje. 2009. "Immigration, Europe, and the 'New' Cultural Dimension." *European Journal of Political Research* 48 (3): 309–34.

Van Kersbergen, Kees, and André Krouwel. 2008. "A Double Edged Sword! The Dutch Centre-Right and the 'Foreigners Issue'." *Journal of European Public Policy* 15 (3): 398–414.

Van Spanje, Joost. 2010. "Contagious Parties: Anti-immigration Parties and Their Impact on Other Parties' Immigration Stances in Contemporary Western Europe." *Party Politics* 16 (5): 563–86.

Velling, Johannes. 1995. *Die Arbeitserlaubnis als Instrument der Arbeitsmarktpolitik zur Steuerung internationaler Zuwanderung auf dem Arbeitsmarkt*. Mannheim: Zentrum für Europäische Wirtschaftsforschung.

Vertovec, Steven. 2007. "Super-diversity and Its Implications." *Ethnic and Racial Studies* 30 (6): 1024–54.

Vertovec, Steven, and Susanne Wessendorf, eds. 2010. *The Multicultural Backlash: European Discourses, Policies and Practices*. New York: Routledge.

Veugelers, John W. P. 2000. "State–Society Relations in the Making of Canadian Immigration Policy during the Mulroney Era." *Canadian Review of Sociology and Anthropology* 37 (1): 95–110.

Veugelers, John W. P., and Thomas R. Klassen. 1994. "Continuity and Change in Canada's Unemploymnet–Immigration Linkage (1946–1993)." *Canadian Journal of Sociology* 19 (3): 351–69.

Veuve, Daniel. 2001. "Mesures d'accompagnement de l'Accord sur la libre circulation des personnes." In *Accords bilatéraux Suisse – UE (Commentaires)*, edited by Daniel Felder and Christine Kaddous, 289–311. Basel: Helbing und Lichtenhahn/Bruylant.

Volpp, Leti. 2015. "The Indigenous as Alien." *U.C. Irvine Law Review* 5 (2): 289–326.

Vuilleumier, Marc. 1992. *Flüchtlinge und Immigranten in der Schweiz: Ein historischer Überblick*. Zürich: Pro Helvetia.

Waever, Ole, Barry Buzan, Morten Kelstrup, and Pierre Lamaitre, eds. 1993. *Identity, Migration and the New Security Agenda in Europe*. London: Pinter Publishers.

Wagner, Stephen T. 1986. *The Lingering Death of the National Origins Quota System*. PhD dissertation, Harvard University.

Wallace, Sophia J., Chris Zepeda-Millán, and Michael Jones-Correa. 2014. "Spatial and Temporal Proximity: Examining the Effects of Protests on Political Attitudes." *American Journal of Political Science* 58 (2): 433–48.

Wasem, Ruth Ellen. February 27, 2013. *Brief History of Comprehensive Immigration Reform Efforts in the 109th and 110th Congresses to Inform Policy Discussions in the 113th Congress*. Washington, DC: Congressional Research Service.

Wasserman, Elizabeth. July 9, 2006. "Media: Pundit Power." *CQ Weekly Online*.

Weisman, Jonathan. April 12, 2006. "Immigrant Bill Fallout May Hurt House." *Washington Post*.

Westerhoff, Horst-Dieter. 2007. "Die Greencard: Zur Wirtschaftspolitik der rot-grünen Bundesregierung." Diskussionsbeiträge aus dem Fachbereich der Universität Duisburg-Essen 161: 1–29.

Westlake, Daniel. 2018. "Multiculturalism, Political Parties, and the Conflicting Pressures of Ethnic Minorities and Far-Right Parties." *Party Politics* 24 (4): 421–33.

Whitesides, John. January 29, 2013. "GOP Immigration Reform Politics Turned 'Upside Down'." *HuffPost*. www.huffpost.com/entry/gop-immigration-reform_n_2572650, accessed August 27, 2019.

Wilkes, Rima, Neil Guppy, and Lily Farris. 2008. "No Thanks, We're Full: Individual Characteristics, National Context, and Changing Attitudes toward Immigration." *International Migration Review* 42 (2): 203–329.

Wilson, James Q. 1980. "The Politics of Regulation." In *The Politics of Regulation*, edited by James Q. Wilson. New York: Basic Books.

Wilson, R. Paul. 2016. "Harper and the House of Commons: An Evidence-Based Assessment." In *The Harper Factor: Assessing a Prime Minister's Policy Legacy*, edited by Jennifer Ditchburn and Graham Fox, 27–43. Montreal: McGill-Queen's University Press.

Wimmer, Andreas. 2001. "Ein helvetischer Komprosmiss: Kommentar zum Entwurf eines neuen Ausländergesetzes." *Swiss Political Science Review* 71 (1): 97–104.

Wishnie, Michael J. 2001. "Laboratories of Bigotry? Devolution of the Immigration Power, Equal Protection, and Federalism." *Faculty Scholarship Series* 933: 493–569.

Witko, Christopher. 2011. "Campaign Contributions, Access, and Government Contracting." *Journal of Public Administration Research and Theory* 21 (4): 761–78.

Wolgin, Philip Eric. 2011. "Beyond National Origins: The Development of Modern Immigration Policymaking, 1948–1968." Unpublished dissertation. University of California, Berkeley.

Wood, John R. 1978. "East Indian and Canadian Immigration Policy." *Canadian Public Policy* 4 (4): 547–67.

World Bank. 2014. *The World Bank Annual Report 2014*. Washington, DC: World Bank.

World Elections. 2015. "Swiss Referendums 2014." *Elections, Referendums and Electoral Sociology around the World*. https://welections.wordpress.com/, accessed June 14, 2019.

Woroby, Tamara. 2015. "Immigration Reform in Canada and the United States: How Dramatic, How Different?" *American Review of Canadian Studies* 45 (4): 430–50.

Wright, Chris F. 2017. "Employer Organizations and Labour Immigration Policy in Australia and the United Kingdom: The Power of Political Salience and Social Institutional Legacies." *British Journal of Industrial Relations* 55 (2): 347–71.

Wright, Matthew, Morris Levy, and Jack Citrin. 2016. "Public Attitudes toward Immigration Policy Across the Legal/Illegal Divide: The Role of Categorical and Attribute-Based Decision-Making." *Political Behavior* 38 (1): 229–53.

Wright, Robert E., and Paul S. Maxim. 1993. "Immigration Policy and Immigrant Quality: Empirical Evidence from Canada." *Journal of Population Economics* 6: 337–52.

Wroe, Andrew. 2007. "The Shifting Politics of Immigration Reform." In *America's Americans: Population Issues in U.S. Society and Politics*, edited by Philip Davis and Iwan Morgan, 263–87. London: Institute for the Study of the Americas.

Wüst, Andreas. 2009. "Bundestagskandidaten und Einwanderungspolitik: Eine Analyse zentraler Policy-Aspekte." *Zeitschrift für Politikwissenschaft* 19 (1): 77–105.

Zaun, Natascha. 2016. "Why EU Asylum Standards Exceed the Lowest Common Denominator: The Role of Regulatory Expertise in EU Decision-making." *Journal of European Public Policy* 23 (1): 136–54.

Zeleny, Jeff. June 28, 2007. "Immigration Bill Prompts Some Menacing Responses." *New York Times*.

Zelizer, Julian E. January 22, 2015. "When Liberals Were Organized: Progressives Seeking a Model for an Effective Congress Could Learn from the Nearly Forgotten History of the Democratic Study Group." *The American Prospect*. http://prospect.org/article/when-liberals-were-organized, accessed September 26, 2020.

Zepeda-Millán, Chris. 2017. *Latino Mass Mobilization: Immigration, Racialization, and Activism*. Cambridge: Cambridge University Press.

Zick, Andreas, Ulrich Wagner, Rolf Van Dick, and Thomas Petzel. 2001. "Acculturation and Prejudice in Germany: Majority and Minority Perspectives." *Journal of Social Issues* 57 (3): 541–57.

Zinterer, Tanja. 2004. *Politikwandel durch Politikberatung? Die kanadische Royal Commission on Aboriginal Peoples und die Unabhängige*

Kommission "Zuwanderung" im Vergleich. Wiesbaden: Verlag für Sozialwissenschaften.

Zolberg, Aristide R. 1999. "Matters of State: Theorizing Immigration Policy." In *The Handbook of International Migration: The American Experience*, edited by Charles Hirschman, Philip Kasinitz, and Joshua DeWind, 71–93. New York: Russell Sage Foundation.

——— 2003. "The Archaeology of Remote Control." In *Migration Control in the North Atlantic World: The Evolution of State Practices in Europe and the United States from the French Revolution to the Inter-War Period*, edited by Andreas Fahrmeier, Olivier Faron, and Patrick Weil, 195–222. New York: Berghahn.

——— 2006. *A Nation by Design: Immigration Policy in the Fashioning of America.* New York: Russell Sage Foundation.

Index

413